AF564392

Human Resources and Gender Issues in Poverty Eradication

Human Resources and Gender Issues in Poverty Eradication

Editors
ROBIN GHOSH
RONY GABBAY
ABU SIDDIQUE

ATLANTIC PUBLISHERS AND DISTRIBUTORS

in collaboration with

The Centre for Migration and Development Studies
Department of Economics
The University of Western Australia
and
International Institute for Development Studies (IIDS)
Australia

Published by
ATLANTIC PUBLISHERS AND DISTRIBUTORS
B-2, Vishal Enclave, Opp. Rajouri Garden, New Delhi-27
Phones : 5413460, 5429987

Sales Office
4215/1, Ansari Road, Darya Ganj, New Delhi-02
Phones : 3273880, 3285873, 3280451
Fax : 91-11-3285873
e-mail : info@atlanticbooks.com
web : www.atlanticbooks.com

ISBN : 81-7156-965-X

Typeset at
APD Computer Graphics, Delhi

Printed in India at
Nice Printing Press, Delhi

Preface

This Volume is the result of an international Conference held at the University of Western Australia in November/December, 1998. The purpose of the Conference was to bring together experts from many disciplines and professions to discuss two broad but inter-related themes in the context of the Indian Ocean Region : (1) Human Resources and Gender Issues in Poverty Eradication and (2) Energy and Services Sectors in Development.

The papers presented in this Volume relate to the first theme viz., Human Resources and Gender Issues in Development. A separate Volume is planned to be published, in which the papers dealing with the other theme viz., energy, tourism and services sectors will be included.

Out of a total of 25 papers presented in the Conference, only 17 papers are included in this Volume on the recommendation of an independent assessor who judged the scholarly qualities of the papers to decide whether or not these could be published. However, as editors, we take full responsibility for excluding several of the Conference papers from publication in this Volume.

We wish to record with thanks the generous financial support from AusAID, Canberra that made it possible to invite several eminent scholars from overseas to attend the Conference in Perth. Generous financial support from the Edith Cowan University in Perth in jointly hosting the Conference with the Centre for Migration and Development Studies, and the International Institute for Development Studies (IIDS) Australia, is also thankfully acknowledged.

As always, Mrs. Glenys Walter, Administrative Officer in the Department of Economics at the University of Western Australia, prepared the camera-ready copy expeditiously and with great professionalism.

A word of thanks to Dr. K.R. Gupta, Managing Director, Atlantic Publishers and Distributors, New Delhi is also appropriate here. Dr. Gupta began his career as a professional economist in a well-known Indian University, but has now made his name and fame as a reputed publisher for scholarly works from all over the world. It was Dr. Gupta's enthusiasm and the dedication of his workers in the publishing house that made it possible to produce this Volume at a short notice.

Finally, we wish to record our appreciation of support from Professor Paul Miller, Head of the Department of Economics at the University of Western Australia, who has always taken a keen interest in the research activity of his colleagues at the Centre for Migration and Development Studies.

Editors
Robin Ghosh
Rony Gabbay
Abu Siddique

The University of Western Australia
Perth

Table of Contents

1 Growth, Development and Sustainable Development

Robin Ghosh
Rony Gabbay
Abu Siddique

The purpose of this introductory paper is to clear up the current confusion over the meaning of certain words which are commonly used in the development literature. There appears to be a good deal of misunderstanding about the exact meaning of the terms : economic growth and economic development. These are often used as interchangeable terms, and indeed as synonymous by the lay people. However, in the professional literature, the term "economic growth" is generally defined in a very specific sense.

Economic Growth

In his *Wealth of Nations*, published more than two hundred years ago, Adam Smith had this to say about the wealth of a nation :

> "The annual labour of every nation is the fund which originally supplies it with all the necessaries and conveniences of life which it annually consumes, and which consist always either in the immediate produce of that labour, or in what is purchased with that produce from other nations. According, therefore, as this produce, or what is purchased with it, bears a greater or smaller proportion to the number of those who are to consume it, the nation will be better or worse supplied with all the necessaries and conveniences for which it has occasion."[1]

When translated into modern terminology, what the above paragraph is supposed to mean is simply this :

Annual Produce = $GDP_t = f(L_t)$, where
GDP = Gross Domestic Product

[1] Adam Smith, *The Wealth of Nations* (Edwin Cannan's edition), Modern Library, New York, lvii.

L = Labour in employment
t = time period.

The index of prosperity (or otherwise) of a nation is then measured by GDP_t/P_t, where P = Population.

Despite the passage of time since Adam Smith wrote his *Wealth of Nations* (1776), the concept of economic growth is still today linked with GDP, which is defined as "the money value of all goods and services marketed in an economy during a given period." Monetary value can, of course, fluctuate, depending upon inflation, or deflation. Hence, an inflator/deflator can be used to arrive at a constant monetary value of GDP. Other things being equal, if this GDP increases over time, a country is supposed to experience positive economic growth. That explains the importance of the concept of GDP in the economic literature.

The measure of economic growth, in terms of GDP, is, of course, very imperfect. First of all, economic activity itself to produce goods and services is likely to create environmental pollution, both in terms of what we take from it and in terms of the disposal of the wastes in the atmosphere and ocean. For example, a newly built brick factory would increase employment and income of the people living near it. But the smoking chimneys of the factory would also add pollution to the atmosphere of that locality. But such pollution is ignored in the calculation of the GDP.[2]

Secondly, many types of activities which are useful and add to the sense of wellbeing of the people have no monetary value, if these are not sold in the market. For example, hobby type gardening, housewives' work at home, and similar non-marketed activities are not included in the calculation of GDP and yet such activities do improve the sense of welfare in the community.

Thirdly, defence expenditure is included in GDP. Now, making bombs does give a sense of security to a community, but defence expenditure does not necessarily improve the living standards of the people. Indeed, defence expenditure is like what Pigou called "exhaustive expenditure."

---

2 See, for example, E.J. Mishan, *The Costs of Economic Growth.*

In brief, if economic growth is measured solely in terms of GDP and population growth, then it would have a very narrow meaning, as it would not take into account the quality of human life.

Growth *versus* Development

As stated earlier, economic growth focuses on increases/ decreases in real income on a per capita basis. It has therefore, a narrow focus. Economic development, on the other hand, has a much broader definition. When economic growth translates into a structural change in an economy, by way of better education, better health facilities and longer life expectancies for the population at large, and more particularly for women, we can then talk about economic development. It means that if a community experiences economic growth over a number of years, and as a result, the real incomes of the members in that community continue to improve, they can then spend more on education, health, arts, music and culture, and by doing so, move from a situation of economic growth to economic development. In the longer term, it is the quality of human life that is more important than an improvement in real income.[3]

It is, however, not necessary that economic growth would always, in the long-term, lead to economic development. There are, of course, certain criteria to assess whether or not economic growth was going in the direction of economic development. These criteria may be summed up as follows :

- *Growth* without distributive justice means growth without *development*. If economic growth were to accentuate inequalities of incomes and wealth, it would be difficult to call it development. A precondition of the development process is the elimination of absolute poverty levels and a reduction in gross disparities of incomes and wealth.

---

[3] For all of this, see R.N. Ghosh, B. Ray and K.C. Roy, "Sustainable Development : Some Issues" in R.N. Ghosh, *et al.* (edited), *Sustaining Development : Human Resources, Gender and Environment,* Atlantic Publishers, New Delhi, pp. 251-64.

- Growth is possible in an authoritarian and totalitarian system. But true *development* can only take place in a democratic political and social organization. Political liberty and economic freedom must be the fundamental precondition for long-term economic development. It is, indeed, difficult to imagine how development would take place in a society that opposes individualism and denies civil rights to its population.
- Gender issues and development of human resources are fundamental in assessing the success of a process of economic development. An improvement in the economic and social status of women is a necessary precondition for development in many Third World countries. Similarly, the process of development is expected to improve the full potential of all members in a community, irrespective of caste, colour, ethnicity, sex and religion.

In brief, development is a broader concept, as compared with economic growth. Development of a society is expected to create an environment for a nicer and nobler life for everybody.

Papers in this Volume

The choice of the papers to be included in this Volume was not easy. Theoretical as well as applied papers were to be included. But the papers were to be somehow relevant to the main theme of the Indian Ocean region. This region is so diverse that it is difficult to give it a precise meaning. Australia, South Africa and India are three of the major players in the region. Mauritius, the Seychelles and the Maldives are comparatively small countries but have enormous significance in terms of tourism for the region as a whole. Then, again, it is not easy to place a country like Bangladesh in the Indian Ocean. Bangladesh has a long coastal line in the Bay of Bengal, which flows into the Indian Ocean, but is still not a member of IORARC. Fiji is certainly not an Indian Ocean country, but being primarily a sugar producing country, faces problems which are similar to those confronting Mauritius.

Despite the definitional problems, we have decided to include many papers which do not directly deal with the Indian Ocean region. In this Volume, we have included sixteen papers which deal with different aspects of growth, development and sustainable development, with some reference to the Indian Ocean region.

Meena Acharya's chapter focuses on the relationship between the inter-generation mode of property transfer and women's empowerment because currently it is still a primary source of economic power for the majority of the people in South Asia. Property rights and control over women's sexuality are viewed as intricately related factors in the determination of women's position in the overall power structure and so in their empowerment.

Empowerment is viewed as a process by which disfranchised and subordinated individuals or groups improve their own position in the overall power structure and social hierarchy. This process may be decomposed in two sub-processes — one directed to improvement in the life-options and opportunities for individual development (human development approach) and strengthening of the role and bargaining power of the disfranchised and subordinated groups in vital decisions affecting their lives and livelihoods. These sub-processes together result in improvement in their position in the power structure. From a gender perspective this process is seen as an inter-play of complex social and economic forces both in the private (domestic) and public arena.

In their chapter, Biman Prasad and Sunil Kumar investigate the impact of the nature of property rights on the welfare of women and their empowerment in Fiji. The welfare and empowerment of women in Fiji is explored in the context of contemporary economic developments, social welfare and values. The main elements of economic transition from inward-looking import substitution strategies of the past to the current outward-looking export-oriented strategy are also discussed in order to argue the origins of gender disparity in employment and social life in Fiji. The issues of inheritance of land and property and the distribution of the same through matrimonial links are also examined in the paper.

Following on their discussion on "Property Rights in Fiji," Biman Prasad, Mahendra Reddy and Sunil Kumar further analyse the trends in poverty, employment and wages in Fiji to conclude that the poverty level in Fiji increased from 15 per cent in 1977 to almost 25.1 per cent in 1991 (See Chapter 4). They argue their case by producing some startling official statistics on employment and wages in Fiji.

D.J.J. Botha's chapter examines the causes of continuing poverty in many African countries. He tends to conclude that politicians could be the greatest obstacles to economic development in Africa. By their commitment to false socialist ideology, politicians in many African States amassed huge personal and family fortunes but allowed the progressive impoverishment of the people.

Peter Longton's chapter is mainly theoretical. He argues that poverty is a multi-dimensional concept, and that it implies raising standards in three basic dimensions of human development *viz.*, physical wellbeing, safe and healthy reproduction, literacy and knowledge. He argues that an assault on poverty cannot be unidimensional and limited to any one mechanism such as the free market, or any other single aspect but must be multi-dimensional and holistic, embracing at least economic, social and political aspects.

Malati Pochun's chapter (7) is generally descriptive of the socio-economic situation in selected countries of the Indian Ocean region, with a special focus on human capital and gender issues. Available statistical data regarding a number of variables such as access to education and health facilities, sanitation, availability of safe drinking water, labour force participation, infrastructures, demographic trends, communication and technology are used to discuss theoretical issues and to recommend policies for eradication of poverty.

In a very interesting chapter (8) Anita Medhekar Smith and Lawson Smith examine the gender-based biases in rural India. They argue that rural women in India face poverty not only in terms of income but also because of gender-based disparities in relation to their capability and wellbeing as measured by social development indicators such as the level of nutritional intake, educational attainment, health, infant and maternal mortality, life expectancy and fertility levels.

K.C. Roy discusses the impediments to women's empowerment in rural India (Chapter 9). He argues that making women economically independent is crucial to achieving women's empowerment, which, in its turn, is essential for achieving sustainable development. In India, the imposition of gender discrimination on women embodied in the 'classic patriarchy' prevents them from becoming economically independent, and tends to keep them under perpetual poverty. Women experience discrimination outside and inside their homes. Women's land rights — both legal and customary — are rarely recognised. They have little control over input and technology, their access to common property resources is continuously being eroded. Therefore, the fundamental needs for women's empowerment are land rights, supply of inputs and removal of cultural barriers.

In chapter 10, Liam Ryan draws some interesting lessons from the impact of recent globalisation on three of the ASEAN countries — Thailand, Indonesia and Malaysia. He examines the negative impact of globalisation by first questioning the extent to which the principle of shared growth was effectively translated into policy, and secondly, by analysing how globalisation contributed to speculative gain-driven capital movements that destabilised and forced the collapse of the currencies in the three South-East Asian countries, thereby causing precipitous price falls in their share markets and massive disruption to their financial and banking systems.

In a more general chapter, Schalk W. Theron discusses how the developing countries could seek to reduce poverty by effectively dealing with crime and violence to create a stable environment for economic activity, streamlining government spending and revenues, and by adopting a brisk privatisation programme, and flexible market reforms targeted at growth and job creation.

In her chapter (12) Begum Zaman specifically focuses on the situation in Bangladesh. As in many other Asian countries, the participation of women in Bangladesh in the labour market has increased in recent years particularly in the export-oriented sectors such as food processing and readymade garments. On the supply side, it is poverty which brings the women to the labour market, while on the demand side, it is the competitiveness of the international market that demands their cheap labour. The goal of Begum Zaman's chapter is to add to the body of knowledge about women's labour market participation and its characteristics in Bangladesh.

S.R. Harrison and F. Moog have a very different theme for their chapter. They review the motivations, methods, progress and problems in livestock dispersal programmes in developing countries. Increase in livestock production has been a priority in many developing countries in Asia and the Pacific. This has led to government programmes to increase livestock ownership, with consequent increased dietary production, reduced expenditure on imports and increased incomes of landholders. To some extent, intensive production systems are appropriate for poultry and swine, and feed-lotting of cattle. However, there is also considerable potential for small-scale production, which offers greater equity and self-sufficiency benefits and enhances social status and credit-worthiness, and can take advantage of underutilised labour and feed resources. As a result, various livestock 'dispersal programs' have been devised to assist smallholders to obtain livestock. These may involve gifts of livestock, loans on favourable terms, or loan of breeding stock. Such programs have great potential for improvement in the welfare of smallholders, and increased output of livestock products. However, they can have high risk for recipients, and require livestock husbandry skills that may not be a tradition, and sometimes the types of livestock introduced are not well suited for the recipients' resource situation.

In a very interesting chapter, Binayak Ray discusses gender and poverty issues in the Indian Ocean rim countries. He points out that about one-half of the world population are women, and yet in many areas of human endeavour they are well behind men. The genesis of the women's movement can be traced to their participation in the war and post-war reconstruction efforts. For historical reasons women's movement in industrialised and developing countries has differences. The UN and the World Bank policies have contributed in bringing women's issues in the main stream global policy agenda. The Indian Ocean Rim Association of Regional Co-operation countries are mostly developing nations. Women's position in these countries as measured in the UN developed Human Development Index (HDI), Gender Development Index (GDI) and Gender Empowerment Measure (GEM), is generally speaking poor.

Ray argues that in an increasingly globalised economy, dynamics of women's movement has been changing rapidly. In an uneven global economic, social and political environment developing countries, in particular, must adopt innovative policies to achieve the movement's objectives. This new environment provides opportunity to women to set their own agenda within the boundaries set by governance and civil society issues, and various rights instruments.

Amir Mahmood discuses the role of education and training in Asian development. He argues that human resource development can be viewed as organised efforts to enhance the productivity of human capital. A major contribution of the new growth theories is their explicit treatment of the role of human capital in determining the rate of (endogenous) technological progress. Investment in human capital has been given credit for an efficient use of productive factors of production and product and process innovations. Investment in education and training is a fundamental precondtion for economic growth.

Mahmood assesses the impact of human resource development strategies on the development and competitiveness of South and East Asian economies by focusing on the role of education, training, skills and gender disparities in education. He contends that, among other factors, higher literacy rate; efficiency of allocation of resources among various education sub-sectors; acquisition and application of new knowledge; rapid accumulation of skills; skill-job requirement linkages; linkages between industry educational/ vocational institutions; and efforts to reduce gender disparities in education, have played an important role in helping East Asian countries to create a conducive environment to achieve rapid economic growth.

In chapter 16, M.E. Qureshi, S.R. Harrison and K.C. Roy discuss the usefulness of Geographic Information Systems (GIS) in storing environmental information, in analysing environmental problems and in decision-making processes, with special reference to sustainable management of catchment areas in India and Pakistan. The paper also contains an overview of natural resource degradation in the two South Asian countries.

The concluding chapter (17) by K.C. Roy, C.A. Tisdell and A. Ghose is centrally concerned with the issues relating to women's empowerment in rural India in the context of Amartya Sen's entitlement theory. The main theme of the paper is to argue the case of access to education to improve the economic and social status of women in India in the long-term.

Development *versus* Sustainable Development

The World Commission on Environment and Development (the Brundtland Commission) defined *sustainable development* as "development that meets the needs of the present without compromising the ability of future generations to meet their own needs." The fuller definition given by the Brundtland Commission is worth quoting :

> "Humanity has the ability to make development sustainable — to ensure that it meets the needs of the present without compromising the ability of future generations to meet their needs. The concept of sustainable development does imply limits — not absolute limits but limitations imposed by the present state of technology and social organization on environmental resources and by the ability of the biosphere to absorb the effects of human activities. But technology and social organization can be managed and improved to make way for a new era of economic growth.... In the end, sustainable development is not a fixed state of harmony, but rather a process of change in which the exploitation of resources, the direction of investments, the orientation of technological development and institutional change are made consistent with future as well as present needs."[4]

---

[4] World Commission on Environment and Development, *Our Common Future*, 1987.

At the Earth Summit in 1992, nations extended the above definition and adopted a set of principles to guide future development. The Rio Declaration on Environment and Development defines the rights of people to development and their responsibilities to safeguard the common environment.[5]

For public policy purposes, there are several core concepts that underpin sustainable development. First, in the context of sustainable development, we have to assess the demographic and social landscape of a country and the rate of its urbanisation. Indefinite population growth in an environment of limited resources cannot surely be sustained. The need for feeding an ever increasing population might lead to deforestation and salinity and the consequent disruption of the ecological system.

Indeed, population growth, combined with the demand for a higher and higher material standard of living, has been the single most important factor in the ecological crisis of the present age. The ecological system in which we live evolved slowly over millions of years. It derives its stability and predictability because of its diversity and complexity. In their desire to maintain an ever increasing population size, human beings are simplifying the complex ecosystem and creating future uncertainties.[6]

Ecological problems are not confined in their effects to local or national frontiers but have implications globally. For example, pollution of a river in one country may have a disastrous impact on a neighbouring country which depends for its drinking water on the same river flowing through its territory. Similarly, deforestation in one country may have an adverse environmental impact on all the countries of that region. Indeed, the destruction of the Amazonian forests would have a global impact on the environment in the long-term.

Secondly, sustainable development must lead to inter-generational equity. The present generation must not overuse

---

5 See the World Resources Institute (1987, 1994 and 1997), *World Resources*, New York.

6 World Summit for Social Development, 1995.

existing resources to adversely affect the potential material living standards of future generations. In this context, it is important that every nation seeks to ensure that its use of renewable resources (such as agricultural methods and technology, is *sustainable*, and that its exploitation of non-renewable resources such as minerals, oil, gas and coal) is geared towards an efficient and optimum inter-temporal use.[7]

Finally, sustainable development assumes a process of an extension of human rights embracing civil and political liberties. Should economic growth and development fail to achieve the so-called "trickle down effect" and create inequalities at national and international levels, the whole idea of sustainable development would be defeated.

> "We are deeply convinced that economic development, social development and environmental protection are inter-dependent and naturally reinforcing components of sustainable development, which is the framework for our efforts to achieve a higher quality of life for all people. Equitable social development recognises that empowering the poor to utilize environmental resources sustainably is a necessary foundation for sustainable development. We also recognise that broad-based and sustained economic growth in the context of sustainable development is necessary to sustain social development and social justice."[8]

Conclusion

In this chapter we have defined economic growth as a short-term increase in per capita real incomes. A continuous process of economic growth should normally lead to economic development in the long-term, which would involve growth with distributive justice, and a general improvement in the quality of life, as measured by the Human Development Index (HDI) such as better education, longer life expectancy and better health facilities, cleaner environment, more leisure hours, greater gender equality and so on.

---

[7] See, for instance, R.N. Ghosh, *Agriculture in Economic Development*, Vikas Publishing, New Delhi, 1977.

[8] World Summit for Social Development, *op. cit., Declaration and Programme of Action.*

Sustainability of development is, however, a broader concept. It involves a pattern of economic development that would be compatible with safe environment, biodiversity, ecological balance, intergenerational and international equity. By definition, therefore, sustainable development can be achieved through global (or international) efforts, or at least by joint efforts of nations which have a common stake in their environment such as forests, rivers and atmosphere. To achieve sustainable development it is, therefore, important for nations to come together to work out a common program for action on issues such as atmospheric pollution, sharing of water, damming of rivers, and construction of common river and electricity grids.[9]

In brief, sustainable development is not possible at a local, or a national level. Trans-national effort involving international cooperation is a fundamental prerequisite for sustaining development. It is true that some issues of sustainable development can be resolved at the local level. That is why it is said that "global is local." But when costs of development at a local or national level exceed benefits, international efforts are needed to ensure sustainability of development.[10]

---

9 *Brundtland Commission's Report.*

10 See, for instance, the Report of the Expert Group Meeting on *Women, Population and Sustainable Development : The Road from Rio, Cairo and Beijing*, Santo Domingo, November 1996.

2 The Role of Property Rights in Women's Empowerment : the Case of Nepal

Meena Acharya

The Analytical Framework

Scope of the Paper

This paper is not concerned with the question of : how women's subordination originated? With the origin of private property as Engels believed? Or, with the start of the agricultural stage as postulated by others (e.g., Martin and Voorhies)? Or, due to some other factors? This paper argues that given the predominance of property ownership and the military might in determination of power relations in the present day world, women with property rights will have a more level playing field.

The social reproduction process which comprises material as well as human reproduction is based on private property rights. Individuals and societies with command over vast resources and militaristic might are able to force their will on the mass of the population with no survival means except their own labor. This power may be exercised through direct or indirect channels. Wealthy household's greater say in all aspects of social and political decision making is well established and accepted in social sciences (*e.g.*, Dahl, 1989, UNDP, 1996). Control of the state apparatus by the haves in general and by trans-national corporations in particular is also a popular subject of discussion in modern political science (*e.g.*, Greider, 1992).

In the case of gender relations, the situation is more complicated by the private-public dichotomy and the patriarchy (see Okin, 1991; Meillassoux, 1981). The domestic community, as Meillassoux (1981) calls it, has its own rules of material and human reproduction, which are conditioned and in its turn conditions the material reproduction process in the public arena. We need to look inside this domestic community in all its multi-dimensional relationships with the outside world. The focus of this paper is on the importance of property rights for empowering women within and outside this domestic community and freeing them from the gender relationship of subordination and domination, given the overwhelming importance of command over all means of production as the basis of power under modem capitalism.

Property and Its Relevance

Property is also a historical concept (see Hirsehon, 1984). At some point of history, it may have included only cattle, slowly encompassing people and women. The concept of women as property has been very persistent until recent times nor is it completely wiped out today. These concepts, however, are outdated in the context of current capitalist mode of production.

Here, in this paper, property rights are defined to include all legal and social traditions of inter-generational transfers in addition to an individual's right to keep the property from his/her own earnings. The first and second components of this complex body of rights need to be distinguished clearly in any discussion about women's empowerment. Theoretically and legally, probably the right to one's one earnings are more or less recognised universally with few exceptions in some developing countries. But the rights to inter-generational transfers vary from country to country and culture to culture. There is a large variation within South Asia (See Bina Agrawal, 1994) and even within a small country such as Nepal.

Currently, in most developing countries the main avenue for acquiring capital and land is intergenerational transfers. Gains from investment in human capital and employment are still limited and not high enough to lead to significant accumulation. Even investment in human capital is dependent on rights to intergenerational transfers. Only rich people with properties or households with high enough salaries can afford to educate their children to a level which may lead to further accumulation. Community property rights which provided equal access to all its members have eroded fast in the process of marketization and privatization. Gender inequality in property transfers is, therefore, a primary factor leading to relative poverty and economic insecurity for women.

Access to economic resources is primary to physical survival and hence a precondition for achieving gender equality in other fields. On the basis of extensive anthology from South Asia, Bina Agrawal (1994) argues this fact convincingly in her recent work. The fact is that women with no access to alternative means of livelihood are more likely to be violated than those women who have independent means of support for themselves (For example see New ERA, 1997 for Nepal).

The Bargaining Model

Using a bargaining model for gender interactions within the household, and outside in the community and the state, Bina Agrawal elaborates in detail how a woman's *defacto* access to land strengthens her bargaining position. The bargaining model used extensively in the theory of the firm in micro-economics, has also been introduced to study the household economy (e.g., Folbre, 1986). Applied to household it postulates that households are not wholly co-operative, altruistic units as assumed by the neo-classical economists, but are composed of individuals whose relationships are characterised by both co-operation and conflict. Their relations may be maintained or changed through a process of contestation or bargaining between individual members. The outcome of bargaining will be affected by the access of individual members to economic, political and social power, which are given by an overall socio-economic structure at a given point of time.

Bina Agrawal also recognises the importance of ideological (e.g., control over sexuality, village endogamy/exogamy, distance to parental home, *purdha* etc.) and other factors (*e.g.,* literacy rate, female labor force participation, total fertility rate, land scarcity etc.) in determination of the situation whether a woman can gain actual control over land even under conditions of her legal entitlement. At the same time she contends that access to land is the crucial factor in strengthening a woman's bargaining power both within and outside the household.

To quote her "... gender relations and women's economic, political and social positions are the outcome of processes of contestation and bargaining... women's ability to improve their positions has, however, been seriously circumscribed by a historical process that has entrenched inequalities in the distribution of property, in the cultural construction of gender and in exclusion of women from processes of public decision making thereby relegating them to the role of takers and not makers of laws, social norms and rules (p. 477)."

Thus, it can be argued that ideological and material factors are interactively reinforcing the relations of gender subordination.

Empowerment — Some Indicators

This article views empowerment as a complex process, which may be decomposed in two sub-processes — (1) directed to improvement in the life options and opportunities for individual development and (2) strengthening of the role and bargaining power of disfranchised individuals and groups in vital decisions affecting their lives and livelihood.

These two sub-processes are interdependent but separate. This distinction even if not very clear in the case of other disfranchised groups, is very clear in the case of women. A poor household will acquire access to property through purchase, if its access to education, knowledge and employment increases. But the same may not be true in the case of women. A woman may acquire education, knowledge and work throughout her life even earning outside the households, but she may have only limited rights even on her own earning and property acquired by herself. Such limitations on her property rights may be legal or social, reinforced by limitation of her rights in other fields, *e.g.*, social control over sexuality. This control over sexuality could be based on social traditions, or it could also be legally codified.

No doubt a woman's empowerment process is linked closely also to the process of empowerment of the household in the public arena. For example, a woman from a rich and socially high status household has more access to resources and higher social status in the public arena. But her status is derived from the socio-economic status of the household head, in which her status *vis-à-vis* the male members of the household is severely limited. This status holds only until she agrees to a subordinated position within the household. Once the rules of this domination — subordinate game — are broken, she has no social status in the public arena. It is important to examine in this context how her access to property effects her social position.

To analyse the relationship between a woman's command over property and her empowerment one needs also to identify some indicators of empowerment both in the private and the public arena. Political power-sharing is one such indicator in the public arena, but it is not an adequate indicator. Legal code and state policies are other such indicators. Access to household resources and the role in the household decision making could be taken as specific indicators of such empowerment within the household. Women's control over their own sexuality and freedom from violence are other important indicators of women's empowerment.

The Case of Nepal

The Status of Women in Nepal study series completed by CEDA during 1977-1981 (see Acharya and Bennett, 1981 for a summary) showed that women with lesser degree of social control over their sexuality had higher mobility and access to entrepreneurial activities and hence access to independent income. In the communities which allowed women independent entrepreneurial activities, women had much higher role in the household decision making (see table 1). It should be noted here that in all communities in Nepal, immovable property is inherited patrilinealy; women have access to husband's share of property but no share of their own either in the parental or husband's households. In spite of this, certain communities do allow a mother's property to pass over to her daughters, but such instances are not too common. Therefore, the source of greater voice in the household decision making in the case of *Baragaunle, Bhote, Rai* and *Magars* are attributed to their entrepreneurial activities, which was facilitated by their easy mobility, less concern about their sexual purity and generally more egalitarian gender relations in their societies. This paper will delve a little deeper and illustrate how denial of inheritance rights and control over women's sexuality (that is, the material and the ideological) are interwoven closely forming a loop in the Indo-Aryan culture. In Nepal, for example, economic rights of women, *i.e.*, access to property and income, fundamentally determine their access to education, employment and political power.

Family Laws

In Nepal a married woman has equal inheritance rights with her male children and husband in her husband's property. This right is conditional on her remaining faithful to her husband and to his clan, even after his death. Thus, a widow may inherit only if she does not remarry.

A woman can demand divorce from her husband on following grounds :

- if the husband marries again,
- because of physical cruelty from the husband,
- if the husband remains separated for a period of three years without keeping any contact with her,
- if the couple is incapable of bearing children because of the infertility of the husband.

A divorcee has the right of custody over her children below five years of age and, as long as she does not remarry, over her children who are not of age (below sixteen). The father has to provide for food, clothes, education and medical expenses for his children. However, if the earnings of the mother exceed that of father, the mother has to share the expenses.

The conditionalities on which a man can bring another wife include :

- if a wife is mentally ill with no possibility of cure;
- if the wife has an infection or incurable venereal disease;
- if the wife is living separate, having acquired her share of the family property (*Ansa*);
- if the wife is invalid and cannot move;

- if she is blind in both eyes and
- if she has no "child" even after ten years of marriage (Earlier the condition stipulated "son" rather than "child", but socially it is still interpreted as "son" even if legally it says "child").

Other legal provisions on family matters include :

- Limit on minimum age of marriage for a girl at 16 years, and for a boy 18 years, if with the consent of their respective guardians. Without the consent of the guardians, the minimum age of marriage for girls and boys are 18 and 21 years respectively.
- Provision of penalty for child marriage, marriage without the consent of the bride, polygamy, marriage between a bride and groom with age difference of 90 years and more. However, marriage once completed cannot be nullified.
- The husband has the right do decide the place of settlement.
- The wife has to have permission of her husband to work outside the home.
- Women can enter into legal contract only in connection with her *Stridhan* (her exclusive property as defined below).

Laws on Property

The *Mulki Ain* (The Law of the Land) specifies that a woman is entitled to two types of property : *Stridhan* and *Ansa*.

This code defines the '*Stridhan*' as well as movable and non-movable property earned by a woman herself or given to her by anybody at the time of her marriage, or before and after as present. She has absolute right over this kind of property and can do as she wishes with it, *Ansa* is defined as the property acquired at the time of division of property among the *coparsonors* (original inheritors). On this *Ansa* she has absolute right over all movable property and half of the immovable property. To sell the remaining half she has to take the permission of her husband or son if married or of her father/brother if unmarried. A woman can get 'Ansa' in following instances :

(i) If the daughter is unmarried till the age of 35 and remains so thereafter, she gets equal share with her brothers in the ancestral property. *Mulki Ain*, however, specifies that if the daughter marries after receiving her *Ansa*, she has to return all of it to other coparsonors. If the daughter or sister is not of 35 years of age at the time of the partition of property but remains unmarried afterwards she may not claim any property. A son, however, has right over the ancestral property as soon as he is born.

(ii) If the father has no wife, son or male descendent on son's line then even the married daughter can claim the parental property.

(iii) A widow over 30 years of age has right over all her husband's *Ansa*. If she is less than 30 years of age she cannot claim *Ansa* unless her in-laws do not provide her food, clothing and some extra expenses for fulfilling her religions needs. Further a widow has to return the *Ansa* to the coparsonors of her husband if she remarries.

(iv) A divorcee cannot claim alimony if she can sustain herself economically. A divorcee without any means of subsistence, has right over alimony up to five years if she does not remarry. However, if the divorce is by mutual consent or on the ground of infidelity of wife, she has no right to alimony. This, of course, puts the women at a very precarious position. If she does not have any *Stridhan* and if she is incapable of working for subsistence, who is to provide for her after five years of divorce? This forces women to remain married at any cost. Therefore, in cases of marriage failure women are frequently forced by economic circumstances to tolerate cowives.

(v) Married woman can demand *Ansa* from her husband only in following situations :

- If the husband does not provide for her living expenses in accordance with his economic standard, which is very difficult to prove.

- If the husband throws out the wife from his house.
- If the husband physically abuses his wife regularly. This point reflects that a husband may beat his wife occasionally.
- If the husband takes another wife, however, the property now will be divided between the husband and all his wives and sons.
- If the woman is 35 years of age and has been married for fifteen years, she can claim her *Ansa* without any reason.

In each of the aforesaid situation the woman has to remain faithful to her husband. It her fidelity is suspected and adultery proved she has to return *Ansa*. A man's fidelity has no bearing on his right to *Ansa*.

Further, while a woman has to have permission to sell even her *Ansa*, a man can sell all moveable property and immovable property without his wife's/daughter-in-law's permission. This provision puts severe limits on women's right to *Ansa*. Because of this provision if a household does not want to give any *Ansa* to a "woman" all the property may be sold before a partition can be effected. Further, the woman has claim over *Ansa* only if she remains married for fifteen years and she is 35 years of age or above. If she has not been married for fifteen years, she cannot demand *Ansa*.

Practical Implications of the Legal Provisions

This discrimination in property rights and degree of legally codified social control over one's own sexuality puts women in a very precarious position. On the one hand, girls/women are expected to compete with men in all walks of life — education, employment, social recognition and political participation. Women are expected to participate on equal footing with man in the public arena while she is a subordinate in relation to men in all aspects of domestic life. The dependency of public/private spheres, which is generally ignored, may be illustrated vividly in the case of Nepal.

For example, girl's access to education and food *vis-à-vis* boys is severely limited by the fact that a married daughter inherits no property in the parental household and correspondingly has no responsibility for looking after parents in their old age. Numerous studies have cited "*Arkako Ghar Jane*" (shifting girls to husbands household on marriage) as one of the major causes why girls are not getting equal opportunities with boys in education, besides poverty and the need of girls' labor at home (CERID, 1986, 1997. Acharya, 1981). The female/male literacy ratio in the country is only 0.34 compared to 0.58 in the SAARC region. This means that there are only 34 literate women to 100 literate men among the adult population in Nepal. The SAARC average, on the other hand, is 58 literate women to 100 literate men among the similar age group of population. In Nepal girls who get to go to school also have one year less schooling than boys.

A girl's worth in the parental home is severely limited by the fact that she carries no responsibility to look after her parents in their old age. So, she is discriminated in food allocation, access to education, health facilities etc. A recent survey, however, found no difference in child (6-36 months) nutrition or breast feeding for girls and boys in Nepal in general. Such data must be more closely examined. We would expect that in communities where women have very little access to property and independent income generating opportunities, gender discrimination in nutritional levels of male and female children would emerge more prominently. Communities with slacker control over sexuality of women and hence with greater access of women to income earning opportunities outside the household will have lesser degree of discrimination against their female children.

Table 1 below features eight villages representing different communities in Nepal which grant various degrees of income earning opportunities to women and have various degrees of control over their sexuality. As far as immovable property is concerned patrilineal inheritance system prevails in all communities in Nepal both legally and socially. Variations, however, are wide in the income earning opportunities allowed to women and movables inherited through mothers. Therefore, the variable on independent source of income is taken as an indicator of some access to property. This access has been rated substantial, moderate and little depending on whether women have wide entrepreneurial activities and some access to income (substantial), just inheritance of maternal property and wage earning opportunities (moderate), just same wage earning possibilities (little) and neither inheritance nor wage earning opportunities (none). Similarly sexual control has also been rated as little, moderate and strict. This variable is a composite of different indicators such as practice of *purdha* (actual veiling) and restrictions on mobility, attitude towards premarital sex, widow remarriages, adultery and illegitimacy etc. While *Parbativa* (even *Brahmin/Chetri*) women are not required to practise *purdha*, their mobility and choice of marriage partners are strictly controlled by rules of the village and the clan. Widow remarriage is not allowed, adultery is strictly punished and illegitimacy is a real problem. Among, the *Baragaunle, Lorong Rai, Kham Magar, Newar/Jyapu, Tamang* and *Tharu* communities — while adultery is not condoned attitudes towards premarital sex and illegitimate children are very liberal. The *Maithili* community is labelled moderate because among the *Yadavs*, widow and second/third marriages are frequent and socially accepted even though they practise veiling. The *Maithili* Brahmin community, on the other hand, practises *purdha* and is very strict in controlling women's mobility. Adultery and premarital sex is strongly condemned and punished with much more severe consequences for women than for men.

In table 1 below, there are two separate columns to show women's contributions to household decision making and awareness about village politics. The decision making variable comprises the per cent of decisions where women are involved. The 1978 data relate to more than 12 thousand decisions taken in a total of 280 households in eight rural communities during the day preceding the interview (in the case of day-to-day decisions on matters such as farm management, food allocations shopping etc.) or the year preceding the field study (for decisions relating to investment or other resource allocations such as sale of land, animals etc.). Similarly, 1993 figures relate to 5,779 decisions of similar nature in 440 households.

The political awareness percentages given in table 1, relate only to proportion of women knowledgeable about village politics without juxtaposing it to male awareness in both surveys. Such female/male ratio would have illuminated other factors such as general politicization of the village, distance to national polities etc. But such comparative data are not available.

Table 1 : Independent Income, Sexual Control, Decision Making Input and Political Awareness

Communities	Ind. Income Source	Degree of Sexual Control	Input in Household Decision Making		Political Awareness	
			1978	1993	1978	1993
Baragaonle	Substantial	Little	62.5	60.2	96.2	75.0
Lorung Raj	Substantial	Little	86.1	45.4	68.7	70.0
Khan Magar	Substantial	Little	64.5	36.8	96.7	91.8
Newar/ Jyapu	Little	Little	43.9	39.8	18.2	36.4
Tamang	Moderate (wage)	Little	53.5	32.9	68.8	44.5
Tharu	Little	Little	37.5	10.2	43.9	63.6
Maithili	None	Moderate (Yadavs)	38.1	18.5	64.4	78.2
Parbatiya	None	Strict	39.1	25.6	37.5	22.7
Overall	Some	Varied	53.8		61.8	61.1

Source : Acharya and Bennett, 1981 for 1978 figures, *Stri Shaktti* for 1993 figures.

The above figures show that generally in the communities with lesser control over women's sexuality higher proportion of women were aware of village politics. However, exceptions are also quite significant as *Newar* and *Tharu* with lesser degree of control showed much lower awareness than theoretically highly controlled *Maithili* women.

Two caveats seem relevant in this respect. First, women's awareness levels depend on many more things such as literacy, level of general politicization of the village, exposure to media etc., than just one factor of control on their sexuality. The Maithili village in this case study happened to be a very politicized village (Acharya,

1981), while the Newar village seemed much oblivious of the political issues even if very near to Kathmandu. Therefore, the more relevant indicator in this case could be female awareness relative to men. But no data was collected on male awareness in the above case studies as mentioned above.

Acharya (1994) extensively analyses how women's political participation are severely limited by lack of access to economic resources and control over her mobility which is taken as one of the indicators of social control over her sexuality. On the national scale women's access to positions of power in Nepal is much lower than in other South Asian countries, even though their economic activity rate is on the higher side in the region (table 2).

Table 2 : Selected Economic and Political Indicators on Women's Empowerment in the SAARC Region

Countries	Female Economic Activity Rate as % of Male Economic Activity Rate 1995	Women in Parliament %	Women's Share of Earned Income
Nepal	68	3.9	Na
India	46	7.3	25
Bangladesh	73	9.1	23
Pakistan	36	2.6	21
Sri Lanka	55	5.3	36
Maldives	73	6.3	35
South Asia		6.3	25

Source : *HDR*, 1998.

It has also been found that women bear domestic violence and abuses stoically because they have no fall back position on leaving the husband's household. How lack of access to alternative means of livelihood, in case of marriage failure, leads to commercial sex activities is vividly illustrated by a recent study (New ERA, 1998). Of the 19 case studies presented in this report more than one third had left their homes because of violence. Another study (Sathi, *et. al.*, 1997) reported that 88 per cent of women had suffered from physical violence in their lives. Majority of 268 commercial sex workers interviewed in Nepal and India in the course of New ERA study, identified poverty and need of money as the primary cause for being in this business.

The decision making column in table 1 above also indicates that women with some access to economic resources and social freedom (*e.g., Baragaunle, Lorung Rai,* and *Kham-Magar*) are involved in household decision making on a larger scale. The *Newar/Jyapu* and *Tamang* women with less access to economic resources but large degree of social freedom had inputs in the household decision making ranging between 44 to 53 per cent in 1978. In the rest of the communities women's decision making roles were much lower. The communities where women have lower access to independent economic resources, also are ranked at the lower end of the scale in household decision making inputs. Relatively higher decision making input of *Parbatiya* women *vis-à-vis Tharus* and *Newars* probably is explained by the fact that a substantial number of low caste women in this community were working as wage earners and had some independent sources of income. Additionally, this village is quite near the Kathmandu valley, with a substantial size of migrating male population. Male migration tends to put more managerial responsibilities on women than in situations of permanent male presence in the household.

Given such situation, the women's movement in Nepal is actively pursuing reform of laws on women's legal right to property as a matter of priority. There has been a strong backlash and the Bill which is pending in the Parliament is directed to eliminating some of the glaring gender inequalities enshrined in the law — such as the age limit on women for inheritance rights both in the parental and the a final household. But a daughter will still lose all her rights in parental property after marriage. Even these mild amendments are pending with no prospect for early discussions as there is no agreement among the major political parties on the various clauses of the Bill.

The strength of the opposition to this Bill itself is an indicator of how this right is fundamental to women's empowerment in Nepal. The strongest argument the opponents have so far produced is that it will fundamentally change the social structure and create havoc in the society. Whether it will create a havoc is not clear, but the fact that it will affect the social structure fundamentally is not in dispute. The whole idea about women's empowerment is to change the social structure fundamentally, leading towards a more egalitarian gender relations in the private as well as public spheres. So far the changes have come only in the civic sphere, *e.g.*, political rights. But women need both economic and social rights for an effective exercise of their political rights.

Freedom from hunger and physical violence are two basic necessities for human survival and primary factors for women's survival. Hence, they form basic elements in the empowerment process. Employment can provide current means of survival but without equal inheritance rights intergenerationally, female of the species will have to start again and again from '0' level in the economic arena, which weakens their competitive strength.

REFERENCES

Acharya, Meena (1981), 'The Maithili Women of Sirsia,' *The Status of Women in Nepal*, Volume II Part , CEDA, Tribhuvan University, Kathmandu.

______ (1994), 'Political Participation of Women in Nepal' in *Women and Politics World Wide* (eds.), Barbara Nelson and Nazma Chaudhari, Yale University Press, New Heaven, USA.

Achaya, Meena and Lylln Bennett (1981), 'The Rural Women of Nepal : An Aggregate Analysis and Summary of 8 Village Studies,' *The Status of Women in Nepal*, CEDA, Tribhuvan University, Kathmandu.

Agrawal, Bina (1994), 'A Field of One's Own : Gender and Land Rights' in *South Asia*, Cambridge University Press, UK.

CERID (1986), Education of Girls and Women in Nepal, T.U. Kathmandu.

______ (1997), 'Gender and Secondary Education : A study Report,' submitted to Secondary Education Project/Cambridge Education Consultants Ltd.

Dahl, A. Robert (1989), *Democracy and Its Critics,* Yale University Press, Newhaven and London.

Folbre, Nancy (1986), 'Hearts and Spades : Paradigm of Household Economics,' in *World Development*, 14(2).

Greider, William (1993), *Who Will Tell The People,* Simon and Schuster, New York, London.

Hirsehon, Renee (1984), 'Introduction : Property, Power and Gender Relations,' in *Women and Property — Women as Property* (ed.), Renee Hirsehon, USA.

Martin and Voorhies (1975), *Female of the Species,* Columbia University Press, New York and London.

Meillassoux, Claude (1975), *Maidens, Meal and Money* : Capitalism and the Domestic Community, Cambridge University Press.

Ministry of Law and Justice (1983), *Muluki Ain*, Law Books Management Board Press, Kathmandu.

New ERA (1997), A Situation Analysis of Sex Work and Trafficking in Nepal with Reference to Children, October 1996. Submitted to UNICEF, Pulchowk, Lalitpur, Nepal.

Okin, Susan Moller (1991), 'Gender, the Public and the Private,' in *Political Theory Today* (ed.), Dasid Hold, Cambridge Polity.

Parliamentary Secretariat/HMG (1996), Bill for Amendine, *The Mulki Ain.*

Sathi and Asia Foundation (1997), A Situation Analysis of Violence of Women and Girls in Nepal, Kathmanclu.

Shtrii Shakti (1995), Women Development Democracy : A Study of the Socio-Economic Changes in the Status of Women in Nepal (1981-1993), Kathmandu, Nepal.

UNDP, *Human Development Report,* 1996 and 1998.

3 Property Rights in Fiji : Women's Welfare and Empowerment

Biman C. Prasad
Sunil Kumar

Introduction

The aim of this paper is to investigate the impact of the nature of property rights on the welfare of women and their empowerment. The welfare and empowerment of women in Fiji is explored in the context of contemporary economic developments, social welfare and values. The main elements of economic transition from inward-looking import substitution strategies of the past to the current outward-looking export oriented strategy are also discussed in order to argue the origins of gender disparity in employment and social life in Fiji. The issues of inheritance of land and property and the distribution of the same through matrimonial links will also be examined in the paper.

Economic policies in many instances have implications for gender disparity. The adverse effects (or neglect) of development policies towards the welfare of women are not emphasised adequately. In Fiji, for example, it can be argued that the lack of empowerment (both social and political) of women and the structures of kin relations may be attributed to the uneven distribution of property rights. The converse of this argument can also be argued to explain the level of participation of women in politics and social life in Fiji.

The women's issue was put on the agenda of world development after the 1975 conference in Mexico in which the period 1976-1985 was declared the UN decade for women. While the agenda gained prominence in many developed countries, governments in developing countries failed to address adequately the women's issues in their development policies. In the last decade, however, women's organisations and non-governmental organisations have highlighted various issues regarding the welfare of women that needs to be taken into consideration by policymakers everywhere including developed countries. Fiji, like many other developing countries, is coming to grips with the need to include women-related issues in its mainstream development policies. This is significantly demonstrated by the action taken by the current government in formulating its policies towards addressing the women's issues. In 1995 the Government of Fiji became party to the Convention on the Elimination of All Forms of Discrimination Against Women in Beijing. The Fijian Government declared its commitment by pledging to adhere to five-point efforts to address women's issues, *viz.,* (1) that it would mainstream women's concerns in the planning process and all policy areas; (2) that it would review laws that disadvantage women; (3) that it would allocate resources to develop women's micro-enterprises through policy implementation in financial institutions; (4) that it would seek to involve women in decision making and assign fifty per cent representation in participation, appointments, training and promotions at all levels of government and (5) that it would campaign to promote a sound and stable environment that is free of violence, especially domestic violence, sexual harassment and child abuse (Ministry of Women and Culture, 1998).

Currently, the statistical evidence on employment shows that women continue to be marginalised in employment but the trends are positive (Jahan and Prasad, 1997). Table 1 shows lack of women participation in Fiji's work-force in various sectors of the economy. However, the overall share of women in Fiji's work-force has increased slightly. In the period 1993 to 1996 it increased by 0.7 per cent (see tables 1 and 4). The manufacturing sector has a high rate of participation (43 per cent), but is basically due to employment in low wage garment industry which has absorbed low skilled women workers since 1987 when the Tax Free Zones (TFZs) were provided by the government to roll the economy back into action after the military coups.

Since the military coups of 1987, Fiji has undergone significant economic, political and social changes. As a result of the coups the 1990 Constitution came into effect which institutionalised racial discrimination and also discrimination against women. This caused outward migration of the high skilled segment of the labour force. However, after 10 years of political uncertainty, a new constitutional arrangement has been reached which provides for ethnic and gender equality.[1]

Table 1 : Employment by Sector and Gender, 1996

FSIC Sector	Male	Female		Total
		No.	%	
Agriculture Forest and Fisheries	1,697	283	14.3	1,980
Mining and Quarrying	2,213	95	4.1	2,308
Manufacturing	14,022	10,613	4.3	24,635
Electricity and Water	1,784	80	4.3	1,864
Construction	5,615	113	2.0	5,728
Wholesale and Retail Trade	13,671	7,059	34.1	20,730
Transport and Business Services	8,114	1,676	17.1	9,790
Financial and Business Services	4,594	2,613	36.3	7,207
Community, Social and Personal Services	24,032	11,807	32.9	35,839
Total	75,742	34,339	149.4	110,081

Source : *Bureau of Statistics, Census Data* 1996 (Unpublished).

The adoption of Structural Adjustment Program (SAP) since 1987 has affected the economy in a significant way. The SAP in Fiji has decisively led the economy away from inward-looking import-substitution to an outward-looking export-oriented strategy. While the economic rationale of these structural adjustment policies was the generation of competition in a neo-classical framework, its adoption has not shown much positive results. The SAP has, on the contrary, created a number of problems such as increased poverty, unemployment and social ills such as higher levels of crime, suicide and malnutrition in lower income groups and also industrial unrest.

---

1 A new Constitution based on multi-party democracy has been accepted and new elections were scheduled for early 1999.

The SAP policy changes in Fiji since 1987 have clearly meant a shift in emphasis away from the primary and rural sectors to the urban sector, the benefits of which have not been obvious (Prasad and Tisdell, 1997).

However, to what extent women have benefited from these policies and whether the position of women in the country has improved is not clear and raises controversy about the effectiveness of SAP. In the case of Fiji, the open market policy options has been seriously marred by institutional constraints such as the nature of property rights in land, and the racial and gender discrimination as institutionalised in the 1990 Constitution.

As pointed out by Agarwal (1994), the question of property rights is vital for understanding the extent of women's empowerment. Since only 10 per cent of land in Fiji is held as freehold, it provides severe constraints to women in terms of property ownership. In most of the South Pacific countries including Fiji, the empowerment of women will be possible by providing them with education and skills on an equal footing with men. It implies women need to be provided with equal opportunities in employment, education and ownership of properties. Furthermore, the role of women is firmly placed in the context of the family. Most reports on women have focused on the idea of strengthening the family unit under the traditional socio-cultural practices.[2] As a result of these approaches to development, the extent of control over resources by women is overlooked, and the discrimination embedded in the traditional patriarchal societies is reinforced and women continue to suffer oppression and exploitation.

This paper, therefore, addresses the question of property rights, in particular the nature of property rights in land and how it affects the economic position of women in Fiji. It is divided as follows : Part 2 provides the theoretical and conceptual issues regarding

---

2 See for example, the *Port Vila Declaration on Population and Sustainable Development* (1993). None of the articles, for example, in recent book on perspective of Pacific Island Women considered the issue of property rights and control of resources by women in general.

women and development and the role of property rights. Part 3 considers some of the indicators of women's development and a brief overview of the situation in Fiji. Parts 4 and 5 discuss the nature of property rights and the extent to which women have rights over property and how it may affect their welfare. Part 6 provides concluding comments.

Women and Economic Development : General Views and Theories

Tisdell (1996) provides a useful account of views and theories of how the welfare of women may have been affected by economic development. On a more pessimistic view he points out that, contrary to common belief, primitive societies are not necessarily egalitarian. However, on an optimistic view, he pointed out that primitive and subsistence societies were largely patriarchal and the development of the market economy could open up new opportunities for women. Tisdell (1996) concludes that the relationship between women's socio-economic status and economic growth may be U-shaped.

In many developing countries the traditional cultures and societies are patriarchal and tend to accord a subordinate status to women. Since in Fiji land ownership rights are entrenched in the Constitution, freeing it up to the market forces as an economic resource is far more difficult than otherwise. To change the legislation guiding the control and use of native land from the grips of the Native Land Trust Board (NLTB) in both the houses of Parliament would require three quarters of the votes of members present. The Great Council of Chiefs, an avowedly patriarchal institution, under the 1990 Constitution holds the veto power in the affairs relating to land and fishing rights. Jalal (1998 : 56) concludes that land rights are entrenched and since the 1990 Fiji Constitution recognises customary law (Article 100), it favours males and thus provide that the land titles be held through the male line. The new 1997 amended Constitution also recognises the customary law (Article 186) and requires the Parliament to make provision for its practice.

Women's organisations world wide and more so in developing countries, as a means of women's emancipation, have advocated the movement of women from the traditional confines of the home into the modern work-force. This, it is claimed will provide women greater choice and freedom for the type of employment they engage in and hence improve their welfare. It is also likely to provide a boost for policies which favour increased participation of women in the economy (Klein, 1984 : Sinclair, 1983). During the 1950s and 1960s many developing countries chose the path of industrialisation based on import-substitution policies. Such industrialisation further marginalised the women's role in developing countries. The growth of the manufacturing and industrial sector in many developing countries led only to the deterioration of women's welfare.[3]

The import-substitution industrial strategy failed to improve growth, and the expected 'trickle down' to the masses, especially to women and children did not take place.[4]

The Keynesian demand management policies became increasingly unsustainable in Fiji as a result of increasing unemployment and inflation which led to the increased incidence of poverty. The debt crises of the late 1970s and the early 1980s required alternative strategies for growth. The supply-side 'structural adjustment' policies are now being actively adopted by many developing countries, as an effective means of accelerated development, as experienced by many South-East Asian countries in the 1970s and 1980s.

The key to the supply-side structural adjustment policies is the opening of economies designed to promote international trade and 'down-sizing' government. The development of export industries such as the garment industry has increasingly led to the feminisation of labour particularly in many of the developing countries (Standing, 1992). However, the conditions and wages for women in the new export industries are a cause for concern. Standing (1992 :

3 See, for example, Anker and Hein (1986); Boserup (1970); Bruton, (1970) : Jaquette (1982); Leahy (1986) : Nash and Fernandez-Kelly (1983); Rogers (1979); Roy (1994); Tiano (1987), Tinker and Bramsen (1976); Tinker (1990).

4 For a summary of the experience of import substitution policies, see *Power* (1966).

351), for example, points out that "young women, particularly in the Newly Industrialised Countries (NICs) in Asia, have been socially and economically oppressed for so long that they have low 'aspiration wages' and low efficiency wages." So, the success of supply-side structural adjustment policies in improving the welfare of women is questionable (Tisdell, 1994).

The encouraging aspect of the debate on the welfare of women is that international organisations such as the UN and the World Bank are increasingly emphasising gender-based development projects. For example, the 1997 Human Development Report points out that "Gender equality is essential for empowering women and for eradicating poverty." A statement of recommendations of the report points out that "if development is not engendered, it is endangered." And "if poverty reduction strategies fail to empower women, they will fail to empower society." The Human Development Report recommends :

- "Focusing clearly on ending discrimination against girls in all aspects of health, education and upbringing starting with survival;
- Empowering women by ensuring equal rights and access to land, credit and job opportunities;
- Taking more action to end violence against women, the all-too-pervasive hidden side of human poverty."

The Human Development Report's inclusion of the Gender Related Development Index (GDI) and the Gender Empowerment Measure (GEM) has also helped to highlight the inequality of development benefits to women. It has also put pressure on governments to actually produce data relating to women's issues. The GDI is calculated using the same variables as the HDI but adjusted for the differences in achievement between men and women. The GEM is based on economic and political participation of women in different countries.[5]

---

[5] For details on the calculations of the Gender Related Development Index and Gender Empowerment Measure see the technical note 2, pp. 123-24 of the *Human Development Report*, 1997.

However, there still remains both methodological and conceptual biases which may cause difficulties in making appropriate policies (Agarwal, 1986). Many non-governmental organisations are also putting pressure on the governments to include gender-based development strategies which may ultimately enhance the participation of women in the economy. In Fiji, the Law Reform Commission is focusing on the women's issues so that the transition of law takes place in such a way that it provides women with equal rights in respect of justice, family life and work. The Law Reform Commission has acted on areas such as equal rights to a marriage, division of property at marriage breakdown, domestic violence, child care and maintenance (Ministry of Women and Culture, 1998 : 36-39).

Gender based equality in property ownership (including land) in Fiji is significantly imbalanced compared to that in developed countries. As in many developing countries, women in Fiji are not the inheritors of property. Jalal (1998 : 57) states that as the Native Lands and Fisheries Commission generally adopts a patriarchal interpretation of customs and the 'mataqali' ownership of land, it places men in full control and management of the land and thus permits women to only temporarily possess and use the land but not control it. Agarwal (1994) argues that one of the most important constraints to women's welfare and empowerment is the 'gender gap' in command over property. She provides a useful account of the nature of land rights that women have in South Asia. Land rights to women fits into the broader question of providing control of resources and income which may be used better for the immediate families (Standing, 1992). Income increases for men, on the other hand, do not seem to be automatically passed on to the family in an effective way (Hanger and Moris, 1973; Palmer, 1977; Young, 1978).

In Fiji the debate on the welfare of women has largely been concentrated on the opportunities for women in employment and violence against women, and has largely taken place in an emotionally charged manner involving mostly women's organisations. For example, the Fiji Women's Crisis Centre has raised with the Courts and the justice system on several occasions, the issues concerning miscarriage of justice against women. The issues of poverty (deteriorating family values), and of social inequalities and the incidents of violence against women are generally closely related. Table 2 below shows the instances of violence against women in Fiji over the last 5 years. There has been a steady increase in violence against women since the 1980s but it escalated in the post-coup era which can be attributed to increasing poverty. The highest incidents of violence against women were reported for the year 1996, when a total of 690 cases was recorded. A similar trend is observed for the data provided by the Fiji Women's Crisis Centre. An annual average rate of increase in cases of violence against women of 43 per cent is observed from the period 1993 to 1996. The highest rate of increase is observed for the year 1995.

Table 2 : Trends of Violence Against Women

Year	Murder	Attempted Murder	Man-slaughter	AWITCGH	AOABH	Common Assault	Other Off-ences	Total (%Increase)
1993	1	0	2	27	177	22	6	235
1994	4	0	0	40	183	39	12	278 (18%)
1995	2	0	0	31	354	72	11	470 (69%)
1996	2	1	1	56	404	211	15	690 (47%)
1997	0	0	0	32	430	85	14	561 (-19%)

Source : *Fiji Police Force, Report*, 1998.

While violence against women has generally increased over the years, cases of domestic violence have also increased in a similar manner. Table 4 shows the trend in domestic violence and child abuse reported to the Fiji Women's Crisis Centre (FWCC) over the years.

Table 3 : Instances of Domestic Violence and Child Abuse Reports to FWCC

Year	Domestic Violence	Child Abuse	Total (% Increases)
1986	35	2	37
1987	58	1	59 (60%)
1988	123	1	124 (110%)
1990	175	1	176 (42%)
1989	212	-	212 (20%)
1991	245	11	256 (21%)
1992	248	8	256 (0%)
1993	241	14	255 (0%)
1994	285	13	298 (17%)
1995	335	33	368 (23%)
1996	469	29	498 (35%)
1997	403	19	422 (-15%)

Source : *Fiji Women's Crisis Centre*, 1998, Data Base.

The above table shows an average annual increase of 25 per cent over the period 1986 to 1997. The highest increase is observed for the year 1988 which could have been caused largely due to job losses as a result of economic downturn after the coups and family disintegration arising from migration.

Changing Role of Women and Economic Performance of Fiji

Fiji's economic performance since Independence based on GDP does not show any sustained level of growth. The economy suffered a major blow after the two military coups in 1987, which adversely affected economic performance. Since then, a radical shift in economic policies has taken place, and the government has actively promoted a policy of exporting more and more of manufactured goods. The tourism sector has also received a good deal of attention from the government and has grown by about 39 per cent since 1991. The earnings from tourism industry increased from $ 407.7 million in 1993 to $ 616.6 million in 1997 at 1990 prices (Bank of Hawaii, Fiji Economic Report, 1998).

Despite the adoption of the new economic policy since 1987, the economic growth of Fiji has remained sluggish. As shown by figure 1-1, the overall per capita GDP Growth averaged at about 1.6 per cent between 1971-1995. GDP growth rate was the highest in 1989 peaking to 12.9 per cent growth rate as a result of some stability provided by a civilian government after the coups, and the opening up of garment factories. Tourism also promoted growth.

Figure 1-1 : Annual Growth Rate of GDP, Fiji : 1971-1995 (Constant Prices)

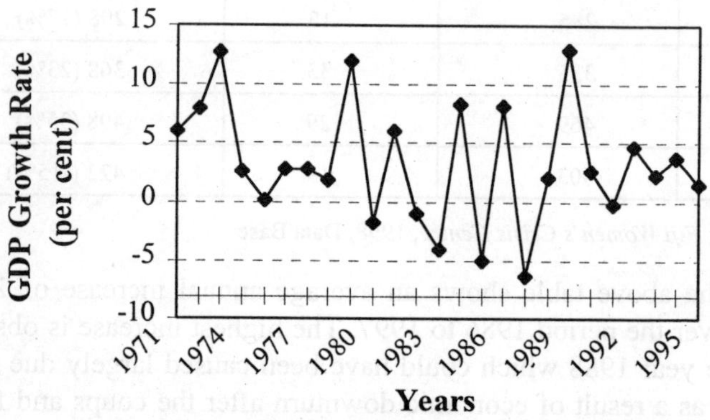

There has been little structural change in the Fijian economy since the 1970s. The agricultural sector, including sugarcane, livestock, forestry and subsistence and fishing now accounts for 21.3 per cent of the GDP (which has only declined slightly after a decade when it constituted 22.2 per cent of the economy). The manufacturing sector while actively promoted has not contributed well towards the growth of the economy. However, within the manufacturing sector, the growth of the garment industry is significant. The growth in this sector is very important since it provides a large portion of employment for women in the country.

Like many developing countries, Fiji also offered incentives such as tax exemptions to the garment industry. The implementation of a thirteen-year tax holiday allowed existing factories to convert to tax free status. Furthermore, it attracted many investors from Australia and New Zealand allowing them preferential access to their home country markets under the South Pacific Regional Trade and Economic Co-operation Agreement (SPARTECA). Investors from other regions including the ASEAN region also took advantage of the tax exemptions and the availability of cheap labour. As a result of all these incentives, the garment industry grew from a mere F$ 2m industry in 1986 to about F$ 160m industry in 1993. This resulted in increased employment, particularly for female workers. To some extent this cushioned the effects of the decline of the construction industry that resulted in serious unemployment amongst men in the urban squatter and low income settlements. The garment industry provided an alternative employment for large numbers of women from mainly these squatter and low income settlements. These female workers absorbed in the garment industry had to work for low wages to cover up for the lost household income. Despite recent increases, the wages offered to the garment workers have remained very low. It has been, for example, pointed out that the initial wages in the garment were only thirty-six per cent of the urban poverty line wage (Ram, 1994). The abolition of the minimum wage legislation after the military coups resulted in gross exploitation of workers in the garment industry. The legislation, however, was restored in 1991 due to vigorous trade union pressure on the government. This resulted in significant improvement of wage rates and working conditions.

Women's role in development is now recognised by the government in its official policy documents. For example, a chapter was devoted to women's issues in the government's 1993 official policy documents for economic growth. It outlined the following policies to enhance women's participation in the economy (Government of Fiji, 1992, 73-74) :

- "involving women as equal partners in the national political, economic and social development of the country, through positive discrimination, where appropriate;
- women to be recognised and valued as resources which can be utilised and assisted to contribute more effectively in an economically productive development process;
- upgrading of training and skill levels and overall human resource development for women in an effort to improve their access to employment opportunities;
- strengthening of collection and dissemination of information on gender basis for policy formulation;
- strengthening of co-ordination of women's activities in the overall development effort;
- examining legislation, including international legal instruments pertaining to women, with a view to safeguarding the interests of women."

A national plan of action has now been included in the development policy framework of the government. At its launching on the 9th of October 1998 the Prime Minister stated, "the Government is committed to increasing women's appointments on boards, committees, councils, commissions and tribunals and with the guidance of the Ministry of Women, is continually trying to identify and promote qualified women."

Table 4 shows the occupational breakdown of men and women in Fiji. It is quite clear that women represent less than one third of the total work force and about forty-two per cent of the total men's employment.

Table 4 : Employment of Women by Occupational Category, 1993 : Fiji

Occupational Category	Male	Female	Total
Professional, Technical and Related Workers	10,584	7,567	18,151
Administrative and Managerial Workers	6,840	522	7,362
Clerical and Related Workers	8,004	8,064	16,068
Sales Workers	3,761	1,605	5,366
Service Workers	8,571	3,536	12,107
Agriculture, Animal Husbandry and Forestry Workers and Fishermen	1,801	143	1,944
Production and related workers, Transport Equipment Operators and Labourers	31,353	9,689	41,042
Total	70,914	31,126 (30.5%)	102,040

Source : *Government of Fiji* (1993), *Annual Employment Survey.*
Note : Figures for 1996 are presented in table 1 for the reason that the occupational categories in the two tables differed at source and could not be aggregated appropriately.

Table 5 shows the changing pattern of female and male wage and salary workers. The analysis by Devi and Chand (1997) shows that while the number of female salary workers increased from 1980-1986, in the post-coup period (1987-1993), it remained unchanged.

Table 5 : Employment Structure in Fiji

	Females				Males				
	Wage Earners	%	Salary Earners	%	Wage Earners	%	Salary Earners	%	Total
1980	6,058	13.9	8,344	30.5	37,557	86.1	19,001	69.5	70,960
1981	6,260	15.4	9,256	31.2	34,433	84.6	20,435	68.8	70,384
1982	6,276	16.6	8,337	28.6	31,541	83.4	20,842	71.4	66,996
1983	6,749	16.7	9,065	30.2	33,715	83.3	20,994	69.8	70,523
1984	7,238	17.1	9,879	30.4	35,002	82.9	22,608	69.6	74,727
1985	7,600	17.1	11,427	34.7	36,762	82.9	21,548	65.3	77,337
1986	8,147	18.1	10,868	34.3	36,761	81.9	20,840	65.7	76,616
AVG 1980-1986		16.4		31.4	33,242	83.6		68.6	
1987	8,698	21.9	10,951	33.2	30,958	78.1	22,035	66.8	72,642
1988	8,845	20.0	10,810	32.6	35,415	80.0	22,330	67.4	77,400
1989	13,240	23.0	11,485	32.3	44,369	77.0	24,105	67.7	93,199
1993	17,366	n.a.	13,760	34.1	n.a.	n.a.	26,546	65.9	n.a.
AVG		21.6		33.1		78.3		67.0	

Source : Devi and Chand, 1997.

Table 7 shows the sectoral composition of the employment of women. Since 1980 the percentage of women employed in the manufacturing sector has increased but more significantly after the military coups of 1987. This is largely explained by the development of the garment factories. It is argued that industrialisation can provide an impetus for equality for women in terms of employment and economic independence. However, the degree to which this happens in developing countries including Fiji depends on a number of factors. In many developed countries working mothers for example have institutional support for child care which allows them to engage in full-time employment. In the absence of such institutional support, employment of more women in the manufacturing sector could disturb the social cohesion and extended family support which usually is available in both the rural and the urban sectors. In Fiji, for example, women workers in the garment industries work for long hours and usually have no institutional support for child care.

Table 6 shows the gender related development index for Fiji. In 1994 the income share of the females was just 21.4 per cent compared to 78.6 per cent for the males. Life expectancy is higher for females while the literacy rate is slightly lower than that of the males. The overall gender related development index is much lower in Fiji, as compared to some developed and developing countries.

Table 6 : Gender Related Development Index : Fiji

Gender Related Development Index (GDI) Rank	Life Expectancy at Birth (Years) 1994		Adult Literacy Rate (%) 1994		Earned Income Share (%) 1994	
	Female	Male	Female	Male	Female	Male
53	74.1	69.9	89.2	93.7	21.4	78.6

Source : UNDP (1997).

Table 8 shows the gender empowerment measure. While the measures used by the United Nations Human Development Report capture the major indicators, more specific measures could shed further light about women's status. One of the measures that could be used is the extent of property rights or property ownership that women have in the society. Lack of property rights over resources by women takes away a significant amount of their empowerment capability. Even, with the measure provided by the Human Development report, it is evident that women still lag behind men. The measure of number of seats held in Parliament by women and the percentage of women administrators and managers is low. This is significant because these measures reveal that men are still predominantly involved in the decision making process. In Fiji's Parliament (1998) there are no elected non-Fijian women. It should be noted that representation in Parliament is associated with a number of factors and the extent of property rights and ownership of resources may have significant influence on their ability to support their election campaign and be elected to the Parliament.

Table 7 : Sectoral Composition of Employment by Gender

Year	Manufacturing		% of Female Employment in Manufacturing	Wholesale and Retail Trade		% of Fem. Emp. in Wholesale and retail sector	Total		Female Employment as % of Total Employment
	Male	Female		Male	Female		Male	Female	
1980	12,495	1,483	10.6	8,621	3,552	29.2	56,588	14,402	20.3
1981	11,151	1,730	13.4	8,905	3,440	27.9	54,868	15,516	22.0
1982	10,144	1,568	13.4	8,392	3,403	28.9	52,383	14,613	21.8
1983	9,645	2,052	17.5	9,454	3,847	28.9	54,709	15,814	22.4
1984	11,427	2,278	16.6	10,115	4,051	28.6	57,610	17,117	22.9
1985	11,065	2,631	19.2	9,872	4,177	29.7	58,310	19,027	24.6
1986	10,826	2,965	21.5	9,319	3,948	29.8	56,721	18,999	25.1
1987	9,881	3,696	27.2	8,367	3,576	29.9	55,277	19,563	26.1
1988	9,901	3,963	28.6	8,068	3,715	31.5	53,291	19,655	26.9
1989	10,730	7,104	39.8	9,237	4,546	33.0	59,520	24,725	29.3
1993	14,320	10,059	41.3	11,588	4,581	28.3	70,915	31,126	30.5
1996	14,022	10,613	43.1	13,671	7,059	34.1	75,732	34,339	31.2

Source : Devi and Chand, 1997; *Census*, 1996 (Unpublished data).

Table 8 : Gender Empowerment Measure, Fiji

Gender Empowerment Measure (GEM) Rank	Seats Held in Parliament (% Women)	Administrators and Managers (% Women)	Professional and Technical Workers (% women)	Earned Income Share (% to Women)	GEM Value
68	5.8	9.6	44.7	21	0.329

Source : UNDP (1997).

Property Rights and Women in Fiji

Fiji has a unique system of land ownership where the indigenous Fijians own eighty-three per cent of the land on a communal basis, seven per cent is freehold owned privately by individuals and ten per cent is owned by the state. The native land is managed by the Native Lands Trust Board (NLTB) on behalf of the Fijian landowners.[6] Currently, about 28 per cent of the native land is leased out for use, the bulk of which is held by non-Fijian sugarcane farmers who pay rent to the NLTB on an annual basis. Most of these leases are on a thirty-year basis which may or may not be renewed after the lease time expires.

Currently, the issue of land leases is a matter of national concern since the bulk of the leases are expiring and there is a pressing demand by the landowners not to renew the leases. Most Fijian landowners are native Fijians, but most lease holders are Indo-Fijians. So, the conflict between landowners and lease holders has an ethnic origin.

The government is now involved in negotiations which is perceived to be undertaken within the provisions of the Agricultural and Land Lords and Tenants Act (ALTA). This issue is particularly important to the sugar industry where seventy-four per cent of the farms are on native land all of which falls under the ALTA legislation.[7] By the year 2024 about ninety-six per cent of the current leases will expire. The current review of the ALTA

6 For more details on land ownership, see France (1969); Durutalo (1985); Nayacakalou (1975); Ward (1995).

7 ALTA legislation was adopted in 1976 under which all leases in the agricultural sector were regulated. For more details on the ALTA, see Prasad and Tisdell (1996).

legislation may imply reform of the land tenure system. This, however, does not question the practices of land ownership in Fiji where the bulk of the land is legally managed by an entrenched communal institution (NLTB), the existence of which has no economic grounding. There is no evidence of any suggestions by the NLTB or other communal Fijian institutions to change the communal nature of the ownership of land in Fiji. While this aspect of land ownership protects the rights of native owners as a group, it may restrict land development and the access of women to land (Jalal, 1998 : 54). Changing the land legislation requires three-quarters votes at the three levels of law making in Fiji : the House of Representatives, the Senate, and the Great Council of Chiefs (Jalal, 1998). She notes that the law making institutions are weighted against women.

The Fijian society is largely patriarchal and thus inheritance and transfer of property is largely patrilineal. Females in the ethnic Fijian society, however, do become inheritors of property and of royalty money if they inherit the chiefly title. Even, in these situations, there is always dispute; and males are generally preferred over females.

The dominant ethnic Fijian women's organisation is the *Soqosoqo Vakamarama* which was formed by the wives of the missionaries operating in Fiji in 1924 (Sovaki, 1996). This organisation is, however, based on the traditional socio-cultural values and has been interpreted as a largely conservative organisation. Historically, for example, the organisation in its submission for constitutional arrangement before Independence argued for special seats for those with chiefly status and a communal system of voting. Alternatives views, however, were also expressed for common roll (Sovaki, 1996). The conservatism within the *Soqosoqo Vakamarama* has forced young educated Fijian women to join more progressive women's groups such as the Fiji Women's Rights Movement and the Women's Crisis Centre.

The current context of land disputes in Fiji has little or no room for gender based discussions. Women in the Fiji society are generally not considered as natural benefactors of property owned by the household where the male head makes the decisions about the property. This is largely the case in the rural areas. In the urban areas, however, the practice is changing as a result of the changing nature of property ownership largely due to economic necessity. Working couples buy or develop property as joint owners since it gives them better access to loans on the basis of household income. There is, however, room for improvement which could provide more equitable share in property ownership to women. Tax laws, for example, often inhibit the development of women's participation in business partnership with their husbands. The Housing Authority and the commercial banks have a policy of not insisting that both spouses' names be on legal titles to property unless the woman is in paid employment and is contributing directly to the loan payments. This policy fails to recognise women's unpaid work in the homes with their husbands (Jalal, 1998 : 55). The current law in Fiji does not recognise business partnership between husbands and wives for tax purposes. In more developed countries like Australia, however, wives and husbands can form partnership and also get tax benefits through income splitting.

Do Women Need Independent Property Rights?

Agarwal, (1994) points out that about two decades ago the issue of independent property rights in South Asia was not even admitted in public policy. She states that "indeed gaining acceptance for the idea that women need independent rights in land itself an area of struggle, an essential first step in the struggle to translate that need into effective rights in practice" (Agarwal, 1994 : 3). In the South Pacific islands including Fiji, this question is still far from any public policy debate. In fact, it is almost taken for granted that family should be a unit of property ownership, however, within the family unit the resources may not necessarily be shared equally (Agarwal, 1994).

Hirschon (1984) and Agarwal (1994) point out several issues regarding property rights and its relationship to the development of women. Agarwal (1994 : 11) in particular provides six inter-related issues which in her view is relevant for the discussion of property rights and women's welfare in any country. These are as follows :

- gender relations and household's property status;

- gender relations and women's property status;
- the distinction between ownership and control of property;
- the distinctiveness of land as property;
- what is meant by rights in land? and
- prospects of non-land based livelihoods.

Agarwal (1994) points out that land rights for women in the rural areas are vital for women's welfare, efficiency, equality and empowerment. The welfare argument relates to the inequality and poverty in the household that could be avoided if women have independent rights over resources and particularly land in the rural areas.[8] While to date there has been no study on the inequality amongst women in households, the figures on poverty show that more women rather than men are living in poverty. Amongst the Indo-Fijian families in rural areas the land is owned and leased by the male head. A survey of rice farmers in Fiji in 1993 showed ninety-five per cent of the land under rice was owned by the male head of the family. The level of income control in the rice growing areas by women is insignificant. Women, however, provide a significant proportion of labour in rice industry, particularly in the form of family labour in the planting and harvesting of the crop.

According to Roberts (1991), the women's nutritional development and requirement in Fiji is below that of men and below the acceptable health standard. Women in the rural areas suffer many health problems including being underweight, more anaemic and the increasing prevalence of non-communicable disease. The poor health of women leads to further problems such as lower weight babies, and a higher rate of infant mortality. Women in the rural areas play an important role in production and distribution; and women's poor health leads to reduced production.

Women also do not inherit property as a result of obvious bias on the grounds of efficiency. Women are generally regarded as not

---

8 Various studies of South Asian countries point out the bias in the allocation of resources in the family and inequality between men and women. See, for example, Agarwal (1986); Dreze and Sen (1989); Harris (1990).

being able to manage the farms and would have difficulty in controlling the family labour and gaining access to credit and other institutional support. Institutional help to counter the gender bias could lead to parity in efficiency between males and females. Furthermore, there is evidence in other countries that credit facilities are better managed by women.[9]

Ownership and property rights over resources including land has important implications for equality and empowerment. Equality in ownership of property is based on the practice where women are not discriminated in the inheritance and share in the household property. The overwhelming argument in recent years for empowering women has been based on employment, education and training. While this has contributed to the improvement of women's welfare, it has not necessarily led to their empowerment. Empowerment as defined by Agarwal (1994 : 39) is more than just providing equal opportunities. "As a process that enhances the ability of disadvantaged (or powerless) individuals or groups to challenge and change (in their favour) existing power relationships that place them in subordinate economic, social and political positions. Ownership of property including land would provide not only economic power but also the power to mobilise resistance to policies and practices which promote and perpetuate gender inequalities. In Fiji, and indeed in most Pacific Island countries, there are no legal barriers to women owning property as individuals or as part of a family but the interpretation of the customary law governing the control and management of land gives power over land mainly to men (Jalal, 1998 : 56).

In Fiji, both the Indo-Fijian and ethnic Fijian societies are patriarchal in which the women's access to ownership of property in 'practice' is subordinate. The subordination arises from the fact that females do not inherit their share in the family property on equal footing with the male progeny. This includes share in land ownership and leased land for farming. The families of Indo-Fijian females who strongly adhere to customary practices, provide gifts and other household valuables and the immediate need of the newly

9 For example, Hossain (1987) points out that Grameen Bank in Bangladesh which provides credit to women has a very high and efficient rate of repayment.

wed at the time of marriage.[10] This is usually the case in rural areas. This practice, however, has faded significantly in the urban areas due to economic and social reasons. Such practice of matrimonial obligations is a serious burden on the families of the female. The monetary value of these obligations sometimes runs into thousands of dollars.

In rural areas propertyless women are employed on farms who earn much less than their male counterparts. Women in these circumstances, are, therefore, disadvantaged in two ways : (1) they lack empowerment due to lack of property ownership and (2) are deprived of equal pay for equal work. Table 7 shows the distribution of earnings by male and females in the agricultural sector in 1978 (National Agricultural Census, 1978). The 1991 agricultural census, however, does not include the statistics on agricultural earnings by males and females in the same manner.

Table 9 : Distribution of Agricultural Earnings, Fiji : 1978

	Males Adults	Female Adults	Youth/ Children	Total
Full time employment	90.7	7.8	1.5	100
Part time employment	83.0	12.8	4.2	100
Indigenous Fijians	20.0	4.0	2.0	26.0
Indian Fijians	57.0	7.0	2.0	66.0
Others	7.0	0.6	0.4	8.0
Sugarcane	52.0	8.0	2.0	62.0
Plantation	4.0	0.2		4.2
Animal Production	18.0	2.0	0.2	20.2
Others	11.0	2.0	1.0	14.0
Traditional Farms	5.0	1.0	1.0	7.0
Modern Farms	77.0	10.0	3.0	90.0
Others	2.0	0.8	0.2	3.0

Source : *Fiji National Agricultural Census* : 1978.

In the agricultural sector farms are predominantly owned by the males. Table 10 shows the distribution and ownership of farms in

---

[10] Gifts are provided in the form of household essentials where the marriage is arranged and sanctioned by the family.

Fiji. Females just make up 5.2 per cent of the total farm ownership in the country. While it is usually argued that the household represents equality for all members in the family, this may not be necessarily the case. The family unit is not an undifferentiated unit as is assumed in the standard economic analysis. This view, however, has been challenged and studies have shown that there is considerable intra-household inequality and women tend to be the ones who suffer the inequality. The ownership of land and property by the male counterparts leave little room for any bargaining for equality within the framework of the household. In both the Indo-Fijian and ethnic Fijian societies in Fiji, the family is conceptualised as unitary and persistent intra-family inequalities in the resource allocation and other activities are concealed. The unitary conceptualisation of the household, however, has been questioned and some of the problems have been highlighted by both economists and non-economists.[11]

In terms of inheritance, women in practice do not easily get their share of the property from their parents. Usually women themselves are reluctant to demand share from their parents' properties due to the fear of creating enmity with their male siblings who are regarded as their protectors in bad times. In Indian society this is even reciprocated by parents and brothers by not drawing or not intending to draw any benefits from married daughters or sisters. As a result of this two-way relationship, daughters, once married, technically lose out completely on any form of inheritance from the family wealth, unless the daughter is the sole inheritor. In the Muslim community the practice is also similar, and women usually do not inherit property once they are married. This is despite the fact that the Islamic law requires females to inherit at least half of what the male inherits. In the indigenous Fijian tradition the practice is somewhat similar to the practice in the Indian community where the female loses the right of inheritance once she is married.

---

11 For a discussion of the problems of conceptualising the family as unitary, see Agarwal (1990); Evans (1991); Fleming (1991); Folbre (1986, 1988); Roberts (1991); Sen (1983, 1990); Wilson (1991).

Table 10 : Farm Ownership in Fiji : 1991

Division	Females	(%)	Males	(%)	Total
Central	669	3.6	17,931	96.1	18,600
Western	2,763	6.5	39,987	93.5	42,750
Northern	1,335	6.1	20,697	93.9	22,032
Eastern	90	0.9	9,816	99.1	9,906
Total	4,857	5.2	88,431	94.8	93,288

Source : *Government of Fiji* (1992).

Table 11 shows the number of workers engaged on farms by sex and category as paid and unpaid. The table shows that of the 135,227 unpaid workers on farms 21 per cent are women and of the 24,661 paid workers only 9.7 per cent are women. Of the 8,715 workers who work for remuneration in kind, 14.4 per cent are women. While in total the farm ownership by women is at 5.2 per cent, 21.2 per cent unpaid workers are women.

The broader question as pointed out by Agarwal (1994) is, why has property ownership by women not appeared as an issue in the mainstream women's economic development? The overwhelming preoccupation of women's organisations and activists who advocate equality is that of access to jobs and parity in wages.

Table 11 : Workers on Farms by Sex and Category (paid and unpaid), 1991.

Relatives without Remunerations				Workers with Remuneration						Total
				In Cash			In Kind			
Division	Male	Female	Total	Male	Female	Total	Male	Female	Total	
Central	25,466	9,300 26.8%	34,766	2,784	285 9.3%	3,069	2,513	89 3.4%	2,602	40,437
Western	48,609	10,283 17.5%	58,892	10,226	864 7.8%	11,090	3,267	962 22.7%	4,229	74,211
Northern	20,112	7,691 27.7%	27,803	8,311	1041 11.1%	9,352	1,139	174 13.3%	1,313	38,468
Eastern	12,326	1,440 10.5%	13,766	955	195 17.0%	1,150	541	30 5.3%	571	15,487
Total	106,513	28714 21.2%	135,227	22,276	2385 9.7%	24,661	1,255	7,460	8,715	168,603

Source : *Government of Fiji* (1996).

According to the Marxists, market capitalism is discriminatory towards women (Tisdell, 1996). So, Engles (1972) advocated the abolition of private property. He believed that in a capitalist economy gender relations are hierarchical where women were economically dependent on men. Engels (1972 : 137) describes the family as follows:

> *"The modern individual family is founded on the open or concealed domestic slavery of the wife, and modern society is a mass composed of these individual molecule. In the great majority of cases today, at least in the processing classes, the husband is obliged to earn a living and support his family, and that in itself gives him a position of supremacy without any need for special legal titles and privileges. Within the family he is the bourgeois, and the wife represents the proletariat."*

To overcome such gender-related discrimination, and for the emancipation of women in general, women need to be part of the labour force. Once, they are in the labour force, the issue of ownership of property really is not a factor. Agarwal (1994), however, points out that Engels' proposition for the abolition of private property rights may have led to the neglect of the question of women's ownership of property.[12] Molyneux (1981) points out that in many of the socialist countries women remained at the lower end of the job hierarchy and had little political participation.[13]

Table 12 shows the distribution of female workers vertically at different levels of salary structure. While the females are under-represented at the lower and middle level of employment, they remain grossly marginalised at the higher salary scale.

---

[12] Others including, Aaby (1977); Barret (1980, 1985); Coward (1983); Delmar (1985); MacKinnon (1989); Molyneux (1981); Reiter, (1977); Sacks (1975),

[13] For further discussion on the position of women in socialist economies see Aslanbeigui, Pressman and Summerfield (1994), Funk (1993); Grapad (1997), Harsanyi (1993); Paukert (1991) United Nations Office at Vienna, Division for the Advancement of Women (1992).

Table 12: Distribution of Salary Employees by Sex, 1996

Salary Range	Male	Female	%	Total
Under $ 7,500	7,852	3,928	33.3	11,780
Between $ 7,500 and $ 25,000	18,554	10,647	36.5	29,201
Over $ 25,000	2,297	393	14.6	2,690
Total	28,703	14,968	34.3	43,671

Source : *Fiji Bureau of Statistics, Census* 1996, unpublished data.

Agarwal (1994) suggests the following if women's welfare is to improve in future :

> *"It is thus time to move beyond a single-minded emphasis on women's employment, which has preoccupied planners and most grassroots groups as the means of improving women's economic position, toward giving centrality to women's ownership and control of land — the means of production itself."*

The effort by the Government of Fiji may be a case in point where it has extended financial assistance through loans for women's participation in commerce. The Ministry of Fijian Affairs' Small Business Equity Scheme provides interest free loans to ethnic Fijians for micro-enterprise projects. This scheme is placed well to help ethnic Fijian women in business. However, the motive of this scheme is more geared towards ethnic balancing rather than gender balancing, as it sets the condition that the applicant be an ethnic Fijian registered in the *Bola ni Kawa Bula* (see Ministry of Women and Culture, 1998 : 58-59). The Women's Social and Economic Development Programme (WOSED) is another institution funded by the Pacific Community and New Zealand Overseas Development Agency that provides loan facilities for women in commerce. This scheme has expanded over the past four years, from 27 loans in 1993 to 251 loans in 1997 (see table 13). However, this financial scheme has also functioned more on the premise of ethnic balancing in commerce than a loan provider for women. Of all the loans provided, 93 per cent went to ethnic Fijian women despite the 1997 Poverty Report indicating that more Indian households fell in the poorest sections of the society (Ministry of Women and Culture, 1998 : 60).

Table 13 : Accumulative Growth of the WOSED Scheme, 1993-1998

Year	No. of groups	Number of Loans	Total
1993	6	27	$ 88,294.00
January 1995	17	83	$ 27,866.00
January 1997	44	251	$ 95,610.00
June 1998	73	393	$ 124,918.00

Concluding Comments and Policy Implications

The impact of structural adjustment policies on poverty, employment and economic growth has been an issue for most developing countries, and Fiji is not an exception. Its impact on the welfare of women in Fiji has largely been discussed within the overall framework of property right analysis, employment and broader macro-economic performance. The overwhelming preoccupation of debates on the role of women in Fiji has been on the extent of female participation in the labour force, equality of wages, and working conditions for women. From the Marxian point of view, the family unit can be conceptualised as an institution of oppression for women if they did not have independent income earning capacities. However, as pointed out by Agarwal (1994) and Tisdell (1996), women's position has not improved despite the progress on enactment of non-discriminatory laws.

In Fiji, the laws are generally non-discriminatory and legally women have equality with men, but the actual practice diverges from the laws significantly. The indicators showing the participation of women in the economy and their empowerment are well below those of men. While women's employment participation has increased as a result of the restructuring of the economy and the development of the garment industry, the majority of female garment factory workers including other service industries, have low paid jobs. Women of both Fijian and Indian ethnicity suffer from the traditional practices and norms which are inherently discriminatory. However, Indian women seem to be worse off, because the government has failed to provide them special loan assistance on equal footing with the ethnic Fijian women.

The whole question of women's property rights, especially in land, should be considered if the extent of women's empowerment and welfare is to be improved significantly in Fiji. The system of land tenure in Fiji itself has to undergo significant reform. Eighty-three per cent of the land is owned by the NLTB on behalf of the indigenous Fijian landowners. While this aspect of land ownership protects the rights of ethnic Fijian owners, it may restrict land development and the access of women to land (Jalal, 1998 : 54). Within the indigenous Fijian community, which owns eighty-three per cent of the land, there is no consensus on the ownership and use rights. The discussion on the Fijian land amongst the indigenous Fijians is largely restricted to males. Reform of the current system of land ownership is needed and the reform must also take into account the bias in the ownership and distribution of land across gender.

The impending expiry of current leases under the ALTA legislation has created increased insecurity amongst the farmers in the agricultural sector. The current discussion is concentrated on the renewal and non-renewal of leases with each ethnic group on each side of the negotiating table. This narrow focus does not address fundamental issues such as the economic efficacy of the current system of ownership and lease. Resolving this land problem may open up a multitude of fronts from which the issue of gender inequality in property rights could be tackled.

Like in many developing countries, women in rural Fiji depend largely on the land for their subsistence and cultivation of minor cash crops. From the welfare point of view independent land rights for women could provide them with the opportunity to have better control and use of land. Ownership of land and other assets can provide women with control on the household income, which can be used for securing credits for further investment, and thus their future empowerment. Empowerment itself is likely to lead to a process of bargaining of power relations both at the local and national levels while the need for gender equity is accepted at the official level, it is not always reflected in the government's policy direction.

REFERENCES

Aaby, P. (1977), 'Engels and Women,' *Critique of Anthropology,* 3(9/10) : 25-53.

Agarwal, B. (1986), 'Women, Poverty and Agricultural Growth in India,' *Journal of Peasant Studies* 13(4) : 165-220.

Agarwal, B. (1990), 'Social Security and the Family : Coping with Seasonality and Calamity in Rural India', *Journal of Peasant Studies* 17(3) : 341-412.

Agarwal, B. (1994), *A Field of One's Own : Gender and Land Rights in South Asia*, Cambridge : Cambridge University Press.

Anker, R. and Hein, C. (eds.) (1986), *Sex Inequalities in Urban Employment in the Third World,* New York : St. Martin's Press.

Aslanbeigui, N., Pressman, S. and Summerfield, G. (eds.) (1994) *Women in the Age of Economic Transformation,* London : Routledge.

Bank of Hawaii, *Fiji Economic Report* (1998), Suva, Fiji.

Barret, M. (1980), Women's Oppression Today : The Marxist/Feminist Encounter, London : Verso Books.

Barret, M. (1985), 'Introduction', in F.A. Engels, *The Origin of the Family, Private Property and the State,* Harmondsworth : Penguin Books.

Boserup, E. (1970), *Women's Role in Economic Development,* London : Macmillan.

Coward, R. (1983), *Patriarchal Precedents : Sexuality and Social Relations*, London : Routledge and Kegan Paul.

Delmar, R. (1985), 'Looking Again at Engel's Origin of the Family, Private Property and the State,' in J. Mitchell and A. Oakley (eds.), *The Rights and Wrongs of Women,* Harmondsworth : Penguin Books.

Devi, P. and Chand, G. (1997, 'Female Employment and Earnings,' in G. Chand G. and V. Naidu (eds.), Fiji : *Coups, Crises and Reconciliation, 1987-1997,* pp. 69-80, Suva : Fiji Institute of Applied Studies.

Dreze, J. and Sen, A.K. (1989), *Hunger and Public Action,* Oxford : Clarendon Press.

Durutalo, S. (1985), *Internal Colonialism and Unequal Regional Development : The Case of Western Viti Levu, Fiji,* Unpublished M.A. Thesis, School of Social and Economic Development, University of the South Pacific.

Engels, F.A. [1884] (1972), *The Origin of the Family, Private Property and the State,* Harmondsworth, Penguin, Books.

Evans, A. (1991), 'Gender Issues in Rural Household Economics,' *IDS Bulletin,* 22(1) : 51-59.

Fiji Bureau of Statistics, *Census* 1996, (Unpublished Data) Suva, Fiji.

Fiji Women's Crisis Centre, *Data on Clients and Service*, 1998, Suva, Fiji.

Fleming, S. (1991), 'Between the Household : Researching Community Organisation and Networks,' *IDS Bulletin* 22 (1) : 37-43.

Folbre, N. (1986), 'Hearts and Spades : Paradigms of Household Economics,' *World Development,* 14(2) : 245-55.

Folbre, N. (1988), 'The Black Four of Hearts : Towards a New Paradigm of Household Economics,' in D. Dwyer and J. Bruce (eds.), *A Home Divided : Women and Income in the Third World,* Standford : Standford University Press.

France, P. (1969), *The Charter of the Land : Custom and Colonisation in Fiji,* Melbourne : Oxford University Press.

Funk, N. (1993), 'Feminism East and West,' in N. Funk and M. Mueller (eds.), *Gender, Politics and Post-Communism,* New York : Routledge.

Government of Fiji (1981), *Report on the Census of Agriculture 1978,* Suva : Parliament of Fiji.

Government of Fiji (1992), *Report on the Fiji National Agricultural Census 1991,* Suva, Ministry of Primary Industries.

Grapard, U. (1997), 'Theoretical Issues of Gender in the Transition from Socialist Regimes,' *Journal of Economic Issues,* 31(3) : 665-686.

Hanger, J. and Morris, J. (1973), 'Women and the Household Economy,' in R. Chambers and J. Morris (eds.), *Mwea : An Irrigated Rice Settlement in Kenya,* Munich : Weltform Verlag.

Harris, J. (1990), 'The Intra-family Distribution of Hunger in South Asia,' in J. Dreze, J. and A.K. Sen, (eds.), *The Political Economy of Hunger,* Oxford : Clarendon Press.

Harsanyi, D.P. (1993), 'Women in Romania,' in N. Funk and M. Mueller (eds.), *Gender, Politics and Post-Communism,* New York : Routledge.

Jahan, N. and Prasad, B.C. (1997), *Labour Participation and GDP : A Case of Urban Women in Fiji,* Paper presented at the VIII Pacific Science Inter-Congress, The University of the South Pacific, Suva (13-19 July).

Jalal, P.I., (1998), 'Law for Pacific Women-A Legal Rights Handbook,' Fiji Women's Rights Movement, Suva, Fiji.

Jaquette, J.S. (1982), 'Women and Modernisation Theory : A Decade of Feminist Criticism,' *World Politics,* 34 : 45-56.

Klein, E. (1984), *Gender Politics : From Consciousness to Mass Politics,* Cambridge : Harvard University Press.

Leahy, M.E. (1986), Development Strategies and the Status of Women : A Comparative Study of the United States, Mexico, the Soviet Union and Cuba, Boulder, CO : Lynne Rienner.

Mackinnon, C. (1989) *Towards a Feminist Theory of the State,* Cambridge : Harvard University Press.

Ministry of Women and Culture (1998), 'The Women's Plan of Action : 1999-2004,' Volume 2, Suva, Fiji.

Molyneux, M. (1981), 'Socialist Societies Old and New : Progress Towards Women's Emancipation,' *Feminist Review,* (8) : 1-34.

Nash, J. and Fernandez-Kelly, M.P. (eds.) (1983), *Women, Men and the International Division of Labor,* Albany : State University Press of New York.

Nayacakalou, R.R. (1975), *Leadership in Fiji, Melbourne,* Oxford University Press.

Palmer, I. (1977), 'Rural Women and the Basic Needs Approach to Development,' *International Labour Review,* 115(1) : 97-107.

Paukert, L. (1991), 'The Economic Status of Women in the Transition to a Market System, The Case of Czechoslovakia,' *International Labour Review,* (130) : 613-633.

Prasad, B.C. and Tisdell, C. (1996), 'Institutional Constraints to Economic Development : The Case of Native Land Rights in Fiji,' *Asia Pacific Development Journal* 3(2) : 49-71.

Prasad, B.C. and Tisdell, C. (1996), Getting Property Rights 'Right', Land Tenure in Fiji, *Pacific Economic Bulletin* 11(1) : 31-46.

Prasad, B.C. and Tisdell, C. (1997), 'Economic Adjustment and International Trade : A Policy Dilemma for Fiji,' in Tisdell (eds.), *World Trade and Development : Economic Integration, Regional Blocs and Non-Members,* Delhi : Atlantic Publishers.

Ram, K. (1994), 'Militarism and Market Mania in Fiji,' in A. Emberson-Bain, (ed.), *Sustainable Development or Malignant Growth? Perspectives of Pacific Island Women,* Suva : Marama Publications.

Reiter, R.K. (1977), 'The Search for Origins : Unravelling the Threads of Gender Hierarchy,' *Critique of Anthropology* 3(9/10) : 5-24.

Republic of Fiji Police Force, Special Report, 1998, Suva, Fiji.

Roberts, P. (1991), 'Anthropological Perspectives on the Household,' *IDS Bulletin* 22(1) : 61-64.

Rogers, B. (1979), The Domestication of Women : Discrimination in Development, New York : St. Martin's Press.

Roy, K.C. (1994), 'Landless and Land Poor Women in India under Technological Change : A Case for Technology Transfer,' in K.C. Roy and C. Clark (eds.), *Technological Change and Rural Development in Poor Countries : Neglected Issues,* New Delhi : Oxford University Press.

Sacks, K. (1975), 'Engels Revisited : Women : The Organisation of Production and Private Property,' in R.R. Reiter (ed.), *Toward an Anthropology of Women,* New York : Monthly Review Press.

Sen, A.K. (1983), 'Economics and the Family,' *Asian Development Review* (1) : 14-26.

Sen, A.K. (1990), 'Gender and Cooperative Conflicts,' in I. Tinker (ed.), *Persistent Inequalities : Women and World Development,* New York : Oxford University Press.

Sinclair, B.D. (1983), The Women's Movement : Political, Socioeconomic, and Psychological Issues, New York : Harper and Row.

Sovaki, M. (1996), 'Women in Fijian Methodism,' in A. Thornley and T. Vulaono (eds.), *Stories of Methodism in Fiji and Rotuma* 1835-1995, Suva : Fiji Methodist Church.

Standing, G. (1992), 'Global Feminization Through Flexible Labor,' in C.K. Wilber and K. Jameson (eds.), *The Political Economy of Development and Underdevelopment,* Singapore : McGraw-Hill, Inc.

Tinker, I. (ed.) (1990), *Persistent Inequalities : Women and World Development,* New York : Oxford University Press.

Tinker, I. and Bramsen, M.B. (eds.) (1976), *Women and World Development,* Washington, D.C. : Overseas Development Council.

Tisdell, C. (1994), 'Conservation, Protected Areas and the Global Economic System : How Debt, Trade, Exchange Rates, Inflation and Macro-economic Policy affect Biological Diversity', *Biodiversity and Conservation* (3) : 419-36.

Tisdell, C. (1996), Discrimination and Changes in the Status of Women with Economic Development : General Views and Theories', in K.C. Roy; C.A. Tisdell, and H.C. Blomqvist (eds.), *Economic Development and Women in the World Community,* pp. 25-36, London : Prager.

UNDP, (1997), *Human Development Report* 1997, New York : Oxford University Press.

United Nations Office at Vienna, Division for the Advancement of Women (1992), *The Impact of Economic and Political Reform on the Status of Women in Eastern Europe and the USSR :* Proceedings of a United Nations Regional Seminar, Vienna, 8-12 April 1991.

Ward, R.G. (1995), 'Land, Law and Custom : Diverging Realities in Fiji,' in R.G. Ward and E. Kingdom (eds.), *Land, Custom and Practice in the South Pacific,* Cambridge University Press.

Wilson, G. (1991), 'Thoughts on the Cooperative Conflict Model of the Household in Relation to Economic Method,' *IDS Bulletin* 22(1) : 31-36.

Young, K. (1978), 'Modes of Appropriation and the Sexual Division of Labour : A Case Study of Oaxa, Mexico,' in A. Kuhn and A.M. Wolpe (eds.), *Feminism and Materialism,* London : Routledge and Kegan Paul.

4 Trends in Poverty, Employment and Wages in Fiji

Biman C. Prasad
Mahendra Reddy
Sunil Kumar

Introduction

The adoption of a structural adjustment program (SAP) in Fiji since the mid 1980's has raised important questions relating to unemployment, poverty and the wages in Fiji. The program was adopted in response to declining levels of economic growth experienced after the military coups of 1987. For example, a recent report by the Bank of Hawaii shows that GDP in Fiji declined by about 2.5 per cent compared to that in 1996. Real per capita GDP also declined by about 3.9 per cent and this is the biggest drop in the 1990s. The report further predicts that the 1998 GDP will decline further (Bank of Hawaii, 1998). The major components of SAP policies include reduction in government expenditure; deregulation of the product, labour and financial markets; corporatisation and privatization of state owned enterprises. With the sluggish performance of the economy and declining levels of government expenditure, unemployment has increased markedly and together with this poverty, income inequality and declining wages have become a central feature of the down turn in Fiji's economy (Prasad, 1998). Furthermore, the increasing poverty level is linked to the deterioration in macro-economic policies of Fiji (Prasad and Asafu-Adjaye, 1998).

This paper explores the extent of unemployment, wages and poverty in Fiji and in particular the situation in the urban areas. The issues of unemployment and poverty are central questions in the face of the increasing globalisation of our economy. The adoption of export-oriented market-friendly policies as opposed to inward-looking import-substitution is now seen as a panacea for all economic ills in Fiji. However, international experiences such as the collapse of the 'Asian Tigers' has affected our economy and the recent 20 per cent devaluation of the Fiji dollar was designed to cushion the effect.

The first part of the paper provides an overview of poverty and unemployment in Fiji. The second part deals with some of the causes of poverty in Fiji and the impact of urbanisation on poverty and unemployment. The third part of the paper deals with the implications of poverty and unemployment; and the fourth and fifth part deal with the impact of poverty and unemployment on the resource use.

Unemployment, Wages and Poverty in Fiji : An Overview

Poverty in Fiji

The last national household income and expenditure survey carried out in 1990/91 was used to examine the poverty scenario in Fiji. Summary results of the poverty analysis are presented in table 1. At the national level, approximately, 24 per cent of the households were earning income below the poverty line income. Relative to the 1977 period, poverty in 1990/91 had increased by 60 per cent. Poverty in urban area is more serious, registering an increase by 150 per cent.

Table 1 : Per cent of Households Under Poverty, 1977/1991

Region	1977	1990/91	Change
Urban	12	30	150
Rural Settlement	20	28	40
Rural village	21	22	5
National	15	24	60

Source : *UNDP* (1997).

Two key issues faced by policymakers in Fiji are that of declining real wages and unemployment. Real wages have been steadily declining since 1977 (table 2). Notable falls in real wages are seen in the manufacturing, construction, transport and services.

A possible direct impact of a declining real income can be that more people would be forced into the poverty trap.

Table 2 : Real Wages Ratios (Per cent of 1977-84 Wages)

Sector	1972-76	1977-84	1985-86	1987-91	1992-96
Agriculture	102	100	87	86	91
Mining	102	100	92	92	114
Manufacturing	90	100	90	72	68
Electricity	83	100	100	89	94
Construction	92	100	91	84	83
Commerce	94	100	91	79	84
Transport	91	100	95	86	84
Services	91	100	92	81	81
Overall	91	100	92	80	79

Source : Chand (1998).

The unemployment situation is a cause of serious concern for a number of reasons. First, Fiji does not have a social security system which can cater for those who are unemployed. Unemployment is also related to broader dimensions of human resource development. In the case of Fiji Islands, the government has initiated the development resource plans, which is intended to develop appropriate skills. However, the development of human resource also needs to be matched by employment growth in the economy. This in turn is related to the population growth and the labour force participation rates.

Table 3 shows the official unemployment rates between 1983 and 1995. These rates do not reflect the actual level of unemployment that may exist in the economy. For example, Chand (1998) points that the actual level of unemployment may be around 25 per cent assuming an underemployment rate of 50 per cent and a 100 per cent female participation rate. The current employment situation in Fiji is serious. The government estimates that there are 15,000 school leavers who enter the market every year in search for jobs. Of these 5,100 are females and 9,900 males. The minimum qualification of the majority of these school leavers is the Fiji School Leaving Certificate. These levels do not equip the persons with appropriate skills to enter the job market very easily. Apart from the school leavers, the government has identified another 2,000 persons entering the job market every year. These include about 500 females and 300 youths who have no formal qualifications and about 1,200 who are the victims of the downsizing in the government sectors and the laying off of workers by commercial enterprises.

Table 3 : Unemployment Rate in Fiji, 1983-95

Year	Unemployment Rate (%)
1983	6.9
1984	7.4
1985	7.9
1986	7.5
1987	10.2
1988	11.0
1989	6.1
1990	6.4
1991	5.9
1992	5.4
1993	5.9
1994	5.7
1995	5.4

Source : *Government of Fiji, Bureau of Statistics, Current Economic Statistics,* various issues.

The real problem of finding jobs for about 17,000 persons annually has to be urgently addressed to counter the growing problems of poverty, crime and other social ills. Most of these unemployed are likely to look for jobs in the formal sector. Even with a very optimistic estimate by the government on the ability of the formal sector to create jobs, it can only generate about 8,000, which would include attrition rates due to retirement and overseas emigration of some workers. It is estimated that only 3,000 new jobs are created annually through increased investment and economic growth.

According to the 1996 census, there is a backlog of about 17,300 unemployed persons who are also seeking formal sector employment. The unemployment problem in Fiji cannot be addressed in the same way as in countries where they have social security for the unemployed. In the case of Fiji, people can be idle if they have others in the family to support them. Others who are not so fortunate are faced to take up low paid part-time employment. While there is no official estimate of underemployment, it could be a major portion of those not included in the official unemployment statistics provided by the government. Table 4 shows the job growth has approximately kept pace with the population growth. However, as pointed out earlier, the official unemployment rate given in table 3 does not represent the true picture of the level of unemployment in the country.

Table 4 : Population and Employment, 1990-1997

Year	Population (000's)	Population Growth (%)	Paid Employment (000's)	Employment Growth (%)
1990	736,000	1.4	90,023	
1991	746,000	1.4	91,729	1.9
1992	758,000	1.6	93,494	1.9
1993	771,000	1.7	95,254	1.9
1994	784,000	1.7	96,336	1.1
1995	790,000	0.8	98,686	2.4
1996	803,000	1.6	100,660	2.0
1997	815,045	1.5	102,170	1.5

Source : *Government of Fiji* (1998).

The provisional 1996 census report shows that population increased from 715,375 in 1986 to 772,655 in 1996 (*Fiji Government,* 1997). The annual average growth rate between 1986-1996 was about 0.8 per cent. Population declined in 1987 for the first time due to a high emigration level amongst Fiji Island's

Indian community. This was largely due to the military coup of 1987 in which ethnic Indians had been a target of abuse and discrimination. Fiji Island's population is projected to reach 821,000 in the year 2000, representing an annual average growth rate of less than one per cent. Fiji has a relatively young population with about 53 per cent of the population below the age of 25 years.

Labour Force Participation

More insight on the causes of unemployment can be obtained by examining the labour force distributions by sector and by time period. The Labour Force Participation Rate (LFPR) for males has remained relatively unchanged. For example, the LFPR for males only increased from 84.6 per cent in 1976 to 86.0 per cent in 1986 and the provisional census report of 1996 does not show much increase. However, that for women has been increasing in the same period. For example, it increased from 17.2 per cent in 1976 to 23.5 per cent in 1986. The LFPR's for women has continued to increase and Fiji's Ministry of National Planning has estimated a net increase in the labour force between 1986 and 1996. It is estimated that the total labour force in the Fiji Islands grew at an annual average rate of 2.3 per cent over the 1986-1996 period, as compared to the population growth rate of 0.8 per cent.

In terms of the sectoral distribution of the labour force, the formal sector represented 36 per cent of the total labour force (table 5). The formal sector includes employment on regular salaries and wages. The informal and the agricultural sectors comprise 58 per cent and the balance of 6 per cent is classified as open unemployment.

Table 5 : Labour Force Distribution by Broad Economic Sectors, 1990, 1993 and 1996.

Employment Sector	1990		1993		1996	
	Number	%	Number	%	Number	%
Formal Sector	84,000	31.9	102,000	36.2	109,000	36.2
Informal Sector and Agriculture	162,800	61.7	163,400	57.9	174,400	57.8
Open Unemployment	16,900	6.4	16,600	5.9	18,100	6.0
Total	263,700	100	282,000	100	301,500	100

Source : *Government of Fiji* (1998).

One of the key issues for consideration is the large percentage of labour force in the informal and the agriculture sectors. Yet government policies in the last ten years have been largely geared towards the urban manufacturing sector. It has been more concentrated in creating formal sector jobs. It must be pointed out that given the economic structure of the Fijian economy, the informal and agricultural sectors are likely to be the key areas for future employment growth, and particularly for those with out appropriate skills.

Unemployment : Regional and Ethnic Dimensions

Unemployment breakdown by region and ethnic dimensions can allow more detailed deduction of policy implications. Table 6 shows the rate of unemployment by region and by different ethnic groups. The rate of urbanisation has been increasing and together with it also the unemployment rate. As shown in table 6 the urban unemployment rate is higher than the rural rate. It has also been increasing over the last ten years. The largest number of unemployed falls between the age of 14 and 24. In the urban areas, unemployment rate amongst ethnic Fijians is much greater than among the ethnic Indians. One explanation for this has been that the adoption of the Structural Adjustment Program (SAP) led to a shift in the economic policy directions away from the agricultural sector to the urban based manufacturing sector (Reddy, 1998).

Table 6 : Unemployment by Region and Ethnic Group and Age, 1996 (per cent).

Age Group	Urban	Rural	Urban		Rural	
			Fijian	Indian	Fijian	Indian
14< x ≤ 19	24.49	13.33	31.44	18.50	11.17	15.78
20 < x ≤ 24	13.24	7.78	17.28	9.20	8.09	7.15
24 < x ≤ 29	7.38	3.87	9.92	4.68	4.60	2.68
29 < x ≤ 34	5.27	2.79	6.90	3.79	3.12	2.02
34 < x ≤ 39	4.14	1.89	5.16	3.23	2.02	1.49
39 < x ≤ 44	3.59	1.98	4.41	2.88	2.02	1.74
44 < x ≤ 49	3.55	1.94	3.77	3.37	1.81	1.95
49 < x ≤ 54	4.30	1.65	3.74	4.87	1.65	1.66
54 < x ≤ 59	5.02	2.03	4.50	6.01	1.89	1.87
59 < x ≤ 64	6.81	2.31	7.93	5.71	2.14	2.68
64< x ≤ 69	8.81	2.57	9.32	6.39	2.68	1.92
69 < x ≤ 74	9.67	3.02	9.22	10.40	2.73	3.44
X > 75	15.75	5.49	16.23	13.07	5.70	4.61

Source : *Bureau of Statistics* (1996).

Population, GDP and Employment Growth Rates : Some Implications

The shrinking agricultural sector in Fiji has led to a significant rural to urban migration. Since 1966, the urban population has increased by 13 per cent due to internal migration. Table 7 shows the changes in the percentage of rural and urban populations. Between 1986 and 1996 urban population increased by about 8 per cent while rural population declined by approximately the same percentage.

Deregulation policies pursued by the government since 1987 adversely affected some of the major agricultural industries such as the rice industry. A significant withdrawal of resources away from the rural sector has not been matched by the growth of the urban sector industries. The contribution of the manufacturing sector has not increased significantly. It has remained between 10-14 per cent of the GDP since 1988.

The major component of the increase in the manufacturing sector's contribution to the GDP has been the garment industry which has been promoted since the economic decline experienced by Fiji after the military coups. The garment industry expanded significantly after the introduction of tax-free status. Garment exports grew steadily since 1988 reaching $ 131 million in 1991, $ 188 million in 1996, and $ 200 million in 1997 and is projected to increase to $ 275 million in 1999.

Table 7 : Urban and Rural Population Growth, 1966-96.

		Population (per cent)	
Division		Rural	Urban
Total Fiji	1966	66.6	33.4
	1976	62.8	37.2
	1986	61.3	38.7
	1996	53.6	46.4
Western	1966	73.0	27.0
	1976	71.9	28.1
	1986	71.9	28.1
	1996	62.6	37.4
Central	1966	40.5	59.5
	1976	35.5	64.5
	1986	32.7	67.3
	1996	27.9	72.1
Northern	1966	86.3	13.7
	1976	85.2	14.8
	1986	85.0	15.0
	1996	78.5	21.5
Eastern	1966	92.7	7.3
	1976	93.0	7.3
	1986	93.2	6.8
	1996	90.8	9.2

Source : *Bureau of Statistics, Household Income and Expenditure Survey* (1966, 1976, 1986, 1996).

Figure 1 : Growth Rates of the Agricultural and Non-Agricultural GDP, 1984-96

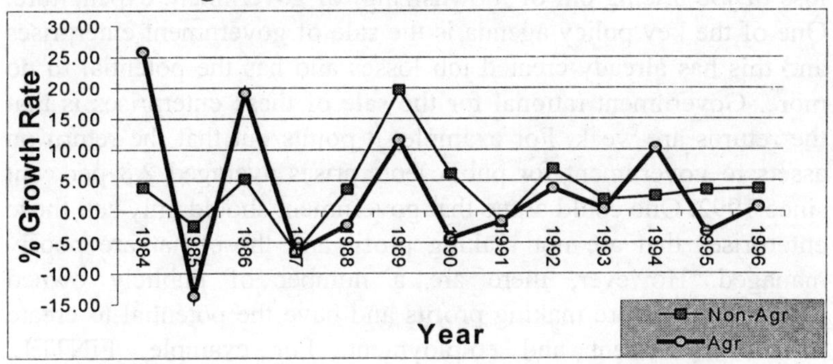

Source : *Bureau of Statistics Current Economic Statistics* (various years).

The decline in the rural (agricultural) sector and the subsequent out-migration of labour requires the non-agricultural sector to expand at a rate which is greater than the decline if unemployment is to be reduced. Results from figure 1 show that the rate of growth of the non-agricultural sector has been slightly greater than the loss in the agriculture sector. The question that arises now is why are all the workers released from the agricultural sector not absorbed in the non-agricultural sector. One reason may be that the non-agricultural sector is not that labor intensive. This proposition can be verified by examining and comparing the employment elasticities of the two sectors. This is done in the next section.

Since 1988, the Fiji Government's economic policies have put a major emphasis on the urban-based manufacturing sector. A lot of incentives have been provided to the private sector. This is in line with government philosophy that the private sector is the engine of growth. The 1999 budget continues with this philosophy and has provided further incentives for private sector investment. These include exchange controls, profit repatriation, and special tax incentives for investors in the tourism industry (*Government of Fiji*, 1998).

The other issue that explains the increase in the level of unemployment in the urban areas is the lack of job creation and the loss of job arising out of 'downsizing' of government expenditure. One of the key policy agenda is the sale of government enterprises and this has already created job losses and has the potential to do more. Government rational for the sale of these enterprises is that the returns are weak. For example, it points out that the return on assets to government for public enterprises averaged 2.8 per cent since 1992. One could argue that government should only sell those enterprises that are not making profit and those that are poorly managed. However, there are a number of publicly owned enterprises that are making profits and have the potential to create further investment and employment. For example, FINTEL, Telecom Fiji Ltd, Air Pacific and the Fiji Sugar Corporation have been profitable and have been paying dividends. Yet the government intends to sell these enterprises. It does not make much economic sense to sell profitable enterprises and reduce employment opportunities in those areas. Another reason that is advanced by the government for the sale of public enterprises is to provide competition and efficiency. In the case of Fiji, most public enterprises are monopolies and provide useful services to the public. However, those that have been sold create private sector monopolies and the services that were provided before are no longer provided in the same quantity and quality.

Employment Elasticities : Overall and Sectoral

Strategies aimed to increase GDP will lead to employment creation. A crucial question that needs to be answered is what sectors need to be promoted to achieve multiple objectives. If one of the crucial objectives is to maximise employment creation, then we need to identify those sectors which have high employment elasticities. Employment elasticities with respect to GDP and individual sectors are presented in table 8. With respect to the overall GDP, a one per cent increase in GDP would lead to an average increase in employment by 0.27 per cent. It is to be noted from the trend in elasticities that since 1977, the rate of increase in employment arising out of a 1 per cent increase in GDP, has been increasing. In the 1977-80 period, the elasticity of employment was 0.17 per cent. In the 1991-96 period, the elasticity of employment increased to 0.39 per cent. Upon examination of individual sectors, the manufacturing sector is most elastic relative to the other sectors (an elasticity of 0.54 per cent). The least elastic response to employment creation is the Electricity Gas and Water sector (with an elasticty of 0.03 per cent). Other sectors, which have potential to generate employment to a large extent are Agriculture, Retail and Trade, Finance and Real Estate and Community and Social Services. If employment generation is seen as key to poverty alleviation, then these values of employment elasticities can be used for governments' resource allocation.

Table 8 : Employment Elasticities with Respect to GDP by Sector, 1977-96.

Sector	1977-80	1981-86	1987-90	1991-96	1977-96
Agriculture	0.18	0.26	0.41	0.51	0.29
Mining and Quarrying	0.01	0.07	0.39	0.28	0.19
Manufacturing	0.39	0.48	0.64	0.63	0.54
Electricity, Gas and Water	0.01	0.02	0.04	0.04	0.03
Building and Construction	0.14	0.23	0.24	0.29	0.21
Wholesale & Retail Trade	0.29	0.31	0.46	0.41	0.36
Transport and Communication	0.12	0.18	0.23	0.29	0.19
Finance, Insurance and Real Estate	0.31	0.43	0.53	0.49	0.44
Community, Social and Personal Services	0.19	0.33	0.35	0.32	0.31
All	0.17	0.25	0.32	0.39	0.27

Source : Raw data on employment and GDP by sector were obtained from Bureau of Statistics, *Current Economic Bulletin* (various years).

Note : Elasticities were computed by first estimating employment equation for overall economy and also for each sectors. The GDP coeficients and means of employment and GDP for each time period were used to compute the final elasticities.

Another interesting result that comes out of the above analysis is that the employment elasticity of the non-agricultural sector (0.28 per cent) is less than that of the agricultural sector (0.29 per cent).[1] Therefore, for the non-agricultural sector to absorb labor released from the agricultural sector, it has to grow at a much higher rate then the rate of decline of the agricultural sector. Furthermore, due to the strong cultural and traditional norms of the society in Fiji, most of the labor employed in the agricultural sector is mainly males. However, the employment generated in the non-agricultural sector, particularly the garment industry, is mainly for females.

Unemployment — Poverty Linkage

The issue of unemployment-employment and its linkage to poverty has been a contentious issue. In Fiji this linkage is somewhat puzzling because if one looks at the official unemployment statistics and the level of poverty, then poverty should really not be that high as is recorded. However, before we look at the situation in Fiji, it is important to highlight conceptually the linkage. According to Sen (1998), given any poverty line, all the usual poverty measures can be estimated if the mean income and the parameters of the Lorenze curve are known. Therefore, the manner in which unemployment or employment affects poverty would depend upon its effects on the mean and its distribution. It is also known that in most cases measures of poverty are insensitive towards the distribution of income for people above the poverty line. Therefore, what matters is the effect of unemployment upon the incomes of people who are on the fringe of the poverty line. In the case of Fiji not all the people who are below the poverty line are employees. In this case it does not make sense to only consider wages and the availability of jobs for the poor. As we pointed out earlier, there is a large percentage of people who work in the informal sector.

---

1 Note that if non-formal employment figures are also used in elasticity computation, then the agricultural sectors employment elasticities will be much larger figure. Since there is no record of non-formal employment in all sectors, only formal employment figures was used in elasticity computation.

There appears to be a strong linkage between the levels of unemployment and poverty in Fiji. According to the 1990/1991 Household Income and Expenditure Survey, the bottom thirty per cent of all income groups earn about ten per cent of total income, whilst the top thirty per cent earn sixty per cent of the total income. Poverty in Fiji has clearly been on the rise since 1987. A government study on poverty in 1996 shows that the level of poverty in Fiji is about 25 per cent. However, small pilot surveys carried out by Fiji Council of Social Services show much higher levels of poverty in Fiji.

In Fiji's case, creation of productive employment is the most efficient way of alleviating poverty because there is no other suitable means through which people can receive assistance when they do not have employment. Government in its 1999 Budget emphasises the development of the private sector and has provided tax relief to taxpayers. Some of the provisions in the 1999 Budget include the increase in the income tax threshold from $ 5,000 to $ 6,500 per year. The government estimates that as a result of this, about 12,648 people will be removed from the tax net (*Government of Fiji*). Apart from this, tax allowances have also been increased and this could provide some relief to the low income earners. However, this does not address the problem of poverty, that is those below the poverty line do not have any relief from the tax concession. The majority of those living below the poverty line are those who have incomes that are already below the income tax threshold.

Poverty Alleviation Fund

On a yearly basis, Government allocates a certain portion of their budgetary expenditure for poverty alleviation. This appropriation is distributed to households under the poverty line income. The total amount of funds distributed in 1993 are given in table 9. Simple arithmetic calculation, presented in table 9, reveals that in both the years, the allocation fell much short of addressing the poverty problem for all households under poverty. For example, in 1993, a total of 38,983 households did not receive any assistance. Similarly, in 1999, using a poverty level of 25 per cent and an average household disbursement rate of $ 20/household/month, only 20,958 households will receive assistance (table 10). This will leave 13,641 households, under poverty, with no assistance at all.

Table 9 : Poverty Alleviation Fund and Households Under Poverty, 1993

	Indian	Fijian
Total PAF Disbursed	43,106.85	123,721.66
No of Recipient Households	240	687
Approx. Number of Households Under Poverty	22,150	17,760
Number of Poverty Stricken Households With No Assistance	21,910	17,073

Notes :

1) Number of recipient households was computed using a monthly allowance rate per household of $ 15 for 1993.

2) Approximate number of households was determined assuming the 1990/91 poverty level of 25 per cent. However, estimates reveal that poverty level has actually increased after 1991.

Table 10 : Poverty Alleviation Fund and Households Under Poverty, 1999

	General Population
Total PAF allocated (F$)	5 million
Number of recipients (approximately) households	20,958
Total number of households under poverty	34,600
Number of poverty stricken households that may not get any assistance	13,641

Notes :

1) PAF allocation obtained from *Fiji Government,* 1999 Budget.

2) Number of households under poverty use a base figure of 25 per cent poverty level. Given the recent sluggish performance of the economy, a larger portion of the households is expected to be under poverty. In absence of data on this, the 25 per cent level is assumed.

Implications of Poverty

Poverty, Land Degradation and Resource Depletion

In a semi-subsistence agrarian community, households under poverty often try to maximise output through intensified use of land. Intensified land use leads to land degradation in various ways. For example, in Fiji's sugar industry, farm size has been declining over time (table 11).

Table 11 : Farm Size Changes in Fiji's Sugar Industry

Year	Size (acres)
1978	12.42
1991	9.33

Source : Reddy (1998). *Production Economic Analysis of Fiji's Sugar Industry,* Unpublished Ph.D. dissertation.

With increasing population at the farm level, with the same amount of land or a smaller portion, the land would be subject to intensified agriculture to meet the food demand from increasing population. Intensified agriculture would lead to a rapid deterioration of soil nutrient base. Such practices would also lead to soil erosion and thus loss of the top fertile soil.

Poverty and Environmental Pollution : Some Intergenerational Concerns

Unsustainable agricultural practices can lead to intergenerational poverty implications. For example, to maintain soil fertility, farmers would intensively use artificial fertilizers. In small island countries, where ground water is directly used through wells, the leaching down of artificial fertilizers to the ground water lens poses serious health risk (Reddy and Chase, 1992). A large number of farmers apply significant doses of pesticides to control pests such as insects and weeds. This again can leach down and contaminate the ground water lens. Furthermore, these chemicals can also be consumed directly through residues in the plant material. The implications of such unsustainable practices can be explained as follows :

- The high amount of artificial fertilizer and pesticide use can increase production cost, reduce profit margin and, therefore, reduce the net disposable income of farm households.
- The health hazard created by artificial fertilizer use and pesticide use can lead to low productivity of labor due to deteriorating health conditions and thus lower farm income of the households. Also in the longer run, it may lead to loss of life, and in such scenario, if the person is the sole income earner, then again there is a danger of sliding into poverty.
- Intergenerational poverty concerns can also arise in two ways. One is that, if a family falls into poverty, then the likelihood of their household to be in poverty is quite high. Secondly, the negative effects of unsustainable use of land are most likely to be felt in the longer run. That is, the next generation will feel the negative effects of the unsustainable practices of the current generation *via* a less productive resource (land in this case).

Poverty can contribute to other problems such as deforestation and global warming. Poor families who cannot afford to consume alternative energy sources (*e.g.*, electricity) or do not have access to these alternative energy sources can resort to using fuel wood to supplement their energy requirement, thus leading to increasing deforestation. This is quite prevalent in developing countries and Fiji is no exception.

Conclusion

The level of unemployment and associated levels of poverty have increased in Fiji in the last ten years. The adoption of the structural adjustment policies since the military coup in 1987 has affected policy direction of the country. Major emphasis and incentives have been provided to the urban based manufacturing sector and at the same time resources were reduced from the agricultural sector. There is evidence that the policy shift since 1987 has led to increased levels of urbanisation and unemployment. Associated problems of urban crime and other social ills have increased at alarming levels in the urban areas of Fiji.

The key issues that we discussed in the paper include the levels of unemployment, wages and poverty. The unemployment level in the country has increased and so has the level of poverty. About 25-30 per cent of the population now live below the poverty line. The majority of the labour force is employed in the informal/agricultural sectors. However, government's job creation efforts have largely been in the formal sector. The government's own statistics show that the formal sector may be able to generate only 8,000 jobs a year, whereas the number of unemployed seeking jobs annually are about 17,000.

The government's overall policy of promoting private sector development ignores the structure of the Fijian economy where the majority of the people do not have formal employment, and are dependent on self-employment opportunities and subsistence. The development of the private sector and the emphasis of export-led economic growth must be balanced with expenditure policies that promote self-employment generating activities. Poverty and unemployment could be tackled through a balanced development of both the agricultural sector and the manufacturing sector.

Another reason why the government's policy shift (which links the growth and development of the economy to the non-agricultural sector) is failing to address the increasing unemployment problem is because the non-agricultural sector is not as labor intensive as the agricultural sector. The employment elasticities computed in this paper should substantiate such view. Furthermore, the rapid growth in the manufacturing sector has provided gender specific employment for females. Therefore, the labor released from the shrinking agricultural sector (mostly males), was not successful in finding employment. If government wants to solve the problem of unemployment within its current economic policy scenario, then the growth rate of the non-agricultural sector should far exceed the rate of decline of the agricultural sector.

REFERENCES

Bank of Hawaii (1998), *Fiji Economic Report*, Hawaii : Bank of Hawaii.

Bureau of Statistics (1996), *Household Income and Expenditure Survey,* Suva.

Chand, G. (1994), The Labour Market and Labour Institutions in Fiji in an Era of Globalisation and Economic Liberalisation, Suva : Fiji Trade Union Congress.

Chand, G. (1998), Labor Market Deregulation in Fiji, Memeo.

Government of Fiji (1998), *Economic and Fiscal Supplement to the* 1999 *Budget Address,* Suva : Ministry of Finance and Ministry of National Planning.

Government of Fiji (1997), "Development Strategy for Fiji : Policies and Programmes for Sustainable Growth," *Parliamentary Paper No. 58,* Suva : Ministry of National Planning.

Prasad, B.C. and Asafu-Adjaye, J. (1998), "Macro-economic Policy and Poverty in Fiji," *Pacific Economic Bulletin*, Vol. 13, No. 1, pp. 47-56.

Prasad, B.C. (1998), "The Woes of Economic Reform : Poverty and Income Inequality in Fiji," *International Journal of Social Economics,* Vol. 25, Nos. 6/7/8, pp. 1073-94.

Reddy, M. (1998), "Structural Adjustment Policies, Agricultural Growth and Rural Poverty in Fiji," *Journal of South Pacific Agriculture*, 5(1) : 61-68.

Reddy, M. and R.G. Chase (1992), "Preliminary Studies on Nutrient Leaching of N and K Fertilizers Applied to Coralline Soils," *Journal of South Pacific Agriculture*, 1(2) : 27-42.

Sen, A. (1998), "Rural Labour Markets and Poverty," In Radhakrishna, R. and Sharma, A.N. (eds.), *Empowering Rural Labour in India : Market, State and Mobilisation,* Delhi : Institute for Human Development.

UNDP (1997), *Fiji Poverty Report.*

5 Poverty in Developing Countries

D.J.J. Botha[1]

Introduction

This paper is limited to aspects of poverty in sub-Saharan countries — *aspects* only, because the subject is extremely wide, and we shall have to economise on details. My comments shall draw on observations from the sidelines only, to which we shall apply basic economic theory, rather than delve into the vast literature of the subject.

It forces me to address briefly only four essential topics : *education, economic growth, protection* and the overriding importance of *politics* in the development process. A brief survey of these will give us an overview of the subject. It will also enable us to ask questions about the prospects of an early reduction in poverty in these countries.

Unchartered Territory

The modern theory of economic development could be said to have received its major impetus, if not its origin, from the de-colonisation process after the Second World War. Suddenly the District Commissioners were gone, and there were no more parades on the town square with the salute taken by a high official in white uniform and plumed helmet. These symbols of Empire retreated to their head offices in London, Paris, Brussels, The Hague and, later, Lisbon, leaving behind them large administrative lacunae in huge areas that were underdeveloped in just about every respect. This was so especially in Africa. Of all the territories de-colonised, those in Africa appear to have the greatest difficulty in standing on their own feet. Dire poverty, high illiteracy rates, indifferent governance

[1] This paper benefited from comments kindly made by Professor Colin McCarthy, Head, Department of Economics, University of Stellenbosch.

by new political masters — all these appear to be more endemic to Africa than to most of the countries in the East.

Western powers at the time were genuinely desirous of assisting in a process of a "take-off into self-sustained growth" in Africa and elsewhere. But they did not grasp the true nature, extent and vast complexity of economic development in these countries. Marshall Aid was thought to serve as a pointer to what could be expected from aid wisely applied. A similar result was expected in Africa. Funds flowed to those countries in substantial volumes. They also benefited handsomely from the rivalry between the West and the Communist world. Each tried to outsmart the other in a bid for the goodwill and political sympathies of the developing countries, with the West supplying most of the funds, the Communists most of the ideology.

The remarkable results of Marshall Aid did not, of course, materialise. Africa was not Western Europe. It was not sufficient merely to supply funds for development. What was needed was the financial prudence and business acumen of the West. These could not be acquired overnight, and they did not automatically accompany political independence. They were also not provided by the IMF and the World Bank. A wider approach was required, which lies outside the province of official institutions. These are usually not geared to deal with matters such as the cultural idiosyncrasies of the people, the unreliability of a newly-created civil service, or the unpredictability of the political scene generally.

The suppliers of funds entered uncharted territory. They did not — nor do we today — have a general and reliable formula that would necessarily set in motion a process of self-sustained economic growth. The Washington consensus gave rise to policies of structural reform, amid rising criticism from countries at the receiving end. This is not surprising. Western ideas for policy reform are often inappropriate, based as they appear to be on perceptions of economic development in advanced countries. For example, some two years ago Jeffrey Sachs from Harvard expressed strong and optimistic views in *The Economist* on the potential of African countries to emulate the performance of the Tigers from the East. We now know better, of course. What is surprising is that

Sachs could say this in the face of the increasing mountain of debt that had been accumulating in Africa over the decades. The extent of that debt was once well expressed by President Kaunda of Zambia in a London television interview. He castigated the World Bank for advancing insufficient funds to his country for that year, adding : "These funds are not even enough to enable us to pay the interest on our existing loans." This, expressed in the late 'seventies, revealed a great deal. It clearly implied an unwise use of loan funds, and ignorance of what is prudent financially. It also well epitomised the economic problem of Africa, as represented in the shocking statistics for many of the economies on that continent.

Africa did not stumble into this predicament by accident. The disastrous accumulation of debt took place over time and against the background of many incisive analyses by economists and a succession of international conferences, many of them under the auspices of the United Nations.

A Parade of Conferences

It is not necessary to provide a catalogue of all of the high-level UN conferences on economic development. We may mention only some of those that had a direct connection with Africa. Most well-known were those held at Lomé on tariff protection for African countries, the provisions of which will be gradually phased out by the Uruguay Round decisions. But there were others, less well-known that dealt with problems around domestic economic development in African countries.

In the sixties the UN General Assembly launched an International Development Strategy for the 1960s, 1970s and 1980s. As many African countries were still under colonial rule at the time, the first development strategy for Africa was announced by the Economic Commission for Africa in respect of the decade of the seventies. This was followed in 1973 by the Declaration on Co-operation, Development and Economic Independence at the tenth ordinary session of the Organisation of African Unity (OAU). In 1977 the OAU adopted the Revised Framework of Principles for the Implementation of the New International Economic Order in Africa.

In February 1979, prominent Africans met in Monrovia to consider what kind of development Africa should aspire to by the year 2000, and by what means it should be achieved. One month later the ECA met in Rabat, Morocco, on an African development strategy, which was adopted three months later by the OAU in Monrovia. This has become known as the Monrovia Declaration of Commitment. It placed the emphasis on endogenous growth for Africa, by means of natural and human resources from Africa. Nine months later, in April 1980, the OAU met in Lagos to make specific recommendations on the principles laid down in Monrovia. This has become known as the Lagos Plan of Action (LPA).

The implementation of these measures was seriously delayed by a variety of unforeseen circumstances. Most important among these were the disastrous drought of 1983-85, problems in administration, and the vicissitudes of international trade. This led the ECA in April 1985, to consider proposals for accelerating the implementation of the Lagos strategy. It was adopted three months later by the OAU and a year later (June, 1986) by the UN General Assembly. It has entered the literature on development as UNPAAERD, or the United Nations Programme of Action for Africa's Economic Recovery, 1986-1990.

These conferences dealt with the wide problem of African economic development. They all had as objective an improvement — a hope for substantial improvement — in the standard of life of the average citizen in the many countries on that vast continent. But there were also other international conferences with a frame of reference wider than the economic well-being of Africa, and whose decisions did little to further the objective of African advancement. The most well-known among these was the Uruguay Round of tariff negotiations from which African countries stood to benefit little, if at all, as we shall see below.

Poverty and Dire Poverty

Countries in sub-Saharan Africa are generally associated with very low per capita incomes inequitably distributed, low rates of literacy, poor health and sanitary conditions, limited markets and poor communications in rural areas, government controls, environmental degradation made worse by periodic droughts, and so on. These, taken together, describe African poverty as an overall concept.

It cannot be measured by income alone. A satisfactory level of income is a necessary condition for economic well being, not a sufficient one. Even if defined by income only, poverty takes many different forms. At the extreme end we find the poorest of the poor, the most lamentable condition of human existence. These are people, usually illiterate, who sleep in rags under makeshift shelters of scrap iron, cardboard and canvas on an empty stomach, with no prospects for the morrow. In fortunate cases, there might be a possibility of the odd menial task with, however, no job security. They are found in their millions in Africa. In South Africa in recent years they have been seeking refuge in huge squatter camps around the cities. These are the people with no particular skills, who migrate from the rural areas in the hope of finding employment of some kind in an urban environment. It adds enormously to the cost and the civic and other responsibilities of the city administration to provide the infrastructure required to accommodate the unexpected and sudden increase in population.

But even the established townships provide their particular problems. While writing this paper the metropolitan authorities of Cape Town announced that R 32 million would be spent on the townships to repair leaking water taps. It has been estimated that some fifty per cent of the water supply to the townships are wasted in this manner.

Higher up from this lowest level is an infinite variety of poverty, all defined with respect to the attainability or otherwise of an increasing level of welfare, an increasing level of satisfaction. Charles Dickens's *Mr. Micawber,* therefore, in fact represents a variety of situations. He can be relatively well-off, or he can be destitute. Whatever the case may be, he hates being in the red, which is a salutary attribute, and one that has the practical effect of staving off bankruptcy.

There is a spectrum of states of poverty. As Nobel laureate Amartya Sen said in an interview recently, "Poverty can be seen as deprivation of basic capabilities — the capability to be well nourished, to receive medical attention and be in good health, to be able to participate in the life of the community and so on."

The most sophisticated form of poverty is that which makes the individual feel deprived of the perquisites offered by society. He may have enough to eat, but he lacks the material resources that would allow him to enjoy and participate in the good things in life. This is the most subtle manifestation of poverty, one which includes a large percentage of the population in both the developed and underdeveloped worlds. Here is the *raison d'être* of the study of economics. We are interested in the material well-being of the individual, a state of affairs that would allow him to satisfy his particular needs.

Poverty in Africa is very elemental. The average individual in the rural areas is not well housed, clothed or nourished. He ekes out a living on the poor soil of a communal property, he is often illiterate and is doomed to repeat the simple lifestyle of his forebears with no prospects for the future.

Poverty is the central theme of the authoritative UN publication *Human Development Report* which has been appearing annually since 1990. Reading any of these reports gives an idea of the many dimensions and intricacies of the problem of world poverty and attempts at furthering economic development. Journal, articles cannot compete with this omnibus publication for coverage, or books for the comprehensive data compiled by its specialist research teams. All the same, the global view taken in these reports necessarily results in many statements that cannot always be applied to the problem of any particular country.

Education

One such example is education, human investment, which in many ways is the very essence of the problem. In fact, it could be said that all development starts with education. Put differently, if we consider the possibilities of development in a country, the first question to ask would be about the labour force — its education and its skills. This is the very key to success or failure. Modern industry requires skills. It is the skilled workman who earns the good wage, the unskilled who gets caught in a vicious circle of poverty with little prospect of advancement.

In some developing countries in Africa a proper and comprehensive programme of education may be too expensive to carry through in full. It also requires planning of a very detailed and sophisticated kind, and an efficient administrative system to run a programme of county-wide dimensions. The planning aspect is a headache in many a country. For an extrapolation must be made of the expected future demand for labour against the estimated number of school-leavers over that period in order to avoid an excess supply arising of young qualified job-seekers. This is a real dilemma, for there is no telling what the future demand for labour will be. It could fluctuate from an excess demand during an upswing in the cycle, to an excess supply during the downswing. It is a problem that has no necessary connection with the level of development of a country. But it could be more acute if a nation-wide programme of education is started in a country with an underdeveloped manufacturing sector that cannot mop up increases in the labour supply during the expansion phases of the economy.

This has been well illustrated by John Knight, Professor in the Centre for the Study of African Economics at Oxford, in an interesting paper on education in Zimbabwe.[2] When the country gained Independence in 1980, the number of school-leavers was under 10,000. Seven years later it reached 100,000, or 50 per cent of the number of 17-year olds. They had hoped to find employment in the formal, non-agricultural sector, in which the average annual increase in employment over the period was only 20,000. This shows the insoluble problems facing educational planners whose ideals of increasing the general level of education — and, it was hoped, productivity — of a country can be constricted by the current level of activity in the manufacturing sector.

---

2 J.B. Knight, "Labour Market Issues in Zimbabwe : Lessons for South Africa," *South African Journal of Economics*, March 1997, pp. 69-98.

A related study has been conducted by Tekaligne Godana, Professor of Economics in the University of Zimbabwe.[3] His findings support those of John Knight, but he draws some startling conclusions. He found that education was not the great equaliser that it has always been reckoned to be, nor does it necessarily cause the redistribution of incomes with which education has been associated in the literature. If there is no corresponding increase in the demand for labour, educational achievements become devalued — the filtering-down effect — without the expected increase in remuneration. The filtering-down happened especially among secondary school-leavers, not primary, as the lower-educated are usually found in the lower-paid job categories.

The question now arises, if this is what empirical evidence shows, could it still be said, as above, that all development started with education? The answer is a qualified yes, provided the manufacturing sector has the potential for expansion, although presently constrained by a shortage of qualified labour. In Zimbabwe it was the other way around : the programme of education led to a sudden increase in the supply of labour, which descended upon a relatively small manufacturing sector. This was in a country that had recently gained Independence, and whose future policy towards private enterprise, for overseas investors, was still uncertain and untested.

It is a situation that may in some respects repeat itself in South Africa. There has recently been a substantial increase in spending on education, something which should have happened decades ago. The ANC government realises the importance of a good general education, so much so that the Education vote has become the largest in the national budget. Although still hampered by a quagmire of poor administration, this could well lead to an increase in the number of job-seekers which the disconcertingly sluggish manufacturing sector may not be able to absorb.

If we now turn to the treatment of this subject in the 1997 edition of the *Human Development Report,* we find little reference

---

[3] T. Godana, "Returns to Education in the Manufacturing Sector in Zimbabwe : Some Empirical Evidence," *South African Journal of Economics,* March 1997, pp. 99-113.

to these obstacles.[4] It advises that countries must "invest liberally in human development so that they are ready to face the challenge of globalization and compete in open markets."[5] The Report is optimistic : "...poor countries can leapfrog several decades of development if they combine their low wages (*sic)* with basic education, technical skills and export-led growth."

This is a very general statement. The authors of the Report seem to overstate vastly the immediate prospect of the underdeveloped countries — at least those in Africa — becoming competitive in world markets in respect of commodities whose manufacture requires education and skills. More problematic is the connection which they lay between that kind of manufacturing, and low wages. Low wages are what everybody would like to see disappear in manufacturing. Also, it is not clear how, and if so, to what extent the process of globalization will in any way directly affect these poverty-stricken countries.

Economic Growth

The purely economic side to development is concerned only with an increase in the material well-being of the individual. It calls for an increase in output per worker over the whole spectrum of economic activity. Education, if wisely planned, could be a means towards this end, a means perhaps towards lessening the inequitable distribution of income. It implies an expansion of output in all industries, primary, secondary and tertiary. In developing countries it relates mostly — initially, at least — to primary and secondary production, expanding (i) agricultural and (ii) industrial output. Both are fraught with problems.

Increasing Agricultural output touches on very complex issues such as land reform, mechanisation and crop selection. It often affects the very livelihood of a conservative people to whom intervention in activities handed down from generation to generation could be a traumatic experience. There is in Africa the

---

4 UNDP, *Human Development Report 1997*, Oxford University Press, Oxford and New York, 1997.

5 *Ibid.*, p. 9.

ever present problem of overgrazing and denudation of the land, to which an obvious solution would be an official limitation on the number of livestock (cattle, goats, sheep) allowed per unit of land, calculated in accordance with the carrying capacity of the land. From the Masai in the North, who regard their cattle as God-given, to the Xhosa on the Southern tip of Africa, for whom cattle are one of their major sources of wealth, this kind of measure would be resented. To enforce it would be costly, if not impossible.

The *Report* takes Malaysia as an example of a country that has launched a successful national anti-poverty programme in agriculture.[6] It centered around four issues, *viz.,* (i) resettlement of the landless, (ii) rehabilitation and consolidation of land, (iii) processing of farm produce and (iv) training of the young for non-farm employment. This called for a concerted national effort. As was said above, private enterprise cannot be expected to perform this kind of national service. The trickle-down process may in the end achieve a similar result, but it would take time. All the same, there are no easy general solutions to the problem of increasing output in the agricultural sector. The many factors involved differ from country to country and call for measures tailored to the needs of the country or region concerned.

Africa is a case in point. A successful agricultural development programme in Africa calls for a substantial, albeit perhaps impossible, land reform. Self-interest plays an equally important role in agriculture as it does in other spheres of economic activity. But with *communal* property rights embedded culturally in a social system, self-interest is smothered, and individualist activity tends to reduce to a minimum. Ethics also comes into play. If the community regards individual success as proof of the exploitation of others, entrepreneurial ambition goes overboard. This is a deadly recipe for eternal stagnation.

But there is another problem. Agricultural produce is sold on world markets that are notorious for wide and sudden fluctuations in prices. This has cost the African countries dearly. A slump in world markets can cause a drastic deterioration of the terms of trade for Africa, with a consequential losses in income. It is a serious

---

6 *Ibid.*, p. 75.

problem for the struggling countries in Africa, for they are exposed to competition with countries the world over — including, of course, Europe — from whom no quarter could be expected. It becomes, in effect, a matter of "charity begins at home," and the best and most efficient win.

Growth through industrialisation raises problems of its own. Most of them could be narrowed down to two general issues :

(a) The first, is the great *sine qua non* of economic growth : the availability of a sufficient number of entrepreneurs. Without entrepreneurs there can be no growth, except State-sponsored growth which, as we know and have seen in Europe, misses that essential dynamic ingredient of self-interest. The dilemma in many sub-Saharan countries is the relatively small number of indigenous entrepreneurs from whom it is expected to initiate a process of industrialisation, or to expand an existing one. Foreign entrepreneurs, one suspects, are a second-best solution, and may in some regions be interpreted as a form of economic imperialism. A leading South African firm that operates internationally has pioneered a successful new approach to foreign investment. It allows local businessmen a substantial representation on the board of directors. In some cases it has gone even further by entrusting them with the majority vote on the board.

The theory underlying this philosophy is that local businessmen, apart from being better informed about the country, would not deliberately follow policies inimical to the interests of the firm, the country and, in consequence, the foreign investor. It is a policy based on trust — trust on the part of the foreign investor in the abilities of local talent, which, in turn, instils trust and confidence in the motives of the investor. In the process local businessmen gain valuable experience in business administration and management.

(b) The second, equally ubiquitous issue connected with the general question of growth through industrialisation is that of capital-intensive *vs.* labour-intensive production. There is very little place in modern economic theory for labour-intensive production, a process which generally shuns modern technology, and is costly because of the low per capita productivity. However, it generates employment of the otherwise unemployable, the less skilled and the unskilled. It raises the possibility of alleviating the pressing problem of unemployment in less developed countries.

Labour-intensive production is favoured by many as best suited to resolving the unemployment problem in developing countries. But it is unlikely to be the most productive. Nor would it be able to withstand the cold blast of international competition for long. This seems to narrow labour-intensive production down to being at most a local affair. In the case of substitute products, however, it would have to contend with foreign competition. Local producers are likely to claim for protection, on pain of retrenching labour or even closing down. We are back at the old principle — and problems — of infant industry protection.

Growth through industrialisation is generally regarded by planners as a tantalising possibility, although often an evasive one due to the ceilings set by shortcomings of various kinds, *e.g.*, skills, know-how (technology), infrastructure and entrepreneurship. There have, of course, been exceptions. Malaysia is again an example of a country that has been successful in this respect. Figures show (*Report*, p. 75) that between 1970 and 1994 industrial production in Malaysia rose from 14 to 32 per cent of total production, which led to an increase in the share of manufactures in exports to increase from 12 to 77 per cent. These are not figures that one would expect to find repeated in Africa.

The Malaysian success story seems to have been the result of systematic planning, correct allocation of priorities and a receptive labour force. These conditions are seldom found together in developing countries. The *Human Development Report* for 1997 implies that this could be seen as the success route for developing countries generally. It states (p. 75) that in its previous (1996) Report it was shown "how a virtuous cycle of economic growth and human development takes over when the pattern of growth is labour-using and employment-generating ..." Perhaps the *Report* was unduly optimistic. For there are many countries in sub-Saharan Africa in which this would not necessarily follow. The absence of a sufficient number of entrepreneurs, a shortage of skills, of risk-capital from overseas and the absence of a general culture of manufacture and competition makes the possibility of a virtuous cycle of growth a fast-receding ideal. Statistics bear this out. Sub-Saharan Africa is one of the poorest regions in the world, which showed a cumulative decline of 21 per cent in real GNP between 1981 and 1989. In 1992 about 45 per cent of people in this part of Africa were classified as poor — and "the situation remains alarming in the 1990s" as the *Report* puts it pessimistically (p. 32). This is a particularly bad omen. One could safely say that the reasons for it are not only economic — perhaps not even economic at all. They appear to be more deep-seated, and to descend to the very roots of society, encapsulated by vague generalities such as the work-ethic of the people and, as we shall see below, the much less vague question of the manner in which some of these countries are governed.

Capital-intensive production raises questions of its own. With it goes the export of the latest technology to the developing country and other capital goods. This need not necesssarily be in the best interests of the receiving country. The more capital-intensive the production process, the less labour is required per unit of output, and although improved skills and pockets of high incomes may result in certain regions, much of the rest of the population may be left to fend for itself. Worse still, the relatively industrialised centres may attract the poor to squatter camps in search of employment of one kind or another.

This is what the "growth-pessimists" point to, plus the finding that a per capita growth of some 3 per cent per year would be required to reduce poverty by 50 per cent over a decade. To a large number of countries in Africa this is presently an unattainable ideal. Again, although there are countries that have been able to reduce the incidence of poverty through industrialisation, it can by no means be seen as a panacea. The varied successes around the world bear testimony to it. Before a country embarks on a national programme of industrialisation a close and circumspect study of the viability of industrialsation, the effects on employment, skills acquisition and the environment should be undertaken. Industrialisation as such is not necessarily a wonder cure.[7]

The euphoria around economic growth cools off considerably if one considers the failures. Not all economic growth benefits the poor. Two examples are quoted in the 1997 *Human Development Report* (p. 75). During a period of rapid capital-intensive growth in India in the 'fifties and early sixties,' regional areas with a high growth rate caused little reduction in rural and urban poverty. In Brazil during the same period the poor also benefited very little from capital-intensive increases in output.

Tariffs

Whether production is capital or labour intensive, a central question that arises is whether industry can survive without a wall of tariff protection. Protective tariffs are a core general question in international trade, irrespective of the stage of economic development of a country. Tariffs serve to keep out international competition during the period when the industry concerned is supposed to find its footing. In many of the developing countries this is a typical example of infant-industry protection, of the kind first advocated by Alexander Hamilton during the early years of the US, in his *Report on Manufactures* of 1791. In Europe, Friedrich List, half a century later, made an extensive case for protection and a customs union, the *Zollverein*, for the States of Northern Germany.[8]

Infant-industry protection, although acting as a shield against well-established foreign competition, blunts the cost-reducing initiatives forced on firms from outside under a system of free trade. As the tariff is paid by importers, the cost of protection is borne by consumers in the home country. The customs receipts constitute income to the government, and could favourably affect fiscal policy

---

7 There was a time, some decades ago, when industrialisation was seen in the literature as the only true road to success for developing countries, with agriculture totally neglected as an occupation suited to backward regions. It was in this era when a student from Africa at a University in England described the need for the industrialisation of his country in rather poetic terms : "to us the smoke from a factory chimney smells sweeter than a rose."

8 F. List, *Das nasionale System der politischen Ökonomie,* 1841, English trans. 1885.

in the form of increased spending on domestic projects, as could also the normal tax receipts. Both take money out of the pockets of consumers. The difference is that while taxation only takes money from consumers, a duty on a commodity, it is hoped, will provide employment in the industry concerned, with multiplier effects in the rest of the economy. Also, it will assist in the acquisition of managerial and craft skills, and increase gross domestic product. It could be seen as a long-term investment for the country, which, indeed, it would be if the tariff was eventually abolished. In the ideal case — which often remains only an ideal — the long-term benefit might outweigh the short-term cost.

Infant-industry protection raises many questions. With the process of industrialisation goes an increase in imports which may outweigh the inflow of investment capital, and so lead to a shortage of foreign exchange and, if it persists, exchange control. Part of the increased imports would be in respect of capital goods to supply the infrastructure called forth by the requirements of industry, such as roads, railways, ports, airports and telecommunications. This requires planning of a high order, and a government and civil service that are equal to the task. This, of course, is question-begging. It partly explains why industrial development in these countries has, on the whole, been rather unspectacular. It also explains why tariff protection cannot generally be associated with economic growth.

There is something ambivalent about tariffs. Many countries are implementing them, including advanced countries. The current view favours a liberalisation of trade world-wide and sees as ultimate ideal the total removal of tariffs. Simple models show how zero tariffs maximise — and protection reduces — welfare. It is a view that widely underlay the discussions of the Uruguay Round of tariff negotiations, which many developing countries have since come to suspect would work to their disadvantage. The *Human Development Report* (1997) puts it bluntly (p. 85) : "The Uruguay Round left intact most of the protection for industry and agriculture in industrial countries, while ignoring issues of vital concern to poor countries — notably the problem of debt and the management of primary commodity markets."

The free-trade theory, however, well argued, cannot disguise the fact that the industrial countries are not the most ardent supporters of the idea of a total liberalisation of trade. They have continued to subsidise production and exports, and practise tariff protection in various sophisticated ways. This was also pointed out by the *Report* (p. 85) : "As successive GATT agreements reduced tariff barriers, industrial countries increasingly switched to non-tariff barriers — quotas, antidumping measures and 'voluntary' export restraints."

It is not only industry that the developed countries are protecting. They also protect agriculture. During the Uruguay Round no steps were taken against the subsidisation of agriculture, which the *Report* also criticises (p. 86) : "Agriculture remains the only area of international trade in which export dumping is accepted as a legitimate trade practice."

Complete trade liberalisation is still clearly only a far-off ideal. This contrasts rather sharply with the confidence in the idea of trade liberalisation that underlies the papers of many international trade theorists. The latest appeared in the *Economic Journal* of September, 1998, *i.e.*, two months ago, by Anne O. Krueger of Stanford University. Her paper is on "Why Trade Liberalisation is Good for Growth," and deals mainly with the question of import substitution *vs.* free trade. Although this does not address the question of poverty in particular, it follows that if free trade stimulated growth, it may also reduce poverty.

The paper throws the net wider by not referring merely to initiating an industrialisation process in a developing economy. It refers to "outer-orientated trade strategies." By this is meant "a trade strategy that is not biassing incentives in favour of import-competing industries and that provides roughly equal incentives to all exporting activities" (p. 1514). This could be seen as referring to semi-industrialised economies attempting to stimulate growth, which is different from starting a process of industrialsation *ab initio* in an effort to reduce poverty in countries with few skills, a poor infrastructure, low per capita incomes and massive unemployment. Import-replacement policies, as Krueger shows, do not have a favourable track record, and have been "associated with increasing costs and slowing growth over time" (p. 1518). The paper argues correctly that trade liberalisation is superior to import-replacement. The question that arises is, why has such a policy not yet been put into practice internationally? Why do the developed countries of the world adhere to tariffs and other trade restrictions? Could it be that, in the final analysis, protection, applied circumspectly, does safeguard employment in the industrialised countries?

This is how politics enters the argument. Mass unemployment undermines the authority of democratically elected governments, which largely explains why they rely on protection despite the rhetoric against it. In developing countries governments go much further : in fact, they could constitute the greatest obstacle to economic growth.

The Political Log-Jam

Development economics does not analyse in depth the role played by politics in the development process. That is as it should be. But it is also not sufficient merely to mention that development takes place within a particular political framework, and that the interests of the politicians may enhance or retard the process. One needs to go one step further. We know how corruption on the scale experienced today in many countries harms the economy in diverse ways. Development economists have been paying attention to this aspect, and a sizeable literature on this slippery subject has been accumulating over the past few decades.

But there is more to the political aspect than that, especially in African countries. The African scene, in many respects, is perhaps unique in the world. Politics in Africa is a serious business, perhaps more so than elsewhere. There is no long-standing Western democratic tradition in Africa. In this respect it does not stand alone. Democracy, imported from Europe, presupposes literacy, tolerance, a free press, opposition parties and a readiness of the ruling party to hand over power if beaten at the polls. None of these comes naturally to Africa. The African politician clings to power. He realises that his party should be ousted, his life-style may crumble. Unless he is a professional man, there may be nothing he can return to. Poverty is likely to stare him in the face.

Perhaps this explains the many undemocratic countries on that continent. In mid-October 1998, Swaziland held a democratic election. But it was an election of a different kind, for Swaziland is a monarchy in which all opposition parties are banned. South Africa is due to hold its next election in 1999. In October 1998, the President and the leader of the ruling ANC party publicly made it known that any majority less than two-thirds would be regarded as a disaster. In the Democratic Republic of the Congo there is no democracy, for the country is ruled by a military despot who overthrew the previous despot — a man with fourteen official vacation mansions — and whose political future is currently being endangered by the activities of yet more rebel forces.

Democracy in rural Africa means something quite different: Wide consultation with the representatives of the people — the headmen — and the policies decided upon subsequently executed by the Chieftain. Open political opposition is regarded as antagonistic to the people and the government, and may be severely punished. This is well illustrated by what has been happening in Nigeria over the past number of years. And Nigeria is the country with perhaps the greatest economic potential in Africa.

The political factor in development has been vividly described by Claude Ake, Professor of Political Science at the University of Port Harcourt, Nigeria,[9] at an international conference held in Abuja, Nigeria, in 1987. Politicians, says Ake, believed and tried to convince others that there was no basis for political opposition. In the course of time, "apoliticism was elevated to the level of an ideology while the political structures became ever more monolithic." One must remember that the political scene before

---

9 C. Ake, "How Politics Underdevelops Africa," in *The Challenge of African Economic Recovery and Development*, A. Adedeji, O. Teriba and P. Bugembe (eds.), London, Frank Cass, 1991, pp. 316-29. Quotations in the text are from pp. 317-23. This omnibus volume of some 800 pages contains papers read at the Abuja conference and covers a large number of topics on African economic development.

Independence was also one of domination. There was no room for political parties, and when Independence came, countries emerged that were "really a hotch-potch of nationalities or people who had little in common with each other before colonialism brought them under a common domination." It was then that the consequences of the Conference of Berlin in 1884 became clear, when areas on the African continent were arbitrarily allocated to the imperial European powers.

Then follows a sentence in Ake's paper that puts a question mark behind a great deal of modern development economics. It also justifies the view that economists should pay more attention to the political constraints in the development programmes in Africa. He says : "The appearances suggest that development is our major pre-occupation. It is not, and cannot be — at least for most of our leaders. They are as it were, in a state of siege and their first concern — sometimes it seems to be the only one — is to survive and to reproduce their domination." This state of affairs affects economic development in many ways. The quest for survival on the part of those in power is incompatible with the objective nature of a development programme. The result is that incompetent people are appointed to key posts, while "competent people are wasted." These appointees are often "overpaid for what they do in order to keep them happy, creating demoralizing disparities between reward and effort."

This is virtually military rule : in "most of Africa" the governments are "for all practical purposes, armies in action." Africa cannot be associated with political stability. It is a situation that is not calculated to smooth the road for developers. Entrepreneurship cannot flourish under such conditions. Worse still, "fairly successful entrepreneurs are watched and harassed for fear that they may become centres of opposition" even when they do not show signs of political ambition. This is a shocking statement coming as it does from an African scholar.

Conspectus

There is a spectrum of developing countries, from the partly industrialised like Brazil, India, Korea and South Africa to, at the other extreme, subsistence economies with little prospect of advancement, like Angola, Sudan, Malawi, the Democratic Republic of the Congo (under military rule), Mocambique and a few others. There is hope for the former group, but not for the latter, at least in the foreseeable future. The picture for Africa is a pretty grim one. The 1997 *Human Development Report* lists all the obstacles to development as well as the policies that might be expected would lead to a reduction of poverty in these countries. But there is an unmistakable undertone of despair. The problems are vast and complex. Throughout the *Report* reference is made to "poverty eradication", a concept that is used *at nauseam*. Of course, poverty cannot be eradicated we shall always have the poor with us. It can only be reduced. It is a process, as the *Report* itself shows convincingly, which is not happening in most of the developing countries.

The present clamour for a cancellation of debts raises the question whether the developed world over the years had thrown money into a bottomless pit. Was it a question of ignorance, or just inept management, on the part of the receivers? Or both? And if the debts were cancelled and a start made all over again, will the old mistakes not recur? Why have the receiving countries always been loath to accept "aid-with-strings?" Would the "strings" not have supplied the necessary financial discipline which was obviously lacking in so many cases? Could this be the key to future success? The answers to these questions can only be supplied by politicians.

This brings us back to the notion of the economic order. The three approaches to the reduction of poverty in Africa cannot be said to have been successful. First, this is not the best terrain for the free market system on any big scale. The political risks have kept out many a potential private entrepreneur. Second, aid within a socialistic framework could not be expected to be more successful than it was in Eastern Europe or the Soviet Union. Although the command economy may be expected to be more to the liking of many African politicians than the uncertainties of a democratic system, the world today knows better than ever before how total planning can run an economy into the ground if the crucial element of self-interest is absent. Third, aid with strings needs looking into as a new approach. The old aversion to it could be met, provided the co-operation of the political order was secured. This is not a territory for economists, but it would appear that if African politicians could be persuaded that economic prosperity would be associated in the minds of the electorate with their benign rule, they might change their attitude to development aid. There is only one danger : the new approach would certainly shipwreck if the professional politicians of Africa realised that most of the aid would then likely be channelled to the grass-roots level.

This also refers to what Mr. Tony Blair had in mind when during his visit to China in October he declared that the two extremes of capitalism and hard core socialism have run their course. The approach of the twenty-first century is along a middle road. The State has a role to play. It must only recognise its limits. The new German Chancellor Gerhard Schröder called it the *neue Mitte,* the new middle way.

6 The Dimensions of and Assault on Rural and Urban Poverty : A Social and Historical Approach

Peter A. Longton

The Dimensions of Poverty

The ultimate aim of this exercise is an assault on rural and urban poverty — an amelioration of common misery — which provokes the question : "What is meant by poverty and how may it be measured?"

Deriving from the notion that a person's material standard of living determines his or her well-being, poverty is conventionally specified in terms of an unacceptably low material standard of living either relative to others or on the basis of some absolute minimum. The absolute poverty approach might thus define a minimum standard of income such as would be required to sustain life : for example, estimating minimum dietary needs and how these can be most cheaply met. The relative poverty approach defines poverty not against an absolute scale but compared to the rest of the community (Pearce, 1983, p. 345).

This traditional treatment of poverty has been found too restrictive for some contemporary studies and modern thought embraces more people-centred and multidimensional notions. Firstly, Sen (1982, p. 30) introduced as a heuristic device, a distinction between notions of well-being based on possession of things and their characteristics, on the one hand, and those based on conditions of people and their characteristics, on the other. The universe of things is made up of goods and services in the usual sense which has been the traditional focus of study in economics. Consumer demand for these commodities has, however, also been interpreted as demand for the characteristics of these commodities in that, for example, demand for beer can be better specified in terms of demand for different degrees of bitterness of the beer, light *versus* dark beer etc. Any well-being then stems directly from the commodities and their characteristics. The elaboration of notions describing people and their characteristics provides an alternative way of viewing quality of life. The "welfarist approach" (Sen, 1979) holds that the standard of living is to be judged in terms of the level of satisfaction or utility for the individuals concerned, while the usage of characteristics of people opens up a non-utility approach to the quality of life in terms of such characteristics as level of nourishment, morbidity, literacy, education, social fellowship and other economic, social and political traits. A further elaboration of this way of thinking is to be found in Sen's (1980) notion of "basic capability" referring to a person's capabilities of functioning in normal life enabling him or her to earn a living, participate in discussion etc., and thus open up the opportunities for living available to him or her.

Quality of life, whether positive well-being or negative poverty or misery, can thus be thought of and measured in terms of goods and services, clusters of commodity attributes, utilitarian pleasure, sets of popular characteristics or bunches of functional traits. As the ultimate objective in the present context is a people-centred notion of poverty that recognizes that human deprivation may occur in a number of important dimensions, income, although an element is merely one factor and, moreover, focuses on means rather than ends.

Lastly, "The capability poverty measure is a multidimensional index of poverty reflecting the percentage of population with capability shortfalls in three basic dimensions of human development" namely living a healthy well-nourished life, with safe and healthy reproduction and being literate and knowledgeable. The three corresponding social indicators of poverty might be the per cent of children under five who are under weight, the percentage of births unattended by trained health personnel and the per cent of women over 14 years who are illiterate (UNDP, 1996, p. 109).

The ultimate aim has been specified in terms of the basic dimensions of a healthy well-nourished life, safe and healthy reproduction and literacy and knowledge, while income was criticized as being unidimensional and focusing on means rather than ends. Nevertheless, the greatest potential lies in economic growth and the main bridge between such growth and opportunities for human development centres around employment, which provides people with the income that enables them to take advantage of a range of goods and services required for an adequate quality of life (the argument seems to have come round in a circle).

The best development strategy and means to this end of poverty amelioration thus lies in promoting employment-generating growth (*Ibid*, p. 87). The argument is well summarised in a "Statute of the Realm" of Elizabeth the First of England in 1598 :

> "Whereas the strength and flourishing estate of the kingdom has been always and is greatly upheld and advanced by the maintenance of the plough and tillage, being the occasion of the increase and multiplying of people both for service in the wars and in times of peace, being also a principal means that people are set on work and thereby withdrawn from idleness, drunkenness, unlawful games and all other lewd practices and conditions of life and whereas by the same means of tillage and husbandry the greater part of the subjects are preserved from extreme poverty in a competent estate of maintenance and means to live, and the wealth of the realm is kept dispersed and distributed in many hands, where it is more ready to answer all necessary charges for the service of the realm" (Hurstfield and Smith, 1972, p. 47).

The Assault on Rural and Urban Poverty

The critical question facing authorities today as indeed faced Queen Elizabeth the First of England in the 16th century is "How is it possible to establish what policies to pursue so as to best achieve employment-creating growth?"

There is a range of broad discovery procedures or modes of research available for exploitation which can be roughly listed as :

1) Evolutionary operation or full scale exploration in the real world proceeding by trial and error as in "learning by doing;"
2) Replication or test operation of a reduced scale pilot scheme;
3) Experimentation with artificial conditions under tight control as in a laboratory;
4) Simulation of the real world with some form of constructed model and lastly
5) Conceptualisation or symbolisation of the real situation in an ideal model.

This range of approaches varies progressively in the degree to which the methods involve the real or an ideal world, provide minimal or maximal control of conditions, produce maximal or minimal authenticity and often vary in commitment of resource and cost.

Taking China as an example, Lea and Chandhri (1983, p. 333) point out that the reorganization of its agriculture into communes was "the outcome of at least 30 to 40 years of small scale experimentation and incremental changes". While Moise (1994, p. 204) considering recent changes remarks that "provincial and local leaders were encouraged to experiment freely and the successful experiments became models for national emulation."

This paper is essentially an exercise in conceptual terms to throw light on what policies to pursue in order to achieve employment-creating growth combining growth with expansion of opportunities in an employment friendly growth strategy (UNDP, 1996, p. 92). A convenient starting point might be to isolate the preconditions for economic growth embracing a wide spectrum of factors. In terms of Braudel's Analysis (Braudel, 1980) at one extreme can be distinguished the structural features of the natural environment essentially constant over a very long time span and here Jones (1981, p. 226) has pointed out how Europe possessed a number of ecological features of site, location and resource endowment, advantageous to the emergence of capitalism within its boundaries. While at the other extreme there are the fast changing "People, Politics and Events" of "Narrative History." Since this is the history of "Kings, Battles and Dates" almost by definition most details of such histories are only of indirect interest to policy formulation.

Neither the unchanging structural features nor the buzzing confusion of episodic incidents, however, has much relevance to the quest for optimal policies, which must involve the Conjunctural Factors of Braudel's intermediate time sector lying between the unmoving structures and the fast moving events. Further categories of determinants : finer distinctions relevant to policy development, again can be distinguished according to the time span they involve within these Conjunctural Factors. Firstly, in the longest time span a given outcome can be attributed to its distant historical (or geographical) roots in a "genetic" explanation. Secondly, a given outcome may be explained as the product of some process over a medium time scale whether evolutionary, functional or purposive, so that "change, unless subject to very large shocks, is perceptible but very slow" (Lea and Chandhri, 1983, p. 333). Thirdly, an observed outcome may depend on (or better be explicable in terms of) the constellation of contemporary and contiguous factors that make up its situation, which forms the realm of scientific explanation whether deductive, statistical or causal. Such situational factors will embrace factors within the control of human agents, others outside that control and throughout a variable stochastic aspect. It is a premise of this paper that, naturally, the controllable elements of the situation form the raw material of intentional action and thus the focus of discussion.

Furthermore it is a second proposition of this paper that these elements partake of a certain structure which can be elicited :

1) by constructing a conjectural model elaborating the predisposing conditions for growth based on the conclusions of theoretical studies of :

   a) the emergence of capitalism in the medieval history of Europe and

b) the development of modern economies in the recent history of East and South East Asian countries.

2) While at the same time comparing any insights resulting from this analysis of the historical dynamics of capitalism with lessons derived from practical projects to ameliorate rural poverty in some successful countries.

This critical discussion leads to the conclusion that the preconditions for growth in a society lie in a melange of causal mechanisms which can be given a certain structure, and where a certain complex of dynamic relations between the various parts of the social system namely the different economic, political, religious and other institutions of a society, is conducive to growth in that society. More specifically, it has been argued in the literature, (Baechler *et. al.*, 1988) and is argued here that growth occurs within a framework with at least three levels, stratified in terms of such criteria as geographical extension, population size, size of unit and intensity of power relations. In this way, can be distinguished :

(1) at a basic level, a multitude of minute micro units of entrepreneurial activity, whether local communities or firms, characterised as being the least extensive and most intensive units of the entire system, conceptualized in economics as the infinite number of infinitesimal entities of the "market;"

(2) at a intermediate level a few medium sized macro units of typically regulatory activities, conceptualised in political terms as the "national state," a principal core of which is a web of rules and laws fostering and sustaining the market and concentrating resources on certain selected lines of activity;

(3) internal to each society can be distinguished a clutch of stakeholder groups, with their relative roles and powers and possible dominance of some over others and the resulting outcomes and

(4) at the most extensive and least intensive level can be found a single overarching megaunit whether a religious church or a secular political power casting a hegemonic umbrella over

all underlying components of the "civilization" and providing an international order and security system.

Any assault on rural and urban poverty requires attention to certain pre-conditions at each and all of these levels of economy, society and civilization. Obviously, there is no universal recipe for job creating growth and each specific case depends on its particular geographical and historical features. Nevertheless, hopefully, the exercise will show some of the major component causal mechanisms that have a role in the growth of a society.

A convenient starting point might be the question as to whether the growth process should be market driven guided by the price signals of a free market in a *laissez faire* economy or government driven guided by administrative fiat of the state in some form of a "command" economy.

Level I : Economy and Market

Turning first to the economic history of Europe to derive some insights on this issue, there seems to be a fairly wide consensus that the European dynamic and the emergence of capitalism was based on "a multiplicity of partly autonomous and competitive, local economic power networks — peasant communities, lordly manors, towns and merchant and artisan guilds" (Mann, 1988, p. 18); so that in the late fifteenth century the most widespread of the forms of late medieval industry was the village industry, descended from the specialised crafts on manorial estates (Parker, 1979, p. 44); while Roberts (1996, p. 217) remarks that before 1800 "manufacturing growth was still largely a matter of the multiplication of small-scale artisan production and its technical elaboration." In Renaissance Italy even the fine arts as painting and sculpture were organized as family businesses just like weaving even grocery (Burke, 1974, p. 73).

This emphasis on the small local unit recurs in the discussion on practical projects to improve rural conditions in many countries. The 1996 edition of the *Human Development Report* (p. 94) states "Agricultural development strategies can favour small over large holdings, following considerable evidence that small holdings produce higher yields than large, mechanised holdings." Lea and Chandhri (1983, p. 337) remarks, "To us it seems that the role of modern inputs, infrastructure and other enabling institutions is important but grossly exaggerated. More important than these inputs is local participation, local organisation and the skilful use of historical experience by the policy makers."

This picture of the economy as a very large number of very small units was idealized, of course, in the concept of the "perfect market" of the economists, ultimately in an abstract plane making it amenable to mathematical treatment and capable of achieving an equilibrium condition (it is only the assumption of an infinite number of players that ensures that an equilibrium is always possible). Members of the neo-classical school have always insisted that only the "Free Market" results in the most efficient allocation of resources, only its prices signal the optimum growth path overtime, and only free trade brings greatest welfare to all, so that government intervention can only lead to inefficiencies and failures (Rodan, 1997, p. 9; Weiss, 1996, p. 174). However, according to other commentators, the neo-classical view of the perfection of the market cannot be substantiated and they make such points as :

(1) the "market" is not completely a naturally occurring phenomenon but depends on certain essential social preconditions *e.g.*, property rights;

(2) the market itself exhibits deficiencies *e.g.*, dealing with collective goods;

(3) unconstrained, especially financial, markets can lead to excessive financial flows around the globe and produce chaos, as in "casino capitalism;"

(4) markets are not necessarily infinite person games with assured equilibrium points;

(5) historical and recent experience shows that markets can be subject to irrational factors such as the "lemming effect" of crowd panic among investors and consumers;

(6) empirical studies of real world economies showed varying degrees of government intervention in the market especially perhaps in early periods of fast growth.

Confronted with so much evidence for government intervention in the economy, some Free Market theorists acknowledge a role for the state but suggest that the various government measures have a self-cancelling or neutralising effect so that the policies are equivalent to no policies, and thus do not alter the basic market forces. These "Simulated Free Market" theorists were thus able to maintain that a liberal trade regime is essential for a successful growth story (Weiss, 1966, p. 175). In a similar vein, Jones E.L. in his study of the "European Miracle" states "An underlying thrust of our argument has been that very long-term growth was less the result of a conjunction of growth-promoting forces than of the removal of impediments."

The jury is still out regarding the question of whether higher political and social authorities can or should intervene in economic markets, topically taking the form of debating how and to what degree domestic authorities should monitor and regulate lending practices of banks and other financial institutions, including the debate over how fast or even whether developing countries should open their financial markets to global capital (Akyuz, 1998).

In dealing with such problems it is tempting to develop and use some set of principles which would give unambiguous solutions and clearly distinguish pro and anti market views, but each situation is complex and easy answers to questions are not readily available by appeal to principles, but rather found by trial and error through experience (Garran, 1998, p. 194).

Certainly the "New Institutional Political Economy" (Rodan, Hewison and Robison, 1997, pp. 9 and 11-13) maintains that the development and efficient operation of markets is contingent upon the establishment of institutional structures which will provide the necessary neutral regulatory framework or web of rules and laws fostering and sustaining the operation of free markets *e.g.*, rules of private rights, regulations for making and exchange, mechanisms for the collection of taxes, solutions to collective problems as free riding and, most fundamentally, to provide law and order. Benson (1993) in an analysis of interorganizational relationships considers "rules of structure formation" which in advanced societies are principally those which relate to the process of capital formation and function of legitimation (Ham and Hill, 1983, p. 177), while the point is also discussed by Offe (1974). Turning to the comparative history of the state, Hall (1986, p. 23) having criticized the role of the Chinese imperial governments adds "This is not to say that the impact of the state upon capitalism must always be negative. A different type of state the European organic state was capable, once capitalist relationships were established of providing crucial services for capitalism." According to Mann (1988, p. 18), one of the power networks promoting the exploitation of agricultural-cum-trading opportunities in medieval Europe was the presence of "small, weak political states, growing in centralized, territorial, co-ordinating and organic powers, but never internally or geographically hegemonic".

In further steps along the road of purposeful intervention in the market, Linda Weiss (1996, p. 178) under the heading of "Governed interdependence theory" reflecting Korea, Japan and Taiwan in the 1990's, describes a system of central co-ordination based on the co-operation of governments and industry which functioned to relieve firms from bearing the entire burden of major risks of raising capital, developing new products and technologies and training skilled engineers and workers. These functions which Linda Weiss attributes to good government are especially interesting in the present context of assaulting rural and urban poverty, as they echo to a remarkable degree the major components necessary in policies for employment-creating growth, as expounded in the *Human Development Report* 1996 of the United Nations Development Programme (UNDP). One lesson of successful experience the Report proposes (p. 98) is "Equitable access to productive assets" whether capital or land, and it mentions bold experiments to provide simple banking services to the poor such as imposing minimum quotas for small enterprises in the lending portfolios of commercial banks. Another lesson the Report emphasizes (p. 95) is "sustained investment in people — to climb the ladder of skills productivity and wages" and it underlines "that high-employment economies have invested heavily in the development of just such human capabilities — from basic education and health to technical education to research and development to in-service training" while earlier in the Report (p. 8) it specifically lists research and development as part of successful employment strategies. In these and other "lessons" the Report emphasizes the importance of strengthening the small scale and informal sector production which is perhaps of particular interest in the context of this paper (UNDP, 1996, p. 8 and 97).

In Free Market Theory and Simulated Free Market Theory the emphasis is on the power of the market to govern economic activity but in Wade's (1990) category of "Governed Market Theory" the role of the market mechanisms is emphasized and that of the state given greater prominence. This theory is based on the belief that the superior performance of developing countries was the result of heavy investment in internationally competitive high growth industries and that this concentration of resources on certain selected lives of economic activity was not such as might have been expected if market mechanisms alone had operated, but rather was the outcome of a set of strategic industrial policies involving export and sectoral promotion consistently pursued by a strong autonomous state (Weiss, 1996, p. 177). The recent economic history of East Asia does seem to exhibit examples of where the "developmental state" was able to beat the market, but conditions have changed with the progress of industrialization and it does not appear to have the same success at a stage of advanced industrialization (Garran, 1998, p. 206).

Level II : Society and Stakeholder Groups

The introduction into the discussion of the idea of co-operation between government and industry leading to intentional action in the form of strategic policy (whether this notion is soundly or falsely based), does introduce a completely new aspect : namely that of the internal dynamics of the society or the politics of groups and their interests. When the free market is considered as the perfect mechanism of resource allocation, giving the optimal answer exactly, then any political conflict is irrelevant, if not harmful, to the outcome. As soon as the rigidity of the system is relaxed and it is recognized that there is more than one way to achieve economic development, then the question of "optimal for whom?" can be asked and the role of stakeholder groups becomes highly relevant (Robison, 1996, p. 13). Internal to every society can be distinguished a clutch of stakeholder groups engaged in a political game where each group has its particular role and where typically power is distributed unequally over the group so that often there is dominance of one group over the others and the outcome of the political game gives undue benefit to the dominant group or elite. It is this game which is critical in determining the specific form of the web of rules and laws supporting the market (Benson, 1993). For example, different approaches to rural development strategies will have different major objectives for the policy makers and will provide major benefits to different groups so that, for example, a technocratic strategy to increase output will mainly benefit the land owning elite, while a reformist strategy to redistribute income as well as increase output will mainly benefit middle peasants, while a radical strategy to redistribute political power, wealth and output will mainly benefit small peasants, and lastly a free market determined strategy will benefit large farmers. The differences can be illustrated by case studies from different Asian countries (Lea *et. al.*, 1983 p. 24).

Level III : Civilization

Previously in this discussion (1) at a basic level, the market of a multitude of minute units of entrepreneurial activity was postulated; (2) then at an intermediate level, macrounits of typically regulatory activities conceptualized as national states were introduced; (3) whose internal structure of stakeholder groups was briefly noted; so now (4) lastly, at the most extensive and least intensive level, an overarching megaunit is supposed, casting a hegemonic umbrella over all of the underlying components of the "civilization" and providing an "international" order and security system. "In every period a certain view of the world, a collective mentality, dominates the whole mass of society. Dictating a society's attitudes, guiding its choices, confirming its prejudices and directing its actions, this is very much a fact of civilization" (Braudel, 1995, p. 22). While more specifically in Charles Kindleberger's view, a hegemonic power provides a range of public goods including relatively open markets, a stable international trading currency and a deterrent force (McLean, 1998, p. 218). In the contemporary world a particular need is an institution with rules and the power to enforce them which will monitor and control the excesses of the global short term flows of capital of "casino capitalism" (Akyuz, 1998, pp. 33-43).

The modern diplomatically regulated multi-state civilization replaced in the history of Europe the span of Christendom (Mann, 1988, p. 18). One of the critical characteristics of medieval European society was the extensive normative regulation supplied by the Church and required by the competition among the actors in the market, since it was basic that they should trust one another to honour their word and also trust each other's essential rationality. Moreover, norms of behaviour must apply "not only in direct interaction but also right across complex, continential chains of production, distribution and exchange (Mann, 1988, p. 11). Hall (1988, pp. 123-6) expresses similar views when he points out that "the rules of the market must be maintained for individual exchanges to proceed; consensus to use the lapidary Durkheimian formation, must precede contract "and he goes on to say that "in this early period there is a sense in which the church was the government in that it made people feel part of a single community." In other words here was a Christian commonwealth.

Conclusion

Following from this note on the traditional role of the Christian Church and as a form of summary, it is significant to note that common people throughout early Europe would derive their identity primarily and most immediately from the kith and kin of their local community, secondly, from being Christian and only thirdly, (and weakly in early European history) from any sense of "national" group. It was similar outside Europe as an Anatolian peasant in the days of the Ottoman Empire would think of himself firstly as a member of a certain village, secondly, as a Moslem and only thirdly, (if at all) as a Turk, so that on the collapse of the empire and the emergence of the modern state Ataturk had to make a persistent effort to instil a feeling of "Turkishness" in his people.

These levels of "village", "nation" and "church" seem quite fundamental and any assault on rural and urban poverty requires attention to certain preconditions at each and every one of these strata, which might more aptly be translated in more modern terms as "economy, society and civilization" as promoted by F. Braudel and the other "Annals" historians.

REFERENCES

Akyuz, Y, (1998), "The East Asian Financial Crisis : Back to the Future" in *Tigers In Trouble* ed. K.S. Jomp, London : Zed Books.

Baechler, J.J.A. Hall and M. Mann (eds.) (1988), *Europe and the Rise of Capitalism,* Oxford : Blackwell.

Benson, J.K. (1993), "Interorganizational Networks and Policy Sectors" in Rogers, D. and D. Whetten (eds.). *Interorganizational Coordination,* Iowa State University Press.

Braudel, F. (1980), translated by S. Mathew as *On History*, London : Chicago University Press.

Burke, P. (1974), *Tradition and Innovation in Renaissance Italy*, Great Britain, Fontana/Collins.

Garran, R. (1998), *Tigers Tamed*, St. Leonards, Australia : Allen and Unwin.

Hall, J.A. (1986), *Powers and Liberties,* Harmondsworth : Penguin.

Ham, C. and M. Hill, 1983, The Policy Process in the Modern Capitalist State London : Harvester.

HDR, See, UNDP.

Hurstfield, J. and A.G.R. Smith (eds.) (1972), *Elizabethan People* London : Edward Arnold.

Jones, E.L. (1981), *The European Miracle* Cambridge : Cambridge University Press.

Lea, D.A.M. and D.P. Chandhri (eds.), 1983 *Rural Development and the State*, London : Methnen.

McLean, I. (1996), *Oxford Concise Dictionary of Politics* Oxford : Oxford University Press.

Mann, M. (1988), "European Development : Approaching a Historical Explanation" in J. Baechler, J.A. Hall and M. Mann (eds.), *Europe and the Rise of Capitalism,* Oxford : Blackwell.

Moise, E.E. (1994), *Modern China* London : Longman.

Offe, C. (1974), "Structural Problems of the Capitalist State" in Von Beyme, K. (ed.), *German Political Studies*, Vol. I, London : Sage.

Parker, W.N. (1979), "Industry" in Burke, P. (ed.), *The New Cambridge Modern History*, XIII, Cambridge : Cambridge University Press.

Pearce, D.W. (1983), Macmillan Dictionary of Modern Economics, London : MacMillan.

Roberts, J.M. (1996), *A History of Europe* Oxford Helicon.

Rodan, G.K. Hewison and R. Robison (eds.) (1997), *The Political Economy of South-East Asia*, Oxford : Oxford University Press.

Sen, A.K. (1979), "Personal Utilities and Public Judgements : or What's Wrong with Welfare Economics?" *Economic Journal*, 89 : 537-58, reprinted in Sen (1982).

______ (1980), "Equality of What" in S. McMurrin (ed.), *The Tanner Lectures on Human Values,* Cambridge: Cambridge University Press, reprinted in Sen (1982).

______ (1982), *Choice, Welfare and Measurement*, Oxford : Blackwell.

United Nations Development Programme (UNDP) (1996) *Human Development Report*, Oxford : Oxford University Press.

Wade, R. (1990), Governing the Market : Economic theory and the Role of government in East Asian Industrialization, Princeton University Press.

Weiss, L. (1996), "Sources of the East Asian Advantage : an Institutional Analysis" in Robison, R. (ed.), *Pathways to Asia*, St. Leonards, Australia : Allen and Unwin.

7 Human resources and Gender Issues in Poverty Eradication : A Comparative Study of Selected Countries of the Indian Ocean Region

Malati Pochun

"Eradicating poverty will always require more than increasing the incomes of the poorest" — Human Development Report, 1997.

Introduction

It is known that while the world is approaching the third millennium, more than one billion people are living on less than a US dollar a day, and another two billion are only slightly better off. Although most of the poor are in the developing countries, poverty pockets exist in the industrialised countries as well.

On the other hand, the progress made in the past fifty years by the world as a whole on several fronts such as per capita income, life expectancy, infant mortality, health, housing and education has created an unprecedented hope for the poor countries that it will be possible for them to eradicate the absolute poverty in their countries within a reasonable time, in the sense of satisfying at least the basic needs of all.

There is growing evidence that a two-pronged strategy of sustainable economic growth, and investing heavily in human capital through improvements in education, health, nutrition and other social services including the family planning services is crucial for achieving further progress in the eradication of poverty. Because, research in several countries has shown that these two strategies together create a 'virtuous circle' of mutually reinforcing improvements to finally replace the earlier 'vicious circle' of poverty generating more poverty. Within the region, Singapore,

Malaysia and Mauritius are striking examples of the success of such policy.

Investing in the education of girls and women is considered as particularly important both for gender equity reasons and also because it is considered as possibly the highest return investment for the developing world. Because, it not only improves the situation of girls and women, but also has a multiplier effect of improving the situation of their families and eventually leading to transformation of societies in the future generations by reductions in fertility, maternal, child and infant mortality, and by increasing both the desire and learning abilities of people for skill development and improved economic contribution.

The countries in the Indian Ocean region differ widely in their GNP per capita (in US $) ranging from a low of $ 90 in Mozambique to a very high of $ 22,500 in Singapore in 1994 (table 1). Six countries in the region, Mozambique, Tanzania, Madagascar, Yemen, Kenya and India are below the poverty line, in ascending order of GNP per capita. Raising the standard of their people and reducing or eradicating poverty would, therefore, be top priority of these countries. Moreover, if the economic and social development is not accelerated sufficiently enough to counteract the continued rapid pace of population growth, their situation could worsen in the coming decades.

This paper would attempt a comparative study of the socio-economic situation in selected countries of the Indian Ocean region with a particular focus on the prevailing human capital and gender issues. Available statistical data regarding a number of relevant variables such as access to education and health facilities, sanitation, availability of clean drinking water, labour force participation, demographic variables and access to media will be used both as a support to the theoretical issues involved and to suggest improvements and policy decisions necessary for eradication of poverty in the coming one or two decades.

The paper consists of six sections. The second section describes the different dimensions of poverty and the Human Poverty Index (HPI) of UNDP. Section three deals with priorities for poverty reduction concerned with human resources and gender issues. A profile of human and income poverty in the Indian Ocean region is presented in the section four. The nature of human poverty in the Indian Ocean region is explored in the section five. Section six shows how gender inequality and human poverty are mutually reinforcing. Section seven is the concluding section. All Tables are given in the Appendix.

Dimensions of Human Poverty

It is now generally realised that human poverty has many dimensions, and it is not just about income poverty, or lack of what is necessary for material well-being. Poverty is reflected in the deprivation that people suffer throughout their lives. It means not having the choices and opportunities which are most basic to human development, and which make it possible to live a long, healthy and self-fulfilling life, to be educated and to have a reasonable standard of living, and also to be able to live in freedom, self-respect, dignity and community respect. Eradication of poverty, therefore, seems to be concerned with addressing the causes of poverty in all its dimensions and not in just reducing income poverty with social safety nets.

Human Poverty Index

Some of the faces of human poverty are manifested in a short life, illiteracy, exclusion and lack of private and public resources, and also in different combinations of these. The Human Poverty Index (HPI) of UNDP combines basic dimensions of poverty and is useful in revealing the differences between human poverty and income poverty. The HPI uses indicators of the most basic dimensions of deprivation, namely, a short life, lack of basic education and lack of access to public and private resources. It cannot, of course, reveal the full extent of poverty in all its dimensions, but it certainly provides a measure of poverty from the human development perspective. It is useful to the policy-makers, since by pointing out causes of poverty in a country it can also provide solutions for eradicating poverty.

Priorities for Eradication by Poverty

Three priorities for eradication of poverty are concerned with the empowerment of women and men, gender equality and pro-poor growth in all countries and faster growth in developing countries among others.

Empowerment of Women and Men

> *'Everywhere the starting point is to empower women and men — and to ensure their participation in decisions that affect their lives and enable them to build their strengths and assets.'*

Given that economic assets of poor people, both women and men, are meagre, their social, political, environmental and personal assets assume much importance for them. Building the assets of the poor and empowering them is thus the starting point for eradicating poverty. Among others such a strategy needs :

- Policy reforms and actions that would enable poor people to have access to assets which would reduce their vulnerability. Housing, land and access to credit and necessary financial services are important in that direction.
- It is also important to ensure education and health care for all, reproductive health services, family planning, access to safe water and sanitation within the shortest possible time.
- Social safety nets should be provided to the poorest and victims of disasters.

Gender Equality

> *'Gender equality is essential for empowering women and for eradicating poverty.'*

It is widely known that women constitute the majority of poor. Gender inequality robs them of the power of decision making both in the household and in the community as well as in national and international forums. Gender equality is thus the starting point for the empowerment mentioned earlier, for eradicating all forms of human poverty. This implies :

- Removing all discriminations against girls starting right from birth, in all aspects of survival, health, education and upbringing.
- Empowering women by giving them equal rights and access to land, credit and job opportunities.
- Taking appropriate action for ending all forms of violence and abuse against women.

Empowering women eventually leads to the empowerment of a society and to its transformation. Empowerment of women is therefore an important part of the strategy for eradication of poverty.

Pro-poor Growth

To ensure that poverty reduction is sustainable, growth in all countries needs to be both pro-poor and accelerated in those developing countries where growth has been slow. Incomes of more than a billion people in the world have actually declined in the last two or three decades. Moreover, even with economic growth, the proportion of people living in poverty can increase, if the growth is not pro-poor.

Growth is pro-poor when employment, productivity and wages of poor people rise and public resources are utilized to promote human development by rapid improvement in people's health and skills. Such pro-poor growth leads to a 'virtuous cycle' of economic growth and human development. If growth is not pro-poor it only leads to further income inequality as manifested in the ratio of the incomes of the richest 20 per cent to those of the poorest 20 per cent. (table 2).

Pro-poor and accelerated annual economic growth of at least 3 per cent per capita can, with equitable distribution, double incomes in one or two decades and halve income poverty, provided, poverty eradication is considered the main priority of a country's economic policy. Malaysia has been successful in reducing poverty by adopting such a policy.

About three-fourth of the world's poorest people live in rural areas depending mainly on agricultural activities. Pro-poor growth should, therefore, be concerned with increasing agricultural productivity and incomes, particularly in the small-scale agriculture, microenterprises and in the informal sector where poor people mostly belong. Growth in these sectors is labour intensive and generates incomes for poor at low cost.

Increased productivity of small-scale agriculture also leads to reduction in food prices and further benefits poor, both urban and rural. Malaysia since 1971 and India in the early 1980s followed this strategy.

Other key priorities for reduction in rural poverty are fostering technological progress for agricultural diversification, reversing environmental decline in marginal regions and increasing the speed of demographic transition so as to achieve low birth and death rates and slower population growth.

Basic education and health care are considered some of the most powerful means for growth. Investments in basic education and health have shown high rates of returns, especially for girls. Reducing human deprivation in education and health for all should in fact precede rather than follow economic growth.

Both the strong pro-poor growth and policies for translating that growth into human development and poverty reduction are needed.

Profile of Human and Income Poverty in the Indian Ocean Regions

This section presents a profile of human and income poverty in the Indian Ocean region. Australia, Singapore, Malaysia and Mauritius have attained high levels of human development (HHD), while Oman, South Africa, Sri Lanka and Indonesia have reached the medium level of human development (MHD); and Kenya, India, Yemen, Tanzania, Madagascar and Mozambique are in a low state of human development (LHD). The HPI is not available for Australia, Malaysia, Oman and South Africa, while Income Poverty measure is not available for Singapore, Mauritius, Oman, Yemen and Mozambique (table 3).

Nearly seven per cent of people in Singapore now suffer from human poverty, followed by Mauritius where a less than 13 per cent are affected by human poverty. Sri Lanka, Indonesia and Kenya suffer moderate levels of human poverty. However, India, Tanzania, Yemen, Madagascar and Mozambique, in that order are the worst cases of human poverty in the region. Around 40 to 50 per cent of their population suffer several forms of human poverty. It is to be noted that between 1970 and 1990 HPI for Mauritius and Sri Lanka declined by 35 and 41 per cent from 19 to 12 and 35 to 21 respectively (table 4).

A comparison of the HPI with income-based measure of poverty of $1-a-day poverty line (table 3) reveals that :

- Both income poverty and human poverty are pervasive in the Indian Ocean region, affecting between 20 and 50 per cent of the people of at least eight countries of the region.
- In the HHD countries, Australia, Singapore, Malaysia and Mauritius, only between 6 and 12 per cent of the people are affected by either income poverty or human poverty.
- Among the MHD countries (excluding Oman for which there is no information), in South Africa nearly a quarter of people suffer from income poverty but the extent of human poverty is not known.
- Sri Lanka has made a remarkable progress in reducing income poverty, now a mere 4 per cent, but now faces a large backlog of 21 per cent in human poverty. On the other hand, Indonesia[1] which has reduced its income poverty to 15 per cent also has the same backlog of around 21 per cent in its human poverty.
- Among the LHD countries Tanzania has made remarkable progress in reducing income poverty to 16 per cent but has a very large backlog of human poverty of 40 per cent.

---

[1] The effects of the economic crisis in Indonesia and Malaysia in 1997 and 1998 have not been taken into account in this paper.

- Kenya has reduced human poverty so that human poverty now affects a quarter of its people, but income poverty is very high at 50 per cent.
- In India and Madagascar also the proportion of people in income poverty exceeds the proportion in human poverty. However, in Madagascar both human poverty and income poverty are at much higher levels than in India.
- In both Yemen and Mozambique human poverty is very high, around 50 per cent, whereas the extent of income poverty is not known.
- Poverty is particularly pervasive in the LHD countries of the region. However, there are some achievements as well.

It is thus seen that some countries have done better in reducing income poverty than human poverty, other countries have done better in reducing human poverty than income poverty. This implies that progress in reducing income poverty and progress in reducing poverty in human choices and opportunities are not always at the same level.

Sri Lanka and Indonesia would need to reduce basic deprivations in choices and opportunities, by further increasing access to basic education and health services. Kenya and India have heavily invested in reducing deprivations in basic human capabilities. But India still has a large backlog of human poverty of nearly 40 per cent. Therefore, India and Tanzania would both need to reduce basic deprivations in choices and opportunities by increasing access to basic education and health services. Yemen, Madagascar and Mozambique would need to reduce drastically the basic deprivations in choices and opportunities by an accelerated increase in access to basic education and health services. Moreover these countries will also need to invest heavily in reducing deprivations in basic human capabilities.

Regression analysis of several developing countries has indicated a weak relationship, between income-poverty index and HPI. Eradication of poverty would therefore need monitoring of progress in reducing poverty both in income and in human choices and opportunities by focusing on extending access to basic education and health services as well as by investing heavily to reduce deprivations in basic human capabilities.

Nature of Human Poverty in the Indian Ocean Region

Human poverty means that people do not enjoy opportunities and choices most basic to human development, being able to live a long life, be healthy, well-nourished, able to participate in the community activities, and so on. This section looks at how the poor and the deprived in different countries of the region are living and the deprivations they face in their lives.

Deprivations in three essential dimensions of human life are considered — longevity, knowledge and a decent standard of living. The variables used for reflecting these aspects are : the percentage of people expected to die before age 40, in other words vulnerable to death at a relatively early age; the percentage of adults who are illiterate, and, therefore, excluded from the world of reading and communication; the percentage of people without access to health services and to safe water; and the percentage of malnourished children under five, all indicating deprivation of a good standard of living.

Deprivation in years of life

A short life is a major indicator of human poverty. People dying before the age of 40 implies lives with severe deprivation. In Australia, Singapore, Malaysia, Mauritius, Oman and Sri Lanka, fewer than 10 per cent of the people are expected to die before reaching the age of 40, and between 15 to 25 per cent in Indonesia, South Africa, India, Kenya and Yemen compared with around one-third in Tanzania and Madagascar and over 40 per cent in Mozambique. Deprivation in years of life in these countries is 10 times or more of that in Australia and Singapore, showing a wide disparity between countries of the region (table 2).

Infant mortality and child mortality also reflect survival deprivation and are often used as indicators of both poverty and development in a country. In 1960-94 the infant mortality rate declined in all the countries of the region by 40 to nearly 90 per cent. In Oman there was a dramatic reduction from more than 200 per 1,000 live births in 1960 to less than 30 in 1994. But in Mozambique the rate is still over 100 per 1,000 live births, being the highest in the region. Kenya, India, Tanzania, Madagascar and Yemen are other countries in the region with high infant mortality rates ranging from 70 to nearly 90 in that order. As against this, Singapore has reached a rate of only 5, *i.e.*, 5 per cent of that in Mozambique, showing the wide disparity in the region.

In 1995 Mozambique's amazingly high under-five mortality rate of 275 per 1,000 live births is nearly 50 times that in Singapore and more than 20 times that in Malaysia. Oman has had the largest reduction among all developing countries, of 91 per cent in under-five mortality rate from 280 to 25 and Singapore the seventh largest reduction of 80 per cent from 30 to 6 between 1970 and 1995. Rates for other countries range from nearly 20 for Sri Lanka to over 100 for Yemen and India and over 150 for Tanzania and Madagascar, once again confirming the immense disparity in the region (table 5).

Maternal mortality has a considerable share in the high mortality in developing countries. A high maternal mortality rate reflects the gender-biased attitude of society in general and the consequent serious neglect of women. It could also be partly due to poor maternal health services in developing countries. However, with some additional investment in maternal health care, maternal mortality can be considerably reduced and even can be avoided. The maternal mortality rate in the developing countries is 471 per 100,000 live births, as against that of a mere 30 for the industrial countries. Yemen and Mozambique have extremely high maternal mortality rates of 1,400 and 1,500 respectively per 100,000 live births, 3 times that of the average for all developing countries, and 140 and 150 times respectively that for Singapore. Maternal mortality rates of seven countries in the region exceed the average rate of 471 for all developing countries. Four of these are sub-Saharan Africa countries (Kenya, Tanzania, Madagascar and Mozambique) plus Indonesia, India and Yemen. It is observed that there is a vast disparity in the maternal mortality rates in the region. Very high rates in the above seven countries reflect severe neglect of women's health and reproductive health, and gender issues involved in survival deprivation in these countries (table 5).

A reduction in each of these rates would imply reduction in survival deprivation which should be reflected in a longer life expectancy. Life expectancy at birth is a good indicator of the level of human development. In developing countries life expectancy rose by 16 years during 1960-94, from 46 years to 62. Singapore's life expectancy at 77, is 15 years more than the developing country average and 3 years more than the industrial country average. Life expectancies in Sri Lanka, Malaysia, Mauritius and Oman are also 10 to 8 years higher than the developing country average, while life expectancies in Kenya, Tanzania and Mozambique are 8 to 16 years lower than the developing country average. Mozambique has the lowest life expectancy of only 46 years (table 1).

Deprivation in Health

People without access to health services suffer or, can even die from sicknesses which could have been cured or avoided. In Yemen, Tanzania, Madagascar and Mozambique a very high percentage of around 60 per cent of the population, do not have access to health services (table 2).

Over 40 per cent of one-year-olds are not immunised against tuberculosis in Mozambique and around 25 per cent in Madagascar. In other countries of the region the extent of immunisation was very high, between 86 and 97 per cent. The immunisation of one-year-old against measles was almost 100 per cent in Oman. In the other countries, excepting Madagascar, Yemen and Mozambique, between 10 and 30 per cent were not immunised. While in Madagascar, Yemen and Mozambique, a high per cent — 40 and 60 each respectively — were not immunised.

AIDS cases reported per 100,000 people in 1995 were very high at 95 in Tanzania, and nearly 30 in Kenya, while in South Africa and Mozambique the rate was 7. Tuberculosis is pervasive in the region and the number of cases reported per 100,000 people range from more than 220 in South Africa and 170 in Mozambique to less than 15 in Oman and Mauritius. Malaria cases where reported, range from over 4,000 cases per 100,000 people in

Tanzania, over 2,000 in Sri Lanka and 800 in Oman, to only 11 in Singapore.

Between 1970-72 and 1990-92 cigarette consumption per adult has risen in all countries of the region excepting Singapore, Sri Lanka and Tanzania. In Indonesia it has more than doubled, while in the other countries the index has risen from around 15 to over 70 per cent, the latter being in Yemen and Madagascar.

Population per doctor reveals extremely wide variation from 33,000 in Mozambique, 20,000 in Kenya to only a little over 1,000 in Mauritius, showing that the population per doctor in Mozambique is nearly 33 times more than that in Mauritius. Higher the population per doctor the lower would be the access of the population to the health services. These numbers are very high compared with the average for developing countries of one doctor for every 6,000 people and, for the industrial countries one for every 350. Population per nurse was much smaller in most countries where information was available, varying from 400 in Mauritius to over 9,000 in Kenya, *i.e.*, over 20 times that in Mauritius. It would seem that people generally have more access to nurses than to doctors, except in India where it was the opposite. Nurses require much less training and cost much less to employ.

Public expenditure on health as a percentage of GDP in 1990 was 4 per cent in Mozambique, 3 per cent in South Africa, Kenya and Tanzania, 2 per cent in Sri Lanka, and only 1 per cent in all other countries except Mauritius and Oman, for which no information was available (table 6).

It is thus observed that the low human development countries are generally characterised by low level of immunisation of one-year-old against infectious diseases, high incidence of infectious diseases among the population, rising consumption of cigarette per adult, high population per doctor and even for nurse. Public expenditure on health as a percentage of GDP is very low in India, Yemen and Madagascar being 1 per cent, against 3 to 4 per cent in Kenya, Tanzania and Mozambique.

Deprivation in Economic Provisions

Between 1975-80 and 1990-96 the share of people in developing countries with access to safe water rose by nearly three-fourths, from 41 per cent to 71 per cent. In Singapore, Mauritius and South Africa, access to safe water was almost 100 per cent. In Malaysia, Oman and India the share of people with access to safe water was roughly 80 per cent. In other countries the percentage of population without access to safe water ranged from around 40 per cent in Sri Lanka, Indonesia, Yemen and Mozambique to nearly 50, 60 and 70 per cent respectively in Kenya, Tanzania and Madagascar reflecting a high backlog in the provision of safe water in these countries (table 2).

In 1990-96 three-fifths of the people in developing countries did not have access to sanitation. In the Indian Ocean countries the proportion of people not having access to sanitation, once again show extreme differences from 1 per cent in Mauritius to around 25 per cent in Oman and Kenya, around 50 per cent in South Africa, Indonesia and Mozambique to over 70 per cent in India and Yemen and almost 100 per cent in Madagascar. It must be remembered that poor sanitation exposes people to various types of infection (table 1).

The proportion of underweight children under five in developing countries declined from 41 per cent in 1975 to 22 per cent in 1990-96. In the Indian Ocean region there was a spectacular decline in the proportion for Mauritius, from 32 to 16 per cent, in the same period. South Africa and Oman had the lowest proportions of 9 and 12 respectively while India had the highest proportion of 53, in 1990-96. Health backlog in the region in respect of underweight children under five is thus enormous with the share of seven countries much above that for developing countries (table 5).

High fertility deprives parents and children from achieving a good standard of living. Having too many children weakens women's health. It also reduces their equality and autonomy, since their options for education, skills and employment or other income-generating activities reduce when they have many children. Generally, poor people have large families as they perceive large families as beneficial to them. Both infant mortality and child-mortality being high in poor communities, parents try to have many children so that some of them would survive and could support them in their old age. Under such circumstances children are perceived as old-age security for parents. Having many children implies increased assets and more security and, therefore, less vulnerability. The reduced opportunities for education and savings for themselves and for their children, however, robs them of the opportunity of escaping poverty. High fertility, therefore, perpetuates poverty in the long term.

Better health conditions leading to survival of more children encourages parents to have fewer children. The total fertility rate for all developing countries is 3.1 as against only 1.7 for industrial countries. While the total fertility rate in Singapore and Australia is comparable to that in industrial countries, the two Arab States Oman and Yemen have extremely high rates of around 7 and 8 respectively. Another five countries, namely, South Africa, Kenya, Tanzania, Madagascar and Mozambique, also have rates much above the developing countries average. It is to be noted that fertility rates of Oman and Yemen are some of the highest in the World (table 9).

Deprivation in knowledge

Deprivation in knowledge is an important dimension of human poverty. It implies being excluded from the world of reading, communication, and full participation in society. Adult illiteracy rate, *i.e.*, percentage of adults who are illiterate is used as a measure of deprivation in knowledge.

Between 1970 and 1995 the adult illiteracy rate in developing countries declined by nearly half from 57 per cent to 30 per cent. Kenya had the fastest decline in the region — from 68 per cent to 22 per cent, a decline of 68 per cent. Indonesia had the next highest decline from 46 per cent to 16 per cent, a decline of 65 per cent. The adult illiteracy rates in 1995 ranged from around 10 per cent in Singapore and Sri Lanka to a high of around 60 per cent in Mozambique and Yemen and 65 per cent in Oman, implying a huge backlog in these countries (table 2).

Children in the poorest families generally do not attend school and start working at a very young age. Even five-year-olds are known to be working. Women in such families are over-worked and do not have time to perform all the household tasks, which are then performed by the young children. Many children also do paid work. Although helping in the survival of the family, it reduces their opportunities for education and their means of escaping the poverty cycle.

In developing countries 110 million children are out of school at the primary level and 275 million at the secondary level. Regional shares differ considerably. At the primary level, nearly half the children out of school are in South Asia and 10 million are in the Arab States. The percentage of children not reaching grade five in 1990-95 was 25 for all developing countries as compared with 2 per cent for industrial countries. In the Indian Ocean region, the percentage ranges from 0 for Singapore and Mauritius to nearly 25 per cent for South Africa, among the high and medium development countries. Among the low development countries Tanzania and Kenya have made much progress and the percentage of children not reaching grade five varies from 17 for Tanzania to 65 for Mozambique, and 72 for Madagascar (table 2).

The combined first and second level gross enrolment ratio in 1992-94 was 74 per cent for developing countries, compared with 98 for industrial countries. There were significant regional variations, the percentage for Sub-Saharan Africa being 53 per cent and that for the least developed countries at 46 per cent. Within the Indian Ocean region also there were wide variations ranging from 35 to little over 40 per cent for Mozambique, Madagascar and Tanzania to around 70 per cent for Yemen, India, Kenya and Oman, and 80 per cent or over for the high and medium development countries excepting Oman.

The combined first, second and third level gross enrolment ratio for all developing countries is 56 per cent against 83 per cent for industrial countries. The least developed countries and Sub-Saharan Africa having a ratio of around 40 per cent. The variations within the region are even more striking. Mozambique, Madagascar and Tanzania have the lowest ratio of 25 to a little over 30, Yemen, Kenya and India over 50, Oman, Mauritius, Malaysia and Sri Lanka 60 and over, Singapore over 70, and South Africa and Australia roughly 80 per cent. Thus the ratio for Mozambique is less than one third of South Africa and Australia, and even less than one-half of the other low development countries Yemen, Kenya and India (tables 1 and 7).

Media plays an important role in expanding people's knowledge and in transfer of information and ideas globally. Developing countries have about 200 radios per 1,000 people, a fifth of the ratio in industrial countries, and 140 televisions per 1,000 people, around one fourth of that in industrial countries. Sub-Saharan Africa has only 30 televisions per 1000 people.

Oman has the highest number of televisions per capita in the developing world, with 730 per 1,000 people. Singapore has the highest number of radios per capita in the region with 645 per 1,000 people. Deprivations in communication amongst the low development countries are revealing. Tanzania has the lowest number of radios and televisions per capita in the region, with 26 radios and less than 10 televisions per 1,000 people. Excepting 192 radios in Madagascar and 270 televisions in Yemen per 1,000 people, other low development countries are not much better off than Tanzania (table 1).

Gender Disparity in Human Poverty

Gender biases in most developing countries lead to unequal opportunities in education, employment and asset ownership for women. Women thus have fewer opportunities and choices. Poverty widens such gender gaps and thus poor women are the most vulnerable. Life expectancy at birth for women is 63 years for all developing countries, three years more than that for men, as compared with 78 and 70 years for women and men respectively in industrial countries.

In the Indian Ocean region life expectancy at birth for women has risen for all countries from around 6 per cent for Kenya to 40 and 50 per cent respectively for Yemen and Oman. It ranges from around 80 in Australia and Singapore and a little less than 75 in Oman, Malaysia and Mauritius in ascending order, to 47 in Mozambique. Although in almost all countries women's life expectancies were more than those for men, the differences varied from seven in Mauritius to zero in India. Countries where women's life expectancies are not much higher than those for men generally reflect poor health conditions of women and their general neglect in the society (table 8).

In developing countries there are 60 per cent more women than men among illiterate adults, female primary enrolment is 12 per cent lower than male enrolment and their share in earned income is less than one-third. Female wages are only three-fourths of male wages and their labour force participation rate is two-thirds that for male.

In the Indian Ocean region only in South Africa men and women are equal among illiterate adults. In Singapore, women among illiterate adults are more than three times of men, while in Mauritius there are a little over 60 per cent more women than men among illiterate adults.

Adult literacy rate for women in developing countries is 60 per cent compared with 78 per cent for men. In industrial countries it was almost 100 per cent for both men and women. Adult literacy rates for women in the region vary widely, the range running from almost 100 per cent in Australia, nearly 90 per cent in Singapore and Sri Lanka to only 22 per cent in Mozambique. While in all countries except Australia adult literacy rates for women are less than those for men, the gender gap is very wide in India and Mozambique, being only a little over one-half and two-fifth respectively of the rate for men (table 8).

In Yemen the female primary enrolment is as low as half that for males, while in Madagascar it is 13 per cent more than male enrolment. In Sri Lanka, Singapore and Oman the primary enrolments for male and female are almost equal (table 5).

Female net enrolment ratio at primary level is 86 for developing countries. In Oman the ratio more than doubled between 1980-92 reaching a little more than 70 per cent. In South Africa, Mauritius, Indonesia and Australia it ranges from 93 to 99 compared with only 37 in Mozambique. No data was available for other countries.

The female net enrolment for secondary level was not available for most countries and ranged from more than 80 for Australia to around 50, 34 and 5 respectively for South Africa, Indonesia and Mozambique, reflecting the extreme disparity between countries.

Female tertiary students per 100,000 women for all developing countries in 1992 are nearly 560 compared with around 3,400 for industrial countries. In the region Australia and South Africa have the highest numbers — more than 3,400 and nearly 2,000, other countries having a range of 750 for Indonesia to 16 for Mozambique, once again showing the extreme diversity in the region. There was no data for Singapore, India and Tanzania. It is to be noted that there has been tremendous progress as compared with the situation in 1980. In 1992 female tertiary students per 100,000 women were almost five times in Mauritius, over three times in Indonesia, Kenya and Mozambique, nearly double in Malaysia and 60 per cent higher in Sri Lanka compared with 1980 levels (table 9).

The combined primary, secondary and tertiary gross enrolment ratio for females in all developing countries is a little more than 50 per cent against 60 per cent for males. In industrial countries, on the other hand, the ratios for females and males are respectively 84 and 81, *i.e.,* somewhat higher for females. Among the high and medium development countries in the region the ratio for females varies from around 60 per cent in Indonesia to around 80 per cent for South Africa and Australia, whereas for low development countries it ranges from around 20 per cent for Mozambique to a little more than 50 per cent for Kenya. In fact the ratios for females exceed slightly those for males in Australia, Malaysia, Mauritius, South Africa and Sri Lanka. In other countries also the female ratios are not much lower than those for males except in India and Mozambique where the female ratios are 75 and 70 per cent respectively of those for males. However, the vast diversity in the region is once again evident with the ratio for Mozambique being one-fourth of that for Australia and South Africa. No data was available for Oman, Yemen and Madagascar (table 8).

Women hold about a quarter of total parliamentary seats in South Africa and Mozambique, while their share was as low as one per cent in Yemen (table 5).

Women's share of unpaid family workers ranged from a high of 88 per cent in Tanzania to a little less than half in Mauritius. On the other hand, female economic activity rate varied from as high as more than 90 per cent of that for males in Tanzania and Mozambique to a mere 20 per cent of the male rate in Oman, reflecting a high gender inequality (table 5).

Women's share of adult labour force (15 years and above) for all developing countries is only about 40 per cent, while in Madagascar, Kenya and Mozambique it is 45 to nearly 50 per cent, in an ascending order. In the other countries excluding Oman, women's share of adult labour force is only between 30 to 40 per cent while in Oman it is the lowest at 12 per cent (table 10).

In the developing countries women are only 12 per cent of all male administrators and managers, compared with 27 per cent in industrial countries, and they are 64 per cent of male professional and technical workers as against 95 per cent in industrial countries.

In Australia women are three-fourths of men administrators and managers and in Singapore a little over half compared with only 2 per cent in India. While women constitute nearly 90 per cent of men in South Africa and 80 per cent in Malaysia among the professional and technical workers, they form only 19 per cent of men professional and technical workers in Singapore. As clerical and sales-workers women range from nearly 80 per cent of men in Indonesia to 24 per cent in Australia. Women service workers on the other hand are more than three times of men in Australia and almost double of men in South Africa and two-third of men in Indonesia, while in Sri Lanka they form only 60 per cent of men (table 11).

These statistics reveal that women are generally concentrated in low-paid, low-skilled jobs in many countries of the region while their share is very low in managerial occupations. No data is available for both Arab States, Oman and Yemen, and the Sub-Saharan countries excluding Mozambique.

Women's share in earned income ranges from 47 per cent in Tanzania to around 40 per cent in Australia, Kenya and

Mozambique and one-third in other countries except India and Mauritius where their share is only around one-fourth (table 8).

High fertility very often has a constraining influence on women's participation whether social, political or economic. Having many children tends to weaken women's health and reduces time available for other activities. As a result, women are left with reduced options for education, skill development and income-earning work. Poor people sometimes perceive having many children as increasing their assets. This, however, creates a vicious cycle in the long run, as, especially girls from such families have their options and opportunities for education and employment much reduced. Consequently, they also may marry early and have many children and the vicious cycle perpetuates.

Over the past 25 years fertility in developing countries has fallen by more than 40 per cent. In Sub-Saharan Africa there is hardly any reduction, while, in industrial countries fertility has fallen by 27 per cent. However, the total fertility rate in industrial countries at 1.7 is about one-half of that in the developing countries. In the region Sri Lanka has had the largest decline in fertility of nearly 60 per cent while Indonesia and India had declines of around 50 per cent.

On the other hand, in Oman and Yemen and Mozambique there was no decline in fertility in 25 years. Yemen and Oman have one of the highest fertilities in the world of more than 7. Other countries of Sub-Saharan Africa also have high fertility rates from 5 in Kenya and nearly 6 or more in Tanzania, Madagascar and Mozambique (tables 9 and 12).

Women would have fewer children if infant and child mortality rates improve and more children survive. When employment opportunities increase women tend to have fewer children and invest more in the education of each child, girl or boy. This leads to a 'virtuous' cycle as educated girls tend to have fewer children and infant and child mortality improve further when mothers are educated. Educating girls is considered the single most important factor associated with lower fertility.

It is even more important to relieve women of their triple burden of child-bearing and rearing, household work and paid work, so that they have more time for leisure and to look after their own health. Improvement in women's status, and their empowerment leads to women having a greater role in household decision-making and to sharing of household tasks by both husband and wife.

When women desire fewer children they need the contraceptive services, especially free services in the poor countries and the cooperation of their husbands, so that they can translate their desires into reality. The contraceptive prevalence rate, using any method, in developing countries is 56 per cent and in Sub-Saharan Africa only 16 per cent, compared with 71 per cent in industrial countries.

The contraceptive prevalence rates (any method) in the region reveal a large variation from around 75 per cent for Australia, Singapore and Mauritius (not available for Malaysia), between 50 and 70 per cent for South Africa, Indonesia and Sri Lanka, in an ascending order, and from around 20 to 40 per cent for Madagascar, Tanzania, Kenya and India to exceptionally low rates of 7 and 9 for Yemen and Oman respectively (table 12).

Lack of personal security is also a kind of deprivation of which women have a large share. Among the world's refugees more than 80 per cent are women and children. Among the worst threats of violence are those against women. A third of married women in developing countries are battered by their husbands during their lifetime. Each year an estimated 1 million children, mostly poor girls in Asia are forced into prostitution.

Gender-related Development Index (GDI) and the Gender Empowerment Measure (GEM) can effectively highlight the gender disparity. The GDI uses the same set of basic capabilities as the HDI, adjusting for gender inequality. The GEM measures gender inequality in key areas of economic and political participation and decision-making (tables 8 and 13).

- The GDIs show that Singapore has succeeded in enhancing the basic human capabilities of both women and men.
- Mozambique which is one of the bottom rank countries, shows that women face a double deprivation : overall

achievements in human development are low in this society and women's achievements are lower than men's.

GDI rankings and values imply that :

- No society treats its women as well as its men.
- Gender inequality is strongly associated with human poverty.
- Gender inequality is not always associated with income poverty. Tanzania has a low incidence of income poverty (16 per cent) by the $ 1-a-day poverty line.
- Gender equality can be achieved at different income levels and stages of development. It can be achieved across a range of cultures and political ideologies.
- There is a strong negative association between the extent of human poverty and opportunities for women (in some countries).
- The link between income poverty and opportunities for women is not always positive *i.e.,* even in income-poor societies, women may enjoy opportunities to participate in economic and political activities (table 8).

Summary and Conclusions

The countries of the Indian Ocean region reveal a vast disparity in respect of both the level of human development attained, and the human resources as well as gender issues involved in poverty eradication. While some countries have attained high human development others are in medium or low development state.

Both income poverty and human poverty in the region vary within wide ranges and are pervasive. Some countries have done better in reducing income poverty while other countries have done better in reducing human poverty. India, Tanzania, Yemen, Madagascar and Mozambique, in an ascending order are the worst examples of human poverty in the region. Around 40 to 50 per cent of their population suffer various forms of human poverty. On the other hand, Sri Lanka has made remarkable progress in reducing income poverty but still has a considerable backlog in human poverty.

Human Resource Issues

It is extremely important to extend the access to basic primary education and health services as well as invest heavily to reduce deprivations in basic human capabilities in the low human development countries and in some of the medium development countries.

- Many of these countries have extremely high fertility rates and are likely to double their population in the coming one or two decades. Educating girls is considered the single most important factor associated with lower fertility. For educated girls marry late and have fewer children. They are then able to invest more in the health, nutrition, education and training of each child. Better health and lower mortality reinforce these decisions leading to a virtuous cycle of prosperity and enabling individuals to escape from poverty, malnutrition, dropping out of school, child labour and poverty in the long run.
- It is thus necessary to accelerate the pace of both economic and social development for the empowerment of men and women, building their human capital and improving their access to land, housing and credit, for the eradication of poverty in these countries.
- Investing in secondary and tertiary education and in skill development and training will be the next step towards increased pro-poor economic growth and prosperity of all people.
- Media has an important role in raising people's awareness of importance of health care as well as in expanding their knowledge and horizons.

Gender Issues

Women constitute the majority among the poor and the illiterates as gender biases reduce women's opportunities in education, skill-development, employment, asset ownership and participation in community affairs. They are generally concentrated in low paid, low-skilled jobs in many countries of the region, while their share is very low in managerial occupations, which results in women having a low share in earned income. High fertility in many of the countries of the region as well as the cultural practices in some countries also have an impact on their participation in economic activities. Most of these women do only the unpaid household work which is neither valued in the house nor in society.

- Gender inequality is strongly associated with human poverty rather than income poverty. Human poverty in turn has a strong negative association with opportunities for women.
- It is important to empower women and end all gender inequality by giving women equal access to land, credit and job opportunities. Their empowerment will also protect them from domestic violence, societal abuse and other deprivations.
- Investing in women is necessary not only for gender equality and equity, but also for the effects it has on their families. Because women's health and education has an impact on their childbearing decisions. It leads to improvement in their children's health and survival, increases their own income-earning capacity and employment opportunities, eventually reducing poverty.
- Furthermore, it is of utmost importance to remove all discriminations in survival, health, education and upbringing of the girl child. Educating girls is considered to be the highest return investment for developing countries. Increased education of girls eventually transforms a society as their sons and daughters benefit from it by way of reduced infant mortality, smaller number of children, and more education and training for each child, and as a result, the children escape poverty. The educated girls themselves have better economic opportunities, their work is valued, they marry later and participate in household decisions, have fewer children and less risk of maternal mortality. On the other hand, when girls are not educated their unpaid

household work is not valued both in the home and outside. They marry early and have more children, and as a result cannot invest much in each child, thus perpetuating the family poverty.

Conclusion

In conclusion it can be said that every country in the region needs policies and strategies for reducing its share of human poverty in the shortest time possible, reducing gender inequalities and eradicating absolute poverty. However, in some countries, particularly in countries with low human development, the process of eradication of poverty needs to be carried out at an accelerated pace.

REFERENCES

Human Development Report, 1997, UNDP.

Building Human Capital For Better Lives — George Psacharopoulos, The World Bank.

Investing in All the People : Educating Women in Developing Countries — Lawrence H. Summers, EDI, The World Bank.

The World Summit for Social Development, 1995, *Recommendations.*

APPENDIX

Table 1 : Profile of Human Development in the Indian Ocean Region

		Population With Access To									
	Life Expectancy At Birth	Health Services %	Safe Water %	Sanitation %	Dailycalorie Supply Per Capita	Adultliteracy Rate	Combined First And Second Level Gross Enrolment Ratio (%)	Daily Newspapers Copies Per 100 People	Televisions Per 100 People	Real GDP Per Capita (PPP $)	GNP Per Capita (Us $)
COUNTRY	1994	1990-95	1990-96	1990-96	1992	1994	1992-94	1994	1994	1994	1994
Australia	78.1	-	-	-	-	-	-	26	48	19,285	18,000
Singapore	77.1	-	100[C]	-	-	91.0	86	36	38	20,987	22,500
Malaysia	71.2	-	78	94	2884	83.0	78	14	23	8,865	3,480
Mauritius	70.7	100[C]	99	99	2696	82.4	80	7	19	13,172	3,150
Oman	70.0	96	82	78	-	-	74	3	73	10,078	5,140
Sri Lanka	72.2	-	57	63	2275	90.1	87	3	7	3,277	640
South Africa	63.7	-	99	53	2705	81.4	100[D]	3	10	4,291	3,040
Indonesia	63.5	93	62	51	2755	83.2	80	2	15	3,740	880
Kenya	53.6	77	56	77	2075	77.0	72	1	2	1,404	250
India	61.3	85	81	29	2395	51.2	72	-	6	1,348	320
Yemen	56.2	38	61	24	2203	-	70	2	27	805	280
Tanzania	50.3	42	38	86	2021	66.8	44	1	(.)	656	140
Madagascar	57.2	38	29	3	2135	45.8	42	(.)	2	694	200
Mozambique	46.0	39[C]	63	54	1,680	39.5	35	1	(.)	986	90

Source : *Human Development Report,* 1997, UNDP.

C Data refer to a year or period other than that specified in the column heading, differ from the standard definition or refer to only parts of the country.

D Less than half the unit shown.

Table 2 : Profile of Human Poverty in the Indian Ocean Region

Rank HPO	Country	People not expected to survive to age 40 (as % of total population)	People without access to health services (%)	Population without access to safe water (5)	Adult literacy rate (%)	Children not reaching grade 5 (%)	Population in Poverty: Poorest 20%	Population in Poverty: Richest 20%	Real GDP per capita (PPP $): (%) $1 a day (PPP $)
		1990	1990-95	1990-96	1995	1990-95	1989-94	1989-94	1989-94
				High Human Development					
	Australia	3.5	-	-	-	1	4,077	39,098	8[b]
4	Singapore	3.2	-	0[c]	8.9	0	4.934	47,311	-
	Malaysia	7.2	-	22	16.5	2	1,923	22,447	6
13	Mauritius	6.2	0[c]	1	17.1	0	-	-	12
				Medium Human Development					
	Oman	8.8	4	18	65.0	4	-	-	-
	South Africa	17.0	-	1	18.2	24	516	9,897	24
22	Sri Lanka	7.9	-	43	9.8	8	1,348	5,954	4
23	Indonesia	14.8	7	38	16.2	8	1,422	6,654	15
				Low Human Development					
32	Kenya	22.3	23	47	21.9	23	238	4,347	50
47	India	19.4	15	19	48.0	38	527	2,641	53
66	Yemen	25.6	62	39	59	-	-	-	-
50	Tanzania	30.6	58	62	32.2	17	217	1,430	16
70	Madagascar	32.1	62	71	-	72	203	1,750	72
72	Mozambique	43.8	61[c]	37	59.9	65	-	-	-

Source : *Human Development Region*, 1997, UNDP.

a) Data refer to 1990 or a year around 1990.

b) Income poverty line is $ 14.40 (1985 PPP $) a day per person.

c) Data refer to a year or period other than that specified in the column heading.

Table 3 : Indices of Human Development, Human Poverty and Income Poverty in the Indian Ocean Region

Country	Human Development Index (HDI) value 1994	Human Poverty Index (HPI) % 1990	Income Poverty – population in poverty (%) $ 1 a day (PPP $) 1989-94
High Human Development (HHD)			
Australia	0.931	-	8
Singapore	0.900	6.6	-
Malaysia	0.832	-	6
Mauritius	0.831	12.5	12
Medium Human Development (MHD)			
Oman	0.718	-	-
South Africa	0.716	-	24
Sri Lanka	0.711	20.7	4
Indonesia	0.668	20.8	15
Low Human Development (LHD			
Kenya	0.463	26.1	50
India	0.446	36.7	53
Yemen	0.361	47.6	-
Tanzania, U., Rep. of	0.357	39.7	16
Madagascar	0.350	49.5	72
Mozambique	0.281	50.1	-

Source : *Human Development Report*, 1997, UNDP.

Table 4 : Human Poverty Index (HPI) Value for the Indian Ocean Region, 1990

HP Rank 1990	Country	HPI 1970	Human Poverty Index Value % 1990	Change in HPI value % 1970-90	HDI* Rank
-	Australia		-		14
4	Singapore		6.6		26
-	Malaysia		-		60
13	Mauritius	19	12.5	35	61
-	Oman		-		88
22	Sri Lanka	35	20.7	41	91
-	South Africa		-		90
23	Indonesia		20.8		99
32	Kenya		26.1		134
47	India		36.7		138
50	Tanzania, U. Rep. of		39.7		149
66	Yemen		47.6		148
70	Madagascar		49.0		152
72	Mozambique		50.1		166

Source : *Human Development Report,* 1997, UNDP.

* Human Development Index

Table 5 : Human Poverty of Women and Children in the Indian Ocean Region

	Year	Australia	Singapore	Malaysia	Mauritius	Oman	South Africa	Sri Lanka	Indonesia	Kenya	India	Yemen	Tanzania	Madagascar	Mozambique
Infant Mortality Rate (per 1000 live births)	1994	-	5	12	17	28	51	16	53	70	74	88	85	87	116
Maternal Mortality rate (Per 100,000 live births)	1990	9	10	80	120	190	230	140	650	650	570	1400	770	490	1500
Children under five mortality rate (per 1,000 live births)	1995	-	6	13	23	25	67	19	75	90	115	110	160	164	275
Underweight children under age five (%)	1990-96	-	-	23	16	12	9	38	35	23	53	39	2[illegible]	34	27
Adult Literacy Female Rate (%)	1995	-	14	22	21	-	18	13	22	30	62	-	43	-	77
Adult Literacy Female rate as % male rate	1995	-	331	200	164	-	101	194	212	219	181	-	210	-	181
Female primary enrolment ratio (as % of male)	1995	-	99	83	-	96	-	100	93	-	78	49	-	113	77
Female secondary enrolment ratio (as % of male)	1993-95	105	-	-	-	95	121	-	87	-	-	-	-	-	63
Children not in primary school (%)	1993-95	1	1	-	5	29	4	-	3	9	-	-	52	-	61
Child economic activity rate (% age 10-14)	1995	-	-	3.2	2.9	0.4	-	2.4	9.6	41.3	14.4	20.1	39.5	35.8	33.8
Parliamentary seats held by women (as % of total)	1996	21	3	10	8	-	24	5	13	3	7	1	17	4	25
Female unpaid family workers (as % of total)	1990	59	77	64	48	-	-	56	66	-	-	69	88	-	82
Female economic activity rate (as % of male)	1995	74	63	59	46	19	59	54	65	86	50	39	95	81	92

Source : *Human Development Report*, 1997, UNDP.

Table 6 : Health Profile of the Indian Ocean Region

Country	One-year-old Fully Immunised against						Population			Public expenditure on health	
	Tuberculosis %	Measles %	AIDS case (per 100,000 people)[a]	Tuberculosis cases (per 1000,000 people)[a]	Malaria cases (per 1000,000 people)[a]	Cigarette consumption per adult (1970-72=100)	Per Doctor	Per Nurse	People with disabilities (as % of total population)	As % of GNP	As % of GDP
	1992-95	1995	1995	1994	1992	1990-92	1988-91	1988-91	1985-92	1960	
Australia	-	-	-	-	-	-			15.6	-	-
Singapore	97	88	2.0	51.3	10.8	64	725		0.4	1.0	1.1
Malaysia	97	81	0.7	59.4	202.5	116	2,564		-	1.1	1.3
Mauritius	87	85	0.6	13.5	-	140	1,176	398	2.6	1.5	-
Oman	96	98	0.3	14.4	797.4	-			-	-	-
South Africa	95	76	6.8	222.7	-	128			-	0.5	3.2
Sri Lanka	90	88	0.1	35.9	2,045.4	94	7,143	1,754	0.4	2.0	1.8
Indonesia	86	70	-	25.5	72.3	236	7,143	2,857	1.1	0.3	0.7
Kenya	92	73	29.1	86.7	-	119	20,000	9,091	-	1.5	2.7
India	96	78	0.1	122.0	241.6	136	2,439	3,333	0.2	0.5	1.3
Yemen	87	40	0.1	80.0	274.9	172	4,348	1,818	-	-	1.5
Tanzania, U. Rep. of	92	82	95.5	119.3	4,261.7	97		-	-	0.5	3.2
Madagascar	77	60	-	74.1	-	170	8,333	3,846	-	1.4	1.3
Mozambique	58	40	7.4	167.6	-	124	33,333	5,000	-	-	4.4

Source : *Human Development Report*, 1997, UNDP.

[a] The number of reported cases in adults in children.

Table 7 : Human Development Index for Countries in Indian Ocean Region

HDI Rank	Country	Life Expectancy at Birth (Years)	Adult Literacy Rate (%)	Combined First, Second & Third Level Gross Enrolment Ratio	Real GDP Per Capita (PPP $)	Human Development Index Value	Real GDP per Capita (PPP $) Rank Minus HDI Rank
		1994	1994	1994	1994	1994	1980
			HIGH HUMAN DEVELOPMENT				
14	Australia	78.1	99	79	19,285	0.931	4
26	Singapore	77.1	91	72	20,987	0.9	- 15
60	Malaysia	71.2	83	62	8,865	0.832	- 13
61	Mauritius	70.7	82.4	61	13,172	0.831	- 30
			MEDIUM HUMAN DEVELOPMENT				
88	Oman	70	81.4	60	10,078	0.718	- 49
90	South Africa	63.7	90.1	81	4,291	0.716	-10
91	Sri Lanka	72.2	77	66	3,277	0.711	9
99	Indonesia	63.5	83.2	62	3,740	0.668	- 7
			LOW HUMAN DEVELOPMENT				
134	Kenya	53.6	51.2	55	1,404	0.463	5
138	India	61.3	41.1	56	1,348	0.446	5
148	Yemen	56.2	66.8	52	805	0.361	14
149	Tanzania, U Rep. of	50.3	45.8	34	656	0.357	21
152	Madagascar	57.2	39.5	33	694	0.35	16
166	Mozambique	46	-	25	986	0.281	- 9

Source : *Human Development Report*, 1997, UNDP.

Note : A positive figure indicates that the HDI rank is better than the real GDP per capita rank (PPP $), a negative the opposite.

Table 8 : Gender-related Development Index (GDI) for Countries in the Indian Ocean Region

			Life Expectancy at Birth (years)		Adult Literacy Rate (%)		Combined primary, secondary and tertiary gross enrolment ratio (%)		Earned Income share %)			
HDI Rank	Country	GDI Rank	Female	Male	Female	Male	Female	Male	Female	Male	GDI value	HDI Ran minus GDI k Rank[b]
			1994		1994		1994		1994		1994	
14	Australia	9	81.0	75.2	99.0	99.0	80.0	77.0	39.8	60.2	0.917	5
26	Singapore	27	79.3	74.9	87.2	95.6	71.0	73.0	30.7	69.3	0.853	-1
60	Malaysia	45	73.5	69.0	77.5	88.2	63.0	61.0	30.2[d]	69.8[d]	0.782	7
61	Mauritius	54	74.2	67.4	78.4	86.8	62.0	61.0	25.4[d]	74.6[d]	0.752	-1
88	Oman	-	72.0	68.0*	-	-	-	-	-	-	-	-
90	South Africa	71	66.8	60.8	81.2	81.4	82.0	80.0	30.8[d]	69.2[d]	0.681	5
91	Sri Lanka	70	74.6	70.0	86.9	93.2	68.0	65.0	34.5	65.5	0.694	7
99	Indonesia	86	65.3	61.8	77.1	89.4	59.0	65.0	32.9[d]	67.1[d]	0.642	-2
134	Kenya	112	54.8	52.3	67.8	85.2	54.0	56.0	42.0	58.0	0.458	2
138	India	118	61.4	61.1	36.1	64.5	47.0	63.0	25.7[d]	74.3[d]	0.419	0
148	Yemen	-	56.7	55.7	-	-	-	-	-	-	-	-
149	Tanzania	123	51.7	48.9	54.3	78.8	33.0	35.0	47.3	52.7	0.352	4
152	Madagascar	-	-	-	-	-	-	-	-	-	-	-
166	Mozambique	139	47.5	44.5	22.1	55.8	21.0	30.0	41.3[d]	58.7[d]	0.262	0

Source : *Human Development Report*, UNDP, 1997.

Notes :

a. Data refer to 1994 or latest available year.

b. A positive figure indicates that the GDI rank is better than the HDI rank, a negative the opposite.

c. No wage data available. An estimate of 75 per cent, the mean for all countries with wage data available was used for the ratio of female non-agricultural wage to the male non-agricultural wage.

*Estimated from the total and female life expectancy.

Table 9 : Women and Capabilities in the Indian Ocean Region

Country	Female net enrolment				Female tertiary students		Female life expectancy at birth		Total Fertility	
	Primary		Secondary							
	Ratio	Index (1980 =100)	Ratio	Index (1980=100)	Per 100,000 women	Index (1980=100)	Years	Index (1970=100)	Rate	Index (1970=100)
	1992	1992	1992	1992	1992	1992	1994	1994	1994	1994
Australia	99	99	82	116	3435	171	81	108	1.9	70
Singapore	-	-	-	-	-	--	79	112	2.0	66
Malaysia	-	-	-	-	640	197	74	117	3.4	61
Mauritius	94	119	-	-	313	482	74	115	2.2*	72
Oman	71	222	-	-	413	-	72	151	7.2	100
Sri Lanka	-	-	-	-	402	158	75	114	1.7	38
South Africa	93	-	49	-	1168	-	67	120	4.0	69
Indonesia	95	115	34	-	751	331	65	134	2.5	47
Kenya	-	-	-	-	102	340	55	106	5.5	67
India	-	-	-	-	-	-	61	127	3.0	54
Yemen	-	-	-	-	147	-	57	138	7.6	100
Tanzania	-	-	-	-	-	-	52	110	5.9	87
Madagascar	-	-	-	-	278	-	59	126	6.1	93
Mozambique	37	112	5	250	16	320	48	110	6.5	100

Source : *Human Development Report*, 1997, UNDP.

* Demographic Digest of Mauritius, 1996, C.S.O.

Table 10 : Employment In The Indian Ocean Region

Country	Labour Force (as % of total population)	Women's Share of Adult Labour Force (age 15 and above)		Percentage of Labour Force: Agriculture		Industry		Services		Real Earnings Per Employee Annual Growth Rate (%)	
	1990	1970	1990	1960	1990	1960	1990	1960	1990	1970-1980	1980-1992
Australia	50	31	41	-	6	-	26	-	68	-	0.5
Singapore	49	26	38	7	0	23	36	70	64	3	5.1
Malaysia	39	31	36	63	27	12	23	25	50	2	2.3
Mauritius	41	20	30	40	17	26	43	35	40	1.8	0.4
Oman	26	6	12	67	45	12	24	20	32	-	-
Sri Lanka	40	25	34	57	48	13	21	30	31	-	1.4
South Africa	39	33	37	38	14	27	32	35	55	2.7	0.2
Indonesia	44	30	39	75	55	8	14	18	31	5.2	4.3
Kenya	48	45	46	88	80	5	7	8	13	- 3.4	- 2.1
India	43	34	31	75	64	11	16	14	20	0.4	2.5
Yemen	30	27	30	82	61	6	17	11	22	-	-
Tanzania	52	-	-	-	-	-	-	-	-	-	-
Madagascar	48	45	45	86	78	4	7	10	15	- 0.8	-
Mozambique	53	49	48	88	83	5	8	7	9	-	-

Source : *Human Development Report*, 1997, UNDP.

Table 11 : Women and Political and Economic Participation in the Indian Ocean Region

Country	Administ-ration and Managers		Profes-sional and Technical Workers		Clerical and sales Workers		Service Workers		Women in Government		
	Female (%)	Female as % of male	Female %	Female as % of male	Female (%)	Female as % of male	Female (%)	Female as % of male	Total (%)	At ministerial level (%)	At sub ministerial level (%)
	1990	1990	1990	1990	1990	1990	1990	1990	1995	1995	1995
Australia	43	76	25	33	19	24	77	339	23.7	13.3	26.7
Singapore	34	52	16	19	-	-	41	69	5	0	7
Malaysia	12	14	45	80	-	-	-	-	6	8	5
Mauritius	14	17	41	71	31	44	41	70	7	4	8
Oman	-	-	-	-	-	-	-	-	4	0	4
Sri Lanka	17	20	25	33	22	28	38	61	9	13	8
South Africa	17	21	47	88	-	-	66	196	7	9	6
Indonesia	7	7	41	69	44	79	58	135	2	4	1
Kenya	-	-	-	-	-	-	-	-	5	0	6
India	2	2	21	26	-	-	-	-	6	4	6
Yemen	-	-	-	-	-	-	-	-	0	0	0
Tanzania	-	-	-	-	-	-	-	-	9	16	5
Madagascar	-	-	-	-	-	-	-	-	0	0	0
Mozambique	11	13	20	26	-	-	-	-	13	4	15

Source : *Human Development Report*, 1997, UNDP.

Table 12 : Demographic Profile of The Indian Ocean Region

	Estimated Population (Millions)			Annual Population Growth Rate (%)		Population Doubling Rate (at current growth rate)	Crude Birth Rate	Crude Death Rate	Total Fertility Rate*	Contraceptive Prevalence Rate, any method (%)
Country	1980	1994	2000	1960-1994	1994-2000	1994	1994	1994	1994	1987-1994
Australia	10	18	19	1.6	1.1	-	-	-	1.9	76
Singapore	1.6	3.3	3.6	2.1	1.6	2,038	18.5	4.8	1.8	74
Malaysia	8.1	19.7	22.3	2.6	2.1	2,027	27.8	5.0	3.5	-
Mauritius	0.7	1.1	1.2	1.5	1.1	2,057	21.1	6.8	2.2 **	75
Oman	0.6	2.1	2.7	4.0	4.2	2,010	43.6	4.5	7.2	9
Sri Lanka	9.9	17.8	18.8	1.7	1.0	2,065	17.8	5.8	2.1	66
South Africa	17.4	40.6	46.3	2.5	2.2	2,025	30.7	8.6	4.0	50
Indonesia	96.2	194.5	212.6	2.1	1.5	2,040	23.5	8.0	2.8	55
Kenya	8.3	26.5	30.3	3.5	2.3	2,024	35.3	11.6	5.0	33
India	442.3	913.5	1006.8	2.2	1.6	2,036	26.3	9.4	3.2	41
Yemen	5.2	14.3	18.1	3.0	4.0	2,011	48.4	11.5	7.6	7
Tanzania	10.2	29.2	33.7	3.1	2.4	2,022	42.6	14.9	5.8	20
Madagascar	5.4	14.4	17.4	3.0	3.2	2,016	42.7	10.7	5.9	17
Mozambique	7.5	16.6	19.6	2.4	2.7	2,019	45.0	18.6	6.5	-

Source : *Human Development Report*, 1997, UNDP.

* Revised Rates.

** *Demographic Digest of Mauritius*, 1996, C.S.O.

Table 13 : Gender Empowerment Measures for the Indian Ocean Region

HDI Rank	Country	Gender Empowe r-ment measure (GEM) rank	Seats held in parlia ment (% women) 1997	Administ-ration and Managers (% women)[b]	Professiona l and technical workers (% women)[b]	Earned Income share (% women)[b]	GEM value
14	Australia	11	20.5	43.3	25.0	40	0.659
26	Singapore	47	2.5	34.3	16.1	31	0.423
60	Malaysia	48	10.3	11.9	44.5	30[d]	0.422
61	Mauritius	49	7.6	14.3	41.4	25[d]	0.419
88	Oman	-	-	-	-	-	-
91	Sri Lanka	70	5.3	16.9	24.5	34	0.307
90	South Africa	22	23.7	17.4	46.7	31[d]	0.531
99	Indonesia	59	12.6	6.6	40.8	33[d]	0.375
134	Kenya	-	-	-	-	42	-
138	India	86	7.3	2.3	20.5	26[d]	0.228
148	Tanzania	-	-	-	-	47	-
149	Madagascar	-	-	-	-	-	-
166	Mozambique	43	25.2	11.3	20.4	41[d]	0.430

Source : *Human Development Report*, UNDP.

b. data refer to latest available year.

d. No wage data available. An estimate of 75 per cent, the mean for all countries with wage data available, was used for the ratio of the female non-agricultural wage to the male non-agricultural wage.

8 Gender-Based Biases in Rural India : Constraining Capability Kavita[1]

Anita Medhekar-Smith
Lawson Smith

Introduction

Poverty involving low independent capability of an individual to achieve well-being[2] is an endemic social phenomenon in relation to rural women in India who are frequently unable to fulfil even the basic necessities of life due to absolute poverty and/or the systematic preferencing of scarce household resources against them.

Rural women face not only poverty as measured by income, but also gender-based disparities in relation to their capability and well-

[1] "Capability Kavita" is posited as the Indian female analogue of Lancelot ("Capability") Brown (1715-1783) who rose from humble origins as a gardener's boy to be, by 1753, England's foremost garden designer. He was dubbed "Capabiltiy Brown", owing to his penchant for saying that certain pieces of land had "capabilities" (see "Brown, Lancelot", Encyclopaedia Brittannica Online [Accessed August 9 1999]. Although Sen (1993, p. 30) asserts that 'Capability is not an awfully attractive word', he nonetheless relied on the expression, 'to represent the alternative combinations of things a person is able to do or be — the various "functionings" he or she can achieve.' The main point is that the antiquated socio-economic milieu of rural India constricts and thwarts the meritocratic aspirations and achievements of highly capable women — individually and collectively — at a discernible cost to Indian society.

[2] As Sen (1993, pp. 42-43) observes, so long as it is possible to identify a minimum level of income corresponding to the minimum accepted capability level, poverty can be defined in terms of either. In the Indian setting, the lack of independent capability to achieve well-being in the lives of poor women, disempowers them in relation to critical household decisions and renders them reliant on the socially mediated, albeit unreliable, altruism of their male off-spring for their on-going welfare (Abadian 1996, p. 1794). For an Aristotelian-based version of the capability approach, see Nussbaum (1993). See also the survey by Qizilbash (1996) in which he advocates Griffin's alternate account of 'well-being and prudential value.' However, it doesn't require the application of a sophisticated measure of well-being to discern that the life-experience of a large proportion of rural women in India, is not far removed from the prospect of being 'nasty, brutish and short.'

being as measured by social development indicators such as level of nutritional intake, educational attainment, health, infant and maternal mortality, life expectancy and fertility levels. According to the Human Development Index (HDI), India's ranking is 135 out of 175, with an absolute value of 0.38, well behind China at 0.64 (Jalan 1992, p. 134).

A number of empirical studies in relation to India have indicated that the extent of anti-female bias across the institutions of household, markets and government is substantially reduced by various factors such as female literacy, paid employment and women agencies and organisations which give rural women more voice and enhance their overall socio-economic standing.

Whilst there are sharp differences in per capita income among Indian states which parameterise the absolute levels of e.g., health and education outcomes for girls, the marked disparity in outcomes for boys and girls has virtually no correlation with per capita income; in other words, gender disparity is not simply a phenomenon of poverty. And contrary to conventional wisdom, there is no evidence of a "nutrition trap" in rural India, because food (in terms of calories) is cheap. Subramanian and Deaton (1996) found that on average, rural Maharashtrian households in 1983, spent less than 1 Rupee per 1000 calories, with the daily wage being about 15 Rupees. That explains, for example, why the inadequacy of the dietary intake of pregnant women in rural India, which has a bearing on pregnancy outcomes, is related not to household income, but to their own educational levels (Panwar and Punia 1998). Across gender, caste and ethnic groups, social indicators for women like life expectancy, adult literacy, health and female morality are significantly lower than for men, and are the worst for women belonging to the scheduled castes and scheduled tribes. While perversely, village studies indicate that in some instances, although rising living conditions have benefited both men and women, the position of women *vis-a-vis* men has deteriorated owing to the process of "Sanskritization," 'whereby high-caste practices (often including those relating to women's lifestyles) are emulated by other castes aspiring to upward social mobility' (Jayaraman and Lanjouw, 1998, p. 39).

This paper is organised as follows. Section 1 of the paper gives an overview of the India's biomass-based subsistence economy and planned economic development strategy with particular reference to the incidence and the nature of rural poverty. Section 2, on the basis of selected indicators, further details anti-female biases in the rural sector using the Human Development Index (HDI), and the variant Gender Development Index (GDI); and section 3 critically examines the intra-household bias against females in relation to the allocation of resources, with reference to the socio-cultural milieu of traditional Indian society and the difficulties of reforming and redesigning structuralised, *i.e.*, socially embedded, informal constraints.

The Agrarian Base of the Economy — A developmental challenge

One of the main challenges facing India's development-oriented politicians and planners since Independence in 1947, has been the biomass-based subsistence economy in which over 70 per cent of the population is rural based, deriving a precarious living from agriculture which comprised over 40 per cent of GDP in 1950 (Dasgupta and Maler 1995). Successive governments have relied on various economic development policy measures and strategies to overcome market failure and self-replicating poverty, thereby facilitating self-sustaining growth.

Recognition by India's new indigenous politicians of the vital role of governments in promoting poverty-reducing economic development and growth, combined with a distrust of free market mechanisms and foreign capital, led to adoption of the socialist model of a centrally planned economy. A system of five year plans[3] was adopted in 1951 by the Indian Parliament to achieve, 'the most effective and balanced utilisation of the country's resources' (Jhingan 1994, p. 626).

In India's centrally planned economy, the target of reducing poverty was addressed through two types of policy instruments : (i) the indirect route of using resources to enhance growth (against a

[3] The Indian economic strategy of a plan frame, the Mahalanobis model and import substitution industrialization, as Nayar (1997, p. 36) explains, did not have their origin in post-World War II economic development, but pre-Independence, 'in Nehru's understanding of the logic of power in the international system, and his admiration for the Soviet model.'

target of 5 per cent per annum) and living standards, an interventionist "pull-up/trickle-down" strategy and (ii) the direct route of the public provision of minimum needs in nutrition, health, education and housing etc. The first approach aimed to generate additional income (then consumption), while the second approach directly provided redistributive consumption, biased towards the poor (Bhagwati, 1988). In 1978-1979 the Integrated Rural Development Program (IRDP) was introduced, 'which is among the world's most ambitious efforts aimed at alleviating rural poverty by providing income-generating assets (including working capital where necessary) to the poorest of the poor' (Paul 1998, p. 117). However, rural poverty programs such as Jawahar Rozgar Yojana (JRY) as initiated in 1989, have been susceptible to widespread mistargeting, besides capture by local interest groups, rampant fraud and corruption (Gaiha *et. al.*, 1998) despite the ongoing imperative of addressing rural poverty by re-configuring the agrarian structure and containing, 'the process of gradual marginalisation and proletarianisation of the peasantry' (Ghosh 1998, pp. 182-83).

It is commonly agreed that the capacity of the centrally planned Indian economy to deliver poverty-reducing growth — especially in the non-agriculture sectors — was retarded over the 1950-90 period, by governments' increasing ill-managed extensive involvement in the economy. First, the poor performance of State Owned Enterprises (SOEs) whose low return on debt-financed investment (crowding out private capital formation, Parker 1995) was partially explicable in terms of self-interest as opposed to common-good models of government including rent seeking by labour (Ghosh and Neogi, 1996) and other pressure groups[4] as well as corruption and the moral hazard accompanying "soft-budget constraints," of SOEs being 'insufficiently motivated to avoid losses by raising efficiency' (Kornai, 1995, p. 142). Secondly, over-regulation of both the public and private sectors (including "the licence raj") which led to low capacity utilisation, a costly input factor mix and low productivity and the related inability of producers to sell additional output — where they had overcome supply constraints — owing to demand constraints (Sarma, 1995; Majumdar, 1996; and Burki, Khan and Bratsberg, 1997).

---

4 Anne Krueger (1974) estimated that rent seeking, the socially costly pursuit of wealth transfers, excluding corruption payments, wasted 7 per cent of India's GNP in 1964; while for 1980-81, it was re-estimated at 25-40 per cent by Mohammand and Whalley (1984), (in Tollison 1996, p. 514).

Although not all of India's post-independent poor economic performance can be explained in terms of market failure, or government failure, or an inward versus outward looking industrialisation policy (Islam, 1992), it is necessary also to consider the structural, cultural and socio-political constraints which impact on development (Stern, 1991).

India's GDP and per capita income growth fluctuated markedly over the 1950-1990 period. With the agricultural sector comprising a large (but diminishing) component of GDP in India's economy (44.5 per cent in 1970, to 30.3 per cent in 1990) and with some 75 per cent of the population living in rural areas, uncontrollable climatic-sourced seasonal output variations had a large impact on total GDP.

For the 40 year period 1950-90, average annual GDP growth per capita was a low 1.55 per cent — due in part to rapid population growth, from 359 million to 844 million — with the effect that annual GDP doubled over the 40 years rather than 27 years as originally envisaged in the *First Plan* of 1951-56. As Dandekar (1992, p. 36) points out, 'clearly the greatest failure has been on the population front.' Furthermore, while India's fixed investment increased by over 75 per cent during the 1950-84 period, the GDP growth rate hardly lifted, that was indicative of an industrial policy framework failure (Majumdar, 1995, 1996; Misra and Saxena 1997; Burki *et. al.*, 1997).

The Incidence and Nature of Rural Poverty

Notwithstanding the growth of non-agricultural sectors in the Indian economy since 1947, poverty remains essentially a rural phenomenon with over 70 per cent of the country's poor in the 1990s, living in rural areas (see Appendix A). India has experienced an especially slow pace of urbanisation, from 10.8 per cent in 1901 to 25.7 per cent in 1991, owing principally, 'to the high pace of rural population growth'[5] (Shinoda, 1996, p. 520). Urban growth has had little impact on rural poverty, especially since India's development strategy from the 1950s stressed capital intensive industrialisation in

---

5 **Although, definitions of urbanization vary markedly across countries, with the upshot that if India adopted a less strict definition as used elsewhere in the region, 'its urbanization level would jump to more than 50 per cent' (Shinoda, 1996, p. 522).**

the urban areas of a closed economy. Rural to urban migration has therefore not been the outcome of transferring resources from agriculture to more productive uses in other sectors, contrary to the developmental process as envisaged. The urban poor, 'are only an overflow of the rural poor, into the urban area. Fundamentally, they belong to the same class as the rural poor' (Dandekar and Rath, in Misra and Puri, 1994, p. 279). As the agricultural sector — in which the poor are mostly located — remains predominant in the Indian economy, fostering growth in the rural economy is pivotal to 'an effective strategy for poverty reduction in India' (Lipton and Ravillon, 1996, p. 19).

Since the 1950s, there have been numerous studies on Indian rural and urban poverty levels using various criteria for estimating poverty. The development of appropriate measures to best ascertain poverty remains a difficult theoretical, statistical and practical issue (Dandekar, 1992, Chapter 5). The World Bank's (1989) study of Indian poverty used a poverty line - the expenditure level at which a minimum calorie intake and indispensable nonfood purchases are assured. The rural and urban poverty lines for 1983 were Rs. 89 and Rs. 112.2 respectively (Datt and Sundharam, 1997, p. 314). In his reassessment of the IRDP over the 1985-1987 period, Paul (1996, pp. 118-19) assessed a family as poor if its per capita family income was less than Rs. 1,180 per annum.

The rural population below the poverty line fell from 53 per cent in 1970, to 44.9 per cent in 1983 and 41.7 per cent in 1988, though in absolute terms the number of rural poor increased from 237 million to 252 million over the same period. The government's increasingly expansive IRDP — which was directed at the poorest rural families — contributed towards that percentage reduction (Paul, 1996). Although, based on an income criterion, the effectiveness of programs such as the JRY, were highly inefficient due to widespread mistargeting, 'as the rural poor who were recruited, made up less than 50 per cent of JRY's workforce in 11 out of 15 of Indian states' (Gaiha *et. al.*, 1998, p. 928).

In any event, by 1993-94, rural poverty levels, according to one measure, had fallen to 36.7 per cent as compared with 30.5 per cent for urban dwellers though the impact of post-1990 stabilisation and structural adjustment related policy reforms on rural poverty levels was not demonstratively positive.

The principal cause of enduring rural poverty levels in India is the low productivity of the agricultural sector, as evidenced by the high correlation coefficient (-0.88) between the poverty gap and average farm yield. Whilst state development spending as well as the growth of non-agricultural output have had some impact on poverty reduction, these have had effects *via* a lagged impact on average farm yield. The low productivity growth of India's agricultural sector has been due, despite the significant benefits of the scale-neutral green revolution, to the failure to get the whole sector up to the metaproduction function, which approximates the innovation possibility curve, the most efficient production point available (Hayami and Ruttan, 1985). In brief, the low agricultural production efficiency of Less Developed Countries (LDCs) such as India, 'is mostly explained by the limited capacity of LDC agricultural research systems to develop a new technology in response to changes in relative price factors, and of farmers' capacity to adopt it' (Hayami and Ruttan, 1985, p. 136.).

For example, in their survey of village studies, Jayaraman and Lanjouw (1998, p. 5) cite the study by Dreze, Lanjouw and Sharma (DLS) of agriculture in Palanpur in 1993, which,

> … was still far from the frontier in terms of productive potential : farmers still sow late; the seeds they use are often adulterated; they are casual about sowing-related details such as timing, depth and spacing; they neglect weeding and so on. DLS suggest that much of this can be explained by the combination of risk aversion, inadequate insurance, expensive credit, and a lack of basic education which has slowed the adoption of new technologies.

The World Bank (1997) report *India : Achievements and Challenges in Reducing Poverty*, was able to draw on the National Council of Applied Economic Research (NCAER) human development profile of India in 1996, to provide a detailed up-to-date account of the characteristics of the rural poor. The main points to emerge from the

NCAER survey, as noted by the World Bank's (1997) report were that the incidence of poverty, confirming its structural socio-economic characteristics as established by prior studies, was as follows :

- 52 per cent for the landless as a whole;
- 68 per cent for landless wage-earners;
- 50 per cent and 51 per cent respectively for the 206 million members of the scheduled castes and scheduled tribes and
- 45 per cent for households in which members were illiterate, compared with 27 per cent for households where both male and female adults can read and write.

Two main factors accounted for such high rural poverty levels. First, high levels of both unemployment and underemployment, with the failure of minimum wage legislation to deliver above subsistence level wages even during employment periods[6]. Secondly, the low asset base of the poor (see table 1) and which in any event is markedly skewed in favour of consumer durable goods (generally obtained on credit from retail shops) as opposed to productive assets such as land, farm implements and livestock (Datt and Sundharan, 1997, p. 322; Bhattacharya *et. al.,* 1991). In any event, there has been no major change in the rural structure of asset ownership since the 1960s, before which an entirely inadequate redistribution of land holdings occurred following independence.

In the post-Independent era, the politically active land owning classes opposed any radical restructuring of rural property relations and were able by a combination of adroit manoeuvring, wholesale avoidance and evasion, outright fraud as well as intimidation and

---

6 Nonetheless, contrary to earlier findings that real wages in rural India had evinced no trend increase, recent analyses indicate an upward trend in most regions of India during the 1970s and 1980s (Bell and Rich, 1994; Ghosh, 1998; Datt and Ravallion, 1998). The 1993 Palanpur village study by Dreze, Lanjouw and Sharma revealed a rising trend in real wages since 1974/75 which is most evident when expressed in terms of the relative price of wheat. A day of casual labour in 1993 earned the equivalent of more than 8 kgs. of wheat compared with below 3 kgs. in 1957/58 (in Jayaraman and Lanjouw, 1998, p. 20). While, in a study of three villages — part of the International Crop Research Institute for the Semi-Arid Tropics (ICRISAT) research program — Pal (1997) found evidence of an increase of up to 60 per cent in real terms of both regular and casual agricultural wages, between 1975 and 1984.

violence, to minimise the impact of various modest land reform measures which endeavoured to abolish intermediaries and impose ceilings on land ownership and redistribute the surplus to landless labourers. Less than 2 per cent of total cultivated land was in fact acquired under land reform measures for redistribution among the landless (J.M. Rao 1997, pp. 127-29; Hanumantha Rao, 1992, pp. 117-18).

Although some 90 per cent of rural households own some land, most have very small plots. And owing to a growing population in agriculture and a low declining rate of growth in agricultural land, there is a declining land-person ratio and very little prospect, owing to political intransigence, of increasing the size of such marginal and small holdings through redistributive land reforms (Ghosh, 1998). Furthermore, there has been a substantial decline in communal resources such as village commons and forests which are important traditional sources of rural livelihood diversification for women, independent of relations with men (Agarwal, 1997, 1998).

Table 1 : Distribution of Assets in Rural Areas

Population Group	Per centage Share of Assets	
	1961	1971
Lowest 10%	0.1	0.1
Lowest 30%	2.0	2.5
Middle 40%	6.1	18.5
Top 30%	79.0	81.9
Top 10%	51.4	51.0

Source : *Sixth Five Year Plan* p. 8, in Rudaar Datt and K.P.M. Sundharan (1997).
Indian Economy (36th revised edition) p. 322, table 12.

To sum up, in India's agrarian economy, arable land is 'the most critical form of property, valued for its economic, political and symbolic importance' (Agarwal, 1997, pp. 2-3). It is strongly associated with security and well-being, with the rural population being divisible into four distinct groups, based on access to land and reliance on agricultural wage income. Landless agricultural and non-agricultural wage labourers and marginal farmers face a significantly higher than average risk of poverty. Nonetheless, adverse trends in landlessness, and a falling land per worker ratio, should not be simply equated with increased vulnerability and poverty — the interaction and changing demographics are somewhat more complex (Jayaraman and Lanjouw, 1998; Pal, 1996, 1997, 1999).

The gender-based variance in poverty and associated social indicators, is discussed below :

The Anti-female Bias in the Rural Sector, Feminisation of Poverty and Inequality

Rural poverty in India, besides being endemic, is somewhat feminised (see Appendix B). As Lipton and Ravillion (1995, pp. 2589-90) explain, young females are typically exposed to excess poverty-related nutritional and health risks, women work longer to obtain the same level of living standards, they bear the brunt of falling living standards, and they are discriminated against in both educational and work opportunities. There is, in other words, 'a systematic anti-female bias in the allocation within rural households of subsistence resources controlled by men, including resources used for food, health care, education and other basic needs' (Agarwal, 1997, p. 27).

The burden of women's work in India outside the household is typically 1.5 to 2.5 times that of menfolk, with rural women (50 per cent of whom suffer from iron deficiencies) working up to 15-16 hours per day during the busy agricultural season, which combined with their domestic chores comprises a double or triple daily burden (Dasgupta and Maler, 1995, p. 2432; Vecchio and Roy, 1998, Chapter 3). They can also spend up to 5 hours per day collecting water in the dry season, accounting for 10-25 per cent of their daytime energy expenditure (See Appendix C).

It is difficult, nonetheless, to accurately specify the range of indicators, which best gauge, the quality of women's lives and their capabilities (Nussbaum and Sen, 1993, p. 5). Among the frequently used indicators of the status of women are sex differentials in : life expectancy at birth; infant mortality rates; school enrolment ratio; school retention rates; the maternal mortality rate; age at marriage;

the working population ratio and the sex-ratio *i.e.,* the number of males per 1000 females (Jalan, 1992, p. 287).

In India, all censuses have shown a deficit of women. The "missing female" syndrome is measured by a variation in the "natural" female-male ratio (FMR, see Appendix A). Dreze and Sen estimated, on the basis of India's exceptionally low FMR of 0.93 in comparison with the European and North American average FMR of 1.05, that, depending on what FMR is most applicable, there were 37 million missing women as at 1986 (in Dreze and Sen, 1995, Chapter 7). The low FMR is most acute in large parts of North India, for example 0.87 in Haryana, while in the south where the social standing of women is much higher, the FMR tends to be above unity and close to European and North American levels, for example, 1.04 in Kerala.

Other indicators of the status of women such as the level of literacy, the mean age at marriage and employment, revealed some improvement. But despite this, Indian women continue to suffer from widespread anti-female bias in regard to health care, nutrition, literacy, choice of spouse, property rights, and freedom of movement and decision-making rights etc. (See Appendices A, B & C). The inferior property rights which women have in relation to land is especially noteworthy, particularly for widows whose economic security which is generally reliant on achieving effective land rights, is subject to a range of severely limiting social, administrative and ideological obstacles and restrictions (Agarwal 1998).

Rural Women, Discrimination and Employment

The poor in India are, as noted above, disproportionately located in rural areas and primarily engaged in agricultural and associated activities as landless labourers, more likely to be women and children than adult males, and are concentrated in the scheduled castes and tribes. The most extreme levels of deprivation exists among women in the scheduled castes and tribes (which account for about 15 per cent of India's population). These doubly disadvantaged women strive for their very survival (Dunn, 1993).

In many Female-Headed Households (FHHs), the low earning capacity of women and limited control over their husbands' income, less access to (unmediated) resource ownership, education, formal sector employment, social security and government employment programs, all contribute to the poor income and well-being state of rural women. Informal estimates suggest that women head nearly 20 per cent of households in India, while Vecchio and Roy (1998, p. 2) found that in tribal areas, the concentration of FHHs was 45-65 per cent. Because the earning potential of women is much lower than their male counterparts, in general, women in female-headed households have less education, lower incomes and high fertility, and lower food consumption levels. The survival strategies of poor FHHs include helping each other (because they typically do not belong to formal support groups), keeping their older children out of school when work is available, taking loans from social networks if possible but otherwise from moneylenders and finally engaging in begging or illicit activities (Vecchio and Roy, 1998, pp. 16-18).

Indian rural women, besides being typically employed on a casual rather than regular basis (Pal, 1996, p. 100) are paid less than men for performing the same agricultural work though their productivity may be equal to or even superior than that of men. For example, in paddy field — which is frequently reserved for casual female gang labour — women have a recognised efficiency advantage. Moreover, controlling for differences in input levels and human capital, the two sexes are equally efficient farm managers (Quisumbing, 1996). However, cultural values and their greater household responsibilities systematically constrain the ability of women to participate in agricultural activities both on their own typically small marginal family landholdings, larger properties and in the wider community.

The issue of whether the ongoing process of agricultural modernisation and related changes in labour arrangements have collectively impacted adversely on the employment prospects of rural women, has attracted considerable interest and engendered some controversy.

In her study of gender and agricultural intensification in south-east Andhra Pradesh, Ramamurthy (1994) found that the highest wages for group activities were for transplanting and harvesting, where both men and women formed groups and were paid the same rates because of peak demand for labour and equal productivity for those tasks. Even at those peak periods however, wage rates remained low at about the family subsistence level owing to tacit agreements among large landowners[7]. Generally, women were paid a lower wage for tasks where there was a clear division of labour. Ramamurthy (1994, p. 205) concluded that agricultural intensification had not improved the welfare of poor rural women, and that, 'the system of patriarchy upholds class exploitation and is linked to the development of agrarian capitalism in an essential way.'

Those conclusions, however, are somewhat difficult to reconcile with other research concerning the socio-economic effects of agricultural development in India.

First, there is clear evidence that, over the 35 year period of 1958-94, higher farm productivity yielded absolute and real gains to poor rural households, though subject to wage sluggishness, insofar as the 'short-run farm-yield elasticity of the real wage is about 0.12 rising to over eight times that figure in the long-run' (Datt and Ravallion, 1998, p. 71). The poor also gained indirectly from lower relative prices of food, while inflation levels adversely affected them. Poor rural women working as casual day labourers shared, albeit on a lagged basis, in these gains.

Secondly, the process of agricultural modernisation and intensification has been associated with the decline of traditional labour services. The rigid caste-based traditional artisan system, has somewhat broken down, with some services becoming extinct and the remaining services being casualised, with caste members thereby being freed up to work as agricultural wage labourers. The decline of traditional labour occupations has been generally associated with reduced, not increased, poverty levels. For example,

7 It is well established that in the informal rural sectors of poor economies such as India's, owing to the lack of trade unions and/or binding minimum wages, in an environment of productivity growth, 'employers will resist wage increases at least initially, and tacit collusion or other forms of resistance on the supply side could also yield downward stickiness. Long-run wage responses to agricultural growth can thus exceed short-run responses' (Datt and Ravallion, 1998, p. 66). This point somewhat contextualises Ramamurthy's (1994) observations regarding the stickiness of rural women's wages.

in the village of Palanpur, 'the decline of traditional labour occupations has preceded rising real wages in the economy including rising agricultural wage rates' (Jayaraman and Lanjouw, 1998, p. 15).

Thirdly, there has been a broadly based two-fold casualisation or "depatronisation" of agricultural labour contracts : (i) daily wage labour contracts have been substituted for regular (seasonal) employment, which in addition to a cash wage, comprised various non-cash benefits and (ii) a shift to piece-rate contracts (often undertaken by gang labour from outside the village) for the more labour intensive irrigation based cash crops, including paddy cultivation (Pal, 1997, 1999; Jayaraman and Lanjouw, 1998). There has also been a growing diversity of alternate labour contracts, including various intermediate group tenancy arrangements, which are preferred by labourers owing to the gains from independent organisation, decision-making and employment flexibility.

The three studies by Pal (1996, 1997 and 1999) of various aspects of the casualisation phenomenon, primarily based on the ICRISAT data from three villages (Aurepalle, Shirapur and Kanzara), indicate that the decline in regular contracts has been caused by rising wages and employment opportunities and an expanded access to formal credit facilities. Traditionally, only men have had access to regular contracts, while casual contracts are available to both men and women. While the regular daily wage is much lower than the casual daily wage, it has been supplemented by various non-wage benefits including *e.g.,* housing, bonuses and gifts and the payment of most of the wages in advance at the start of the annual contract, with no formal interest charge being levied. These arrangements are more suited to landless labourers than labourers with small holdings who may also wish to work part-time in the casual labour market.

Daily regular wages are much lower than casual wages because, in addition to (i) being discounted for the probability of unemployment, there is, (ii) an implicit interest charge on advances which in the three villages studied by Pal, ranged between a low of 8 per cent in Kanzara, 130 per cent for Shirapur, and a high of 258 per cent in Aurepalle. These rates reflected the availability or otherwise of formal credit in the village from credit agencies, as well as non-agricultural employment opportunities. Landless labourers who were unable to access cheaper credit because of their inability to provide collateral security, had little choice but to take up a regular contract, while landed labourers with access to credit, preferred the flexibility of more highly paid casual contracts. There was, however, evidence of an upward trend in wages in response to the growing reluctance of labourers to take up regular contracts. Pal (1997, p. 134) was able to argue that, 'workers' choice between casual and regular contracts in rural India is guided by the marginal cost of credit and opportunity cost of time.'

How the trend to wage casualisation and piece-work impact on poor rural women, must depend on the almost infinitely variable interaction of a veritable constellation of micro-level factors with the possibility of an adverse combination generating the sort of adverse outcomes detailed by Ramamurthy (1994) including :

- whether wages are paid mostly in cash or in kind;
- village/individual access to formal/informal credit facilities;
- the exact agronomic characteristics and dynamics of the village;
- the use of labour from outside the village and
- non-farm employment opportunities.

Where a village has benefited from the green revolution, including irrigation and the opportunity of multiple cropping, then besides benefiting as casual labourers from long-run productivity gains, its poor women should obtain casual employment for more days in each year, and even be preferred, at the margin, over landless male labourers. In a village with an expanding agricultural sector but which is still somewhat credit constrained, women casual labourers may be preferable from the viewpoint of medium farmers, to landless male labourers hired under regular contracts, if such farmers can thereby avoid incurring the nonwage component of the traditional regular contract, combined with the cash flow advantage of paying wages during a shortened contract period, as opposed to payment of discounted wages up to a season in advance, subject, however, to being able to maintain the quality of non-monitorable tasks for which regular labour is typically hired. And if the village is not credit constrained, then it would be even more advantageous for medium farmers to hire women under intermediate contractual arrangements, than landless labourers under either regular or casual contracts. In many labour-intensive agrarian settings, it ought to be cheaper, at the margin, to substitute female labour for male labour; however, social norms may inhibit this type of contractual innovation. This viewpoint is consistent with the observation by Pal (1999) that family, regular and casual labour is used by the larger more labour intensive farms as close substitutes, irrespective of the choice of crop, and that those farms incur otherwise avoidable costs by using regular labour for monitorable tasks, retaining it during slack periods of production. Clearly, a good deal more micro-household and village level research is necessary across the disparate regions of India, to obtain a more comprehensive, detailed account of the socio-economic impact of agricultural modernisation and intensification on poor rural women.

Household Failure — Gender Bias In Resource Allocation and Bargaining

In this part we sketch out and try to account — within the development imperative — for the recurrent failure of households (especially the poorer households) in rural India to efficiently and equitably allocate scarce resources amongst household members, with reference to the persistence of obsolete socio-cultural arrangements and schemes of recurrence (institutions) which curtail individual autonomy *i.e.*, agency, and the difficulty of redesigning them owing to the systemic failures and limitations of individuals, groups, the community, markets and government.

There are three notable forms of household or family failures : (i) the distribution of essential resources; (ii) non-traded family production (*i.e.,* household maintenance, reproduction and child care) and (iii) externalities in human capital formation — education and skill acquisition (Kabeer and Humphrey, 1991). In sum, the systematic privileging of households male members at the expense of female members, is allocationally inefficient, diminishes the capability and well-being of females and in turn the collective welfare and output of the total household (Behrman, 1997, Chapter 4). This diminished capability, well-being and output has adverse market consequences because : (i) it stems the flow of household sourced educated labour and capital flows to market activities and (ii) it reduces in turn the ability of markets to override the consequences of family failures.

Household failure in rural India should not however be appraised in isolation but contextually, with reference to its historical antecedents[8], path-dependence and the societal-wide level of socio-economic advancement in relation to the nation's self-imposed scheme of social modernisation and economic development. Contemporary rural Indian society is readily characterised as "traditional" because, 'biological reproductivity has been in comparative context a defining characteristic of female roles to an extreme degree' (Clark, 1994, p. 11), where the two norms for men and women, 'produce strongly enforced actual divisions of activities and ways of living' (Annas, 1993, p. 280). Although there is considerable variation between states, the south-western state of Kerala has perhaps the most equal gender status and relations while in the north-western states, patriarchy is most socially embedded, gender relations the most uneven and women's capability, well-being and agency-freedom as measured by *e.g.*, the *human development index* or *gender development index*, are the lowest in the Indian subcontinent, independently of income levels (Dreze and Sen, 1995).

The evident household and societal bias against rural Indian women which has no basis in biological gender differences thereby reducing the level of their 'human flourishing and the good life'

---

[8] It is noteworthy that women have not always held a subordinate position in Indian society (Dunn 1993, p. 54). In ancient pre-Aryan India, the social structure was matriarchal. Following the Aryan invasion, the socio-economic status of women went into a long slow decline, although in Vedic times, 'a woman was considered a puritan, a *Sati Savitri* or *Sita*, embodiment of virtue, dedication and sacrifice' (Mehta, 1997, p. 409). Women retained quite high socio-economic status despite the presence of Aryan patriarchal ideology until about 1000 A.D. when Muslim invaders imposed a rigid patriarchal governance system on socio-economic relations (Roy and Tisdell, 1996, pp. 97-98).

(Nussbaum, 1993, p. 327) can be easily repudiated on numerous cogent philosophical and practical commonsense grounds. What entitlements rural Indian women deserve, reduces to an issue of social justice, to which end established distributive justice rules such as *equity, equality and need* can be applied (Major, 1993, p. 142). But leaving aside idealised and relativised theories of justice which would seem remote from the viewpoint of disempowered rural Indian women, O'Neill (1993, p. 318) posits instead the simple justice principle of asking, 'to what extent the arrangements which structure vulnerable lives are ones that could have been refused or renegotiated by those whom they actually constrain'. This perhaps constitutes a practical threshold application of Sen's (1993) measure of the quality of a person's life expressed in terms of his/her capabilities. It also encapsulates the central tenet of the feminist/institutionalist economic model of the household in which '*gender is the central mediating phenomenon* of all household activity, from the formation of household economic goals to the allocation of basic household resources such as labour and income' (Katz, 1991, pp. 53-4). An application of O'Neill's (1993) legitimate consent test to poor women in rural India, would typify much of their household interaction and market transacting as non-consensual or coercive to some degree.

Women in India's poorer rural households may well be experiencing the worst outcomes of an evolutionary transition of institutions :

- subordination to a set of social norms which in the limit are more or less binding for them to enjoy precarious access to what Pettit (1998, p. 64) terms "attitude-dependent goods" (and services which social networks provide) but which over time are shrinking due to an expanding market economy and
- limited capability and well-being, owing to the household's gender-biased allocation of scarce resources including schooling and healthcare services as well as the extension of restrictive social norms and trade practices etc. into the market economy, to take full advantage of the potential for economic gain and "action-dependent goods."

The intra-household bias in its resource allocation against women is however not just a simple matter of, 'relations of power between women and men' (Agarwal, 1997, p. 1). It has to be analysed with reference to the vexed issue of gender role socialisation and the supposed internalisation by rural women (*i.e.*, adoption as valid and binding) of social norms, rules and values which are at face value inimical to their own individual welfare, self-perception and well-being — expressed by Sen (1990) in terms of whether women suffer from false perceptions. Whether or not gender-oppressive norms are internalised by women is not a matter of mere semantics but has important ramifications because if they are internalised, women may be complicit in perpetuating gender inequality by "secondary internalisation" — transmitting them to other victims (Papanek, 1990). Such a proposition may seem contrary to Harsanyi's widely accepted version of rational choice theory which posits, 'self-interested desires for social acceptance, side by side with self-interested desires for economic gain' (cited in Pettit, 1998, p. 65). Granovetter (1985, p. 506) makes much the same point that, what seems like nonrational behaviour, 'may be quite sensible when situational constraints, especially those of embeddedness, are fully appreciated.' A classic example of this in rural India is the fact that, 'many women forego their shares in parental land in favour of brothers for the sake of their potential economic and social support' (Agarwal, 1998, p. 31).

Several additional points can be usefully made. First, some scholars (*e.g.*, Agarwal, 1997) approach the issue of self-perceptions, altruism and self-interest by emphasising the various forms of resistance which women can take to oppressive gender relations which indicate that gender-oppressive norms are not internalised. The upshot of this is that what looks like engagement in oppressive household arrangements, may for example, on closer scrutiny comprise a long-run self-interested exercise of maintaining the household's welfare and in particular that of male offspring because of their dependence on sons in widowhood or old age (Albian, 1996; Agarwal, 1998). Secondly, there are also culturally-specific variations in the constructions of individual and collective (*i.e.*, household) welfare which are apt to mislead. In contrast to Anglo-American countries and their former colonies, India is a collectivist society which involves the subordination of individual to collective goals — described at the individual level as "psychological collectivism" (Dion and Dion, 1993, p. 55). The Indian penchant for personal collectivism is described by Roland (Dion and Dion, 1993, p. 56) as relational rather than autonomous, which developed,

> *... in hierarchical relationships within the extended family in which the following qualities were present : strong emotional interdependence, reciprocal demands for intimacy and support, mutual caring, and a high degree of empathy and sensitivity to another's needs and desires in the family structure.*

Furthermore, the relational sense of self is especially descriptive of Indian women's self-construal, and after marriage,

> *... relationships with female relatives were traditionally a major source of concern and attention for married women rather than the relationship with the spouse. Another source of emotional intimacy was the mother-child, especially the mother-son relationship. (Dion and Dion, 1993, p. 62)*

Agarwal (1997, p. 42) makes a similar point. She cites Aileen Ross's (1961) grading of emotional closeness with respect to 11 relationship types among Hindu joint families in Bangalore. That placed the mother-son and sister-brother relationship in the top 2 positions and the husband-wife relationship as second-last. This divergent prioritisation of relationships in Indian households throws up different patterns of self-interested patterns of behaviour than the naive (Western) observer might otherwise expect. In any event, any account of gender relations and intrahousehold resource allocation, rational choice theory and value internalisation with reference to rural India, has to account for the following social practices which do not align with the simple gender divide :

- the lack of solidarity between women in joint households and between kin/marriage related households — particularly the notorious lack of agency freedom and subordination of young married women in relation to their mother-in-law (Jeffery and Jeffrey, 1994);
- the selection of an offspring's spouse being undertaken to advance the perceived interests of the entire household rather

than the intersubjective preferences — agency freedom — of the offspring;

- bargaining for payment of an ever-escalating though legally prohibited dowry[9] — which together with marriage costs can amount to 3-4 times the value of a poor household's assets (J.M. Rao, 1997, p. 101) — and which if not fully satisfied can lead to endless harassment and even ultimately the death of the young woman at the hands of female members of the household (Roy and Tisdell, 1996, p. 10). Dowry payments also prejudice inheritance rights in land (where they actually exist by customary right or legislative enactment) *vis-a-vis* male siblings and other relatives especially where the woman leaves her village to join her husband's household elsewhere so that the lack of proximity prejudices her capacity to retain those rights by direct enforcement and
- dowry payments from a young married woman's family are not received by the husband's joint household in trust as an inheritance for her benefit but are frequently applied for the separate purposes of the husband's parents and other household members, including reciprocal payment of dowries (Agarwal, 1994, p. 136).[10]

There is irrefutable evidence that conflict among women in households is endemic in rural India, especially between a young married woman and the female members of her husband's household in the affinal village (Jeffery and Jeffery, 1994). The on-going bargaining after marriage for further dowry payments (though legally prohibited) is a common source of conflict. The losses sustained by being oppressed as a young married woman can only be recouped by imposing a similarly repressive financial and service regime on the

---

9 As Agarwal (1994, p. 481) explains, although taking and giving dowry was made illegal by the Dowry Prohibition Act 1961, as amended in 1984 and 1986 to eliminate loopholes, demands for ever-increasing dowry payments continue to be made (owing to a marriage squeeze and larger cohorts of younger women in the marriage market) and in an increasingly coercive and extortionary manner.

10 Interestingly, the topic of intra-gender conflict is somewhat absent in accounts of gender contested land rights (*e.g.*, Agarwal, 1994, 1997, 1998).

incoming spouses of her male offspring. This vicious cycle can only be stopped on an individual family basis if the older generation is prepared to accept a distributional loss by foregoing their recoupment of prior gender-related inequalities, losses and imposts.

Bargaining in the Household

Our poor rural household, whose members' continuing well-being is typically precarious owing to the scarce resources at its command, in order to maximise its long-run prospects in a society in which many types of transactions remain "oversocialised" and are of variable or even indeterminate value, faces the difficulty of choosing co-operative persons with whom to form social alliances (including careful selection of a spouse for its offspring (Becker, 1981, pp. 32-4)) as well as to engage in various economic exchanges, where many hazards exist. The external environment in which the household has to bargain in promotion of its continued well-being occurs in an environment known for its lack of "social capital" *i.e.*, lack of trust, dishonesty, fraud, corruption, and violent resolution of conflict (Woolcock, 1998).

The intra-household allocation of resources can be explained, for analytical purposes, in terms of a bargaining process. Becker (1981) treated the household as a single entity or firm with a production and consumption function, and governance structure (an altruistic head, who allocated resources on a Pareto-optimal basis), engaging in both economic activities and nontraded household activities. Alternatively, and more realistically, intra-household relations can be described in game theoretic terms in which its members explicitly bargain, cooperate or fail to cooperate to varying degrees over household income, production, exchange and consumption. In these alternative co-operative and non-co-operative approaches to household decision-making, the separate resources which each spouse controls are important sources of bargaining power because they delimit opportunities outside the family (*i.e.*, "fall-back" positions). Non-co-operative examples of household bargaining, at the most extreme, still have areas of "joint consumption" (*e.g.*, child rearing) which are important sources of co-operative gains to the husband and wife as well as "separate spheres of activities" with minimum co-ordination of activities which in the limit, comprises 'a division of labour based on socially recognised and sanctioned gender' and which comprises the threat point at which bargaining commences (Lundberg and Pollak, 1993, p. 994).

The non-co-operative models would appear to be most useful in analysing the gender-biased intrahousehold allocation of resources in rural India because they do not literally require personal non-co-operation, but rather, allocation of resources according to recognised and sanctioned gender roles *e.g.*, internalised social norms, which as described above, do not do justice to female members of the household. Although all models of intrahousehold resource allocation have difficulty dealing with the prospect that marital bargaining processes comprise 'complex loosely structured interaction' (Lundberg and Pollak, 1993, p. 994) and with different types of resources (*e.g.*, child care, health and education costs, home labour and market labour) being allocated according to different rules, so that 'unitary, cooperative and non-co-operative decision-making rules may all co-exist in the same household'(Katz 1997, p. 37).

Feminist economists as well as institutionalists while noting that noncooperative models address three key features of family life — asymmetrical information, enforcement problems and inefficiency — which drastically limit the "voice" and "exit" options of *e.g.*, poor rural women in India, seek to better characterise the institutional features of the intrahousehold allocation through an interdisciplinary approach. That task involves, in order to parameterise the gender based differences in the ability to bargain (the "voice" option), resort to threat points and the viability of an exit strategy, obtaining,

> ... *culturally-specific information about factors such as interpersonal behavioural norms, the acceptability of noncooperation and separation, subjective valuation or perception of threat point assets, reference groups and seclusion, and the likely sources of variation in these across households.* (Katz, 1997, p. 37).

Agarwal (1997) undertakes an exercise of this type in order to ascertain, what determines the power of a rural Indian woman to bargain for subsistence within the family. She outlines eight factors as determining a rural person's bargaining strength, including : ownership of and control over assets, especially arable land; access to employment and other income-earning means; access to traditional social support systems; and social norms. Owing to the primacy of land as an ongoing source of income, welfare and security as well as a reduction in traditional social support, Agarwal (1994, 1997, pp. 12-13), predictably gives primacy to, 'effective command over landed property.' Women are not less motivated to advance their perceived self-interest (which here extends to the household's welfare especially that of children) but their bargaining is constrained by social norms, which is, therefore, a "contested area" in addition to, 'contestation over subsistence resources.' Agarwal's analysis (1997, p. 9), however, is not strictly confined to a formal application of a cooperative or noncooperative bargaining model in which separate resources determine a person's fall-back position (*i.e.*, their ability to fulfil subsistence needs outside the family), the same set of separate resources also influence, 'her/his ability to make contributions within the relationship.'

The role of social norms is particularly important in Agarwal's (1997) analysis : these are perceived as being both exogenous and endogenous constraints which set limits on a rural woman's bargaining power in relation to contests for access to welfare-enhancing property rights but also in some circumstances can be bargained over, in which case a woman's overall status, existing property and social support network can provide sufficient power to negotiate otherwise binding norms. However, the analysis of contested areas remains problematic. It appears difficult though, using Agarwal's analytical description, which she claims can be formally modelled, to predict with certainty the contests in which women pursuing effective property rights would succeed and those which would prove intractable to the bargaining endeavours of rural Indian women.

Concluding Comments

No society has been indifferent to whether a person is a male or female. Rather, 'there are everywhere two actual norms for human life' (Annas, 1993, p. 280) that is inadequately accounted for by biological sex differences. In traditional rural India, enforcement of two such distinctive norms causes grave injustice to women. They are subject to pervasive, systemic gender-based inequality in relation to the allocation of typically scarce household resources and which drastically curtails their capability, agency freedom, overall well-being and quality of life. Suggestions that Indian women accept as legitimate intra-household inequality *i.e.*, suffer from "false consciousness" are difficult to sustain because, it cannot be that women whose prospects are so limited that they cannot conceive of better and happier alternatives. It is also a fact that 'women's desires have expanded with the expansion of alternatives open to them' (Annas, 1993, p. 282).

Gender-biased intra-household allocation of resources in rural India, as well as opportunities for women outside the household, are based in an entrenched at best slowly evolving set of traditional social norms, customary rights and practices in a patriarchal society, whose anti-female values are to some extent retransmitted by women themselves. These norms, rights and practices, developed as practical solutions to social arrangements, and had effect because of their conjunction with power. This explains their continuance, despite their probable original deviation from rationality. It also accounts for their resilience and tendency over the longer cycle owing to an ineffective process of critical appraisal and reform, and 'the distorted dialectic of community' (Lonergan, 1978, p. 226) to increasingly diverge from optimal schemes of recurrence which would maximise the potential quality of life for men and women.

Furthermore, within that set of obsolete schemes of recurrence, there is considerable scope for individuals to deviate further from what are at most inferior solutions, because people are not as smart as it is typically assumed (Kreps, 1993). Household arrangements and family-related transactions in rural India such as the practice of arranged marriages and the subjugation of a young married woman, cut off from her own family, to the broad interests of her spouse's extended family and the imposition of all manner of intrusive social norms, customs and practices, are unlikely to economise on altruism, virtue and emotional sentiments (Brennan and Hamlin, 1995). Such households may well perpetuate weak levels of altruism owing to the failure to develop a pro-social tendency in children (Staub, 1991, p. 151). These would seem to constitute intractable social problems.

To remedy them, not only would all relevant obsolete schemes of recurrence have to be entirely re-devised — that is, structure and the rules of the game, particularly those relating to the intrahousehold allocation of resources — but also, all household members would have to fully internalise the altered gender-neutral rules and accept any adverse distributional effects. Regrettably, *Capability Kavita* is unlikely to experience the prospect of gender-neutral agency freedom and the related opportunity to decuple her quality of life from the pervasive socio-economic and cultural milieu of rural India, anytime soon.

REFERENCES

Abadian, S. (1996), "Women's Autonomy and Its Impact On Fertility," *World Development* Vol. 24, No. 12, pp. 1793-1809.

Agarwal, B. (1994), *A Field of One's Own : Gender and Land Rights in South Asia,* Cambridge University Press, Cambridge.

Agarwal, B. (1997), "'Bargaining' and Gender Relations Within And Beyond The Household", *Feminist Economics* Vol. 3 No. 1, pp. 1-51.

Agarwal, B. (1998), "Widows *versus* Daughters or Widows as Daughters? Property, Land and Economic Security in Rural India," *Modern Asian Studies*, Vol. 32, No.1, pp. 1-48.

Annas, J. (1993), "Women and the Quality of Life", in M. C. Nussbaum and A. Sen (eds.), *The Quality of Life*, Clarendon Press : Oxford, pp. 279-302.

Becker, G.S. (1981), *A Treatise on the Family*, Harvard University Press, Cambridge MA.

Behrman, J.R. (1997), "Intrahousehold Distribution and the Family," in Mark R. Rosenzweig and Oded Stark (eds.), *Handbook of Population and Family Economics,* Elsevier, Amsterdam, Volume 1A, Chapter 4.

Bell, C. and Rich, R. (1994), "Rural Poverty and Aggregate Agricultural Performance in post-Independence India," *Oxford Bulletin of Economics and Statistics*, Vol. 56, No. 2, pp. 111-34.

Bhagwati, J.N. (1988), 'Poverty and Public Policy', *World Development,* Vol. 16, No. 5, pp. 539-55.

Bhattacharya, N., Chakraborty, P., Chattopadhya, M. and Rudra, A. (1991), "How Do the Poor Survive," *Economic and Political Weekly*, February 16, 1991, pp. 373-79.

Brennan, G. and Hamlin, A. (1995), "Economizing on Virtue," *Constitutional Political Economy*, Vol. 6, pp. 35-56.

Burki, A.A., Khan, M.A. and Bratsberg, B. (1997), "Parametric tests of allocative efficiency in the manufacturing sectors of India and Pakistan," *Applied Economics,* Vol. 10, No. 3, pp. 451-85.

Clark, A. W. (1994), "Introduction", in Alice W. Clark (ed.), *Gender and Political Economy : Exploration of South Asian Systems*, Oxford University Press, Delhi, Chapter 1.

Dandekar, V.M. (1992), "Forty Years After Independence," in B. Jalan (ed.), *The Indian Economy : Problems and Prospects*, Penguin Books, New Delhi, Chapter 2.

Dandekar, V.M. (1996), *The Indian Economy* 1947-92, Volume II : *Population, Poverty And Employment*, Chapter 10, Sage Publications India Pvt. Ltd., New Delhi.

Dasgupta, P. and Maler, K-G. (1995), "Poverty, Institutions, and The Environmental Resource-Base," in J. Behrman and T. N. Srinivasan (eds.), *Handbook of Development Economics* Vol. IIIB, Elsevier : Amsterdam, Chapter 39.

Datt, G. and Ravallion, M. (1998), "Farm Productivity and Rural Poverty in India," *Journal of Development Studies*, Vol. 34, No. 4, pp. 62-85.

Datt, R. and Sundharam, K. P. M. (1997), *Indian Economy*, 36th revised edition, S. Chand and Co. Ltd : New Delhi.

Dion, K. and Dion, K. L. (1993), "Individualistic and Collective Perspectives on Gender and the Cultural Context of Love and Intimacy," *Journal of Social Issues*, Vol. 49 No. 3, pp. 53-60.

Dreze, J. and Sen, A. (1995), *India : Economic Development and Social Opportunity*, Oxford University Press : New York.

Dunn, D. (1993), "Gender Inequality in Education and Employment in the Scheduled Castes and Tribes in India," *Population Research and Policy Review,"* Vol. 12, No. 1, pp. 53-70.

Gaiha, R., Kaushik, P.D. and Kulkarni, V. (1998), "Jawahar Rozgar Yojana, Panchayats, and the Rural Poor in India," *Asian Survey*, Vol. 38, No. 2, pp. 928-48.

Ghosh, M. (1998), "Agrarian Structure and Rural Poverty in India," *Journal of Contemporary Asia*, Vol. 28, No. 2, pp. 175-85.

Ghosh, M. and Neogi, C. (1996), "Liberalization in India : Quality Differentials Between Public and Private Companies," *The Developing Economies*, Vol. 34, No.1, pp. 61-79.

Granovetter, M. (1985), "Economic Action and Social Structure : The Problem of Embeddedness," *American Journal of Sociology* Vol. 91, pp. 481-510.

Hayami, Y. and Ruttan, V.W. (1985), *Agricultural Development : An International Perspective*, John Hopkins University Press, Baltimore.

Islam, I. (1992) "Political Economy and East Asian Economic Development," *Asian–Pacific Economic Literature* Vol. 6, pp. 69-97.

Jalan, B. (ed.) (1992), *The Indian Economy : Problems and Prospects*, Penguin Books, New Delhi.

Jayaraman, R. and Lanjouw, P. (1998), *The Evolution of Poverty and Inequality in Indian Villages*, Working Paper No. 1870, The World Bank, Washington DC.

Jeffery, R. and Jeffery, P.M. (1994), "A Woman Belongs to Her Husband : Female Autonomy, Women's Work and Childbearing in Bijnor," in Alice W. Clark (ed.), *Gender and Political Economy : Exploration of South Asian Systems*, Oxford University Press, Delhi, Chapter 3.

Jhingan, M. L. (1994), *The Economics of Development and Planning*, 27th edition Konark Publishers, New Delhi.

Kabeer. N. and Humphrey, J. (1991), "Neo-liberalism, Gender, and the Limits of the Market," in C. Colclough and J. Manor (eds.), *States or Markets?: Neo-liberalism and the Development Policy Debate,* Clarendon Press, Oxford, Chapter 4.

Katz, E. (1991), "Breaking the Myth of Harmony : Theoretical and Methodological Guidelines to the Study of Rural Third World Households," *Review of Radical Political Economics*, Vol. 2, Nos. 3-4, pp. 37-56.

Katz, E. (1997), "The Intra-Household Economics of Voice and Exit," *Feminist Economics*, Vol.3, No. 3, pp. 25-46.

Kornai, J. (1995), Highways and Byways : Studies on Reform and Post-Communist Transition, The MIT Press, Cambridge Massachusetts.

Kreps, D.M. (1993), *Game Theory And Economic Modelling*, Oxford University Press, Oxford.

La Rue, C.S. (ed.), *The Indian handbook, Prospects into the 21st Century*, 1997, p. 200, table 13 : 4, Fitzroy Dearborn Publishers, USA.

Lipton, M. and Ravillion, M. (1995), "Poverty and Policy," in J. Behrman and T.N. Srinivasan (eds.), *Handbook of Development Economics*, Vol. IIIB Elsevier : Amsterdam, Chapter 41.

Lipton, M. and Ravillon, M. (1996), "How Important to India's Poor Is The Sectoral Composition of Economic Growth?" *The World Bank Economic Review*, Vol. 10, No. 1, pp. 1-25.

Lonergan, B.J.F. (1978), *Insight : A Study of Human Understanding,* Harper and Row, New York.

Lundberg, S. and Pollak, R.A. (1993), "Separate Spheres Bargaining and the Marriage Market," *Journal of Political Economy* Vol. 101, No. 6, pp. 988-1010.

Major, B. (1993), "Gender, Entitlement and the Distribution of Family Labor," *Journal of Social Sciences*, Vol. 49, No. 3, pp. 141-59.

Majumdar, S.K. (1995), "Public, Joint and Private Sectors in Indian Industry : Evaluating Relative Performance Differences,' *Economic and Political Weekly* 18-25 February, pp. M-25 - M -32

Majumdar, S.K. (1996), "Fall and Rise of Productivity in Indian Industry," *Economic and Political Weekly,* 30 November, pp. M-46 - M-53.

Mehta, S.R. (1997), "Postscript : Can India Attain Sustainable Development Through The Pangs of Poverty and Population Growth?", in S.R. Mehta (ed.). *Poverty, Population & Sustainable Development*, Rawat Publishers : Jaipur, Chapter 21.

Misra, S.D. and Saxena, K.K. (1997), "Structural Change in Cost Shares of Primary Inputs of Indian Industries : An Input-Output Approach," *The Indian Journal of Economics,* Vol. 77 Part 4, pp. 43-472.

Nussbaum, M.C. (1993), "Non-Relative Virtues : An Aristotelian Approach," in M.C. Nussbaum and A. Sen (eds.), *The Quality of Life*, Clarendon Press, Oxford, pp. 242-76.

Nussbaum, M.C. and Sen, A. (1993), "Introduction", in M.C. Nussbaum and A. Sen (eds.), *The Quality of Life*, Clarendon Press, Oxford, pp. 1-6.

O'Neill, O. (1993), "Justice, Gender, and International Boundaries," in M.C. Nussbaum and A. Sen (eds.), *The Quality of Life*, Clarendon Press, Oxford, pp. 303-23.

Pal, S. (1996), "Casual and Regular Contracts : Workers' Self-selection in the Rural Labour Markets in India," *Journal of Development Studies* Vol. 33, No. 1, pp. 99-117.

Pal, S. (1997), "An Analysis of Declining Incidence of Regular Labour Contracts in Rural India," *Journal of Development Studies*, Vol. 34, No. 2, pp. 133-56.

Pal, S. (1999), "Tasked-based Segmentation of Rural Labour Contracts : Theory and Evidence", *Bulletin of Economic Research*, Vol. 51, No. 2, pp. 67-88.

Panwar, B. and Punia, D. (1998), "Nutrient Intake of Rural Pregnant Women of Haryana State, Northern India : Relationship between Income and Education," *International Journal of Food Sciences and Nutrition*, Vol. 49, No. 5, pp. 391-400.

Papanek, H. (1990), "To Each Less Than She Needs From Each More Than She Can Do : Allocations, Entitlements and Value," in Irene Tinker (ed.), *Persistent Inequalities : Women and World Development*, Oxford University Press, New York, Chapter 10.

Paul, S. (1998), "The Performance Of The Integrated Rural Development Programme In India : An Assessment," *The Developing Economies*, Vol. 36, No. 2, pp. 117-31.

Pettit, P. (1998) "Institutional Design and Rational Choice" in R.E. Goodin (ed.), *The Theory of Institutional Design*, Cambridge University Press Cambridge, Chapter 2.

Parker, K. (1995), "The Behaviour of Private Investment," in A. Chopra, C. Collyns, R. Hemming and K. Parker, *India : Economic Reform and Growth,* Occasional Paper No. 134, International Monetary Fund, Washington DC, Chapter 6.

Ramamurthy, P. (1994),"Partiarchy and the Process of Agricultural Intensification in South India," in Alice W. Clark (ed.), *Gender and Political Economy : Exploration of South Asian Systems*, Oxford University Press, Delhi, Chapter 6.

Rao, C.H. Hanumantha (1992), "Agriculture : Policy and Performance," in Bimal Jalan (ed.), *The Indian Economy Problems and Prospects*, Penguin Books New Delhi, Chapter 4.

Rao, J. M. (1997), "Agricultural Development Under State Planning," in Terence J. Byres (ed.), *The State, Development Planning and Liberalisation in India*, Oxford University Press, Delhi, Chapter 4.

Roy, K. and Tisdell, C. (1996), "Women in South Asia with Particular Reference to India," in K.C. Roy, C. Tisdell and H.C. Blomqvist (eds.), *Economic Development and Women in The World Community,* Prager : Westport, Connecticut, Chapter 2.

Sarma, A. (1995), "Performance of Public Enterprises in India," in Dilip Mookherjee (ed.), *Indian Industry : Policies and Performance*, Oxford University Press, Delhi, pp. 289-321.

Sen, A. (1990), "Gender and Co-operative Conflicts" in Irene Tinker (ed.), *Persistent Inequalities : Women and Development*, Oxford University Press, New York, Chapter 8.

Sen, A. (1993), "Capability and Well-Being," in M.C. Nussbaum, and A. Sen (eds.), *The Quality of Life*, Clarendon Press : Oxford, Chapter 2.

Shinoda, T. (1996), "Morphology of India's Urbanization," *The Developing Economies*, Vol. 34, No. 4, pp. 520-49.

Staub, E. (1991), "A Conception of the Determinants and Development of Altruism Ad Aggression : Motives, the Self and the Environment", in C. Zahn-Waxler, E.M. Cummings and R. Iannotti (eds.), *Altruism and Aggression : Biological and social origins*, Cambridge University Press, Cambridge, Chapter 5.

Stern, N. (1991), "Public Policy and the Economics of Development", *European Economic Review*, Vol. 35, pp. 241-71.

Subramanian, S. and Deaton, A. (1996), "The Demand for Food and Calories," *Journal of Political Economy*, Vol. 104, No. 1, pp. 133-62.

Vecchio, N. and Roy, K.C. (1998), *Poverty, Female Headed Households, and Sustainable Development*, Greenwood Press, Westport.

Woolcock, M. (1998), "Social Capital and Economic Development : Towards a Theoretical Synthesis and Policy Framework," *Theory and Society* Vol. 27, No. 2, pp. 151-208.

World Bank, (1989), *India, Poverty, Employment, and Social Services*. Country Economic Memorandum, Washington D.C.

World Bank, (1997), India : Achievements and Challenges in Reducing Poverty, World Bank : Washington DC.

APPENDIX A

Selected Indicators for Major Indian States

State	Population 1991 (Million)	Life expectancy at birth 1990-92		Death rate for 0-4 age group 1991	Total Fertility Rate 1991	Female-male ratio 1991	Literacy rate in 7+ age group 1991		Rural literacy rate in 10-14 age group 1987-88		Incidence of poverty 1987-88 (Head-count ratio)	
		Female	Male				Female	Male	Female	Male	Rural	Urban
Kerla	29.1	74.4	68.8	4.3	1.8	1,036	86	94	98	98	44.0	44.5
Himachal Pradesh	5.2	n/a	n/a	19.3	3.1	976	52	75	81	95	24.8	3.3
Maharashtra	78.9	64.7	63.1	16.3	3.0	934	52	77	68	86	54.2	35.6
Tamil Nadu	55.9	63.2	61.0	16.1	2.2	974	51	74	71	85	51.3	39.2
Punjab	20.3	67.5	65.4	17.0	3.1	882	50	66	69	76	21.0	11.2
Gujarat	41.3	61.3	59.1	23.3	3.1	934	49	73	61	78	41.6	38.8
West Bengal	68.1	62.0	60.5	20.6	3.2	917	47	68	61	69	57.2	30.6
Karnataka	45.0	63.6	60.0	23.6	3.1	960	44	67	56	74	42.3	45.0
Assam	22.4	n/a	n/a	32.4	3.5	923	43	62	78	83	53.1	11.4
Haryana	16.5	63.6	62.2	23.0	4.0	865	41	69	63	87	23.2	18.3
Orissa	31.7	54.8	55.9	39.0	3.3	971	35	63	51	70	65.6	44.5
Andhra Pradesh	66.5	61.5	59.0	21.3	3.0	972	33	55	42	66	31.6	40.0
Madhya Pradesh	66.2	53.5	54.1	44.5	4.6	931	29	58	40	68	49.8	46.0
Uttar Pradesh	139.1	54.6	56.8	35.6	5.1	879	25	56	39	68	47.7	41.9
Bihar	86.4	58.3	n/a	22.8	4.4	911	23	52	34	59	66.3	56.7
Rajasthan	44.0	57.8	57.6	30.9	4.6	910	20	55	22	72	41.9	41.5
INDIA	846.3	59.4	59.0	26.5	3.6	927	39	64	52	73	44.9	36.5

Source : J. Dreze and A. Sen (1995), *India : Economic Development and Social Opportunity*, p. 47 table 3.3, Oxford University Press, New Delhi.

APPENDIX B

Human Development Index (HDI) and Gender-related Development Index (GDI) for Indian States

	Population (millions)	Female-male Ratio	Life expectancy at birth (years)		Adult literacy rate (%)		Share of earned income (%)		Per capita state domestic product (Rs./year)	Human development index (HDI)	Gender-related development index
			Females	Males	Females	Males	Females	Males			
	1991	1991	1990-92		1991				1991-92		
	(1)	(2)	(3)	(4)	(5)	(6)	(7)	(8)	(9)	(10)	(11)
1. Kerala	29	1036	74.4	68.8	80.6	91.7	12.4	87.6	4,618	0.603	0.565
2. Maharashtra	79	634	64.7	63.1	44.2	74.4	29.4	70.6	8,180	0.523	0.492
3. Gujarat	41	934	61.3	59.1	41.8	70.4	26.8	73.2	6,425	0.467	0.437
4. Himachal Pradesh	5	976	64.2	63.8	35.5	64.4	37.5	62.5	5,355	0.454	0.432
5. Punjab	20	882	67.5	65.4	41.8	60.5	5.9	94.1	9,643	0.529	0.424
6. Karnataka	45	960	63.6	60.0	37.7	65.3	25.4	74.6	5,555	0.448	0.417
7. Tamil Nadu	56	974	63.2	61.0	35.8	65.0	21.4	78.6	5,078	0.438	0.402
8. West Bengal	68	917	62.0	60.5	42.8	69.3	8.0	92.0	5,383	0.459	0.399
9. Andhra Pradesh	67	972	61.5	59.0	27.3	52.4	27.2	72.8	5,570	0.400	0.371
10. Haryana	16	865	63.6	62.2	27.0	64.3	7.0	93.0	8,690	0.489	0.370
11 Assam	22	923	53.8	54.6	33.9	62.4	23.7	76.3	4,230	0.379	0.347
12. Orissa	32	971	54.8	55.9	29.0	62.5	19.1	80.9	4,068	0.373	0.329
13. Madhya Pradesh	66	931	53.5	54.1	24.3	56.6	25.4	74.6	4,077	0.349	0.312
14. Rajasthan	44	910	57.8	57.6	17.5	52.7	23.0	77.0	4,361	0.365	0.309
15. Bihar	86	911	58.3	60.4	18.2	55.3	21.8	78.2	2,904	0.354	0.306
16. Uttar Pradesh	139	879	54.6	56.8	20.6	53.6	12.9	87.1	4,012	0.348	0.293
INDIA	846	927	59.4	59.0	33.9	62.4	23.2	76.8	5,583	0.423	0.388

Source : C.S. La Rue (ed.), *The Indian handbook, Prospects into the 21st Century*, 1997, p. 200 table 13 : 4, Fitzroy Dearborn Publishers, USA.

APPENDIX C

Number of women participating in specified activities per thousand of women usually engaged in household duties (principal status), 1987-88 (all India rural).

Activities		Per 1000 Women		
		Subsidiary Activity		
		With	Without	All
(1)		(2)	(3)	(4)
1.	Maintenance of kitchen garden, etc.	217	149	163
2.	Work in household poultry, etc.	536	279	330
Sub-total	1 and/or 2	593	336	387
3.	Free collection of fish, etc	321	184	212
4.	Free collection of firewood, etc.	593	359	405
Sub-total	3 and/or 4	633	384	434
Sub-total	Any one or more of 1 to 4	841	536	597
5.	Husking of paddy (own produce)	203	171	178
6.	Grinding of foodgrains (own produce)	185	172	175
	Preparation of gur (own produce)	12	9	9
	Preservation of meat, etc. (own produce)	8	7	7
	Making baskets, etc. (own produce)	30	24	25
Sub-total	Any one or more of 5 to 9	289	248	256
Sub-total	Any one or more of 1 to 9	869	614	665
	Husking of paddy (acquired)	71	73	72
	Grinding of foodgrains (acquired)	128	103	108
	Preparation of gur (acquired)	45	71	66
	Preservation of meat, etc. (acquired)	49	71	67
	Making baskets, etc. (acquired)	49	72	67
	Preparation of cowdung cakes	596	500	519
	Sewing, tailoring, etc.	206	192	195
	Tutoring of own children	32	37	36
	Bringing water from outside household premises	714	582	608
19.	Bringing water from outside village			
	(a) Distance up to 1km	40	24	27
	(b) Distance 2-5 km	2	2	2
	(c) Distance 6+km	2	1	1
	(d) All	44	27	30
Total	Any one or more of 1 to 19	928	865	877
Number of women engaged in household duties per 1,000 women		69	279	348

Source : V.M. Dandekar (1996) *The Indian Economy* 1947-92, *Volume* II : *Population, Poverty And Employment*, Chapter 10, Sage Publications India Pvt. Ltd., New Delhi.

9 Impediments to Women's Empowerment in Rural India : Access to Employment, Land and Other Resources

K.C. Roy

Introduction

In India, slightly over seventy per cent of total population live in rural areas. Slightly less than fifty per cent of total population are females. This would mean that nearly 700 million out of 1 billion people live in rural areas. Generally, people in the rural areas are poorer than those in the urban areas because of the absence of non-agricultural employment opportunities. Amongst males and females, females are poorer than males because the technological change in agriculture displaces females from many of their traditional jobs, and now agricultural employment opportunities are more limited for females than for males. Also due to gender restriction, illiteracy and ignorance, rural women are unable to go outside the surroundings of their homes in search of employment. Making women economically independent is crucial to achieving women's empowerment, which is central for achieving sustainable development. Improvement in the socio-economic status of women can reduce population growth which can reduce pressure on the environment, which in turn can lead to sustainable development.

Increases in women's income and income earning opportunities improve the family's living standard, enhance the family's social status, raise the age of marriage, reduce the pressure on women's health and time and on them to have more children. Property rights, availability of credits, inputs, and marketing facilities make poor women more independent economically and facilitate the process of sustainable growth and development of the country. In this paper we examine the issues affecting rural women's access to employment, land, other resources and markets.

Gender Discrimination and Poverty of Rural Women

Poor women in rural societies appear in one way or another to be prisoners of social taboos which make them lose their self-confidence, control over their own income and even control over their own lives. (Hartman and Boyce, 1983). Despite considerable class, cultural and regional differences, rural households in all counties in the sub-continent, tend to exemplify a 'classic patriarchy' which implies the shelter of women in a highly hierarchical domestic realm. It also implies control by men of some of the joint patrimony in land, animals or commercial capital (Kandiyoti, 1985). Thus, the imposition of gender discrimination on women embodied in the 'classic patriarchy' prevents them from becoming economically independent and tends to keep them under perpetual poverty. Apart from experiencing discrimination outside their homes, women also experience intra-family discrimination. The degree of anti-female bias in poor families tends to be inversely related to the female's effective contribution to the total family income and to the amount of dowry that her family members would be required to pay at the time of her marriage. The female's contribution can be considered effective if her work is socially visible and socially recognised as valuable. However, as Agarwal (1989) notes, agricultural fieldwork, which is more visible than home-based work, and work which brings in earnings which is economically more visible than collection of non-market goods from CPRs and PPRs and household duties appear to be given a higher social valuation.

Sen and Sengupta (1983) note that higher gender discrimination was found among those landless families in which boys are more involved in socially visible and recognised earning activities, whereas the girls were engaged in processing goods from CPRs, although the total time spent in both activities did not differ much between the sexes. Also, it was found that in small peasant households with the improvement in economic conditions, when the female members were withdrawn from productive field-work, the marriage price of socially perceived unproductive female members increased, although they simply switched their work from field to indoor (Epstein, 1973). Apart from these disadvantages, women also experience intra-family discrimination. Agarwal's (1989) study indicates the pressure of (i) gender based inequalities in the distribution of resources for fulfilling the basic needs, (ii) differences in household spending patterns, with women's earnings much more than men's going to the family's basic needs in poor households and (iii) of a strong link in poor households between the nutritional status of children and the mother's earnings. It was also found that within the family, adult females, adolescent girls and small female children receive less vitamins and minerals through food allocations in both North and South India and also receive less protein and calories in parts of North India than their male counterparts (Harris, 1986).

During illness men receive medical treatment more promptly than women and more females than males receive no treatment at all (Dandekar, 1975). In a survey it has been found that in Bihar ninety per cent of the Landless Labourers interviewed, felt that they did not get enough food and over half of them suffered physically and from malnutrition in varying degrees. During crisis periods such as floods, malnutrition was found to be higher among girls than boys (Prasad, 1981).

The type of agricultural work undertaken by women exposes them to greater health risk than men. Thus, during the rainy season, rice planting, which is done mostly by women, can make them suffer from intestinal infections, arthritis, rheumatic joints, leech bites etc. (Mencher and Saradamoni, 1982). Also, due to the total absence of leisure from their daily routine, poor women are more susceptible to diseases than men.

Extensive research (Roy, Tisdell and Blomqvist, 1996; Roy and Clark, 1994; Roy and Tisdell, 1993a, b; Agarwal, 1989; Bhalla, 1989; Chambers, 1988; Chen, 1989; Duvvury, 1989; Rao, 1991; Roy, Tisdell and Sen, 1992; Jodha, 1986; Roy and Tisdell, 1996) on women's socio-economic status in rural India, found that these women have reached the end of their carrying capacity and that the empowerment of women is a fundamental requirement for sustainable development. The above noted review of gender discrimination faced by women and of poverty of rural women would seem to suggest that in their struggle for subsistence, poor rural women suffer from (i) their diminishing access to common property resources (CPRs) and minor forest produces (MFPs); (ii) lack of control over land; (iii) lack of command over inputs and technology and (iv) cultural barriers which stem from social customs, prejudices, taboos and institutional biases towards men.

Access to Employment

Women generally are much more disadvantaged in their access to employment than men for the following reasons :

(1) Women's job mobility is limited because they have to take care of their children, they are confined to the surroundings of their homes due to the "ideology of seclusion" and they are vulnerable to class and caste related sexual abuse;

(2) Because of their lower literacy levels, lesser access to mass media and lesser interaction with the market place, women have limited access to information on job opportunities;

(3) Men are hired for permanent work such as ploughing, buying inputs, selling products, and for night work such as irrigation and guarding crops. Women are socially excluded from such work;

(4) Introduction of mechanised cultivation has displaced women who have hardly been trained in the use of machineries and have thus remained confined to manual tasks (Agarwal, 1988).

These factors also explain why women are concentrated in casual agricultural work and in the informal sector in some non-agricultural work such as petty trading in markets closer to their home, although they could obtain better income at distant markets and in the formal sector in industrial employment (Banerjee, 1985).

Female-headed households appear to be more adversely affected by gender biases in employment and wages and, in general, are found to have much less access to and control over land, greater dependency on wage labour for employment, and a lower level of education and literacy than households headed by men. Widespread sexual exploitation by landlords, employers and creditors to whom the household is indebted, also appear to take place in the rural sector.

Female Labour Force Participation

A World Bank Study (1992) reveals that female labour force participation rates range from 47 per cent in Maharashtra to 4 per cent in Kashmir. The highest overall participation ratios are in the south, the western, and the central states which are not all rice producers but have large semi-arid areas suitable for coarse grain production or with irrigation, for industrial crops such as sugarcane and cotton. The wheat producing North, and specifically, the leading "Green Revolution" states of Haryana and the Punjab, have very low rates of female participation. But so do the agriculturally stagnating rice producing states of Bihar and West Bengal. This trend is noticed despite the fact that the percentage of population below the poverty line in only 15 per cent in Punjab and 25 per cent in Haryana, but 57 per cent in Bihar and 52 per cent in West Bengal. Therefore, we would have expected that the female labour force participation rates would be higher in Bihar and West Bengal.

On the other hand, in the two Northern states where subsistence agriculture is still dominant, Rajasthan and Himachal Pradesh, women's participation rates are also extremely high.

Overall since the beginning of the 1970s, female labour force participation rates have shown a small but unmistakable increase for all India and in most of the major states. While this has been true in both urban and rural areas, increases have been greater in rural areas than in urban areas. The proportion of female to male workers has also increased though again the shift has been more noticeable in the rural areas. While the sex ratio of all females to male workers increased since the 1970s, the ratio in agriculture moved from 25 to 32 between 1971 and 1981 (World Bank, 1992). This may have been due to the combined effects of HYV technologies (at least in the first phase of the green revolution) which appear to have led to greater overall use of female than male labour, and the movement of men into non-farm employment. Given the deep socio-cultural preferences to keep women out of the workforce, this rise in female agricultural labour participation may be a supply-driven phenomenon and a sign of economic distress. However, more recent studies indicate that the rise in female labour force may be positively related to higher growth in agriculture. Also the rise in real agricultural wage rates, evidence of shorter work days and the narrowing of the gap between male and female wage rates suggest that the increase in female workforce participation rates may also be demand driven. Along with the rise in women agricultural workers, there has also been a rapid increase in the proportion of women cultivators who work as unpaid family workers in field crop production.

However, despite the increase in female labour force participation rates, female agricultural labourers are among the poorer sections of the Indian society with the lowest wage levels and highest unemployment. With 61 per cent below the poverty line, female casual labourers in rural areas show the highest incidence of poverty of any occupational category, male or female. Because of their relative lack of mobility or marketable skills as 90 per cent of them are unskilled and 88 per cent are illiterate, these women are the most vulnerable to seasonal fluctuations in labour demand (World Bank, 1992).

However, what is necessary for women's empowerment is opportunities for more permanent employment, but such opportunities unfortunately have not been created. Rural women are also not being absorbed in many of the jobs outside agriculture that are developing in the rural areas, partly because this employment often requires mobility and specific skills that women do not have, but also because women have not been socialised to seek out and adapt to non-traditional work situations. However, women's capacity to acquire skills and increase mobility may also be constrained by the force of the "ideology of seclusion."

Even if a woman possesses adequate skills she may not be able to leave the confines of home to look for some permanent employment elsewhere due to the "ideology of seclusion."

Field Survey

A field survey was undertaken by the author to ascertain how the "ideology of seclusion" acts as an impediment to women's search for employment and social mobility. The survey was undertaken in Shalboni — a village in a tribal area in Midnapore District in West Bengal, India. Only educated females with university degrees were chosen for the interview. Among the respondents there were both tribal and non-tribal females. Since a road connects Shalboni to the district town, Midnapore, local females are able to travel daily by bus to Midnapore (26 kilometres away) to complete their university degree in colleges and in the university. 36 degree holder females were interviewed. All had bachelor degrees. The results of the survey are presented in table 1.

It can be seen from the table that for all the questions relating to the impediments to search for employment, the affirmative response was 100 per cent. All the 36 respondents agreed that (i) the "ideology of seclusion" prevents women from obtaining information about employment; (ii) in rural areas, due to derogatory social customs, women's travel to distant places is prevented; (iii) even if an offer of employment is secured, the offer may not be accepted because of the force of the "ideology of seclusion;" (iv) the "ideology of seclusion" keeps latent qualities of women relatively undeveloped and (v) that due to their gender, women could not undertake job oriented technical education at places which are at considerable distance from their homes.

Table 1 : Impediments to Educated Rural Women's Search for Employment and Social Mobility

		Search for Employment	Total Interviewed (1)	Yes Response (2)	Not Responded (3)	2 as % of 1 (4)
1		"iedology of seclusion" prevents women from obtaining information about employment	36	36		100
2		In rural areas, due to derogatory social customs, women's travel to distant places to search for employment is prevented	36	36		100
3		Even if an offer of employment is secured, the position may not be accepted because of the force of the "iedology of seclusion"	36	36		100
4		"iedology of seclusion" keeps women's latent qualities relatively undeveloped	36	36		100
5		Because one is female - one could not take job oriented education at distant places	36	36		100
6		**Social Mobility** Is the freedom of movement necessary for a female to utilise opportunities for her development	36	36		100
7		Your family does not allow you much freedom	36	26	10	72.2
8		What would be the consequences if you decide to move freely?				
	i	Unemployed neighbourhood youths will jeer you	36	16	00	44.4
	ii	Village and neighbourhood elders will circulate slander and gossip about you	36	22	14	61.1
	iii	Parents would be subject of neighbourhood gossip	36	25	11	69.4
	iv	Parents will be scolded by your grandparents	36	26	12	72.2
	v	Your loss of freedom and tension may affect your mind and health and you may feel that you are a burden on your family	36	26	12	72.2
	vi	Parents also would feel that you are a liability to them	36	26	12	72.2

In answer to the questions relating to the impediments to social mobility, 100 per cent said that it is necessary for them to have freedom of movement without which they cannot utilise opportunities for their development. Slightly over 72 per cent agreed that their families do not allow them that freedom. In response to the question : what would be the consequences if you decide to move freely, 44.4 per cent said, unemployed youths of the neighbourhood will jeer at them. More than 61 per cent agreed that village and neighbourhood elders would circulate slander and gossip about them. More than 69 per cent agreed that their parents would be the subjects of neighbourhood gossip. More than 72 per cent agreed that (i) their parents will be scolded by their grandparents; (ii) their loss of freedom and the consequent tension may affect their mind and health and they may feel that they are burdens on their families and (iii) most parents also would feel that they are a liability to them.

This field study, therefore, suggests that women's access to employment is seriously compromised by the presence of the "ideology of seclusion" in the rural sector. Hence, measures must be taken along with others to weaken the force of the "ideology of seclusion."

Access to Land

Customary access to land has been largely confined to male household members. Agarwal's study (1988) based on ethnographic information culled from village stories, gives an idea of women's customary land access across regionally among 145 village communities where the households had some access to land as owners or tenants. The study shows that in 131 or 90 per cent of the communities the access to land is clearly patrilineal. Only in 10 communities or 7 per cent of the villages the access to land is matrilineal. This is found in North East India, particularly in Meghalaya and Assam, and in South West in Kerala. Under the old and traditional Hindu law women did not have inheritance rights to land but could enjoy life interest in ancestral property as widows and daughters in son-less families. However, with respect to agricultural land, in most states, the religious law was superseded by regionally prevailing customary law under which women were usually excluded. Among some of the matrilineal tribal communities such as Garos and Khasis in the North East, the Nayans and Mapphilas in Kerala and the Nagudi Vellaras in Tamil Nadu, women's legal inheritance rights to land were conditional on women remaining in their parental home or village and the husband joining or visiting her there. However, over time even these traditional rights have been systematically eroded (Agarwal, 1989). The decline in matriline in the North-East among the Garos was due to changes in state practice and in agricultural practice from shifting cultivation to settled agriculture. This shift from shifting cultivation to settled agriculture and land privatisation has, to a considerable extent, been responsible for the marginalisation of female labour, the registration of private plots in male names and the systematic deprivation of Garo women of their traditional land rights (Agarwal, 1987).

Other Barriers to Women's Access to Legal Shares in Land

Although women's legal rights to land are being recognised since Indian independence, the nature of these rights seem to vary according to the personal laws of different religious communities and regions. As a result, women's legal rights are not applied uniformly throughout the country and are still not on equal terms with men's everywhere. Furthermore, circumstances prevent women from exercising even their limited ownership rights to land and their right to control and independently farm land to which they do have access.

For example, in Northern India where village exogamy and long distance marriages are widely practised, such personal and religious laws impose limitations on women's capacity to exercise direct control over the land they may have inherited or obtained as a gift from their natal villages and also make them dependent on their brothers to maintain a link with their natal village to have access to their land after their fathers' death to provide social, economic and even physical security in the case of ill-treatment by their husbands and marriage breakups — as well as to play the ritual role of maternal uncle in their children's weddings. Recently women, to maintain the link with their mothers, tend to give up their rights in favour of their brothers (Argarwal, 1989).

There are examples of cases where women as sisters and daughters did not voluntarily give up their rights of inheritance in favour of their male kins, they had resorted to various methods of circumventing modern laws such as forging father's wills after his death (Parry, 1979) or appealing to revenue authorities with the argument that their sister is wealthy and does not need land or that she is an absentee landlord (Mayer, 1960). Unmarried and widowed women become subject to various forms of harassment by their male kin. These may involve expensive litigation which may force them to mortgage their land to pay for legal expenses or threats against their lives if they want to pursue the rights to land through the court. There are examples where direct violence was resorted to to prevent women from filing their claims or from exercising their customary rights. (Kishwar, 1987). Official policies also tend to strengthen the traditional attitude which has antifemale bias. These tend to affect court judgement and implementation of government policies. For example, when landless women in Udaipur district in Rajasthan claimed a part of the village wasteland to grow herbs and fodder, the local official said that land would not be allotted to women. In answer to the question why not, the answer was that women had never been allotted land, that is why they won't allot land to women (Lal, 1986). Even among the Garos in North East India, although women had inheritance rights, under the land privatisation programme of the state government, the title deeds granted to individuals have been in names of males (Agarwal, 1989).

Access to Resources, Land Management

First we discuss the issues relating to poor women's access to land. Even when poor women do inherit land, it is difficult for them to exercise control over the land. For example, in villages where village exogamy and long distance marriages are the norm, women who inherit land as daughters may find it very difficult to cultivate the land from their husbands' homes which are located at considerable distance from their natal villages. The "ideology of seclusion" by restricting their interaction with male strangers

(Afshar and Agarwal, 1988) makes it difficult for them to obtain information on agricultural practices, purchasing inputs, hiring labour and machinery to plough the fields and selling the produce etc. On the other hand, since men's movements are not restricted, their contact socially with other men enables them to obtain labour and other inputs in time or to seek help from other cultivators. Also because, women cultivators cannot provide reciprocal labour as men cultivators, they cannot easily obtain labour of their relatives. Women's ability to obtain credit and other agricultural inputs is severely restricted because of their inability, due to the "ideology of seclusion," their ignorance and illiteracy, to travel to towns where most credit institutions, input-co-operatives and Development Block offices are located. At the same time it is difficult for them to get loans from the village money lenders due to their perception that men have greater capacity to repay the loan as they can get wage work to repay the debt. However, such impediments to women's access to resources are not so prevalent in North Eastern states and Southern states of India where females' participation in agricultural field work is much higher than in other parts of India and females are less confined to the surroundings of their homes. Women's ability to self-manage land is also generally limited due to their lack of financial capacity to purchase agricultural technology, other inputs and taboos against women ploughing which almost totally makes them dependent on men for cultivating their land and thereby reduces significantly their ability to become independent farmers.

Credit Availability

Access to credit and agricultural extension are therefore the most fundamental requirements for women to become successful cultivators and to be productively self-employed. However, since land has been the main source of collateral, women's lack of land ownership has prevented them from having access to the formal financial system, thus limiting their ability to acquire other productive resources such as cattle, poultry, looms or working capital for trade in farm or forestry purchase, food processing etc. However, since the disbursement and repayment statistics are not available separately for men and women, it is not possible to get precise national, state or institutional data on women's relative access to the formal credit system. National data of the government of India's credit-based poverty alleviation scheme (IRDP) relate to the number of female beneficiaries not to the actual disbursements.

These data show that although female coverage rose by 5 per cent over 1985/86, less than 15 per cent of the beneficiaries were women in 1986/87 — barely half of the target of 30 per cent. Furthermore, a study of credit flows by gender in a regional rural bank branch and a commercial bank branch, in one district in Andhra Pradesh suggests that even in other government-sponsored credit programmes, women's access to credit is still lower and disbursements to women ranged between 6 per cent and 12 per cent overall, but dropped to zero for agricultural term loans and agricultural cash credit (World Bank, 1992). In such a situation, women's access to credit can be improved by (1) introducing fundamental changes in the banking system and (2) establishing a special women's credit fund. Banks would need more autonomy, responsibility and an interest rate which will make it profitable for them to serve the poor. The IRDP credit also should allow the poor ongoing access to finance system in return for repayment and should include deposit facilities and other services.

Agricultural Extension

As far as the agricultural extension programmes are concerned, the present system largely by-passes 48 per cent of India's self-employed farmers who are women. Making the states' agricultural extension services more accessible and responsible to women farmers, is clearly necessary to increase returns on government investment. Most of the pilot projects which were able to reach women, had hired female extension workers. This would tend to suggest that this approach won't be necessary throughout the country for all projects. However, in areas where male extension workers serve female clients, there may be the need for initial assistance from female "spearhead" to help reorganise groups of farmers. There is also the need for specially trained female Subject Matter Specialists (SMS) who would monitor the needs of local farmers, communicate those to research scientists and propose a special extension service that responds to women's problems with the best technology available (World Bank, 1992).

To make extension services serve both men and women farmers, it is necessary to make all research and extension staff aware of the important role women play in the production system and of the loss of efficiency that would result from the failure to reach them directly. While it may be more difficult to reach women in northern India because of the widespread practice of 'Purdah' in U.P. as well as of the increasing technical and managerial complexity of farming in Harryana and Punjab, the extension system, especially if it works through local women's groups formed and supported by NGOS, producers' cooperatives etc., can reach women who are confined to the surroundings of their homes, and have the lowest level of access to services and resources among all groups. Agricultural extension by enhancing women's social interaction increases their exposure to new agricultural technologies, new processes of decision-making and thereby can increase women's ability to manage their farms effectively.

Agricultural Research and Technology

Agricultural research and infrastructure development to support agricultural intensification and diversification can increase the overall demand for labour and reduce seasonal fluctuations. Thus increase in irrigation coverage by shifting to less water-intensive crops and a wider and more careful distribution of water resources, can increase females' employment. Also other measures such as production of female labour-intensive cotton crop, high value non-cereal crops, vegetables, fruits, nuts, non-timber products and expansion of allied enterprises such as poultry farming and dairying can considerably increase the demand for female labour. However, in regard to the development of technology the interests of female labourers and female cultivators are different. While female labourers want greater development and application of labour intensive technology, female cultivators want labour-saving technology which will make less demand on their own time and reduce the need for hired labour. However, in agricultural research priorities, if greater emphasis is placed on agricultural diversification, it will be beneficial to both women labourers and small and marginal farmers.

Concluding Remarks

In this paper we have examined impediments to women's empowerment in rural India and discussed the issues affecting women's access to employment, land and other resources. The forces of the "ideology of seclusion" and the associated constraints on women's access to resources seem to be stronger among the upper caste Hindus than among secluded caste and tribes and stronger among land-holding cultivators than among marginal farmers and landless labourers. But changes in women's socio-economic status which would help the empowerment process, can be brought about by appropriate policy changes and effective implementation of policies — which create employment opportunities, grant effective land rights to women, and provide access to credit, agricultural extension and research and technology etc. However, women's capacity to become economically independent, would remain severely constrained unless the forces of the "ideology of seclusion" are weakened. The efforts which facilitate unlimited access for women to investments in human capital, to the factors of Production, to productive assets and product markets and to social organisation that facilitate such access, are important. Access to investments in human capital includes, education, health care, skill training and extension advice.

In the long run, access to education is the most powerful tool to equip women for effective interaction with both the social service and productive dimensions of the outside world. However, it has to be noted that except in Kerala and perhaps in a few other states, hardly any education is imparted in schools in the vast rural hinterlands of India. Moreover formal education of younger children would not reduce the force of "ideology of seclusion" unless those who enforce those gender restrictions were also educated. This would require non-formal community education of family and village elders. But NGOs would need to be involved in the implementation of such schemes. Access to factors includes access to credit, entry to and mobility within labour markets, and ownership of and effective utilisation rights to land. However, efforts to grant women effective rights to land would continue to face still resistance and opposition. Without appropriate institutional charges such forces cannot be weakened, but only appropriate community education can gradually weaken these forces. Access to assets includes technology, inputs and raw materials and access to markets includes their ability to buy essential goods and services and sell their final products at true market prices.

In this paper we have examined the more important issues affecting women's access to employment, land and their access to credit and other resources. Action is necessary in all these areas if women's empowerment process in rural India is to succeed. Professor Anartya Sen (The Asian Age, 1996) said that the solution to India's problems of population and development lies in social development in a gender sensitive way. That social development can only come through women's empowerment.

REFERENCES

Afshar, H. and Agarwal, B. Eds. (1988), Women, Poverty and Ideology in Asia : Contradictory Pressures, Uneasy Resolutions, London : Macmillan.

Agarwal, B. (1987), "Maternity in Transition : The Garos, Khasis and Lalungs in North-East India" (Mimeo) New Delhi : Institute of Economic Growth.

Agarwal, B. (1989), "Rural Women, Poverty and Natural Resources," *Economic and Political Weekly*, 24(43).

Agarwal, B. (1988), "Who Sows, Who Reaps? Women and Land Rights in India," *The Journal of Peasant Studies*, 15(4).

Banerjee, S. and Kothari, S. (1985), "A General Profile of Food and Hunger in India," *The Ecologist*, 15(5, 6).

Bhalla, S. (1989), "Technological Change and Women Workers, Evidence From the Expansionary Phase in Haryana Agriculture," *Economic and Political Weekly*, 24(43).

Chambers, R. (1988), "Poverty in India : Concepts, Research and Reality," Discussion Paper 241, University of Sussex : Institute of Development Studies.

Chen, M. (1989), "Women's Work in Indian Agriculture by Agro-Processing Zones : Meeting Needs of Landless and Landpoor Women," *Economic and Political Weekly*, 24(43).

Dandekar, K. (1975), "Has the Proportion of Women in Indian Population Been Declining?" *Economic and Political Weekly*, October 18.

Duvvury, N. (1989), "Women in Agriculture : A Review of the Indian Literature," *Economic and Political Weekly*, 24(43).

Epstein, T.S. (1973), South India Yesterday, *Today and Tomorrow*, London : Macmillan.

Harris, J. (1987), "Capitalism and Peasant Production : The Green Revolution in India," in Shanin, T. (ed.), *Peasants and Peasant Societies*, Oxford : Blackwell.

Hartman, B. and Boyce, J.K. (1983), A Quiet Violence : View from a Bangladesh Village, London : Zed.

Jodha, N.S. (1986), "Common Property Resources and the Rural Poor," *Economic and Political Weekly*, 21(27).

Kandiyoti, D. (1985), Women in Rural Production Systems, Paris : UNESCO.

Khandekar, S.R. and Binswanger (1989), "The Effect of Formal Credit on Output in Rural India," PHR Working Paper Series, Washington D.C. : World Bank.

Kishwar, M. (1987), "Toiling Without Rights : Ho Women of Singbhum," *Economic and Political Weekly*" 24 (31).

Lal, I. (1986), "Goats and Tigers; A Video Film by Ian Lal," New Delhi : ILO.

Manimala (1983), "Zameen Kenkar? Jote Onkar", Manushi No. 14, January-February.

Mayer, A.C. (1960), Caste and Kinship in Central India — A Village and Its Region, London : Routledge and Kegan Paul.

Mehra, R. and Saradmoni, K. (1983), *Women and Rural Transformation*, New Delhi : Concept Publishing Co.

Mencher, J. and Saradamoni, K. (1982), "Muddy Feet and Dirty Hands : Rice Production and Female Agricultural Labour," *Economic and Political Weekly*, December 5.

Parry, J.P. (1979), Caste and Kinship in Kangra, New Delhi : Vikas Publishing House.

Prasad, P.H. Rodgers, E.B. Gupta, S.L. Sharma, A.N. and Sharma, B. (1981), "The Pattern of Poverty in Bihar," World Employment Program Working Paper, No. 152, Geneva : ILO.

Rao, C.H.H. (1991), "Rural Society and Agricultural Development in Course of Industrialisation : Case of India," *Economic and Political Weekly*, 24(11,12).

Rath, N. (1985), "Garibi Hatas : Can IRDP Do It?" *Economic and Political Weekly*, February 9.

Roy, K.C. and Tisdell, C.A. (1996), "Women in South Asia with Particular Reference to India," in Roy, K.C. Tisdell, C.A. and Blomqvist, H.D. eds. (1996), *Economic Development and Women in the World Community*, C.T. and London : Praeger.

Roy, K.C. Tisdell, C.A. and Blomqvist, H.E. ed. (1996), *Economic Development and Women in the World Community*, C.T. and London : Praeger.

Roy, K.C. and Clark, C. ed. (1994) *Technological Change and Rural Development in Poor Countries* : *Neglected Issues*, New Delhi : Oxford University Press.

Roy, K.C. and Tisdell, C.A. (1993a) "Poverty Amongst Females in Rural India; Gender Based Deprivation and Technological Change," *Economic Studies*, 31 (4).

Roy, K.C. and Tisdell, C.A. (1993b), "Technological Change, Environment and Poor Women, Especially Tribal Women in India," *Savings and Development* 17(4).

Roy, K.C. and Tisdell, C.A. and Sen, R.K. eds. (1992), *Economic Development and Environment* — A Case Study of India, Calcutta : Oxford University Press.

Sen, A.K. and Sengupta, S. (1983), "Malnutrition of Rural Children and the Sex Bias," *Economic and Political Weekly*, Annual No. May 6.

Tendler, J. (1987) "Whatever Happened to Poverty Alleviation?" New York : The Ford Foundation.

The Asian Age, (1996), Calcutta, August 17.

World Bank (1992), *Gender and Poverty in India*, Washington, D.C. : World Bank.

10 Lessons from Victims of Globalisation : Thailand, Indonesia and Malaysia

Liam Ryan

Introduction

Wiseman (1998) observes that 'globalisation is the most slippery, dangerous and important buzzword of the late twentieth century,' and after a critical exploration of the ideological underpinnings of a range of policies and practices that are subsumed by the term, cautions against the eager embracing of globalisation without conducting "...a grounded critique of the real costs and dangers of taken-for-granted forms of the unregulated free-market globalisation of the Australian economy" (p. 149).

Garran (1998), writing in the immediate wake of the Asian financial/economic crisis, issues a pointed warning against the neo-classical orthodoxy observing "…one key lesson of the Asian crash is that liberalising markets is not a panacea, and that if done badly it can have damaging consequences" (p. 206).

As the casualty count from the Asian crisis continues to rise, the negative aspects of globalisation are becoming more apparent, particularly in those economies worst-smitten by the original collapse — Thailand, Indonesia, Malaysia and the Philippines in South-East Asia, and South Korea in North-East Asia.

This paper explores the downside of globalisation from the perspective of the newly industrialising economies of Thailand, Indonesia and Malaysia, three recent victims of the destabilising influences of US-based hedge fund speculator and investor activity.

Anatomy of Globalisation

Over the past decade, influential international agencies such as the World Bank (WB), the International Monetary Fund (IMF), the World Trading Organisation (WTO), the General Agreement on

Tariffs and Trade (GATT), the Organisation for Economic Co-operation and Development (OECD), the Association of South-East Asian Nations (ASEAN), Asia Pacific Economic Co-operation (APEC) and the Asian Development Bank (ADB), have been strong advocates of the progressive globalisation of the world economy. In this concerted push they have been supported by many national leaders, corporate executives of international companies, eminent economists and the international banking elite.

It has been persuasively argued that globalisation is inevitable and can be advantageous to all parties, yielding substantial efficiency gains that can lead to the eradication of poverty and improved global socio-economic welfare. The only threat that has been associated with this high-powered globalisation advocacy has been to those countries who, for a variety of reasons, need time to consider the pros and cons of fully opening up their economies to the powerful forces of the global economy.

Globalisation has been packaged to make it appear intrinsically good and desirable, and like the biblical 'seed that fell on good ground,' capable of yielding fruit a thousandfold.

But what does the term mean apart from the literal meaning of moving towards becoming part of a single, integrated global economy — a drive towards economic homogeneity with increased interdependence between nations? It is basically about economic openness and increased international competitiveness. It is a race into the future where those nations that cannot maintain the necessary pace of change will slide backwards in relative economic terms — a sort of economic Darwinism.

Globalisation requires the elimination of protectionism and a standardisation of regulation so as to minimise the obstacles to the shifting of investments and production to any part of the world. Does complete globalisation, then, involve the total removal of national borders and the cessation of government intervention in the economy leading to the unfettered operation of market forces? So the true champions of the globalisation would have us believe. The globalisers stress, as neo-classical economists do, the indubitable benefits of free trade as dictated by the law of comparative advantage in a perfectly competitive environment, itself a construct founded on a cluster of heroic abstractions from reality. In addition, they are adamant that only good can flow from the complete deregulation of financial markets.

But taken to the extreme, globalisation involves the loss of national policy–making sovereignty. The processes through which this global homogeneity is supposed to evolve include deregulation, restructuring, privatisation and global competition policy — processes that usually involve job losses, plant closures, reduced service levels and homogeneity in consumption as evidenced by the spread of fast food chains such as Kentucky Fried Chicken, McDonalds and Sizzlers around the globe. The strongest advocates of globalisation occupy the right end of the political spectrum. Like the arguments put forward in favour of the privatisation of Government-Owned Enterprises (GOEs), those of the globalisation champions are persuasive and often biased in favour of international corporate rentseekers who, by virtue of their power, position, and influence, stand to reap the lion's share of the benefits while being effectively insulated from the negative effects.

What Is New In Globalisation?

Although the now ubiquitous term has a comparatively recent currency, many of its ingredients have existed throughout history. The Roman conquest, occupation and attempted homogenisation of the then known world, within its technological context, had many of the attributes of globalisation — good and bad.

Wiseman (1998) notes that "…the search for new trade routes, resources markets and sources of cheap labour was the driving force behind the sixteenth-century explosion of European exploration and colonisation" (p. 14). Substituting the information highway for trade routes, the same driving force recipe fits the current globalisation surge including the persistent search for sources of cheap labour.

The British Empire was established through the use of superior technology and military 'know how' or expertise. Britain's maritime superiority opened up numerous trade flows, foreign investment flows and technological transfers — key elements of the contemporary globalisation concept. Even the financial transactions side of international trade was greatly simplified and the cheap labour solution achieved by moving people *en masse* to sugar, banana and tea plantations. This was an earlier version of globalisation within a specific, pre-modern technological context.

Regionalism or regionalisation is a microcosm of globalisation but lacks some of the exploitative and vulnerability elements. The European Union (EU) and the North American Free Trade Agreement (NAFTA) have many of the same objectives as globalisation but the benefits are confined to member countries with a common policy stance taken against non-members. Krugman (1991) viewed these regional arrangements as the 'building blocks' for the future formation of an integrated global system. They could just as easily become bulwarks against full integration as indicated by the lukewarm support of the United States and the European Union for multi-lateralism (Young, 1994 : 182).

The new aspects of globalisation derive from the information technology revolution and the greater openness in international capital movements achieved by international monetary agencies. Along with a host of efficiency benefits comes the vulnerability threat as noted by Wiseman 1998 :

> *"The extraordinary speed and spread of global flows, particularly in relation to information and financial transactions, has threatened the capacity of people and governments to regulate, resist, or even fully comprehend the local impact of transformations that result from actions and decisions taken on the other side of the globe."*

It is this vulnerability that through no fault of theirs, made Thailand, Indonesia and Malaysia victims of the economic debacle that struck Thailand with remarkable speed and severity in July 1997. The profit-motivated actions of hedge fund managers exacerbated already volatile situations by generating investment withdrawal panic.

Thailand : A False Sense of Security

Thailand, from the mid-60s, adopted a strategy of export-oriented industrialisation and achieved a rapid expansion of exports from average annual growth rates of 6 per cent in the 1960s and 11 per cent in the 1970s to over 16 per cent in the 1980s (Hewison, 1997 : 104).

From 1992 to 1995, Thailand's economy grew at an average annual rate of 8.3 per cent but growth slumped to 5.5 per cent in 1996 when international investor confidence began to falter. Thailand experienced negative growth of –0.4 per cent in 1997 (ADB : 1998). In no uncertain terms, the bubble had burst. Those managing Thailand's economy in 1996 and early 1997 had no inkling of the impending disaster. They had been lulled into a sense of false security by well-meaning international financial agencies including the WB, the IMF and the ADB. Thailand was being commended as a champion for having followed the dictates of these international agencies and had been rewarded by achieving sustained high economic growth rates. The 1996 stumble was seen as a mere 'correction' that would iron itself out as Thailand's 'economic fundamentals' were deemed to be in robust shape.

The net flow of Foreign Direct Investment (FDI) into Thailand between 1986 and 1990 had been massive as indicated by table 1. After 1990, the rate of inflow slowed down but it was still substantial.

Table 1 shows that Japan was the main source of FDI for Thailand both prior to 1987 and in 1988-89 with the United States occupying second place. The investment sourced from the 'Four Asian Tigers' shows the strength of the Chinese financial/ commercial network across Asia.

Indonesia's prime FDI source was also Japan both prior to 1987 and in 1988-89, but Hong Kong occupied second place ahead of the United States.

Malaysia was far less reliant on FDI but Japan was again the primary source and adjacent Singapore occupied second position. Taiwan and Hong Kong were ahead of the United States as an FDI source.

As FDI is usually committed to infrastructure and plant and equipment, it contributes to export growth and is relatively stable in that it is allocated for the long haul as against short-term speculative gain. No doubt, sound returns on FDI were obtained because of the prosperity generated in these economies over the period in question.

Table 1 : FDI Sources : Thailand, Indonesia And Malaysia ($ US M)

Host/Source	Total	Japan	United States	Taiwan	Hong Kong	Singapore	South Korea
Thailand							
Up to 1987	11,536	2,773	1,910	675	445	351	9
1988-89	7,868	4,431	570	530	278	408	66
Indonesia							
Up to 1987	17,284	5,928	1,244	144	1,876	299	222
1988-89	11,159	1,304	783	1,126	867	489	728
Malaysia							
Up to 1987	4,200	1,741	202	34	262	594	0
1988-89	3,690	967	179	1,314	138	231	49

Source : Compiled from table 10.4, p. 120 *Petrer in Garnaut & Drysdale,* 1994.

Portfolio investment can be shifted quickly. Table 2 provides details of portfolio investment as well as net FDI flows from 1990 to 1996.

Table 2 : Net FDI And Portfolio Investment : Thailand, Indonesia and Malaysia — 1990-1996 ($ US Billion)

	1990	1991	1992	1993	1994	1995	1996	TOTAL
Thailand								
Net FDI	2.3	1.8	2.0	1.6	0.9	1.2	1.4	11.2
Net Portfolio Investment	-	-0.1	0.9	5.5	2.5	4.1	3.5	16.4
Indonesia								
Net FDI	1.1	1.5	1.8	1.6	1.5	3.7	7.4	18.6
Net Portfolio Investment	-0.1	-	-0.1	1.8	3.9	4.1	1.9	11.5
Malaysia								
Net FDI	2.3	3.8	4.7	4.3	3.0	2.7	5.1	25.9
Net Portfolio Investment	-0.3	0.2	-1.1	-0.7	-1.6	-0.4	4.1	0.2

Source : Compiled from tables 7.1, p. 210, table 11.1, p. 321 and table 8.13, in *Asia Pacific Economic Group* (1999).

For Thailand in particular, and Indonesia to a lesser extent, 1993 was the take-off year for portfolio investment inflow. The trend continued through to 1996 with a total of $ US 15.6 billion entering Thailand over the four year period. Thailand was more exposed to portfolio investment than was Indonesia which had FDI of $ US 7.1 billion in excess of portfolio investment in contrast with Thailand's portfolio investment excess of $ US 5.2 billion over FDI.

This would have shown up clearly to hedge fund operators as an imprudent balance between FDI and portfolio investment for Thailand.

Cautious Malaysia, in contrast to both Thailand and Indonesia, had not liberalised sufficiently to permit portfolio investment inflow until 1996 and had a dominant FDI excess of $ US 25.7 billion over the relatively minor $ US 0.2 billion portfolio investment over the seven year period.

It must have seemed ironic to Thai authorities, having followed WB, IMF and ADB advice in opening up the Thai economy to international capital flows, that these very capital flows were now wrecking the economy. That advice was reiterated in the WB's influential 1993 Policy Research Report titled 'The East Asian Miracle,'

> *"Openness to direct foreign investment (DFI) has speeded technological acquisition in Hong Kong, Malaysia, Singapore and more recently, Indonesia and Thailand" (p. 21), and, "in the 1980s, Indonesia, Malaysia and Thailand have adopted a wide variety of export incentives while gradually reducing protection. Exchange rate policies were liberalised and currencies frequently devalued, to support export growth. Overall, these policies exposed much of the industrial sector to international competition and resulted in domestic relative prices that were closer to international prices than in most other developing economies" (p. 22).*

Thailand had assiduously followed the IMF, WB and ADB policy advice. In addition, the bhat was pegged to the US dollar which should have led to restraint in borrowing on the bond market and international financial market credibility in the Thai authorities' ability to keep inflation in check. The strategic alliances between big business, (including the banking sector), and government were strong — a factor that had contributed to Thailand's economic success. There appeared to be no obvious fissures or fault lines when viewed from within but the speculators detected some 'anomalies' and struck with a sudden speculative attack on the bhat in May 1997 which the Bank of Thailand successfully defended. With its foreign exchange reserves depleted, Thailand succumbed to the second speculative strike and allowed the bhat to float on 2 July 1997 resulting in a depreciation of 15 per cent in the first week. This triggered the panic that spread quickly across the region. By January 1998 the Thai bhat had depreciated by 53 per cent, the Indonesian rupiah by 80 per cent and the Malaysian ringgit by 42 per cent (ADB 1998 : 20). Without urgent action from the IMF, the sheer magnitude of these currency collapses were capable of generating a global catastrophe.

The Hedge Fund Speculators

The contagion spread quickly to South Korea and the Philippines and has continued to cause economic and political turmoil across the region and has come close to causing the collapse of the world economy.

Stokes (1998), conscious of the enormous clout possessed by the big US-based hedge funds suspected of being key players in the Asian crises, observes :

> *"These are times when speculators and investors — glorified global gamblers — deal in numbers 10 times the world's total currency reserves each day. They can break the banks of nations — big and small"* (*Weekend Australian* 10-11 October 1998 — p. 19).

Earlier in October 1998, Dr. Alan Greenspan, Chairman of the US Federal Reserve, had been desperately seeking some means of controlling massive international movements of capital by US-based hedge fund managers who panicked at the prospect of capital movement controls and caused an unprecedented slump of 14c in the US dollar against the Japanese yen. What chance had Thailand,

Indonesia or Malaysia in the face of such an assault? Herein lies the source of vulnerability that accompanies sudden movements of large amounts of portfolio investment.

Whilst Malaysia's Dr. Mohamad Mahatir was quick to blame his country's woes on US-based hedge fund operators, including the flamboyant George Soros, Manager of the Quantum Group, a more likely and far more powerful target would have been John Merriweather, President of Wall Street's most successful bond trader up to September 1998 when it went bust — Long Term Capital Management (LTCM). Even in the giant US economy with its sophisticated financial sector, Alan Greenspan felt obliged to mount a rescue mission for LTCM because of the massive damage and confidence loss that its collapse would have caused. In Greenspan's words, such a collapse "…could potentially have impaired the economies of many nations including our own" (*Weekend Australian* 24-25 October 1998, p. 30).

The clear message given by Alan Greenspan was that the large international hedge funds were out of control and LTCM's close brush with collapse had come hazardously close to causing a crash in investor confidence that would have shaken the mighty US economy. Unless hedge fund operations were brought under tight control they were capable of causing irreparable damage to the global financial system now confronted with a new phenomenon — huge sums of footloose speculative funds seeking likely targets to make a 'killing.'

There was a serious questioning of the orthodox economic conviction that unfettered financial markets, guided by Adam Smith's 'invisible hand', would unfailingly restore equilibrium. The Asian financial /economic crisis, however, was more than a mere 'correction' — it was a confidence shattering catastrophe.

James D. Wolfensohn, President of the World Bank Group, in his October 1998 address to the Bank's Board of Governors, displayed an acute awareness of the harshness of the reality, noting that in 1997 in East Asia alone, an estimated 20 million people fell back into poverty and "… at best, growth is likely to be halting and hesitant for several years to come" (p. 2) and that South Asia in early 1997 contained 35 per cent of the world's poor and was stumbling, but no one was predicting the degree of the fall (p. 182).

In relation to the inadequacy of the present international monetary system, Wolfensohn (1998) cautioned "... we cannot pretend that all is well. We cannot close our eyes to the fact that the crisis has exposed weakness and vulnerabilities that we must address. We must be bold but we must also be realistic. We will not devise a new architecture in two days, or even two weeks (p. 6).

Alan Greenspan was also concerned that giant-hedge funds like LTCM had spread their tentacles far and wide to the extent that its possible demise could cause the collapse of national economies around the globe. This is the seamy side of globalisation but it certainly lends support to Dr. Mahatir's original allegations which, possibly because they were couched in anti-Semitic language, brought no official response from the US at the time.

In mid-October 1998, under the aegis of the Federal Reserve, an emergency bankers/hedge fund managers meeting was convened in Bermuda, with a view to finding a means of controlling large capital movements that could destabilise the economy of the parent nation as well as those of host nations. This in itself was a recognition and admission that the unrestricted capital movements advocated by the globalisation champions could have a detrimental effect on world trade and international relations. Some regulation or set of agreed protocols was needed. The initial title given to the planned Bermuda conference was, "*How to handle the flood of assets coming in*." The possibility of some questioning of the origin of this unprecedented 'flood of assets' could have been embarrassing in the light of the asset flight from Asia, so to avoid ruffling Asian sensitivities the conference was dubbed with the more mundane and less emotive title, "*Crisis and corrections: implications for hedge funds*." It is not known if a workable solution emerged from this conference or whether it was an exercise in moral suasion designed to give the impression that the issue of sterilisation of large capital movements, if not under control, was being given serious consideration.

Selecting the Victims

Tables 1 and 2 showed how FDI and portfolio investment moved into Thailand between 1986 and 1994. From $ US 39.6 billion in 1992, Thailand's external debt rose to an estimated $ US 75 billion in 1996 (ADB, 1995 : 120). Over the same period the Current Account deficit rose from $ US 6.4 billion to $ US 7.9 billion (ADB, 1998 : 106). Merchandise exports, after growing by 24.8 per cent in 1995 collapsed to cause a decline of 1.9 per cent in 1996 (ADB, 1995 & 1998). There was another phenomenon that should have caused concern — a meteoric rise in foreign-sourced portfolio investment in both absolute quantity and relative to FDI (ADB, 1995 : 46).

It is surprising that the IMF or the Thai authorities did not draw comparisons between these trends and those in evidence in Mexico's economy before its collapse in 1994. Similar situations, but not as volatile, existed in Indonesia and Malaysia.

In terms of real GDP growth rates throughout the 1960s and 1970s, Thailand's performance had been superior to those of Malaysia and Indonesia. Table 3 shows that in 1996, Indonesia with 8 per cent growth and Malaysia with 8.6 per cent were still experiencing economic expansion whereas a slow down had occurred in Thailand with only 5.5 per cent growth in real GDP.

Furthermore, Malaysia's high growth continued into 1997 with 8 per cent whilst Indonesia's slipped significantly to 4.7 per cent and Thailand's plummeted to negative growth of –0.4 per cent.

Table 3 : Real GDP Growth Rates — Thailand, Indonesia & Malaysia

	1960-1979 % Per Annum	1979-1995 % Per Annum	1996 % Per Annum	1997 % Per Annum
Thailand	7.6	7.8	5.5	-0.4
Indonesia	5.7	6.2	8.0	4.7
Malaysia	6.8	6.8	8.6	8.0

Source : Jolley, 1995, Summers and Heston, 1992 as cited by Sheehan and Tikhomirova, 1996 and *Asia Pacific Profiles,* 1998.

Table 4 : Critical External Indicators

Indicator	Thailand		Indonesia		Malaysia	
	1995	1996	1995	1996	1995	1996
Current Account Balance $ US bn	-13.6	-14.4	-7.0	-7.0	-8.7	-4.9
Official Foreign Exchange Reserves $ US bn	36.9	38.7	18.6	22.4	25.1	25.9
External Long-Term Debt $ US bn	33.5	36.1	86.0	89.0	27.5	28.5
External Long-Term Debt Service Ratio (% Exports)	22.4	26.8	32.8	32.9	7.2	6.3

Source : *Asia Pacific Profiles* 1998, pp. 214, 332 & 346.

Table 4 shows that, on the threshold of the meltdown, Thailand was experiencing current account deficit problems; its external long-term debt and debt service ratio were worsening but it had what appeared to be a comfortable reservoir of foreign exchange reserves.

Indonesia, carrying a much higher level of long-term debt with a corresponding high debt service ratio, had a current account deficit approximately half those of Thailand. It had a much lower foreign exchange buffer — about half that of Thailand.

Malaysia's external position was the strongest of the three in terms of foreign debt and the debt service ratio. Its current account deficit had been reduced from $ US 8.7 billion in 1995 to $ US 4.9 billion in 1997 and it had ample foreign reserves — enough to cover 4.3 months' imports.

This explains why the currency speculators set their sights on Thailand which was clearly the most vulnerable of the three.

Accustomed to absorbing sustained increases in FDI and a recent surge in foreign-sourced portfolio investment, the Thai banks engaged in imprudent and often high-risk lending to prestigious developments that could not contribute to foreign exchange earnings. The heavy reliance on the export of electronic and communication industry components made these economies extremely vulnerable when demand for final products in US and Japan was falling well short of projections. As the US dollar appreciated, due to the pegged currency arrangement export earnings were progressively eroded, while debt servicing costs increased resulting in worsening balance of payments situations. These were propitious signs for hedge fund speculators searching for likely victims and prepared to instigate a massive capital withdrawal to protect their US investor clients and maintain their own reputations by being able to quickly quit markets where prospects of future profitability had diminished.

The globalisation to which the successes of these high-performing South-east Asian economies were largely attributable had become a two-edged sword that now scuttled the dream that was the Asian economic miracle. And to a large extent the worst-affected economies — the victims of the meltdown — were passive players in this global game. They may have been lured into becoming global players, and the wealthy dynastic families with 'crony capitalism' connections may also have managed to move a lot of their wealth to safe havens, but the emerging middle class and the working class had no scope to hedge. Globalisation has the capacity to 'pull the plug' without notice and inflict misery hard on the heels of the promise of a rapid ascent to affluence, and to turn comparative political harmony into turmoil and chaos.

One would expect that consistent with their advocacy of free and open global capital movements, that globalisation champions would also favour free international labour movements and flexible exchange rate regimes. Not so, it appears.

The Myth of Labour Market Flexibility

Flexible labour markets, in globalisation terminology, mean regulated industrial relations to prevent the emergence of unionised labour, and in some instances, the conscious use of child labour in appalling working conditions (New Internationalist, 1997) Leggett (1993 : 25) notes in relation to Singapore, that the future of the Singapore economy depended upon multi-national corporate investment and therefore required; "...that employee unions forego such comparative bargaining advantage that collective solidarity might have offered them and assured potential investors of a stable wages structure, non-confrontational procedures and a co-operative stance towards productivity growth."

The so-called 'selective interventions' in labour markets in Thailand, Indonesia and Malaysia were also not-too-subtle authoritarian devices for mobilising labour for the economic growth push.

Towards A New Global Financial Architecture

Globalisation has an unattractive side that has tended to be overlooked in the euphoria surrounding the spectacular economic growth achievements of the dynamic economies of Southeast and North-East Asia in the 1970s, 1980s and early 1990s. It has to be treated with extreme caution as demonstrated by the recent unfortunate experiences of Thailand, Indonesia and Malaysia. A new global financial architecture is needed to support the open and liberal system of capital flows demanded by globalisation. The new system has to be developed urgently drawing on the lessons provided by the dramatic collapses of the currencies of Thailand, Indonesia and Malaysia following the initial July 1997 crash.

In February 1998, addressing the Group of 24, Michael Candessus, IMF Managing Director, stated "The task before us is very simple : to keep the crisis from becoming a catastrophe of global proportions" (p. 65). The Group of 7 called for the development of a code of conduct to be 'enforced' by the IMF so as to prevent the recurrence of crises such as that experienced in Asia in 1997.

The emerging view was that although large hedge fund operators may have behaved ruthlessly in defending the interests of their clients, the target economies were remiss in having developed vulnerabilities through imprudent financial practices.

In March 1998, Stanley Fisher, IMF First Deputy Manager observed :

"One of the broad policy issues emerging from the Asian crisis is the appropriate speed with which the capital account should be liberalised in view of the potential for shifts in market sentiment. Successful capital account liberalisation requires that certain preconditions be in place and that the process of liberalisation be a gradual and orderly one. In the meantime emerging market countries need to find ways to protect their economies against undesirable surges in short-term inflows" (p. 99).

This may be asking a bit too much of emerging economies not previously exposed to the potential hazards of an open capital movements policy. How are they expected to identify, *ex ante* which investment surges are desirable and which 'undesirable'. If they possessed that degree of discriminatory expertise it is unlikely that their economies would exhibit the vulnerabilities that attract professional currency speculators.

A more forthright admonition might have been to maintain a prudent ratio between FDI and portfolio investment; to hedge the risks associated with short-term borrowing in foreign-denominated currencies; and, unpopular as some of the measures may be, to insulate the domestic economy against any adverse effects arising from the appreciation of the currency against which the host country's currency is pegged. In short, prevent the overexposure that lures the speculators.

In May 1998, Michael Candessus, aware of a growing disillusionment with the IMF's continued faith in the merits of globalisation despite the Asian Crisis, asserted :

"The question before us is straightforward: how to utilise the full potential of globalisation to improve the living standards of all — particularly the poorest — while containing the risks it entails, such as those we have seen materialise so brutally in Asia, and those at least equally pernicious, even if less spectacular, of the continuous marginalisation of the poorest countries" (p. 157).

At last, there is an acknowledgment that the Asian crisis had exposed the risks of globalisation and that apparently, the IMF hierarchy are on the same learning curve as the decision-makers in the worst-affected economies.

It is difficult to envisage any solution based on voluntary compliance by hedge fund operators with a new set of protocols introduced under the surveillance of the IMF. The IMF's credibility is at stake while it continues to defend globalisation, including the continued liberalisation of capital markets, while fumbling around for a solution to a destabilising phenomenon that is itself an integral part of the globalisation process.

REFERENCES

Asian Development Bank, *Asian Development Outlook*, 1995, 1996 and 1998 issues, Oxford University Press, New York.

Asia Pacific Economics Group (1999), *Asia Pacific Profiles 1998*, Australian National University, Canberra.

Garran, R. (1998), *Tigers Tamed : The End of the Asian Miracle*, Allen and Unwin, Sydney, Australia.

Hewison, K. (1997), "Thailand : Capitalistic Development and the State," in Roden, G., Hewison, K. and Robison, R. (eds.), *The Political Economy of South-East Asia*.

International Monetary Fund (1998), *IMF Survey*, Vol. 27, No. 5 March.

International Monetary Fund (1998), *IMF Survey*, Vol. 27, No. 7 April.

International Monetary Fund (1998), *IMF Survey*, Vol. 27, No. 10 May.

Krugman, P. (1991), "Regional Blocks : the Good, the Bad and the Ugly," *The International Economy*, November/December.

Leggett, C., "Singapore" in S.J. Deery and R.J. Mitchell (eds.) (1993), *Labour Law and Industrial Relations in Asia : Eight Country Studies*, Longman Cheshire Pvt. Ltd., Melbourne.

Peter, P. (1994), "The East Asia Trading Block : An analytical history," in Garnaut, R. and Drysdale, P. (eds.), *Asia Pacific Regionalism*, Harper Education in Association with The Australia Jap Research Centre, Australian National University : Canberra.

Sheehan, P.J. and Tikhomirova (1996), *Diverse Paths to Industrial Development in East-Asia and Asean*, Centre for Strategic Economic Studies, Victoria University, Australia.

The New Internationalist (1997), "Child Labour", No. 202, July.

The Weekend Australian, 10-11 October 1998 (p. 19).

The Weekend Australian, 24-25 October 1998 (p. 30).

Wiseman, J. (1998), *Global Nation? Australia and the Politics of Globalisation*, Cambridge University Press, Cambridge, U.K.

Wofensohn, J.D. (1998), "The Other Crisis." Address to the World Bank Group Board of Governors, Washington DC, October.

World Bank (1993), *The East Asian Miracle*, Oxford University Press, Washington.

Young, S. (1994), "Globalism and Regionalism : Complements or Competitors?" in Ross Garnant, Peter Drysdale and John Kunkel (eds.), *Asia Pacific Regionalism*, Harper Educational in association with The Australia-Japan Research Centre, Australian National University, Canberra.

11 Poverty and Inequality and the Eradication Thereof

Schalk W. Theron

Introduction

Poverty is a profoundly political issue. Wilson and Ramphele (1989) state that thousands of South African babies are dying of malnutrition and about two million children are growing up stunted for lack of sufficient calories in one of the few countries in the world that exports food. Owing to the migrant labour system tens of thousands of men are spending their entire working years as lonely labour units in single sex hostels whilst their wives and children live generally in great poverty in overcrowded rural areas.[1]

Wilson and Ramphele (1989 : 4) evolved four reasons why poverty is significant :

1. Poverty inflicts damage on the individuals who must endure it.
2. Its sheer inefficiency in economic terms : an economy where a large proportion of the population is very poor has a structure of demand that does not encourage the production and marketing of the goods that are most needed.[2]
3. Poverty is also the manifestation of great inequality. The existence of too great a degree of inequality makes it impossible to have a harmonious community.
4. Poverty in many societies is itself symptomatic of a deeper malaise as it is often the consequences of a process which simultaneously produces wealth for some and impoverishment for others.

---

1 The *apartheid* regime called these rural areas reserves.

2 Hungry children cannot study properly and malnourished adults cannot be fully productive as workers.

Poverty is the carcass left over from wealth acquisition (Kurien, 1978). Nowhere is this more true than in South Africa where poverty is deep and widespread and where the degree of inequality is as great as in any other country in the world. Poverty is not confined to South Africa. Grinding poverty is to be found in many different parts of the world, including countries of the Indian Ocean rim. But the Gini coefficient[3], which measures the degree of inequality consistently is stark indicator of South Africa's unequal distribution of income. The Gini coefficient in South Africa is about 0.58 which is extremely high indicating a very skewed distribution of income (*Poverty and Inequality in South Africa*, 1998).

Hamburg (in Wilson and Ranphele, 1978) argues that poverty is a matter of income and partly a matter of human dignity. "It is one thing to have a very low income but to be treated with respect by your compatriots, it is quite another matter to have a very low income and to be harshly depreciated by more powerful compatriots". In South Africa that harsh disrespect is embedded in the very structure of the society in many different ways including the migrant labour system, and a set of laws that both classifies and discriminates against people according to racist criteria that are unacceptable anywhere in the world (Wilson and Ramphele, 1978; Giliomee and Schlemmer, 1985).

Definition

Poverty is generally being characterised by the inability of individuals, households, or entire communities to command sufficient resources to satisfy a socially acceptable minimum standard of living (*Poverty and Inequality in South Africa*, 1998). According to Kaufman (1994) devising a definition of poverty needs both an absolute income poverty measure and a relative income poverty measure.

The absolute income poverty measure refers to the minimum of income a family needs to be able to purchase the bare necessities of life. The relative measure assumes a family is in poverty if its income is below the average income of all families by some specified amount *viz*, a family might be defined as poor if its

3 A Gini coeficient of 0 signifies equality and 1 indicates absolute concentration.

income were less than half of the median family income (Kaufman, 1994 : 697).

The Council of Economic Advisors (CEA) formulated an absolute income measure of poverty and define the poverty line as the income threshold below which a family is poor. Since consumption data indicated that low or median income families spent about one third of their income on food, the CEA establish the poverty line at approximately three times the cost of what they considered to be a minimum nutritionally adequate diet (Ruggles, 1990).

The Poverty and Inequality Report (*Poverty in Inequality in south Africa*, 1998) views poverty to include :

1. Alienation from the community — the poor are isolated from the institutions of kinship and community;
2. Food insecurity;
3. Crowded homes;
4. Lack access to safe and sufficient sources of energy;
5. Lack of adequate, paid, secure jobs; and
6. Fragmentation of the family.

Defining what is meant by INEQUALITY within the social context requires consensus on what is meant by equality. The *Poverty and Inequality in South Africa* (1998) views equality as a state of social organisation that enables/gives equal access to resources and opportunities to all its members. It cites a number of possible objectives for policy that aims at reducing inequality :

1. Increasing the relative income share of the least well off;
2. Lowering the ceiling;
3. Improving mobility;
4. Promoting economic inclusion;
5. Avoidance of income and wealth crystallisation — this implies the disproportionate advantages in education,

influence, political power etc., that goes hand-in-hand with higher income; and

6. Comparison against international yardsticks as a country takes as its goal that it should be no more unequal than other comparable nations.

Causes of Poverty

Poverty is not confined to South Africa. Poverty is found in many parts of the world and inequality between rich and poor is visible virtually everywhere. Kaufman (1994) advanced four explanations for poverty. One explanation is that poor people bring to the labour market low levels of productivity. Kaufman (1994) argues that much of the earnings a person receives from work is a return to human capital; and therefore it is not surprising that high school dropouts have few job skills and do not generally earn much because they cannot contribute much to the production and profits of the business. Limited labour market opportunities that certain segments of the population face is a second explanation. Individual productivity has less to do with some people's low incomes than the fact that the economy does not generally provide sufficient jobs for everyone who desires to work and the types of jobs available at the bottom are characterised by low wages, few training opportunities and little employment security. A third explanation is that the attributes, values and aspirations of poor people keep them poor. The reason some people are poor is frequently attributed to poorly developed work ethics, low self-esteem or cultural attributes that lead to a sense of dependency and a lack of initiative. A fourth explanation for some people's poverty is that they suffer unforeseen life events that substantially reduce either the economic resources available to them or their income earnings ability.

Dynamics of Black Poverty in South Africa

There are a number of important differences between the factors that generally generate poverty and those operating in South Africa and especially operating in the rural areas. Natrass (1985) argues that there is a strong relationship between growing, relative and/or absolute levels of rural poverty, the process of urban-rural migration and the level of urban unemployment. Rural poverty generates increased migration to towns and, in the absence of a rapid rate of employment creation in the urban areas, this leads to growing urban unemployment. The *apartheid* system of influx control also caused poverty to build up in the rural areas. The political institutions enforcing the policies of racial separation, while not necessarily the original cause, were the major engines for generating poverty in the rural areas.

Natrass (*op. cit.*) distinguished five factors which contribute to high levels of poverty in the black rural areas, all of which have their roots firmly fixed in the historical patterns of South Africa's economic development, viz the inadequacy of land supply in relation to the agricultural needs of the black population, lack of capital, the failure of technology in the sense that farming techniques have not been adequate to meet the needs of the changing relationships between land and population, rapid population growth, and the growth and persistence of the migrant labour system.

The *Poverty and Inequality in South Africa* (1998) concurred with the above view stating that most of the poor live in rural areas. The poverty share of South Africa's rural areas i.e., the percentage of poor individuals living in rural areas is 70 per cent. The poverty rate in rural areas, *i.e.*, the percentage of individuals classified as poor is about 70 per cent compared with 30 per cent in urban areas. Living standards are also closely related with race in South Africa. While poverty is not confined to any one racial group in South Africa, it is concentrated among blacks, particularly Africans.

Programs to Reduce Poverty

Uprooting poverty demands radical action. The uprooting of poverty implies not only a transformation of agriculture including redistribution of land but also a restructuring of the relations between capital and labour. "Questions of power and ownership are crucial. So too is ideology" (Wilson and Ramphele, 1989 : 5). The point of departure for an appropriate policy framework for the reduction of poverty and inequality in South Africa is the underlying economic structure of the country. The *Poverty and Inequality in South Africa* adopted an approach of breaking the forces that have perpetuated the vicious circle of poverty. The *Poverty and Inequality in South Africa* approach is based on the following five interlocking proposals :

1. Economic growth and human development should be linked and have the aim of achieving sustainable improvements in the quality of life of all South Africans.
2. This is best achieved through enhancing the capabilities of disadvantaged communities, households, and individuals by improving their access to a wide range of assets both physical and social.
3. Increasing emphasis should be placed by the South African Government on redistribution measures in order to assure the long term well-being and the prosperity of the population.
4. To achieve this a more assertive role will be required of government in facilitating the transfer of assets and services from the wealthy to the poor through effective and appropriate social investment.
5. The collection of social, economic, and demographic information for the purpose of monitoring the extent and nature of change should be prioritised to ensure that the reduction of poverty and inequality is managed on a sustainable basis.

The arguments underpinning these programs require elaboration especially those relating to economic growth and human development, and employment and growth and redistribution.

Economic Growth and Human Development

The capabilities approach examines the factors that shape the ability of people to realise their full human potential over time (*Poverty and Inequality in South Africa*, 1998 : 6). Education and training are sources of earnings differentials and types of human capital investment. The analysis of the labour market effects of education and training is the province of human capital theory (Kaufman, 1994 : 301). The essence of human capital theory is the idea that expenditures on education and training are investments that individuals make on themselves to increase their market skills, productivity, and earnings. There is a very strong correlation between educational attainment and standard of living. Education is viewed as a priority area for the improved access for the poor and its relevance is seen primarily in terms of the likelihood of eventual success to employment (*Poverty and Inequality in South Africa*, 1998 : 33). Two separate rates of return to education are estimated as private rate of return and social rate of return. The private rate is the yield on the investment in education by the person making the investment. The social rate of return measures the yield to society from the resources devoted to education. The theory of human capital predicts that wages should be greater than average annual earnings for persons with successively more years of education (Kaufman, 1994 : 312).

Employment and the Eradication of Poverty

Unemployment is one of the most serious and pervasive problems in the labour market. Unemployment is a key indicator of the cyclical performance of the economy. The number of jobs in the economy is directly related to the level of production and spending and an increase in unemployment rate, therefore, is often a harbinger of recession as firms cut back on new hiring or begin layoffs in response to falling demand. Unemployment also imposes a substantial cost on individual workers and their families. There is the loss of income going with unemployment. There is also the scarring effect that a prolonged period of joblessness can impose a significant hardship on workers and on their chances of getting new jobs and resuming their movements up a career ladder.

Kaufman (1994) distinguished between frictional, structural, and cyclical unemployment. Frictional unemployment refers to a constant flow of people between jobs and into and out of labour force due to imperfect information in the job market. Structural unemployment arises from a mismatch, due to skill, education, geographic area or age, between the type of jobs that are available and the types of people who are seeking jobs. Cyclical unemployment is the insufficient aggregate demand in the economy to generate enough jobs for those who seek one. Lack of employment is a significant contributor to poverty. Male unemployment has a negative impact on the survival techniques of women in the absence of alternative productive roles for men or the reallocation of responsibilities for reproductive activities (*Poverty and Inequality in South Africa*, 1998 : 81).

One solution to the poverty problem is to increase the aggregate demand in the economy so that the poor have a wider range of job opportunities. Another solution to poverty may be a social safety net of government transfer programs. Economic development programs aims to foster the development of firms likely to hire disadvantaged workers (Kaufman, *op. cit.*). Mears (1998) argues that small business is the key component of any local economy as it provides the life blood of the capitalist system. Most small businesses are locality bound and rely on local resources of raw materials, skills, and markets. The employment and leadership base in the host communities render small business enterprises a valuable asset in any local community while their ability to create jobs make them a key component in any initiative for the reduction of poverty and inequality locally.

REFERENCES

Giliomee, H. and L. Schlemmer (1985), *Up Against the Fences : Poverty, Passes and Privilege in South Africa*, Capt Town : David Philip.

Kaufman, B.E. (1994), *The Economics of Labour Markets*, Fourth edition, San Diego : The Dryden Press.

Kurien, .T. (1978), *Poverty, Planning and Social Transformation*, Bombay.

Mears, R. (1998), "Natural resources and sustainable economic development in South Africa," *The South African Journal of Economics*, 66(2) : 256-272.

Natrass, J. (1985), "*The Dynamics of Black Rural Poverty in South Africa*," in Giliomee, H and L Schlemmer (1985), *Up Against the Fences : Poverty, Passes and Privilege in South Africa*, Capt Town : David Philip.

Poverty and Inequality in South Africa (1998), Report prepared by the Office of the Executive Deputy State President, Durban : Fishwicks.

Ruggles, P. (1990), Drawing the line : Alternative poverty measures and their implication for public policy, Washington DC: Urban Institute

Wilson, F. and M. Ramphele (1989), *Uprooting Poverty : The South African Challenge*, Cape Town : David Philip.

12 Women in the Urban Labour Market : The Situation in Bangladesh

Begum Meherunnessa Zaman

Introduction

In Bangladesh, as in other Asian countries, the participation of women in the labour market has increased in recent years particularly in export-oriented sectors such as food processing and readymade garments. On the supply side, it is poverty which brings the women to the labour market, while on the demand side, it is the competitiveness of the international market that demands their cheap labour. The goal of this paper is to add to the body of knowledge about women's labour market participation and its characteristics in Bangladesh.

The specific objectives of the paper are to (a) review the urban labour market situation, particularly the gender differences therein; (b) examine whether the job markets are segregated and if so, to what extent; (c) explore the earning differentials by gender and (d) briefly discuss the gaps in providing institutional support to women in the labour market.

Data and Methodology

This paper is mainly based on data drawn from the Labour Force Survey (henceforth LFS) 1995-96 and 1996. Other sources include the Census of Manufacturing Industries 1991/92, 1997, and the Household Expenditure Survey 1995/96 and 1998. Certain information from a micro survey conducted by the author is also presented. The analysis pertains mainly to the year 1995/96. The study is mostly based on tabular techniques. For examining the gender differentials, the popular Duncan Index (DI) is be used. DI is also known as the dissimilarity index[1] and is given by :

$$DI = 0.5 \sum Abs (M_i - F_i)$$

where $\sum$ stands for summation, Abs stands for absolute value, and the M_i & F_i stand for the proportions of men and women.

Labour Force Participation

Aggregate Labour Force Participation

Labour Force Participation Rate (LFPR) or refined activity rate in Bangladesh in 1995-96 was slightly below 50 per cent (table 1). It is slightly higher in the rural areas than in the urban areas. However, IFPR by gender widely varies both in the rural and urban areas. Thus, in the rural areas while 17 per cent of women take part in the labour force, the proportion is almost 80 per cent for men. The difference is almost as wide in the urban areas.

Once the usual or conventional definition of labour is expanded to include various economic activities within the household, the LFPR for all groups increases. But, it rises more in the rural areas and more for women than for men. This is because mostly women carry out the economic activities, which are usually home-based, and it is easier to carry out those in the rural compared to urban areas. As a result, under extended definition, the LFPR for rural women increases more than three-fold, while for rural men it hardly changes. In the urban areas, the LFPR for women increases by almost 8 per cent, but for men it again remains static.

LFPR by Age and Sex

LFPR by age groups for men and women are presented in Table 2. For men, the rate is relatively low at lower age group — 37.7 per cent for the age group of 10-14 years. It then picks up and reaches maximum at the age group of 50-54. It begins to fall at the age group of 55-59, although remains at a high level. Without doubt the early entry into the job market and exit at older age are both symptoms of poverty. The poor cannot afford not to work, as even a

[1] The maximum value DI can take is 1 or 100 per cent which means that the men and women are completely segregated. A value of zero means that the distributions for men and women are exactly the same.

meagre income is better than no income. Similar patterns are found in other South Asian countries (Horton : 1996, p. 10).

For women, let us first consider the pattern under the "usual definition." The LFPR for girls under the age of 15 is nearly 30 per cent. But then it begins to decline and stabilises around 15 per cent up to age 59 when it falls again. What this means is that as girls attain the marital age, they withdraw themselves from the labour market and get married. They tend not to return to the labour market later in their life. Lack of employment opportunities may be one reason. Another reason may be that due to traditional values, married women do not work that much outside the home.[2]

Even if women do not or cannot work outside the home, it does not debar them from involvement in economic activities inside the home and thus earning an income. When such activities are accounted for under the "extended definition" of LFPR, the picture becomes quite different. The pattern of LFPR for women becomes similar to that for men although at any age group, it is lower than that for men. The highest rate for women is 62 per cent that is only two-thirds of that for men in the same age group.

How do these figures compare with those for women elsewhere? The pattern appears to be similar to that of India (Acharya : 1996, p. 46) under the "usual definition." Indeed, the pattern in Bangladesh is pretty much like what one finds in the late nineteenth century America (Blau and Ferber : 1992, p. 75). The relevant data indicate that the patterns in the rural and urban areas are similar for the nation as a whole (under the two definitions). Also, the LFPR for women in the rural areas under the "extended definition" is higher than that for the corresponding age-group in the urban areas.

Employed persons

In 1995-96, the total estimated number of employed persons aged 10 years and above (under "usual definition") was more than

2 For a review on the relationship between tradition and work and lack of work opportunities for women in the rural areas. See (Westergaard : 1993). Also see the references cited therein.

40 million. Of this, only 18 per cent were women.[3] Under an extended definition, however, the total number of the employed persons rises to more than 54 million of whom 38 per cent were women.[4] These proportions compare favourably with those in India and Thailand (Horton : 1996, p. 10). This distribution by sex is similar in rural and urban areas and also for persons of 15 years of age or over.

Sectoral distribution of employed persons

In Bangladesh, most of the people are employed in agriculture.[5] Under the extended definition of labour force participation, more than one-half of both men and women are employed in agriculture (table 3). The gender-gap in agricultural employment is quite large. Three-fourths of women are employed in agriculture compared to only half the men. However, as table 3 indicates women are represented not adequately in most other sectors (except manufacturing). Similar results are found in India (Acharya : 1996, p. 62).

A Duncan index of dissimilarity has been calculated as a composite measure of the difference between the sexes in their representation across sectors. The index (including agriculture) is found to be 0.244. The low index apparently suggests low gender-gap in employment across the sectors. It is known, however, that if there is a heavy concentration of labour in one sector its inclusion may swamp whatever differences there are between the sexes. It is argued therefore that such sectors should not be considered in calculating the index (Acharya : 1996, p. 63, Horton : 1996, p. 22). A re-estimation of the Duncan Index excluding agriculture raises its value to 0.438, a fairly high figure indicating wide gender-gap across the sectors.

Under the "usual definition", the picture alters drastically, particularly for women. While men still are employed mostly in agriculture, less than 40 per cent of women are so employed while nearly 20 per cent are in manufacturing industries. The estimated

---

3 BBS, *LFS,* 1996, tables U11 and U10, p. 152.

4 BBS, *LFS,* 1996, tables E10 and E11 p. 114-115

5 Agriculture is defined here broadly to include production and related activities in crop, livestock, fisheries and forestry.

Duncan indices also become higher. Excluding agriculture, the index rises to 0.57, which indicates high segregation of women by sector.

Urban Labour Market and Employment

This section and those following shall concentrate more specifically on the urban areas and on patterns according to the "usual" definition. As the extended definition affects mostly the agricultural sector in the rural areas[6] the loss in information is unlikely to be serious.

Sectoral distribution of urban employment

In the urban areas, women are concentrated mostly in community and personal services sectors followed by manufacturing. Together they account for 68-78 per cent of employed women depending on the cut-off age one uses (table 4). Men are concentrated mostly in trade and catering followed by community and personal services.[7] Yet, their employment is more diversified as the two sectors account for just above one-half of the jobs they hold. Then again as the total size of male employment is much higher than that for women, the number of women in, say, manufacturing is only about one-half of that of men although the proportion of women in manufacturing is double of that for men. In any case, the high sectoral concentration of women compared to men equates to a fairly high Duncan Index (table 5).

Occupational characteristics of urban employment

Sex segregation is more pronounced in case of occupational categories. Women tend to concentrate in categories such as production worker and service workers. They are conspicuously

---

6 The figures under extended definition will, of course, be more useful if one wants to understand the prospects for employment generation in the medium term future. Although very important from this perspective, the issue is not examined here. This is a major gap in the literature as one hardly finds this particular issue in policy analysis and discourse.

7 The Labour Force Survey does not clearly define what these services are. But, very possibly these include educational and health services and various other odd jobs that people do for others against payment (such as drivers of vehicles owned by private citizens or as gate keepers in people's houses).

absent in administrative and managerial positions and are also rare in sales and clerical work, the two major areas of women's employment in many countries (Blau and Ferber : 1992, p. 120, Fuchs : 1988 p. 14) (Meulders *et. al.* : 1997, p. 89). On the other hand, one finds comparatively more women in professional and technical categories. One can only speculate why this is so.

One line of reasoning may be as follows : Women from poor households enter the labour market mainly as production workers or service workers (including jobs as housemaids). Women from relatively affluent households who are also likely to be better educated may have professional and technical training (including those as engineers and in the medical profession) to be in such jobs. The sales and clerical jobs are most likely to be held by women with at most high school education and those coming from lower middle class families. In fact, it is here that conservatism and adherence to traditional values is probably the strongest.

Unfortunately, the data in the LFS is not sufficiently disaggregated to allow testing the correlation between initial family situation (income and education) and occupational categories. But whatever information is available appears to be consistent with the hypothesis regarding educational background. Thus, of the 342 thousand service workers aged 15 years and above, 86 per cent are without any education (BBS : 1996, p. 157). Among production and transport workers, only about 40 per cent are illiterate while about 30 per cent have schooling of at most 5 years. Almost certainly they have come from poor background (see the following discussion on micro evidence). Of the clerical workers, two-thirds have an education at least up to the school final. Among professional/technical categories (which of course also include semi-literate but experienced technical hands in garages, as electricians, sanitary technicians etc.), the proportion of those having a college level education or beyond is 33 per cent.

Women's employment in manufacturing industries

Distribution by industry : Earlier it was shown that manufacturing is a major sector employing women. Not all manufacturing industries, however, are equally important.

Data produced in Table 6 indicate that for both men and women, but more so for the latter, the highest concentration is in the textiles manufacturing. Food and beverage industries constitute a poor second.

Textiles, however, include ready-made garments which alone accounts for 91 per cent of the total female employment in the textile industry and 76 per cent of all manufacturing industries. For men it is much more diversified. Thus, while ready-made garments accounted for only 6 per cent of all textiles jobs for men, the shares of other textiles in men's employment were 19 per cent for jute textiles, 16 per cent for cotton textiles and 15 per cent for handloom textiles (BBS : 1997, p. 103-104).

Occupational segregation of women in manufacturing : Women are practically absent from administrative, clerical and sales jobs (Table 7). They are mostly production workers. So are men. But, men also have a fair share in mid-level jobs and high level positions.

Characteristics of women workers

The LFS is silent about certain characteristics of the labour force, particularly those related to women workers in major sectors such as manufacturing. Here I reproduce some pertinent information from my own micro survey on ready-made garment workers.[8]

Age pattern : Women in the garments factories are mostly young compared to the general urban working women. Sixty two per cent of the RMG working women are in the age-groups 15-19 and 20-24 years divided equally between them while there are few girls aged 14 years or less. In contrast, the general age pattern for urban, women labourers shows that girls in the 10-14 age groups are the most numerous, 22 per cent of the total urban women labourers while all other age groups have a fair share in the distribution

8 The survey was conducted in 1997 in 22 ready-made garments factories among 260 women workers and a control group of 130 non-workers of similar background. The objective of the survey was to investigate the economic and social changes in the women workers' households as a result of their work outside the home. These information are now being analysed as part of my Ph.D. thesis at the University of Waikato in New Zealand.

(BBS : 1996, p. 147). While it may sound odd that there are few child workers in RMG factories, note that such factories now discourage employment of child labour.[9] In fact, earlier surveys also indicated a rather low percentage of girls (only 13-14 per cent) aged 14 years or less (Zohir and Paul-Majumder : 1996, p. 25-26).

Educational Background : Data in Table 8 demonstrate that the level of education demanded in RMG is somewhat higher than what one usually finds among such workers while there are very few illiterate workers compared to that found from the LFS 1995-96 (39 per cent), the proportion of high school graduates is also higher among the RMG workers than what has been found in the LFS (p. 157). During the survey, it has indeed been observed that the managers wish to employ literate women, the more education, the better. This is so because they must understand simple English written on packaging materials and also have to understand the patterns supplied by the buyers from Western countries.

Migratory characteristics : The rise in the urban population of Bangladesh is the net result of both rural-urban migration and natural population increases. So far, it is hypothesised that the migration factor exerts a stronger influence than the latter.[10] In such a situation one may hypothesize that migration will have a similar influence on the urban labour situation. There are two types of evidence to back up the claim.

At the macro level, the population figures for the last several censuses indicate that women are migrating to the towns in greater number than before. Between 1981 and 1991, the sex ratio in urban areas has fallen from 126 to 119.[11] This is part of an over-all falling

---

9 This was in the wake of the so called Harkin Bill moved in the US Congress to restrict the importation of commodities where their production depends among others on employment of child labour. After much negotiation, a tripartite memorandum of understanding was signed between the Bangladesh Garments Manufacturers and Exporters Association (BGMEA), the ILO and the UNICEF to discontinue employment of child labour in garments factories and arrange for schooling with stipends for the displaced child labourers (BGMEA, 1995). How far this has become effective in rehabilitating the children remains anybody's guess as the value of the stipends (Tk. 300 or so per month) are much less than what the children would have earned in the factories.

10 See (Asaduzzaman : 1989) for review of the urbanisation issue and relative weights of the two factors now and in the future.

11 Sex ratio is usually defined as the number of men per one hundred women.

trend. Yet, for the adolescents (10-14 years), teenagers (15-19) and the young (20-29 years) the fall in the sex ratio has been rather dramatic.[12] That means that women in these age groups must have been migrating to the towns in much larger numbers compared to men. Prospects of finding jobs in specific sectors such as the ready-made garments must have been a magnet drawing them in. In higher age groups the sex ratios have similarly fallen but not so drastically. That means the migration of young women have been a comparatively recent phenomenon as is the rise of the RMG industry.

As to the micro level evidence, of the 260 respondents (in Author's survey), 233 (90 per cent) were migrants. In 1990, a similar survey found the proportion to be 68 per cent (Zohir and Paul-Majumder : 1996, p. 23). Thus, migration for jobs has increased among women. As to the initial motives for migration, seventy four percent of women stated that they had come for a job, more specifically a garments job. Some 27 per cent moved because the family itself migrated. Others reasons were numerically insignificant.

Nature of Employment

Employment status

The status of employment in the Labour Force Survey means whether somebody is self-employed or a wage labourer or an unpaid family labourer. The last category is important in understanding employment in agriculture in rural areas where it is very significant (Hye : 1993). But it may also be so in towns in case of informal and petty occupations.[13] Be that as it may, it is found that under the extended definition, more than 77 per cent of women are employed as unpaid family worker (BBS : 1996, p. 128). Under the usual definition the percentage falls but still remains the largest category at 34 per cent. Apart from this difference, the patterns for

---

12 The falls had been for 1-14 years age group : 112 to 108; for 15-19 years age group : 120 to 107 and for the 20-24 years age group : 132 to 108 (BBS : 1996).

13 The importance of informal occupations in the urban areas has been long recognised. For an analysis of informal employment in urban areas see (Amin : 1986).

men and women are similar as is also evident from the rather low Duncan indices.

In the urban area, in contrast, the employee (*i.e.*, wage labourers) category is the most important for women under the usual definition (table 9). Under an extended definition, its relative importance falls and the category of unpaid family helper becomes somewhat more important. For men, the pattern is different. Here the self-employed category appears to be the most important group followed closely by paid workers. There is, however, little change in the pattern of men when the extended definition is used. The pattern for men indicates the importance of informal occupations such as vendors in open markets, shop-keepers, various types of repair services etc. Very possibly, women in their households help these men out to a considerable extent in organising their trade which may partly explain the increased importance of unpaid family help in the case of women employment under the extended definition. Unfortunately little is known about the empirical relationship between the two and thus remains a major area of future research.

Weekly hours worked

There is a great difference between men and women in the time devoted to employment for income earning. Even under the usual definition, nationally, half of the women put in less than 30 hours of work a week (BBS : 1996, p. 167). The corresponding proportion for men is only 15 per cent. Under the extended definition, the proportion of women working for at most 30 hours increases to 74 per cent (BBS : 1996 p. 129), but that for men remains unchanged. The reasons are quite obvious. Women, unless they work outside the home, combine their employment with other home-based work and in activities (such as vegetable gardening, poultry raising) which do not need continuous attention. Thus the length of time they devote to employment is less than for men who generally work outside the home.

In the urban areas the intensity of work is higher, both for men and women. Indeed, more than one-half of women are found to work (under the usual definition) for at least 40 hours a week (table 10). The proportion remains substantial at 38 per cent even under an extended definition of work. Again for men there is hardly any change. Note, however, that there is a substantial proportion of both men and women who work very long hours (more than 60 hours a week) and the proportions are similar for men and women. This may have to do with employment status. Men are mainly in self-employed activities and women work both as wage labourers and as self-employed persons. Those in self-employment would, of course, like to work long hours to maximise income particularly as such activities tend to have low productivity. On the other hand women in wage labour particularly in manufacturing industries such as RMG are known to work very long hours.[14]

Thus, the patterns of employment by working hours are similar across gender. The result is a rather low Duncan index of dissimilarity, only 0.27, under the usual definition. Under an extended definition, the index, however, rises somewhat to 0.41. The patterns and the indices remain broadly similar when only persons at least 15 years of age are considered (not shown).

Income and Earnings

A caveat

The LFS does not provide any aggregate earnings profile of the participants in the labour force. Only information on earnings by employment status is available. This creates a problem as there are people such as unpaid family workers who do not earn any direct cash or kind income but get to share the income of the household. This is important for understanding the income position of the women and their control of their wages as unpaid family workers constitute a large proportion of the total employed women. Given this caveat I shall look at the earnings profile of wage earners.

---

14 Many women interviewed by me work for 12-14 hours a day which includes 3-5 hours of overtime. Overtime is mandatory as factories have to honour their contracts with the foreign buyers for timely supply. On the other hand, workers do overtime because this helps them, earn extra income. They also usually receive snacks and night meals or cash payments for meals on such occasions.

Earnings profile

Table 11 shows the distribution of men and women under usual definition in the rural and urban areas. It is quite obvious that women earn much less than men both in the rural and urban areas. Otherwise, the patterns for both men and women are similar in the rural and urban areas with the exception that there is a concentration of men, and, to an extent, of women in the urban areas in the topmost earnings category. Yet the fact remains that men earn as wage, on average, twice or more of that of a woman.

Wage employment for women is quite important in the urban areas. To test whether the wage differentials are widespread I estimated the average wage rates for men and women for all types of employees and production workers. The results are shown in table 12. These indicate that the wage differentials are not that different in the manufacturing industries, at least not in all. In RMG for example, the figures suggest a differential of 14-15 per cent in favour of men as also found earlier (Zohir and Paul-Majumder : 1996, p. 46-47). While these do not deny that there may be discrimination (see below), this may partly reflect the fact that some of these industries are also in the public sector where wage differentials on the basis of sex are unlikely. It may be noted that one industry where the differentials are wide is tea processing which is wholly privately owned.

Income from self-employment shows patterns similar to that for wage income (table 13). Men earn roughly twice that of women. Also the patterns are similar in rural and urban areas.

Sex discrimination

The published LFS figures do not reflect any clear analysis of sex discrimination in earnings. But Zohir and Paul-Mazumder (1996, p. 50-51) argue that there may be such discrimination. Controlling for skill, job category, education and such other background characteristics, the earnings differences remain statistically significant and men have been found to earn 23 per cent more than women. The higher earnings, however, may have to do with higher productivity of men as observed by both men and women. During my own survey, women respondents have made similar observations.

Conditions of Work : Institutional Support and Social System

The earlier section has found that women are in a weak position compared to men in the labour market. Thus there is a pressing need for implementing appropriate policies for the protection of women. In the urban areas, a major area of intervention must be the improvement of the working conditions of women in factories.[15] This section discusses these issues rather briefly.

The Issues

There are many issues of institutional support of concern to the women's labour market. Only two broad issues will be discussed due to space limitations and limited scope of the paper. These are laws related to Protection and Equity. The Protective legislation (ILO Convention, 89 (1948)) relates to women's maternity benefit and protection against hazardous and night work. The Equity Promotion deals with existence of equal opportunity (ILO Convention, 100 (1951)), and provisions in the UNCDAW 1988 *i.e.*, removal of all forms of discrimination against women which covers 'marriage bars' to employment, sex-segregated job advertisement and discrimination in retirement age.

Maternity benefits

The first Maternity Benefit Act was passed in 1939 and enforced in January 1940 (Khan : 1995, p. 527). The act is comprehensive in its provisions for dissemination of information (see Appendix 1), eligibility for receiving benefits and safeguards against abuse etc. There is confusion in the literature regarding how this law is interpreted by private entrepreneurs.[16] The author found

---

15 Of course, women's employment issues go far beyond this. Owing to space limitations, however, I am concentrating on legal and institutional measures in urban wage labour market.

16 There is little research on this concept in relation to the labour market. One study (Paul-Majumder : 1993, p. 17) finds that 14 percent of employers (from paper products, printing and publishing, and metal products and machinery) find maternity leave to be a serious problem, but 60 per cent did not find it a problem. However, the author did not mention whether these 60 per cent of industries are in the private or public (Government) sector. If maternity benefit laws are implemented in the public sector; it does not imply a similar situation in privately owned factories. The same document mentioned (p. 120) that

(in her survey) that no where in the factories are the provisions of the Act exhibited as required by law. Also when asked, the factory management clearly stated that they grant the leave (see Appendix 1), but no maternity benefit. If women return, they in some cases get their job back. Although this may be at lower pay.

This is not the place to go into the details of the reasons for non-payment of maternity benefits. But the fact remains that a major reason for a lack of maternity benefits is a lack of awareness and poor implementation mechanism by the Government. A similar situation obtains elsewhere such as India (Acharya : 1996, p. 74). There is a case for investigating this issue more clearly to find loopholes in the law, in its formulation, implementation and the possible effects on women's employment and productivity and efficiency in the factories including their competitiveness in the world market.

Other benefits

It is not clear if night and hazardous works are explicitly prohibited by law for women in Bangladesh.[17] But legally no worker is allowed to work more than 48 hours a week. If a worker exceeds the limit, the worker is entitled to have an overtime allowance at the rate of twice his/her ordinary rate of wages (Khan : 1995, p. 238). In garment factories where overtime hours are the norm, no women worker gets this rate. In most cases they get fifty percent of their basic wages for extra work (own survey).

"... maternity benefit is listed in the labour laws, but Bangladesh has not yet ratified the ILO Convention and therefore the law is not enforced." Ratification of a Convention means a change is made in domestic legislation. If the legislation is there, it is there, whether or not ratification has been done or not. Another study (Zohir and Paul-Majumder : 1996, p. 106) documents that some firms grant maternity leave to women without clarifying whether it is with or without pay. Rahman (1993, p. 71) finds maternity leave to be one of the major concerns of employers against employing women. But she finds "... no way to verify whether the leave is with pay or for how long." The same document records that 94 per cent of employers find women are more sincere about their work than men and 84 per cent of employers admit that they accept lower wages than men. Therefore, they take advantage of women's ignorance and weak economic condition and lack of organisation.

17 In a study on seven Asian countries, only India and Philippines have been found to be signatories to the ILO Convention on night work while in Japan and Korea there is domestic legislation against it (Horton : 1996).

The Constitution [Government of Bangladesh, 1996, p. 14] declares equal rights of all citizens in the public sphere (Appendix 2). So for equal work there should not be any discrimination on wages. But as discussed earlier, there is evidence to the contrary. Similarly there should not be any marriage bar in employment. But in practice, entrepreneurs prefer to employ unmarried or widowed women as that may save them from the discontinuity of work due to maternity leave and other leave due to family obligations.

There is minimum wage legislation in general and in particular for the garment industry.[18] But this is not properly observed (Zohir and Paul-Majumder : 1996). I had a similar experiences during my survey. Women work at the discretion of the employer and temporarily, as they do not have any written contact. Thus, there is no security of employment which may partly explain partly the low wages they receive.

There are other provision in law such as provision of facilities for keeping children aged six years or below in every factory where there are more than 50 women workers. None of the garment factories have this facility.

Thus, domestic legislation is of limited value, if it is not enforced properly. In a country where women have less access to resources than men because of social, cultural and religious laws (such as those pertaining to property rights) (Rahman and Schendel : 1997, p. 49), their access to employment and earned income may not bring them enough respite because of faulty laws, and inadequate enforcement. Poverty forces them to work, but with long hours of work without much legal protection, only the household (and men who control the household) may gain. As result a women can not always continue for long in employment and probably ends up again in poverty.[19]

---

18 Bangladesh Gazette Extraordinary, Thursday, December 27, 1984. For details see (Zohir and Paul-Majumder : 1996, p. 53).

19 Women often have said that they are dog-tired and cannot continue and most apparently retire after a few years. Little knowledge exists about what happens to them afterwards.

Summary and Concluding Remarks

Summary of findings

The findings in the foregoing sections may be summarised as follows :

i. Labour force participation by women is lower than that for men. But if their home-based economic activities are considered, it becomes substantial. The pattern of LFPR by age is similar to what has been observed in other developing and developed (to some extent) countries at similar stages of economic growth.

ii. Women are employed mostly in certain sectors as opposed to men and only in certain occupations. In urban areas, they are concentrated, among others in manufacturing and particularly in RMG factories as workers. Such women are somewhat better educated than the general women labourers are.

iii. While many are paid workers, amongst women in urban areas, there are a very substantial proportion of women who work as unpaid family helpers.

iv. Women are found to devote far fewer hours to earning an income than men, possibly because, they have to combine housework with income-earning work and also because home-based activities need continuous attention. Where it does, many are found to work very long hours.

v. Possibly as a result of a very large group of women being unpaid labourers and also because of possible discrimination, women earn far less than men. But, in manufacturing sector the wage differentials are very high particularly in dynamic sectors such as RMG.

vi. There is little protection offered to women even in the formal labour market. It is not the absence of laws, but their poor implementation, which is partly responsible.

Concluding Remarks

There are many obstacles to improving the economic status of women. Usually, employment generation is thought to be the way out. Unfortunately, this is easier said than done because of the biological and social reproductive roles of women. They are penalised for these roles. But even when society tries to redress the problem somewhat, it is at best a half-hearted effort. The problem is further compounded due to lack of adequate knowledge and analysis of certain problems. Some, which need to be studied include, among others,

- a rigorous analysis of sex-discrimination in the work place in terms of compensation;
- impact of effective minimum wage legislation and provision of other benefits such as maternity leave with pay on women's employment, productivity and competitiveness of industries concerned and
- the economic and social situation of women when they leave their jobs in the formal labour market.

REFERENCES

Acharya, S. (1996), "Women in the Indian Labour Force : A Temporal and Spatial Analysis," in Horton, S., *Women and Industrialization in Asia*, Routledge, London and New York, p. 43-80.

Amin, N. (1986), "Urban Unemployment and Underemployment," in Islam, R. and M. Muqtada, *Bangladesh* : Selected *Issues in Employment and Development*, ILO/ARTEP, New Delhi.

Asaduzzaman, M. (1989), "Feeding Our Future Towns : An Overview of Urbanisation and Associated Food Policy Issues," in Planning Commission, Government of Bangladesh, *Food Strategies in Bangladesh : Medium and Long term Perspectives*, University Press Limited, Dhaka, p. 177-95.

Asaduzzaman, M. (1997), "Role of Micro Credit in Poverty Alleviation in Bangladesh : A Comparison of NGO and Government Intervention," in Rahman, R.I., *Poverty and Development : Bangladesh Perspectives (in Bengali)*, Bangladesh Institute of Development Studies, Dhaka, p. 197-215.

Asaduzzaman, M. (1997a), Employment Generation, unpublished manuscript.

Bakht, Z. (1993), "Review of Rural Non-Farm Activities," in Asaduzzaman, M. and Kirsten Westergaard, *Growth and Development in Rural Bangladesh : Critical Review,* University Press Ltd., Dhaka, p. 119-56.

Bangladesh Bureau of Statistics (BBS), (1996), *Report on Labour Force Survey in Bangladesh* 1995-96, Government of Bangladesh, Dhaka, p. 364.

Bangladesh Bureau of Statistics (BBS), (1997), *Report on Bangladesh Census of Manufacturing Industries* CMI 1991-92, Government of Bangladesh, Dhaka, p. 369.

Bangladesh Bureau of Statistics (BBS), (1998), *Household Expenditure Survey* 1995-96, Government of Bangladesh, Dhaka.

BGMEA, UNICEF and ILO, (1995), Memorandum of Understanding (MOU), The Placement of Child Workers in School Programmes and the Elimination of Child Labour.

Blau, F.D. and Ferber, M.A. (1992), *The Economics of Women, Men and Work*, Prentice-Hall, Inc., Englewood Cliffs, p. 355.

Chowdhury, O.H. (1997), "Nutrition, Physical Growth and Poverty," in Rahman, R.I., *Poverty and Development : Bangladesh Perspectives (in Bengali)*, Bangladesh Institute of Development Studies (BIDS), Dhaka, p. 98-112.

Duncan, O.D. and Duncan, B. (1955), A Methodological Analysis of Segregation Indexes, *American Sociological Review*, 20, p. 210-17.

Fuchs, V.R. (1988), *Women's Quest for Economic Equality*, Harvard University Press, Cambridge Ma, London, p. 171.

Government of Bangladesh, 1996, The Constitution of the People's Republic of Bangladesh, Dhaka, p. 180.

Horton, S. (1996), "Women and Industrialization in Asia : Overview," in Horton, S., *Women and Industrialization in Asia*, Routledge, London and New York, p. 1-42.

Hye, S.A. (1993), Review on Labour and Employment, In Asaduzzaman, M. and Kirsten Westergaard, *Growth and Development in Rural Bangladesh : A Critical Review*, University Press Ltd., Dhaka, p. 261-394.

Khan, A.A.P. (1995), *Bangladesh Labour and Industrial Law*, Pravati Prakashani, Dhaka, p. 797.

Meulders, D., O. Plasman, *et. al.* (1997), "A Typical Labour Market Relations : In The European Union," in A.G. Dijkstra and J. Plantenga, *Gender and Economics : A European Perspective*, London and New York, Routledge, p. 75-85.

Organisation (ILO) — Asian Regional Team for Employment Promotion (ARTEP).

Osmani, S.R. (1997), "Economic Growth and Poverty Alleviation : Some Thoughts on their Relationships," in Rahman, R.I. *Poverty and Development : Bangladesh Perspectives (in Bengali)*, Bangladesh Institute of Development Studies, Dhaka, p. 13-29.

Paul-Majumder, P. and Salma Chaudhuri-Zohir (1993), Employment and Occupational Mobility Among Women in Manufacturing Industries of Dhaka City : Bangladesh Findings from a Survey of Employees, New Delhi, Asian.

Rahman, M.M. and Schendel, W.V. (1997), "Gender and the Inheritance of land", in Schendel, Willem van and Kirsten Westergaard, *Bangladesh in the 1990s : Selected Studies,* The University Press Limited, Dhaka, p. 167.

Rahman, R.I. (1993). Employment and Occupational Mobility Among Women in Manufacturing Industries of Dhaka City, New Delhi, International Labour.

Rahman, R.I. (1997), Poverty and Development : Bangladesh Perspectives (in Bengali), Bangladesh Institute of Development Studies, Dhaka, p. 236.

Westergaard, K. (1993), "Review on Women and Gender Issues," in Asaduzzaman, M. and Westergaard, *Growth and Development in Rural Bangladesh : A Critical Review*, University Press Ltd., Dhaka, p. 407-511.

Zohir, S.C. and Paul-Majumder, P. (1996), *Garment Workers in Bangladesh : Economic, Social and Health Condition*, Bangladesh Institute of Development Studies, Dhaka.

APPENDIX 1

The following Rules are quoted from Khan, A.A. (Prof.) 1995 (Khan : 1995, p. 527– 28).

15. Abstract of Maternity Benefit Act and the rules thereunder to be exhibited. An abstract of the provisions of this and the rules thereunder[20] (Bengali) shall be exhibited in a conspicuous manner by the employer in every part of the place of work in which women are employed.

Abstract (relevant part) of the Bengal Maternity Act, 1939 and Rules framed thereunder (Rule II of the East Bengal Maternity Benefit Rules, 1953).

1. Under the Maternity Benefit Act, 1939, every woman employed for a period not less than nine months immediately preceding the date of her delivery is entitled to receive from her employer maternity benefit at the rate of her daily wages or Taka one a day, whichever, is greater, for a period of 12 weeks at every child-birth, *i.e.*, 6 weeks immediately preceding and 6 weeks immediately following the child-birth.

2. Every pregnant woman should give notice to the manager or employer of her expectation of confinement within 6 weeks. If such notice is not given before the birth of a child, it must be given within seven days of its birth. The notice may be given either orally in person, or in writing in form B appended to the

20 Substituted by Act, LIII of 1974.

East Bengal Maternity Rules, 1953, if before birth, and in form C appended to the said rules, if after birth.

3. A woman must not work during the period for which she received maternity benefit. Failure to adhere this will render both the woman and the employer or the manager employing her liable to prosecution.
4. Maternity benefit is payable to the woman entitled to receive it. If she dies, but her child survives, the benefit due is payable to the person who takes care of the child. If both the woman and the child die the benefit due is payable to the woman's nominee or her legal representative.
5. [21]All payments against claims for maternity benefit shall be made in cash and receipts, therefore, shall be taken. Any claim refused or accepted only in part shall be reported to the Deputy Labour Commissioner, Dhaka.

APPENDIX 2

Bangladesh Constitution

Article 19 (1) : The State shall endeavour to ensure equality of opportunity to all citizens.

Article 20 (1) : Work is a right, duty and a matter of honour to every citizen who is capable of working, and everyone shall be paid for his work on the basis of the principle "from each according to his abilities to each according to his work."

Article 28 (2) : Women shall have equal rights with men in all spheres of the State and of public life.

Article 29 (1) : There shall be equality of opportunity for all citizens in respect of employment or office in the service of the Republic.

---

[21] Only relevant part of the Act is mentioned that is needed for the paper in the original document this is in number 6. It is difficult to ignore the consecutive number. So it is mentioned in number 5.

Tables

Table 1 : Refined Activity Rates by Location and Sex (% of Population Age 10 Years & Above)

Locality	Usual definition			Extended definition		
	Both sex	Male	Female	Both sex	Male	Female
National	48.3	77.0	18.1	64.8	78.3	50.6
Urban	46.4	71.1	20.5	50.6	71.6	28.6
Rural	48.9	78.8	17.4	69.1	80.4	57.3

Source : Bangladesh Bureau of Statistics (BBS), *Report on Labour Force Survey in Bangladesh (LFS) 1995-96,* 1996, Tables 3.20 and 3.10, pp. 36 & 29.

Table 2 : Labour Force Participation by Age Groups and Sex (% of Population 10 Years & Above)

Age Group	Participation rate (Usual definition)			Participation rate (Extended definition)		
	Both	Male	Female	Both	Male	Female
10 – 14	33.3	37.7	28.3	33.3	37.7	28.3
15 – 19	41.7	61.3	18.0	57.5	65.5	47.8
20 – 24	43.5	78.8	15.8	68.9	82.0	58.7
25 - 29	50.2	93.5	16.0	75.9	95.5	60.4
30 – 34	55.4	98.3	15.8	79.8	99.2	61.9
35 – 39	59.9	98.4	18.2	81.4	99.3	62.0
40 – 44	62.3	99.0	17.0	81.9	99.2	60.4
45 – 49	60.9	98.8	14.3	81.1	99.2	58.9
50 – 54	57.4	98.0	14.3	78.4	98.4	57.1
55 – 59	57.9	96.1	14.4	74.6	96.6	49.6
60 – 64	55.2	88.6	11.4	68.2	88.4	41.0
65 +	43.7	70.2	8.4	52.3	71.2	27.1
Total	48.3	84.6	18.1	64.8	78.3	50.6

Source : BBS, *LFS,* 1996, tables 3.21 and 3.11, p. 37 &29.

Table 3 : Employed Person 10 Year and Over by Major Industry and Sex (all Bangladesh)

Major industry	Extended definition		Usual definition	
	Men (mn)	Women(mn)	Men (mn)	Women(mn)
Agriculture	18.4 (54.4)	16.1 (75.2)	17.9 (53.6)	2.8 (38.9)
Manufacturing	2.6 (7.6)	1.5 (7.0)	2.6 (7.8)	1.4 (19.4)
Power & Gas	0.1 (0.3)	0 (0)	0.1 (0.3)	-
Construction	0.9 (2.7)	0.8 (3.7)	0.9 (2.7)	0.1 (1.4)
Trade	5.6 (16.6)	0.5 (2.3)	5.5 (16.6)	0.4 (5.6)
Transport	2.3 (6.8)	0 (0)	2.3 (6.9)	-
Finance	0.2 (0.6)	0 (0)	0.2 (0.6)	-
Community services	3.3 (9.7)	1.7 (7.9)	3.3 (9.9)	1.7 (23.6)
Household & NAD*	0.4 (1.1)	0.8 (3.7)	0.4 (1.2)	0.7 (9.7)
All	33.8	21.4	33.2	7.1

Source : BBS, *LFS,* 1996, p. 44 and table U.15, p. 159.

Notes :
1. * NAD = not adequately defined.
2. Figures in parentheses are percentages of column totals.
3. "-": less than 50 thousand.
4. mn means million.

Duncan index (incl. agriculture) - Extended = 0.24.
Duncan index (excl. agriculture) - Extended = 0.44.
Duncan index (incl. agriculture) - Usual = 0.27.
Duncan index (excl. agriculture) - Usual = 0.57.

Table 4 : Sectoral Distribution of Urban Employed Persons (' 000) (Usual definition)

Major Industry	Aged 10 years & above		Aged 15 years & above	
	Male	Female	Male	Female
Agri, forestry, fisheries	862 (12.3)	184 (9.8)	746 (11.5)	98 (6.6)
Mining, quarrying	11 (0.1)	1 (0.05)	11 (0.2)	1 (0.07)
Manufacturing	1044 (14.9)	530 (28.1)	927 (14.3)	451 (30.5)
Electricity, gas, water	46 (0.6)	6 (0.3)	46 (0.7)	6 (0.4)
Construction	277 (4.0)	15 (0.8)	277 (4.3)	15 (1.0)
Trade, hotel & restaurant	2055 (29.4)	124 (6.6)	2055 (31.8)	124 (8.4)
Transport, storage, communication	974 (13.9)	19 (1.0)	933 (14.4)	19 (1.3)
Financial, business service	137 (1.9)	10 (0.5)	137 (2.1)	10 (0.7)
Community & personal services	1485 (21.2)	742 (39.4)	1292 (20.0)	713 (48.3)
Household sector & NAD	109 (1.6)	254 (13.5)	35 (0.5)	39 (2.6)
Total	7000	1885	6459	1476

Source : BBS, *LFS,* 1996, table U 15 (p. 159) and U 17 (p. 163) and own computation.

Notes :

Figures in parentheses are percentages of column totals. These may not tally due to rounding.

Duncan index for Urban age 10 & above = 0.43.

Duncan index for Urban age 15 & above = 0.47.

Table 5 : Occupational Distribution of Urban Employed Persons ('000) by Sex (Usual Definition)

Occupation	Aged 10 years & above		Aged 15 years & above	
	Male	Female	Male	Female
Professional, technical	442 (6.3)	241 (12.8)	417 (6.4)	231 (15.7)
Administrative managerial	145 (2.1)	6 (0.3)	145 (2.2)	6 (0.4)
Clerical workers	625 (8.9)	67 (3.6)	614 (9.6)	66 (4.5)
Sales workers	2130 (30.4)	111 (5.9)	2003 (31.0)	103 (7.0)
Services workers	350 (5.0)	537 (28.5)	289 (4.4)	342 (23.1)
Agri, forestry, fisheries	862 (12.3)	204 (10.8)	732 (11.3)	101 (6.8)
Production, transport, labourers	630 (9.0)	575 (30.5)	561 (8.7)	495 (33.5)
Not adequately defined	1816 (25.9)	146 (7.7)	1698 (26.3)	133 (9.0)
Total	7000	1887	6459	1477

Source : BBS, *LFS,* 1996, Table U11 (p. 152) and U14 (p. 157) and own computation.

Notes : Figures in parentheses are percentages of column totals. These may not tally due to rounding.
Duncan index for Urban age 10 & above = 0.51.
Duncan index for Urban age 15 & above = 0.53.

Table 6 : Distribution of Employed Persons in Manufacturing Industry (Two Digit Level) by Sex and Industry, 1991/92

Industry	Male	Female
31 : Food and beverage	182901 (16.2)	21662 (10.9)
32 : All textiles	706535 (62.6)	166018 (83.7)
33 : Wood and wood products	14688 (1.3)	3668 (1.8)
34 : Paper & pulp	34882 (3.1)	353 (0.2)
35 : Drugs & chemicals	55279 (4.9)	2396 (1.2)
36 : Glass & ceramics	55711 (4.9)	2016 (1.0)
37 : Iron, steel, copper	17515 (1.6)	175 (0.1)
38 : Metal products & machineries	57989 (5.1)	1049 (0.5)
39 : Miscellaneous	3405 (0.3)	1080 (0.5)
Grand Total	1128905	198417

Source : BBS, *CMI*, 1997, table - 16, pp. 103-08.

Notes : Figures in parentheses are percentages of grand total under relevant columns.

Totals may not add up due to rounding.

Table 7 : Distribution of Employed Persons in Manufacturing Industry by Sex and Occupation (1991/92)

Occupation	Male	Female
Admin. Clerical Sales Worker	169447 (15.0)	1965 (1.0)
Production related Worker	809881 (71.7)	174911 (88.2)
Director/Partner & Proprietor	21181 (1.9)	512 (0.3)
Hired Worker (Daily basis)	115644 (10.2)	18972 (9.6)
Unpaid Family Workers	12752 (1.1)	2022 (1.0)
Total	1128905	198382

Source : BBS, *Report on Bangladesh Census of Manufacturing Industries (CMI)* 1997, table-16, p. 108.

Notes : Figures in parentheses are percentages of relevant total employed persons.
The percentages may not add up to 100 due to rounding.

Table 8 : Educational Levels of RMG Women Workers

Education level	Number of workers	Per cent of workers
Illiterate	6	2.3
Can sign name only	60	23.1
Up to 5 years of schooling	86	33.1
6-10 years of schooling	64	24.6
High school graduate	37	14.2
Above high school	7	2.7
All	260	100.0

Source : personal survey.

Table 9 : Urban Employed Persons 10 Years and Over by Employment Status and Sex ('000)

Employment Status	Usual Definition		Extended Definition	
	Male	Female	Male	Female
Self employed/own account workers	2918 (41.7)	358 (19.0)	2920 (41.4)	357 (13.3)
Employer	66 (0.9)	5 (0.3)	66 (0.9)	5 (0.2)
Employee	2439 (34.8)	1049 (55.6)	2439 (34.6)	1049 (39.0)
Unpaid family helper	543 (7.8)	306 (16.2)	593 (8.4)	1110 (41.3)
Day labourers	1034 (14.8)	167 (8.9)	1030 (14.6)	169 (6.3)
Total	7000	1885	7048	2690

Source : BBS, *LFS*, 1996, p. table U 20 (p. 166) and table E 19 (p. 128) and own calculation.

Notes : Figures in parentheses are percentages of column totals. Totals may not add up due to rounding.
Duncan index of employment status (usual definition) : 0.29.
Duncan index of employment status (extended definition) : 0.37.

Table 10 : Employed Persons (10 years and over) by Weekly Hours Worked and Sex in Urban Areas (' 000)

Weekly hours	Usual Definition		Extended Definition	
	Male	Female	Male	Female
Less than 15 hours	296 (4.2)	167 (8.9)	301 (4.3)	274 (10.2)
15 – 19	99 (1.4)	137 (7.3)	103 (1.5)	291 (10.8)
20 – 29	363 (5.2)	319 (16.9)	379 (5.4)	712 (26.5)
30 – 39	681 (9.7)	262 (13.9)	692 (9.8)	388 (14.4)
40 – 49	2126 (30.3)	355 (18.8)	2137 (30.3)	376 (14.0)
50 – 59	1452 (20.7)	229 (12.1)	1453 (20.6)	231 (8.6)
60 – 69	734 (10.5)	212 (11.2)	735 (10.4)	211 (7.8)
70 and over	1244 (17.8)	207 (11.0)	1246 (17.7)	207 (7.7)
Total	7000	1885	7048	2688
Av. Hours worked (10 - 14 years)	34.3	42.3	34.3	42.3
Av. Hours worked (15 + years)	51	41	51	34

Source : BBS, *LFS*, 1996, p. 167 table U 23 and p. 129 table E 22.

Note :

1. Figures in parentheses are percentages of column totals. Totals may not add up due to rounding.
2. Av. means average in both the rows.

Duncan Index of Weekly Hours Worked (Usual definition) by Aged 10 Years & above = 0.27.

Duncan Index of Weekly Hours Worked (Extended definition) by Aged 10 Years & above = 0.41.

Table 11 : Distribution of Salaried Persons (15 years +) by Weekly Income, Sex and Residence ('000) — (Usual definition)

Weekly income (Taka*)	Rural		Urban	
	Male	Female	Male	Female
1-25	370 (16.8)	376 (61.6)	156 (7.0)	353 (43.9)
25-500	811 (36.8)	141 (23.1)	690 (30.9)	240 (29.9)
501-750	441 (20.0)	56 (9.2)	439 (19.7)	76 (9.5)
751-850	141 (6.4)	15 (2.5)	111 (5.0)	23 (2.9)
851-950	67 (3.0)	11 (1.8)	67 (3.0)	15 (1.9)
951-1050	119 (5.4)	2 (0.3)	194 (8.7)	38 (4.7)
1051-1150	17 (0.8)	- (-)	21 (0.9)	2 (0.2)
1151+	236 (10.7)	9 (1.5)	554 (24.8)	57 (7.1)
All	2202	610	2232	804
Average income (Taka)	708	308	958	480

Source : BBS, *LFS*, 1996, p. 176 table U28.

Note : Figures in parentheses are percentages of relevant column totals. Totals may not add up due to rounding.

* Taka is Bangladesh currency. US $ 1 = 46 Taka at present (1998).

Table 12 : Average Wage Rates in Selected Manufacturing Industries in 1991/92 — Taka/Per Year (' 000')

Industry	All Employees		Production workers	
	Male	Female	Male	Female
Rice milling	12.36	8.11	10.28	8.02
Tea/coffee processing	17.01	10.41	12.73	9.79
Bidi manufacturing	8.25	4.21	7.37	4.17
Cotton textiles	22.42	17.65	19.67	16.89
Handloom	11.56	10.31	11.12	10.31
RMG	16.73	11.76	13.09	11.73
Bamboo & cane	9.06	7.66	7.99	7.52

Source : Estimated from BBS, *CMI,* 1997, table-15, p. 96-97.

Note : Bidi is a kind of hand-spun cigarette using leaves from a plant and tobacco.

Table 13 : Self Employed Persons Aged 15 Years and Above by Monthly Income, Sex and Residence ('000) — Usual definition

Monthly income (Taka)	Rural		Urban	
	Male	Female	Male	Female
Taka 1 – 749	1127 (9.9)	783 (65.0)	201 (7.0)	204 (58.3)
Taka 750 - 1000	1315 (11.6)	192 (15.9)	213 (7.4)	65 (18.6)
Taka 1001 - 1500	2467 (21.7)	74 (6.1)	418 (14.5)	37 (10.6)
Taka 1501 - 2000	2430 (21.4)	65 (5.4)	531 (18.5)	15 (4.3)
Taka 2001 - 2500	1120 (9.8)	22 (1.8)	236 (8.2)	8 (2.3)
Taka 2501 - 3000	1287 (11.3)	19 (1.6)	433 (15.1)	7 (2.0)
Taka 3001 - 3500	424 (3.7)	13 (1.1)	101 (3.5)	3 (0.9)
Taka 3501 - 4000	482 (4.2)	26 (2.2)	229 (8.0)	8 (2.3)
Taka 4001 - 5000	376 (3.3)	4 (0.3)	182 (6.3)	2 (0.6)
Taka 5001-8000	300 (2.6)	6 (0.5)	231 (8.0)	1 (0.3)
Tk. 8000+	52 (0.5)	- (-)	102 (3.5)	- (-)
Total	11380	1204	2877	350
Average income	2073	821	2900	848

Source : BBS, *LFS*, 1996, p. 179, table U 32.

Note : Figures in parentheses are percentages of relevant column totals. Totals may not add up due to rounding.

13 Livestock Dispersal Programs in Developing Countries : Social-Economic Benefits for Human Resource Development in the Rural Sector

S.R. Harrison
F.A. Moog

Introduction

Promotion of livestock industries has been accorded high priority in many developing countries in Asia and the Pacific. "One of the strategies which has been used by the countries [in South-East Asia] ... has been to import live cattle to distribute to feedlot operators and to the numerous small backyard farmers who have relied upon traditional crops and traditional technologies for their livelihood" (Riethmuller and Smith, 1994, p. 1). While intensive production systems play an important role, for some livestock species (particularly cattle) backyard production remains the major sector of the industry. Small scale livestock offers greater equity and self-sufficiency benefits, and can take advantage of underutilized labour and feed resources. Tokrisna and Panayotou (1982) have observed that for the individual farmer, livestock provide an effective means of converting agricultural wastes and under-employed labour into capital.

Livestock "dispersion" or "distribution" programs, sometimes linked to agrarian reform, have been implemented widely in developing countries, to introduce a range of livestock species[1]. A frequently used format is to give smallholders breeding females,

---

[1] The terms dispersal and distribution are sometimes used synonymously, while in some cases dispersal is taken to mean a lower level of monitoring.

from which they return some offspring. Target recipients include farmers in depressed regions, ethnic minority groups and rural women.

Livestock dispersal programs have considerable potential to expand livestock industries and production of meat and other products. They can be particularly effective if a livestock industry is seriously underdeveloped, an unexploited niche in the production system is recognized, or a new production opportunity is identified (such as fish farming in rice paddys). However, it is to be noted that increased production from livestock industries frequently is not the major motivation for livestock dispersal programs. Rather, they may be designed primarily for welfare purposes, to improve the lot of smallholder families who could not afford to acquire animals through savings of loan finance. For the smallholders, livestock distribution programs yield private benefits in terms of producing saleable products, owning assets against which to borrow, and perhaps increased social standing. Considerable externality benefits may also arise, such as genetic improvement in national herds, greater food security and reduced welfare support for the rural poor.

Sometimes livestock are transferred from a well-developed production system to one in a different location, with a more severe climate, and are placed in the hands of farmers who may have little experience in livestock production. A good deal of thought and experimentation in design is necessary to maximize benefits from these programs.

This paper reviews experience in livestock distribution programs in China, Indonesia and the Philippines, with particular emphasis on beef cattle programs. A case study is presented which examines the socio-economic performance of the current Philippines Bureau of Animal Industry supervised cattle distribution program. Some observations are drawn concerning requirments for successful programs.

The potential socio-economic contribution of livestock dispersion programs

Livestock distribution programs are usually motivated on grounds of welfare for low-income communities and expansion of livestock industries as an effective means of rural development. Improvement in genetic quality of livestock may be an important motive. Funding is provided from international donors (including government aid agencies and NGOs) and domestic governments. An impressive example of these programs is the Heifer Project International in China, some details of which are provided below. As noted here, livestock distribution programs can have substantial social (as distinct from private) benefits, hence justifying government expenditure.

Objectives and Outcomes of Heifer Project International in China

HPI-China commenced in 1985 with three projects in Sichaun Province to help rural farm families improve sustainable food production and income generation. Today HPI/China focuses on creating viable communities, increasing dignity, promoting diversified and integrated farming systems, building local institutions, promoting and using the skills and resources of indigenous people, reducing urban migration and caring for the earth.

The Programe has expanded to include 24 projects. Each project family is assisted in buying high-quality animals locally or from other provinces. By the end of 1997, a total of 14,312 households from Han, Yi, Miao, Tibet, Hui, Uygur and Qiang ethnic groups have been provided with "the gift" of 960, 310 animals/poultry including cattle, yaks, dzo (yak x cattle), sheep, goats, pigs, rabbits, chicken, ducks, pigeons, geese and silkworms, as well as appropriate training in their care. Each family in those projects "pass on the gift" by sharing one or more of their animals' female offspring and knowledge gained in training with other needy families to ensure project continuity and multiplies the benefits of the original gift for generations.

By all means, the original inputs have been multiplied many times. Many families have doubled or tripled or quadrupled their income. In the Dayi Rural Rabbit project, for example, the original four families who received 200 imported rabbits have passed on the offspring to new families. This chain of sharing has been keeping going on for 17 generations within 12 years and now reached more than 2,649 families with 16,284 rabbits passed on. This project even passed 30 rabbits on to the poor farmers in Nepal. And we also sent 254 dairy goats to North Korea last year, and have another 60 goats ready for the next shipment.

The vision for HPI-China is for an ever-expanding number of rural communities to achieve a sustainable livelihood. Our program aims for the highest quality standard for participatory development and rural transformation. This is being achieved through our maturing relationships with local organizations and groups, our training and exchange programs, and our ongoing internal and external reviews. Our goal is to help rural families create community life that is healthy, fulfilling and profitable. Heifer Project has been bringing hope, opportunity and quality of life to many needy families in Sichuan, Chongqing, Xinjiang, Jiangsu and Qinghai Provinces of China.

Source : Chen Taiyong (1998).

Problems arising in livestock dispersal programs

In a sense, livestock dispersion programs are a classic case of economic development. For example, consider the case presented below :

Cattle distribution as a classic development assistance program

A smallholder is given a beef cow, and required to return the first calf to the government — to be distributed to another farmer — after which the smallholder obtains full ownership of the cow. The cow grazes plantation weeds, which would otherwise have to be controlled by manual means, and crop stubble which would have been burnt causing soil erosion and air pollution. There is sufficient unused labour capacity to manage the cow, which in any case is considered a pleasant activity. On obtaining ownership, future calves are sold for cash or kept for breeding.

A development expert would soon recognise this as a rather idealized picture. Programs to distribute livestock to smallholders are not without risk. Adverse outcomes might include :

- the weeds for grazing are not nutritious or are toxic;
- the cow escapes from its tether, and destroys vegetable gardens;
- the cow fails to breed, because the owner is unable to determine when to take it to a bull;
- the cow is unhealthy due to inadequate control of ticks and internal parasites;
- during the dry season, there is a scarcity of feed, hence, feed has to be cut and carted from long distances or concentrates purchased;
- the smallholder and his family do not have time to look after the cow, because the imperative is to obtain off-farm income to survive now, not to increase farm income in several years time;
- the cow dies or is stolen and
- the smallholder borrows against the cow, so that once he obtains ownership he is forced to sell it immediately to meet debts.

Although these are genuine risks, and some livestock dispersion programs would have to be judged as failures, other programs have been highly successful. The lesson from this is that programs have to be designed from the head, not from the heart. A careful review of past programs and considerable experimentation is needed to choose a suitable stock type for distribution and to devise appropriate business arrangements for the program, selection criteria and training for recipients, and continuing technical support and monitoring activities.

Previous livestock dispersal programs and their performance

Livestock dispersal programs have been implemented widely in developing countries. Table 1 summarises some of the features of four such programs, in China, Indonesia and the Philippines. It is apparent that a variety of design arrangements have been adopted.

Heifer Program International in China

As indicated above, HPI-China has been a major program of livestock distribution, covering a range of species, from large animals to silkworms. Further general details of the program have been provided by Professor Pu Jiabi, Director of HPI in China (Pu, 1998). Heifer Program International is a US-based ecumenical, non-government non-profit organisation, established in 1944, which raises funds in the US for poverty alleviation worldwide. HPI first donated cattle to China in 1947 through the Relief and Rehabilitation Agency of the United Nations. More recently, a group of projects in China commenced in 1985, with a strong focus on human and community development. Nearly one million livestock and poultry have been passed on to over 14,000 poor farm families covering six ethnic groups. Animals are purchased locally and from other provinces. Some further points made by Professor Pu include :

- "According to the Sichuan Provincial Bureau of Animal Husbandry, the value of the HPI China program has now reached 5 times as much as the original input."
- An objective in the program has been genetic improvement, and in this regard "[t]he milk and meat production of the crossbred goats are 90 percent higher than that of the local breed. More than 10,000 heads of fine offspring have been sold outside the project area as breeding animals. Project animal offspring have been distributed in more than 20 provinces and autonomous regions… [and] made great contributions to animal improvement in China."
- Women have played an important role in HPI projects in China, and 40 per cent of those attending training sessions are women.
- The cattle project is the biggest of the 20 HPI projects in China, and the most beneficial to project participants.
- Money is loaned to project participants, who are contracted to return the same amount of money plus a reasonable

interest rate. The returned money is converted to number of cattle, based on the local cattle price.

- Improvement in living standard and cash income, and human dignity, stand out among all projects.

Livestock Distribution Programs in Indonesia

Patrick (1996, p. 10) comments on "various projects distributing all forms of livestock" in Indonesia (p. 10), and "the vast range of options available to organisations undertaking livestock distribution projects" (p. 25), and notes that cattle are the most popular species distributed[2]. There is a particular emphasis on supporting "sustainable animal production for poorer farmers and village women." He notes that poverty alleviation is a more important aim than improving efficiency and productivity in livestock industries.

Of particular interest here is the World Bank NTASP cattle distribution program. According to Salisbury (1994, App. 1), in this program, criteria were set for both project locations and for selection of participants. Locations require year-round road access, land slope less than 15 per cent, high rainfall, relatively low cattle and buffalo ownership, absence of particular livestock diseases, proximity to an animal health post and agricultural extension office, and majority of farming community below the poverty line. Participants must be adult, married, of good behaviour, landowners or with right of use of land, and able to provide forage. Priority is given to farmers below the poverty line.

Further details of the program have been provided by Patrick (1998). Farmers were required to return two calves before gaining ownership of cows; ownership thus took three or more years, and if the cow missed a calf it could take five years. Cows were distributed in groups of 20, with two bulls. An extension officer was provided for each distribution group. Prior to receipt of cattle, farmers were required to commence forage production, mainly based on tree legumes.

---

2 Ian Patrick was an economist with the AusAID team which evaluated the program during 1990-95.

The main breed used was Bali cattle, well suited to tropical conditions but not to dry areas. Both intensive and extensive production systems were adopted. The initially wild cattle were quickly tamed. Most cattle were tethered in the more fertile cropping areas, although some cattle were run as a herd. Evaluation of welfare benefits was difficult, with confounding by many other factors, including drought conditions during the evaluation period.

Cattle were seen as a status symbol and asset, rather than a productive item. Some of the recipients who were amongst the lowest income group were identified as excellent cattle managers, with well developed forage systems, and it was anticipated they would continue with an efficient cattle raising operation. However, once they gained stock ownership, they immediately sold the cows, having borrowed heavily using them as collateral.

Salisbury (1994) found that productivity (defined as calf production and survival to 12 months) was related to land availability and parasite control. According to Salisbury (1994, p. 10),

> *"The criteria for selection of the NTASP cattle distribution sites are sufficient to ensure that the correct sites will be chosen. However the CHAPS [Cattle Health and Productivity Survey] has shown that in reality all the criteria have not been met, particularly with regard to feed availability throughout the year ...".*

With regard to gender or recipients, Patrick (1996, p. 22) observed :

> *"Althouth it is argued that women are not physically strong enough to handle cattle, this is probably not the case ... [and cattle should be considered] for distribution to women's groups. The major reason for male domination of cattle is their use for ploughing (which is men's work) and the fact that income is highly visible and use of this money can enhance the status of the farmer within the village e.g., donation to mosque, education of children etc. Money from small animals tends to be used for household requirements;*

men, therefore, are more prepared to give control of small livestock to their wives."

Programs in the Philippines

A variety of livestock distribution programs have been implemented in the Philippines. These include the Bureau of Animal Industry (BAI) supervised cattle distribution program (discussed in more detail as a case study below), other concurrent and past cattle dispersion programs, and programs for swine, sheep, chickens and ducks. As far back as 1964, the Congress of the Philippines enacted the *Cattle Dispersion Act* (Salita, 1997).

The BAI has been involved in cattle distribution programs since 1953. These have involved relatively large numbers of cattle — several thousand a year throughout the Philippines. When first set up, farmers repaid the loan for cattle purchase "in kind", but the emphasis has switched to loans administered by Rural Banks and farmer cooperatives, under the control of the BAI. Under the present Multi-Livestock Distribution Loan Program (MLDLP), farmers can obtain a loan to purchase livestock at an interest rate of 10 per cent and repayment term of five years. Loans are supervised by a bank technician and Local Government Unit (LGU) agricultural technician. The smallholder gains property rights to the animal when payment is completed. Credit for livestock acquisition has been provided under the MLDLP for about 3000 farmer clients and financed purchase of 10,000 animals.

Table 1 : Features of Some Livestock Dispersal Programs

Characteristic	Cattle distribution programme			
	Philippines BAI	Indonesian NTASP	Philippines MLDLP	HPI-China
Target recipients	Low-income smallholders	Priority to farmers below the poverty line	Poor farmers	Low income families and ethnic groups
Eligibility criteria	1 ha, convenient to monitor, agree to establish pasture	0.5 to 2 ha, year round road access	Co-operatives preferred	
Group size	10 head	20 head	No restriction	
Repayment method	Return dam when offspring 8 mths. old	Surrender first two offspring	Cash, 5-yrs. amortization	Local value of one animal
Extension and training	BAI , DA-RFU and local government	One extension officer/group	Rural Bank Technicians	Many training sessions
Period to full property rights	Typically about 2 yrs.	Typically 3-5 yrs.	Full payment of loan or 5 yrs.	About 2or more yrs.
Action reqd. prior to receiving animal	Build cattle shed	Establish forage trees		
Action reqd. after receiving animal	Estab. 0.4 ha imp. past.			
Extensive or intensive system	Intensive	Both	Intensive	Intensive
Farmer pays insurance on animal	Yes		Loan cattle mortgage with bank	
Scale of program to date	247 head			Thousands of head

Another program has been the Gintong Ani : Barangay Livestock Breeding Loan Program, targeted at the country's 21 poorest provinces, *viz.*, Muslim regions and the coconut growing provinces which are often hardest hit by typhoons. This program follows the original scheme of repayment; the farmer pays one female calf and retains the dam.

The Land Bank of the Philippines also runs a program called the Cattle Financing Program for Farmer Co-operatives. This is a breeder dispersal program, with the objectives of giving low-income farmers a secondary source of income and rebuilding the cattle population (Riethmuller, 1997). Over the period 1992-94, about 28,000 cattle were imported from the Northern Territory in Australia and dispersed to 540 cooperatives.

In retrospect, experience with cattle distribution programs in the Philippines suggests that the requirement of returning a calf is not ideal — the return rate has been lower than anticipated, and performance of the programs appears to have been adversely affected by ineffectual monitoring. Similarly, loan programs have faced difficulties, with administrative emphasis on repayment of the loan rather than livestock husbandry. Riethmuller (1997) notes a 6 per cent annual mortality rate in these programs, and problems associated with nutrition and breeding.

Private companies and NGOs operate pig distribution programs in the Philippines. For every breeder piglet distributed, two repayment female piglets are collected (and occasionally three). A supervised swine distribution program was implemented by the Bureau of Animal Industry. The program aimed to "provide additional income to farmers as part of the countryside development program of the government" and also to "save the struggling tenants and farmers from the widespread practice of the "PAIWI" system or the traditional method of financing concocted by the landlords or capitalists" (Samiano *et. al.*, 1992). This was an experiment in replacing the 2-3 month old weaners normally provided, with older rearing gilts and ready-to-breed gilts. Recipients were selected on the basis of personal characteristics (good and trustworthy character, industrious), presence of animal housing, capacity to purchase feeds and experience in animal production. "Farmers' classes were held before the distribution of animals to discuss their responsibilities in the project and give them pointers on how to properly raise the pigs." (Samiano *et. al.*, 1992, p. 3).

Case study : the Philippines BAI supervised cattle distribution program

An Australian Centre for International Agricultural Development (ACIAR) project is being developed to carry out a socio-economic analysis of the Philippines Bureau of Animal

Industry (BAI) supervised cattle distribution program. An inspection of this program was carried out in September 1998 (Harrison, 1998). As context for discussion of this program, it is useful to comment briefly on the current state of livestock industries in that country.

Livestock production in the Philippines

Statistics on livestock numbers for the Philippines over the period 1981 presented in table 2 indicate that cattle and carabao numbers have been relatively constant, while there has been a gradual increase in swine and goat numbers.

Table 2 : Populations of Selected Livestock Species in the Philippines, 1981-96

Livestock species	Livestock population by year (1000)						
	1981	1991	1992	1993	1994	1995	1996
Cattle on commercial farms	n.a.	191	153	159	167	186	199
Backyard cattle	n.a.	1,485	1,577	1,754	1,769	1,835	1,929
Cattle — total	1,940	1,677	1,731	1,914	1,936	2,021	2,128
Carabao	2,850	2,647	2,577	2,576	2,560	2,708	2,841
Swine	7,758	8,079	8,022	7,954	8,227	8,941	9,026
Goats	1,696	2,122	2,306	2,562	2,633	2,828	2,845

Source : 1981 figures from Franco (1993), 1991-96 figures from BAI (1998b).

There has been a strong increase in cattle numbers on "backyard farms" in some provinces. Surprisingly, carabao numbers have not declined, as in some Asian countries. Livestock dispersion programs have had some (perhaps small) impact on stock numbers, both through distribution of imported animals and by creating a greater interest in livestock by landholders. Some large-scale intensive production of pigs and poultry takes place, although as indicated in table 2 only about 10 per cent of cattle numbers are found on commercial farms. Further, stock numbers per farm are small, *e.g.*, Franco (1993) found a modal number of one head and a mean of approximately two heads in a sample of 85 smallholders.

In the Philippines, many low-income smallholders have experience in raising livestock (including cattle but often for other owners), have free family labour resources for much of the year, and are able to cut otherwise unwanted grasses and graze animals of crop stubble which would otherwise be burnt.

In that many livestock dispersion programs in developing countries have faced major difficulties, there is much to learn from this apparently highly successful program. Expansion of the program in the Philippines and extension to other countries could provide important markets for live tropical cattle from Australia. High live cattle prices at markets in the Philippines (about $ A2/kg LW) mean that cattle can be purchased from Australia and landed at below the local market price.

Motives for expansion of Philippines livestock industries

The Philippines' BAI has a mandate to expand livestock production, under Executive Order 292 (the Administrative Code of 1997) (Gutierrez, 1997). There would appear to be various reasons for this government priority, *e.g.*,

- improved human nutrition;
- import replacement and export of products such as leather goods;
- use of underutilized resources (land unsuited to crops, labour, grasses);
- utilization of crop stubble and failed crops;
- value adding to crop production;
- replacement of livestock production lost through land conversion due to urbanisation and industrialisation;
- food security (less at risk due from typhoon or drought);
- stock as an asset and source of security and
- transport and draught.

Most of the BAI's recent activities have revolved around implementing the Medium-Term Livestock Development Plan (Gutierrez, 1997). This plan serves as a framework for policy making over a five-year period. The agency's primary concern is to "develop better breeds of livestock through improved genetics, better feeds, and better care of animals" (Gutierrez, 1997, p. 8). Genetic improvement is taking place through the National Cattle Breeding Program. The BAI is progressing with an AI program for cattle, swine and other small ruminants. Programs are in place to improve animal health. Assistance for livestock industry development has been provided by AUSAID, JICA (Japan) and RP-GTZ (Germany).

The current BAI supervised cattle distribution program

In 1997, the BAI commenced a supervised livestock distribution program of *Bos indicus* breeding cattle to smallholders in Luzon. The program uses cattle of high genetic quality imported from Australia, obtained on commercial terms (not as an aid program). Cattle distribution is co-ordinated by the BAI of the Department of Agriculture (DA) with the DA-RFU and the involved Local Government Units (LGUs) in Southern Tagalog and Bicol Regions. It has been designed carefully to meet the needs of selected smallholders, based on considerable experience with livestock introduction. The cattle grazing system involves use of improved pastures under coconut palms. Selection criteria include that :

- at least 10 farmers must be located in contiguous areas close to the main road and
- each farmer must have at least 1 ha of coconut land, with 0.5 ha to be planted with improved pasture, such as Napier grass, Guinea grass or Signal Humidicola.

Each farmer in a cluster is provided with a single heifer. Animal must be dedicated to "breeding and reproduction, to enable the project to extend its economic benefit to other farmers" (BAI, 1998). Ownership of animals is retained by the BAI. Farmers are required to insure animals against death in favour of the BAI with a member insurance company of the Livestock Insurance Pool or other reputable insurance company. If an animal dies, a report from the Provincial Veterinarian is required. Farmers appear to carry liability in the case of theft. Cows are to be returned to the BAI once a farmer takes ownership of the first offspring, at eight months of age. Female calves must not be marketed until they in turn have calved. BAI through its research division staff in collaboration with DA-RFU and LGU staff provide assistance to farmers on pasture development. Approximately 250 Australian brahman cows have now been distributed to smallholders.

An early problem with the program has concerned reproduction. In an effort to overcome slow conception, the BAI provided local *Bos indicus* bulls, one per cluster, with the recipient charging a service fee. Even then, difficulties have arise with respect to heat detection and timely mating, and in some areas hormone treatment for heat synchronization and artificial insemination are now being used.

Performance of the BAI supervised cattle distribution program

The question arises as to how successful the program has been. To judge this, some measure of performance is required. Salisbury (1994, p. 3) chose as a measure of "productivity" for the Cattle Health and Productivity Survey in Indonesia "[a] cow's ability to produce a live calf that can survive to 12 months of age," *i.e.*, a measure of reproduction rate critical to the success of the dispersal program. For the Philippines BAI program, a broader approach using a number of indicators seems preferable. Some relevant indicators include :

- cow mortality rate;
- average turnaround time (from receipt of an animal to redistribution to another smallholder);
- livestock husbandry standard;
- animal condition score;
- smallholder satisfaction rating with the program;
- private profitability;
- private non-production benefits and
- overall social cost-benefit performance of the program.

The mortality rate has been relatively low in this program, and deaths have typically occurred soon after distribution, suggesting this is a matter of choosing suitable recipients. It is too early to determine average turnaround time, since only four weaner calves (from cows in calf at the time of distribution) have been redistributed, although a number of calves have recently been borne. Short turnaround time will depend on successful mating or artificial insemination.

On the pre-project trip, a large number of distribution cattle were observed, and the quality of livestock management was impressive. Many recipients had built housing for stock (out of coco-lumber with thatch roof), tick control was widely adopted, and a number were feeding concentrates.

Animal condition is perhaps expressed in terms of an index, of factors such as quietness, body weight and freedom from injury. Most of the distribution cattle observed were of sufficiently quiet demeanour to be touched by owners (in contrast to their wild state on arrival); few were in poor conditions, and only minor injuries were observed.

Smallholder satisfaction with the program could be assessed in terms of a number of variables, relating for example to inputs they make to the enterprise, outputs in terms of livestock performance, stated degree of satisfaction, willingness to participate in another program, and whether others would like to participate in a program. Recipients appear very proud of their animals and of their achievements in managing them (Harrison, 1998). The program was compared favourably against the traditional "PAIWI" system where smallholders raise cattle for others and receive only part of the revenue from stock sales.[3] The level of success of the program appears to vary between provinces. Where recipients have been selected carefully, and are visited frequently, the program appears to have been an outstanding success. Where this is not the case, stock are not in good condition and there have been some mortalities.

---

[3] Under the PAIWI system, for cattle fattening the net return — after purchase price and other costs met by the owner — is shared equally. For ready-to-breed females, proceeds of sale of offspring are shared equally, with ownership of the dam unaffected. For young females, the smallholder may share in the incremental value of the breeder if sold.

While initial observations are highly positive, a more thorough probability sampling approach to carefully designed questions is required to investigate this performance measure. Research is also required to determine private and social cost-benefit performance of the program, but some observations are possible as discussed below. In order to examine these economic aspects, it is necessary to develop a conceptual model of the cost-benefit performance of a livestock distribution program.

Model of cost-benefit performance of a livestock distribution program

The Net Present Value (NPV) of a livestock distribution program may be represented as

$$NPV = PB - PC + SB - SC$$

where PB and PC are private costs and benefits, and SB and SC are other social costs and benefits, all expressed as discounted sums over a number of years, and aggregated over all participants in the program. In deriving PB, annual benefits of individual smallholders have to be considered. From the individual farmer's perspective, the annual benefit of owning or having breeding rights to an animal might take the form :

$$VA = PV + SV + OB$$

where

VA is annual benefit value of the animal to the individual smallholder;

PV is product value or market value of the animal and services provided by it;

SV is the satisfaction or status value of livestock ownership or possession and

OB are the other family benefits of being a livestock recipient.

This value will accrue in particular from raising a calf, although property rights to distribution cows may also make a contribution. The livestock value in PV could include saleyard value of a local animal of equivalent carcass weight plus breed premium for imported high quality *Bos indicus* animals (associated with greater productivity of offspring). Private and social benefit categories are summarised in table 3, and components discussed in the following sections.

Table 3 : Preliminary Categorisation of Private and Social Benefits of the Supervised Cattle Distribution Program

	Private benefits
Production	Breeding of an animal for income or reproduction Weed control in plantations Manure as a fertilizer for vegetable crops
Personal	Pleasure of having animals of impressive appearance (amenity value)
Satisfaction and status	Personal satisfaction with stock management (taming, raising, breeding) Satisfaction with raising a calf Increased social standing as a livestock owner, pleasure of showing animals to others Status as a member of stock owner group Gaining of livestock management skills
Other family Benefits	Creditworthiness from inflation-proof asset Emergency source of cash or food Desirable activity for family members (therapeutic value) Idle family labor put into productive activity
Social benefits	
Production	Reduced need for livestock imports Improved genetic quality hence greater productivity of the national herd Demonstration effect encouraging other smallholders to raise cattle
Govt. revenue	Government taxation and charges (*e.g.*, revenue from stock insurance)
Welfare Benefits	Greater self-sufficiency hence reduced welfare expenditure Assistance to disadvantaged groups (rural poor, women, teenagers)
Regional security	More settled rural population, less insurgency and reduced urban migration

Financial profitability of the supervised cattle distribution program to smallholders

Table 4 presents estimated costs and returns of the cattle enterprise to smallholders (VA values in the above conceptual model). A Discounted Cash Flow (DCF) analysis approach is employed, with incremental cash flows derived over a 10-year planning horizon. The "without project" case assumes farmers have no cattle nor stock housing, improved pastures or equipment for handling cattle. In the "with project" case, a heifer is retained (or exchanged with a bull calf) for breeding purposes. The data for this analysis are a composite for the various provinces rather than applicable to a specific site.

Table 4 : Indicative DCF Analysis for Smallholder Cattle Enterprise

Parameters	
Number of days feeding/year=	60
Daily feed cost =	10
Labour requirement (hours/day) =	0.5
Labour cost (pesos/hour) =	7.5
Yearling price (pesos) =	8000
Cow value (pesos)=	14000
Real discount rate =	12%

Discounted cash flow analysis											
Cost or revenue category	Amount by year (pesos) -->										
	0	1	2	3	4	5	6	7	8	9	10
Cost item											
Pasture establishment, planting material	1000										
Stock housing	2000										
Gear (ropes, buckets, syringes, etc.)	500										
Insurance of animal	200	200	200	200	200	200	200	200	200	200	200
Concentrate feed	300	600	600	600	600	600	600	600	600	600	300
Hormone treatment	300	300		300	300		300	300		300	

Mating or AI fees	400	400		400	400		400	400		400	
Pesticides and vet. Medicines	200	200	200	200	200	200	200	200	200	200	200
Labour	685	1370	1370	1370	1370	1370	1370	1370	1370	1370	685
Total annual expenses	5585	3070	2370	3070	3070	2370	3070	3070	2370	3070	1385
Revenue item											
Sales of yearlings			8000		8000	8000		8000	8000		8000
Stock on hand											14000
Annual net cash flow	-5585	-3070	5630	-3070	4930	5630	-3070	4930	5630	-3070	20615
Net present value =	8786										

Assumptions :

1. Recipients individually build shed to house their stock, *e.g.*, at night, during the wet season.
2. Improved pastures are established immediately on receipt of a cow.
3. A female calf is obtained by the end of the first year, or a bull calf is exchanged for a female calf.
4. Due to difficulty in "heat detection", proglandin injections are used to bring on estrous for mating/AI.
5. Six calves are obtained in 10 years (*i.e.*, two every three years after the first year).
6. Natural increases are sold as yearlings.
7. No taxation is paid by smallholders.
8. The opportunity cost of labour is 7.5 pesos/hour, about half of the minimum award wage rate.

The financial analysis relies on a number of assumptions. The within-year timing of feed and labour costs is allocated such that half the cost is at the beginning of each year and half is at the end of each year. The opportunity cost of labour is taken as half the minimum wage rate of 120 pesos per day. A real discount rate (net of inflation) of 12 per cent is adopted. Further assumptions are indicated in the parameters and table footnotes. A net present value (NPV) over 10 years of about 9000 pesos is obtained ($ A1 ≈ 23 pesos).

Two of the most critical parameters in this analysis were found to be labour cost and duration of supplementary feeding, and a sensitivity analysis with respect to these factors is presented as table 5. If labour input is limited to one hour per day, the cattle enterprise is able to support supplementary feeding at a cost of 10 pesos per day; at two hours labour per day charged to the enterprise the NPV is negative even if there is no purchase of concentrate feeds. A number of smallholders appear to spend two or more hours per day looking after their cow, which would not appear to be justified on financial grounds. However, if working with cattle is an activity which yields satisfaction in itself, of if cattle labour displaces weed control labour, then a zero opportunity cost for labour would be appropriate, in which case private profitability appears assured. Shared stock housing and self-building further reduce cash outflows. It is to be noted that even if the program is not financially profitable from a private perspective, the project may be attractive to smallholders on the basis of non-production benefits.

Table 5 : Private NPV with Respect to Labour and Feed Inputs

	Labour requirement (hours/day)				
	8786	0	0.5	1	2
No. of	0	20582	12379	4176	-12231
days	30	18786	10582	2379	-14028
feeding	60	16989	8786	582	-15825
per yr.	120	13395	5192	-3011	-19418

Non-production benefits to smallholders

Non-production benefits (SV and OB) are forms of consumer surplus, estimation of which requires application of *non-market valuation* techniques. In the case of the BAI cattle distribution program, since smallholders typically have little savings, they do not have *effective demand* for cattle. Hence, willingness-to-accept compensation (WTAC) rather than willingness-to-pay is the relevant measure of wellbeing. In that the original cows are only on loan, the asset is real only when a calf is produced, so the estimation needs to be applied to calves rather than dispersal cattle. (It is notable, however, that some pleasure and increased standing may arise from possession of dispersal cows, prior to breeding.)

The simplest way to estimate WTAC for calves is to ask smallholders how much they would be prepared to accept in compensation if they were to give up the calf, i.e. what offer would induce them to sell an animal. Theoretical and practical problems arise with direct questioning of smallholders about this amount :

- They may not know what prices cattle bring in the market, against which to relate their WTAC.
- Relevant amounts may be larger than they are accustomed to considering, e.g. a calf may be worth 6000 pesos (about $ A250) and an adult beast 20,000 pesos, and they may lack experience with transactions involving such large amounts.
- They may think that the question is how much a beast such as the one they own would realise in the markets, rather than what they would be prepared to accept to part with it for. This issue appeared to arise in the pre-project field trip, and is essentially a matter of communication.
- They may not wish to appear greedy, given that the cattle dispersion program is relatively generous, and hence may report a conservative estimate.

These considerations suggest the contingent valuation method (using a dichotomous choice survey approach) or choice modelling (Harrison, in press) would be the most suitable methodology to estimate WTAC, and hence private non-production value of livestock. Research proposals are being developed along these lines. However, preliminary experiments have been conducted in which recipients of distribution cattle were asked what price they would be prepared to accept for their calf. For calves at three to four months of age, values ranged up to about 20,000 pesos. Even allowing for the high genetic value of calves, this is about three times the market value, suggesting high non-production benefits.

Overall cost-benefit aspects of the supervised cattle distribution program

The overall economic performance of this program cannot be judged at present, but an ACIAR research program is being designed to investigate social cost-benefit aspects. The conceptual model and benefit categories as in Table 2 provide a framework for this evaluation.

Some lessons learned from livestock distribution programs

The motivation for examining various livestock dispersion programs is to determine whether these programs are worthwhile public sector investments, and to explore how these programs can be designed and managed to ensure high socio-economic performance. In the latter context, it is useful to review various aspects of the programs discussed.

Design of distribution programs : It is apparent that considerable care is needed in program design, and that there no single optimal design. According to Patrick (1996, p. 25), in relation to the various programs in Indonesia, "[e]very group is different, with different social structure, range of skills and resources. A thorough understanding of each is required before any distribution program can begin." Patrick (1996, p. 26) goes on to make an interesting comparison of NGO versus other (domestic government and World Bank) programs :

> *"In general the NGOs have been more successful in implementing successful distribution programs although measuring success has tended to be a purely subjective judgment. NGOs have undertaken more detailed needs analysis and have included the farmers more closely in the decision making process. Farmers choose their own stock and have flexible repayment schedules."*

Selection criteria for recipients. A concern which arises in livestock distribution programs is that sometimes they are politically motivated and livestock specialists are not given the opportunity to select the areas for distribution or the farmer recipients : "... often animal dispersal is effected through the requests of mayors, governors and non-government organisations or through resolutions of barangay [village] and municipal councils" (Samiano, 1990, as cited by Samiano *et. al.*, 1992, p. 2).

Farmer group formation and integration with community life : In the Philippines, cattle are often distributed to farmer groups, and members work together to solve management problems. In Indonesia, "farmers were often told … that they would receive a certain type of livestock on offer [only] if they formed a group" (Patrick, 1996, p. 10). In one program, the extension officer "was in regular contact with the group and would run meetings once a month on a Friday after prayers at the mosque" (*Ibid*, p. 23). Many NGO programs in Indonesia have livestock distribution as part of integrated community and agribusiness development, with assistance in purchase of land and subsidised credit (*Ibid*, p. 11). Greater involvement by livestock recipients in the program and group mutual support is likely to ensure greater commitment and better management of animals.

Monitoring of recipients : It is apparent from experience in the Philippines and Indonesia that careful monitoring of participants — frequent visits promoting interest and encouraging sound management, and providing technical support — is critical in program success. Convenient all-weather access to recipients is necessary for regular monitoring.

Feed supplies in the dry season : The Indonesian program in particular points to the need to ensure adequate feed supplies in the dry season. Pasture availability or an agreement to establish pasture of fodder trees needs to be stipulated at the time of arranging contracts with farmers. It may be necessary to provide planting material and assistance to establish fodder production.

Repayment method and scheduling. Typically, in cattle distribution programs, the farmer is required to return one or two calves. In relation to the NTASP program in Indonesia, Salisbury (1994, p. 11) concludes that "[f]armers must not be forced to return the first two calves but must have the opportunity to select when repayment should occur, ensuring that two calves are repaid within six years or receiving the cattle." In the HPI-China program, each family is required to "pass on the gift by sharing one or more of their animal's female offspring … with other needy families." The Philippines BAI supervised cattle distribution program differs in that the cow is passed on, and the calf retained. This allows ownership to be gained more quickly, and maintains the genetic quality of the animals being passed on. A drawback is that the farmers may become attached to their cows, and be stressed at having to part with them. However, they also become attached to calves, and the cows are likely to be redistributed in the same district. A problem with programs where the cow is retained, particularly where two calves have to be returned, is that if any breeding problems arise the cow will be relatively old when full property rights are obtained, which can reduce interest by the recipient (Patrick, 1998).

Relative priorities on production and holding an asset : The importance of cattle ownership for smallholders may be viewed in terms of production and asset value of animals. In this context, Salisbury (1994, p. 7) noted "[f]armers who valued their cows as an asset rather than as a production unit, produced less calves". According to Salisbury (1994, p. 10) in relation to the selection criteria for cattle recipients in the Indonesian NTASP program,

> *"The criteria ... in themselves do not ensure that farmers, after fulfilling their obligations to the project, will continue in cattle production. ... Even though the productivity at Sambelia was the highest in the project area, farmers did not wish or could not afford to keep their stock after their obligations were completed. The poorest farmers in the areas therefore were not able to take advantage of the long term benefits of cattle production because their short term needs were more important."*

Based on this recommendation, Salisbury (1994, p. 10) makes the recommendations :

> *"If long term cattle productivity is a goal of the distribution program farmers must be educated to understand that the major benefit of cattle ownership is breeding value and not asset value."*

A drawback with this perspective is that smallholders may place great stock on the asset value of livestock. Livestock provide a relatively inflation-free store of wealth, a source of creditworthiness, and social status for the livestock owner, and in some countries are the major form of personal assets. It may be difficult to have a son or daughter married, or married to advantage, without asset ownership. In Indonesia, farmers who had not "repaid their calves" were using their cattle as collateral to buy basic necessities, for ploughing and for renting to other farmers for ploughing (Patrick, 1996, p. 22). Hence placing greater priority on livestock ownership than reproduction may be rational economic behaviour. The Philippines BAI project stipulates that animals be for "breeding and reproduction". It is notable that production (of a calf) is required for the smallholder to realise the asset benefit. In this sense, the program may provide strong incentives for both production and asset benefits, which could be a significant improvement in design relative to other livestock distribution programs.

Attention to reproduction rate : Failure of cows to conceive will delay gaining of livestock ownership and reduce farmer interest in the program. A recommendation from the Indonesian program is to "[e]nsure that bulls have access to cows at the right time — encourage communal housing of female cattle with the bull" (Salisbury, 1994, p. 19). Similarly, Riethmuller (1997, p. 8) notes for the Philippines that "… farmers are unable to detect when the cow is in heat. … Often by the time the cow was brought to the bull, the heat had passed and the cow did not become pregnant. … cows must be kept with the bull at night in an enclosure. Low productive performance is a fairly general problem … The general view in the Philippines is that this is related to feed management."

Concluding comments

Livestock distribution programs have the potential to greatly improve the livelihoods of low-income farmers and tenants, and to assist disadvantaged and minority groups. Well thoughtout design and management of these programs is critical for their success. Considerable experience has now been gained in program design in various countries. The current Philippines BAI supervised livestock distribution program appears to provide an innovative and effective model for design of livestock dispersion programs in developing countries. Both production and asset values of livestock are usually important to smallholders. While these asset values are difficult to quantify, they need to be recognized as of significance in social cost-benefit considerations.

REFERENCES

BAI (Bureau of Animal Industry) (1998a), *Animal Distribution Contract*, Department of Agriculture, Quezon City.

BAI (Bureau of Animal Industry) (1998b), *Livestock Population,* 1991-96, unpublished statistics provided by the BAI, Manila.

Chen, Taiyong (1998), Information on Heifer Project China, Deputy Director of HPI.

China, Chengdu, email communication.

Department of Finance (1991), *Handbook of Cost-Benefit Analysis*, AGPS, Canberra.

Franco, M.A.P. (1993), "The Economic Analysis of the Use of Artificial Insemination as Compared to Natural Breeding in Beef Cattle in the Philippines," M. Agr. Econ. thesis, The University of Queensland, Brisbane.

Gutierrez T.V. (1997), "The Bureau of Animal Industry : Towards Breeding Better Livestock," *Agribusiness News*, 8(5) : 8-10.

Harrison, S.R. (1998), Report to ACIAR on pre-project trip to examine the project "Socio-Economic Analysis of Supervised Cattle Distribution Under Coconuts" in the Philippines during the period 10-18 Sept., The University of Queensland, Brisbane.

Harrison, S.R. (in press), "Progress in Estimation of Intractable Non-Market Values," in S. B. Dahiya, ed. *The Current State of Economic Science*.

Patrick, I. (1996), Eastern Islands Veterinary Services Project, Phase II, ARECS, Armidale.

Patrick, I. (1998), University of New England, Armidale, personal communication.

Pu, Jiabi (1998), Director, China Office of Heifer Project International, Chengdu, Sichuan Province, email response to questions by S. Waldron, The University of Queensland.

Riethmuller, P. (1997), "Philippine Livestock Industries," Report prepared for the Australian Centre for International Agricultural Research, The University of Queensland, Brisbane.

Riethmuller, P. and Smith, D. (1994), "The South East Asian Cattle Industries : An Australian Perspective," *Journal of International Food and Agribusiness Marketing*, 6(4) : 1-16.

Salisbury, R. (1994), *Outcomes of Cattle Health and Productivity Survey (CHAPS) Seminar* May 1994, Eastern Islands Veterinary Services Project, Mararum NTB, Indonesia. (Revised in 1995 by R.B. Wirdahayati.)

Salita, G.C. (1997), *Geography and Natural Resources of the Philippines*, 2nd edn., JMC Press, Quezon City.

Samiano, A.M., Moog, F.A., Valenzuela, F.G., Raymundo, S.G., Agpaoa, E.V. and Fevidal, M.U. (1992), "Modified and Supervised Pig Distribution Scheme in

Selected Areas of Laguna and Batangas," Paper presented at the Department of Agriculture — Bureau of Agricultural Research (DA-BAR) National R&D Symposium, Quezon City.

Tokrisna, R. and Panayotou, T. (1982), "The Economics of Rural Livestock in Thailand : the Case of Buffalo and Cattle," Department of Agricultural Economics, Kasetsart University, Bangkok.

14 Gender Issues, the Women's Movement and the Indian Ocean Rim Countries[1]

Binayak Ray

Gender Issues

There is no universal definition of what constitutes a *gender issue.* Is women's deprivation a gender issue? Are men's issues considered gender issues? Men often feel aggrieved when preference is given to women in particular human activities. Is it a gender issue? The perception varies between persons, and between and within communities. Broadly, gender issues are defined as those issues that directly relate to women and women's movement.

Collectively women have remained dispossessed from many things to which men have had access for ages, although they constitute one half of the world population. This has been the situation in spite of widespread recognition of interdependency of sexes for a healthy relationship, development and progress.[2]

Women's unpaid contribution to the global economy is enormous, which includes subsistence agriculture; care for children, the elderly, and the disabled; provision of clothing and primary health care; cooking; cleaning etc. One study estimates that in 1985 women's unpaid contribution to the global economy was about $ 4 trillion, and they also work longer hours than men (World Resources, 1994-95 : 46; Shivard 1985). This was significant when

---

[1] I gratefully acknowledge the research assistance provided by Mr. K. Sanyal in preparing this paper. My sincere appreciation is also due to Emeritus Professor Reg Appleyard of the University of Western Australia, Dr. Ron May of The Australian National University, Dr. Brian Lockwood and Ms. Ann Marks for their useful comments on an earlier draft. However, all deficiencies in this chapter are mine.

[2] Shivnath SASTRY, an Indian scholar, philosopher and social reformer in the early 20th century strongly expounded this philosophy in his book *Grihadharma* (Domestic Bliss). Cited by Bose in *Discourse of Family and Reordering of Domestic Practices of Women,* (ed.), *in* Samaddar (1997), p. 32.

compared with the estimated global GDP (at 1993 prices) of $ 12,334,550 million in the same year (World Tables 1995). On average women worked 70 and 63 hours a week respectively in Africa, and in the Asia and Pacific during 1970-90, compared to 55 hours by men.

Over the last few decades, fundamental shifts in global economic policies and political realignment have occurred. Women everywhere felt the impact of these changes in varying degrees. Notwithstanding these changes, women's critical roles as reproductive agents, unpaid family and community level workers have yet to receive the recognition they deserve (Moser, 1991).

Complexities in measuring the degree of *women deprivation* have largely contributed in the lack of a focussed policy response to women's issues until recently. The compilation of the Human Development Index (HDI), Gender Related Development Index (GDI) and Gender Empowerment Measure Index (GEM) by the UNDP in 1990 opened the way for a sharper policy response to women's issues.[3] The methodology used in measuring these indexes has since been substantially refined (UNDP, 1998 : 107-10).

---

3 HDI measures overall achievement in a country in three basic dimensions of human development : longevity (measure by life expectancy), knowledge (measured by educational attainment) and a decent standard of living (measured by adjusted income).

GDI captures inequalities in achievement between women and men. The greater the gender disparity in basic human development, the lower a country's GDI compared with its HDI.

GEM measures gender inequality in key areas of economic and political participation, and decision making. It differs from the GDI, an indicator of gender inequality in basic capabilities. It reflects women's capacity to empower through self-reliance, by building new political, economic and social structures similar to those of men. GEM recognises women as agents of change and stresses the need for women to organise themselves for effective voice in determining their role in the development process (Rathgeber, 1990). Drawing on the work of other researchers, the UNDP found that most importantly this enabled women to challenge the perception of those in authority and begin to change their attitudes towards women and rework the development agenda (Institute of Development Studies, 1996; Attwood, 1996). Interestingly, the empowerment concept, as an approach to address women's issues has strong roots in Africa, the poorest of all continents (Steady, 1987).

These indexes provide important tools to objectively measure gaps between men and women in various categories of human endeavour. Some scholars, however, have questioned aspects of the methodology. Goetz and Baden (1997), for example, consider that aspects of the methodology used in developing these indexes are highly culturally loaded. Despite their reservations, in the absence of an alternative, they offer significant scope for adopting a more focussed policy approach to achieve gender related development objectives.

In a significant way, and in spite of war horrors and devastation, the Second World War and Independence struggles in various colonies can be considered important catalysts for bringing women's issues in the forefront of the global policy agenda.

For example, while men were engaged in war fronts, women in large numbers provided back up services, at the front by their participation in defence medical corps and in the domestic economic sectors. This participation directly exposed women to the outside world and contributed in broadening their horizon, and in their increased confidence to seek equal opportunities with men in all walks of life. These paved the way for the growth of women's movement in the post-war years.

Women in increasing numbers also got involved, and were affected by the Independence struggles in many countries, which again exposed them to wider non-domestic issues. On independence, most of these countries enshrined a policy of equal opportunity for all, irrespective of sexes, in their constitutional and legal statutes. Notwithstanding that these policies have largely remained in statute books in many countries, it is undeniable that formal recognition of equal opportunity policy opened a new horizon to women. Higher level of women empowerment in South Africa and Mozambique is an example (table 4).

The United Nations also contributed in focussing on and crystallising issues, which inhibited women's progress in economic and social arena, with support from high quarters, including the then first lady of the United States. It could take this position as there existed subliminal acknowledgement that to achieve long-term development and peace, the needs and rights of entire population must be addressed; not just rights and needs of one-half of the population, leaving the other half in the lurch.

The post-war reconstruction activities opened up opportunities to women to supplement their family income, and encouraged many women to join the labour market. Also, the post-war communist countries' special focus on women's issues worked as a worthwhile reference-point for many women, in the newly independent Asian and African countries.

These are individually small elements and on their own may not have necessarily contributed in achieving women's movement's objectives. Collectively, however, they were catalysts for women seeking equal rights and opportunities in the post-war societies.

In addition, personalities such as Germaine Greer also contributed significantly into the movement by focussing attention to women's poor status and subordinate role in the society, both in developed and developing countries (Chipp and Green, 1980). At the same time Non-Government Organisations (NGOs) in Western countries started asserting their role within their communities by highlighting the disadvantages suffered by women and confronted the *establishment* to remove these disadvantages.

In the initial post-war years, urban and educated class dominated the NGO leadership. This elite leadership, in spite of its inherent weakness, was quick in grasping the complexities and interrelationship of many women's issues. Through their own experience they realised that development and gender-related issues are 'inextricably' linked (Sen, 1991 : 15). This prompted them to broaden their horizon to include issues such as health, poverty, education and environment in the *movement's* agenda.[4]

Nexus between poverty and environmental degradation is a critical issue for many developing country women.[5] For example,

---

4 The role of Global Assembly of Women and the Environment : Partners in Life (Washington DC) and World's Women's Congress for a Healthy Planet (NY) in bringing the women's and the environment movement together is well recognised, and encouraged many NGOs to come together and forge alliances.

5 This nexus is clear from a Nigerian example. A poor farmer in 1987, for a payment of $ 120 a month, agreed to store a barrel in his farmhouse. The

the rural women in developing countries spend more time fetching water and collecting fuel for cooking, and in most instances at the expense of their education (Herz, Subbarao, Habib, *et. al.*, 1991), a situation unlikely to improve in the near future. Due to environmental degradation the water supply per capita in developing countries today is only one third of what it was in 1970 (UNDP, 1997 : 32).

Genesis of women's movement in industrialised and developing countries has some strong differences. Historically, concern for developing country women did not eventuate for any altruistic reason. Generally speaking industrialised countries (read colonial powers) were largely concerned with self-interest such as accessing colonies' resources and, in some cases religious. Consequently, women's issues hardly received any prominence or sympathetic place in the wider scheme of things, and even when there were attempts to improve the wellbeing of their subjects, these were often paternalistic and the needs were assessed through colonial eyes (Mohanty, 1991).

Colonial rule impacted heavily on the entire socio-economic fabric of colonial societies, and irrevocably changed the relationship between the pre-colonial, colonial and post-colonial communities (Koczberski, 1998). Researchers agree that they may not fit well into moulds shaped on the basis of the experience of their former colonies in European and North America (Migdal, 1988; Jolly and Macintyre, 1989). Women's movement in many IORARC countries confirms this situation.

The UN and the World Bank

The UN and the World Bank have also contributed in bringing women's issues in the main stream global policy agenda, particularly in recent decades. Focus of their respective roles, however, varies. The UN's role has been more towards setting agenda for the improvement of women's status and position. It

farmer, without knowing what it contained, grabbed the opportunity to earn this extra income. Soon after the farmer and the members of his family died. At the insistence of an investigative journalist, the Government launched an inquiry with international assistance. The inquiry found that the barrel contained highly toxic waste and the village soil and water were also contaminated beyond use (Morna, 1992).

encourages women to take initiative in whatever way they can to further their own position. The Bank, on the other hand, has adopted a more down to earth approach, although many have reservations about its approach. In spite of their different approaches, at the end contributions of these two agencies are undeniable in promoting women's position in the society.

The UN Commission on the Status of Women was established in 1946 to formulate guidelines and actions to improve women's status in economic, political, social, cultural and educational fields. However, until the 1970s its approach was more protective and not focussed in the mainstream status and development-oriented issues (Anand, 1992). By declaring 1974, the International Year of Women, the UN, in practical terms, raised women's issues in the main stream policy agenda.

At the same time a number of other activities also contributed in successfully bringing women related issues to the forefront of global economic, social and political agenda. Some of these were :

- Declaring 1976-85, the UN Decade for Women,
- Adoption of the Convention on the elimination of all forms of discrimination in 1979,
- Mexico City (1975), Copenhagen (1980), Nairobi (1985) and Beijing (1995) global meetings exclusively focussing on women's issues and
- Establishment of the UN Fund for Women and the International Research and Training Institute for the Advancement of Women.

The Percy Amendment to the US Foreign Assistance Act, requiring US bilateral assistance programs to give particular attention to integrating women into national economic activities in the aid recipient countries also made the task easy for the UN. In the 1960s the US was a major aid provider and had a strong policy influence in multilateral funding agencies and European donor countries

The Bank's approach was focussed on economic issues impacting on women. It took the view that policies such as structural reform, market focussed economic policies are key to achieve improvements in women's socio-economic position (Mitchell, 1995). Its 1987 focus on special needs of women in its funded projects confirms this strategy. This approach was considered paternalistic. It treated women as a homogeneous and vulnerable group in need of economic assistance and failed to recognise the differences between and within countries and communities.

In particular, it ignored that women's lives are affected by multiple variables, such as race, ethnicity, history or class, which should be an integral part of any policy relevant to women's development (Rathgeber, 1995). Studies confirm that development projects, despite good intentions, could have disastrous effects on communities with strong-rooted ethnic traditions and cultural differences. For example, '... the negative effects that mining has had on living standards in the Pacific, including the poverty it has generated, are especially problematic for women given their traditional responsibilities as caretakers of the family' (Emberson-Bain, 1994). This led scholars, sympathetic to women and developing countries' positions, to argue that the initiative was nothing but a strategic tool of capitalist expansion (Chowdhry, 1995).

The Status of Women in the IORARC Countries

Fourteen countries have formed the Indian Ocean Region Association for Regional Co-operation (IORARC), similar to the Asia-Pacific Economic Co-operation (APEC), but without a formal treaty or binding agreement.[6] The countries are : Australia, India and Sri Lanka, Indonesia, Malaysia and Singapore, Kenya, Madagascar, Mauritius, Mozambique, South Africa and Tanzania, Oman and Yemen.

Only Australia is classified as an industrialised country (table 1). Singapore is classified as a developing country, but in reality with a 44 per cent higher per capita real GDP than Australia

---

6 For an analysis of events leading to the development of a regional dialogue, see Chintamani Mahapatra *Co-operative Efforts in the Indian Ocean Region*, Australian Defence Studies Working Paper No. 41, 1996 and Indian Ocean Network News, Vol. 1 No. 3, Indian Ocean Centre, Curtin University, Perth.

in 1997, Singapore is closer to industrialised countries (table 3). Madagascar, Mozambique and Yemen are classified as least developed countries, and the remaining 10 countries as developing countries (UNDP, 1999).

These countries had an estimated population of 1,382 million in 1997, nearly one fourth of the World's population of 5,744 million (table 1). A little more than 87 per cent of these populations live in India, Indonesia and South Africa.

Trade liberalisation amongst member countries remains the focus of IORARC, although the global trade has been declining in recent years. In 1996, the world trade increased by only 3.3 per cent compared to 20 per cent in 1995. It is estimated that in 1998 it increased by only about 3 per cent, compared to 4 per cent in 1997.[7] Collectively IORARC countries experienced decline in external trade even before the full impact of the Asian economic crisis was felt. The export and import growth rates of 8.6 and 6 per cent in 1996-97 were substantially lower than the aggregate growth rates of 177 and 192 per cent during 1980-96, a period of sluggish economic activity (UNDP, 1999 : 45 and World Development Report, 1998/99 : 218-20).[8]

Many reasons could be attributed to this decline. Fall in consumer demand caused by high and persistent unemployment in major industrialised countries is a significant one. In 1997 collective unemployment rates in industrialised countries were 7.3 and 8.5 per cent respectively for males and females (age group 15-64), and the youth (15-24) unemployment rate was 16 per cent (UNDP, 1999 : 236). The rates would have been worse, but for the low unemployment rate in North America. Compared to North America, it remained consistently high in the European Union, Western and Southern Europe, Nordic countries and Japan, world's second largest economy (UNDP, 1998 : 192).

---

7 *The Economic Times* (New Delhi), 11 February 1998 (Economic Intelligence Unit estimate).

8 Singapore, Oman and Yemen have been excluded from this calculation, as consistent data were not available for these three countries.

Japan, a major trading partner of many IORARC countries, is not showing any sign of economic recovery. Unemployment in Japan at the end of 1999 FY was 4.7 per cent, highest since 1954 and is increasing. For the new entrants in the labour market it was 12 per cent. The household expenditure was down for third successive year in 1999-2000.[9]

Indices to Measure Development

Of the three indexes developed by the UN, HDI is a unisex index, which measures achievements in three basic dimensions of human development. GDI reflects women's position *vis-à-vis* men within this context. GEM, on the other hand, reflects the depth of gender inequality in basic capabilities such as economic and political participation, and decision making.

In 1997, only two IORARC countries ranked within the first 50 HDI placing covering 174 countries (table 4). Four countries ranked between 50 and 100, and the remaining eight countries ranked between 100 and 174. As HDI focuses on life expectancy, education and a decent standard of living, the position of majority of these countries in the lower half of the index is not surprising.

Collectively, these countries' GDP is not showing significant improvements, compared to industrialised countries. Their combined GDP growth was 21 per cent lower than the world growth rate during 1980-1997 (table 3). Twelve of these countries recorded a growth rate of 143 per cent compared to the world growth rate of 164 per cent.[10] Growth comparison in percentage terms, however, could be very misleading as majority of these countries started from a very low economic base in 1980. Two of these countries' per capita real GDP declined significantly and one country's income remained stationary.

In real terms, only Singapore recorded a higher per capita real GDP growth than the average of the industrialised countries. In 1997 Singapore's per capita growth was about 20 per cent higher than the industrialised countries' average. Comparatively, Australia, the only industrialised country in the group, recorded nearly 20 per

9 Peter Martin, the Australian Broadcasting Corporation Economics Reporter in Japan, 28 April 2000.

10 No comparable data were available for Tanzania and Yemen for the year 1980.

cent lower growth rate than the industrialised countries. Oman, Mauritius, Malaysia and South Africa did reach a level of more than one third of the industrialised countries' growth rate and the remaining seven countries' per capita real GDP remained significantly low.

Overall, female per capita real GDP remains lower in all countries, including industrialised countries, which recorded women earning only 59 per cent of male income (table 3). This percentage was significantly higher in four of the Sub-Saharan African countries (except South Africa and Mauritius). South Africa's per capita female income compared to men was little lower than Singapore's. In this area, the gender disparity was somewhat less in the Sub-Saharan countries, compared to industrialised countries.

The low HDI ranking is consistent with the high incidence of poverty level in most of these countries (table 4). During 1989-94, 43 percent of the IORARC population were living below the income poverty line.[11] Even Australia, the only industrialised IORARC country, had about 8 percent of its population living below the poverty line.[12] However, the percentage of people living below the poverty line is believed to be higher, if the number is measured on the basis of the national poverty line deemed appropriate by respective country authorities (UNDP, 1999 : 146-48).

Both proportionately and in absolute numbers, largest number of people was living in poverty situations in India, Kenya, South Africa, Tanzania and Mozambique (no data for Mozambique, world's one of the poorest countries, were available). The Asian economic crisis has also put large number of Indonesians into the poverty situation. It is estimated that about 80 million Indonesians

---

[11] Based on the concept of absolute poverty line, expressed in monetary terms ($ 1 a day, PPP basis) : the income or expenditure level below which a minimum nutritionally adequate diet plus essential non-food requirements are not affordable.

[12] In Australia's case the figures refer to 1989-95 period. Also, an income below $ 14.40 a day (1985, PPP $) is considered to be income poverty line in Australia (UNDP, 1999 : 149).

are now living below the poverty line (more than 39 per cent of the country's population). It has also made about 30 million unemployed, 65 per cent of children below the age of three anaemic, and more than half the children under age two malnourished.[13] Analysts believe that this downturn will make it impossible for one Indonesian generation to come out of the poverty gap.[14] Situation in Mozambique has also worsened significantly since the devastating floods in early 2000.

Besides income level, literacy rate also contributes in determining HDI ranking. India, Mozambique and Yemen have very large adult illiteracy rates. Other countries, particularly the Sub-Saharan countries have a better than the average women literacy rate, in spite of their low level of economic development. Higher literacy rate enables the population to have a better knowledge base, and contributes in their capacity to readily adjust in a rapidly changing technological and economic environment (Bhagwati, 1996).[15]

It is worth noting that while growth contributes in poverty reduction, it has no direct relation to human development and gender equity. It is, at the same time, unrealistic to assume that contributing elements to human development can be sustained in a slow or non-growth economic situation. In latter situation, men are more likely to succeed because of their long experience of playing a dominating role in all walks of life. In such an environment, women naturally suffer more than men (Majumdar, 1991).

GDI reflects gender disparity in relation to HDI measures. While some improvements in basic human development areas have been achieved, overall the situation remains poor in most IROARC countries. Notwithstanding a comparatively average higher literacy rate, HIV, the largest killer in Africa and the fourth largest in the

---

13 Downer, Alexander (1998), Australian Foreign Minister at a television interview (Channel 9) in Australia, 1 November.

14 *The Australian Broadcasting Corporation* (1998), 27 October.

15 It is widely acknowledged that one of the important reasons for South Korea's and Taiwan's spectacular economic growth during last two decades was due not only to high education level, but also due to their high quality primary education. This enabled the workers to quickly adopt the new opportunities brought by the technological revolution.

world and malaria, accounting for one million deaths in Africa in 1998, will remain major constraints in Sub-Saharan countries achieving a higher HDI and GDI measure.[16] India and Indonesia, two largest member countries are not affected at same levels, but have other disadvantages limiting their capacity to achieve higher HDI and GDI measures.

Amongst IORARC countries, Mozambique and South Africa have a relatively higher GEM ranking. In 1997 Mozambique ranked 59, compared to its HDI and GDI ranking of 169 and 138. Similarly, South Africa's GEM raking was 18, compared to 101 and 84 in other two categories. Australia and Singapore, which ranked high in HDI and GDI categories, ranked below in GEM category, ninth and 32nd respectively. These examples confirm that gender inequality or empowerment issues are not simply a function of standard of living or educational levels.

One plausible explanation for south Africa's and Mozambique's high GEM rankings could be that women assumed decision-making responsibilities, when men were engaged in the liberation struggles in previous decades. In South Africa's case, the incorporation of a Bill of Rights in the post-apartheid constitution and the establishment of an Office of the Status of Women should have also contributed in achieving this higher ranking.

The situation in Australia has improved considerably in recent years, particularly in the political front. About 26 per cent of the members in the Australian Parliament are now women. This improvement has been achieved within the span of last two elections. While one of the major political parties have agreed in-principle to select women candidates in 35 per cent of the winnable seats, the other party does not have that arrangement, but it actively encourages women to nominate for pre-selection. Government initiatives at all levels have also contributed in this improvement. The establishment of an Office of the Status of women, Human Rights Commission, Anti-discrimination Commission and

16 A WHO official interviewed by the BBC World Service (news) on 12 May 1999.

Commonwealth Affirmative Action Agency are few of such initiatives, though success varied from sector to sector and state to state.

India and Indonesia, two of the largest countries in the group, have not shown any significant improvement in women's position. In terms of legislation passed and enacted, India has a good record. Fundamental rights in India are guaranteed irrespective of sex, caste or creed, but they are mainly civil, political and legal in nature. None of these incorporates economic or social rights. These latter rights cannot be legally enforced (Mukherjee, S. and I., 1995). There are many reasons, both open and subtle, for this poor achievement. Researchers on women's issues broadly agree that four factors hinder the development of the Indian women. These are a feeling of dependency, a fatalistic attitude, social constraints and superstitions, and poverty (Vohra and Sen, 1986). While all these may be valid reasons for the poor plight of women in India, it is undeniable that lack of effective education remains a stumbling block in improving women's position. Even after more than 50 years of independence and a series of development plans a little more than 60 per cent of the adult women remain illiterate.

Indonesia was one of the first countries to ratify the 1995 Nairobi Declaration on the Advancement of Women. It has a 90 per cent enrolment rate for girls in primary schools, in many areas higher than the boys. The Ministry of Women's Affairs is within the Cabinet Office of the Government. Notwithstanding this, serious deficiencies remain in a number of areas. There exist wage differences between men and women for similar work, and women remain vulnerable to exploitation of various forms, including the security of employment and sexual harassment. Violation of labour laws is common (Buchori and Bianpoen, 1996). The fall of the dictatorial regime and the establishment of a democratic government are expected to assist in the development of women in Indonesian. However, it would be naïve to expect that these can be achieved overnight, given the economic and political situation in the country, it will take a long time.

Inferior Status of Women

The reasons for women's poor position in the IORARC countries are many, some are of global nature, and others are country specific.

Thirteen of the IORARC countries are either developing or least developed countries. During the last two decades the economies of most of these countries suffered for reasons over which hardly they had any control. These external factors inhibited their capacity to achieve economic growth, and this, in turn, adversely impacted on women's position. Some of these are :

- Although the ratio of global trade to GDP has been increasing, it fell in 44 developing countries during the past decade,
- Foreign direct investment have by-passed more than half the developing countries,
- Real commodity prices in the 1990s were 45 per cent lower than in the 1980s. As the primary sector dominates developing countries' economies, they suffer more because of this decline in price. Even Australia, the only industrialised country in the group, also suffered because of lower commodity prices and
- Terms of trade for least developing countries have declined a cumulative 50 per cent over the past 20 years (UNDP, 1997 : 9).

These countries have also large external debts. The net debt of 10 member countries[17] increased by 2.2 per cent from $ 122,917 million in 1985 to $ 311,496 million in 1997 (UNDP, 1999 : 193-95). The debt burden of the countries in the Sub-Saharan Africa (six of the IORARC countries are in this region) are so heavy that even the World Bank doubts whether they will ever be able to come

[17] Excluding Singapore, Australia, Sri Lanka and South Africa. Comparable figures for Sri Lanka and South Africa for 1980 were not available and hence these two countries have been excluded from the assessment of the growth of external debt.

out of this situation.[18] Their debt burden, high population growth rates and a primary-sector-dominated economy did not contribute in achieving a higher standard of living.

Besides the poor growth record, the women's movement in most developing countries suffered from poor direction and leadership of the Western NGOs, who were considered better equipped and strategists. Unfortunately, the leadership failed to fully appreciate the importance of differences in women's interests between and within the communities. Even at the operational level western NGOs frequently organised their program delivery through local government officials and village headmen (who, often had strong vested interest) and, more often than not, were guided by them. The people at the grass roots regrettably were not involved (Tendler, 1982). As a result, often without understanding the context, many made faulty analysis of social and economic issues, arrived at dangerously inaccurate conclusions, which contributed in poor strategy formulation and unsatisfactory outcomes.

Daly's[19] study on Indian Suttee[20] highlights the problem. Besides questioning the fundamental validity of Daly's assertions, Narayan (1997), a well-known researcher asked how could it be that *suttee*, and all other problems affecting Indian women that Daly mentioned, managed to remain entirely insulated from the tremendous changes of the last hundred and fifty years. She went on to imply that such studies reflected colonial legacies and ignorance of the history of the creation of a racially distinct and oppressed population within some western countries. She found partial support from other works : 'Western feminists suffer from an explicit sense of cultural superiority; 'western views in general are perceived as hegamonistic, and hence are devalued.' Even in the US, the African Americans and other minority women groups tend to support Narayan's position, arguing that race, culture and class must be

---

18 Edward (Kim) Jaycox, Head of the African Bureau in the World Bank in 1990.

19 Mary Daly claimed that the lot of Indian women had not changed substantially since 1829 (which has been soundly criticised by many researchers, such as Mohanty) in her book *Gyn/Ecology* : The *Metaethics of Radical Feminism* (1990), Beacon Press, Boston.

20 Hindu widow, who immolates herself on her husbands funeral pyre. The British Government with strong support from Indian social reformers declared the practice illegal in 1829.

incorporated into feminist analysis (Marchand and Parpart 1995 : 1-22).

Many in the women's movement also suffered from a false sense of achievement. The election of few women as heads of governments and the appointment of some women in senior executive positions made them to believe in the success of the movement. They overlooked that women who make it to the top show little gender difference in motivation and performance (Kanter, 1977, Franklin and Sweeny, 1988). They forgot that the prospect of female empowerment also threatens many along with those women who have a stake in existing male privilege (Staudt, 1990). They also failed to understand that few scattered individual achievements on their own do not always provide the guarantee of assistance to the cause of women (Sobhan, 1992 : 68).

The failure to recognise the pluralistic nature of women's movement and its inability to speak with one voice and the propensity to engage in hair-splitting debate on trivial issues also adversely affected women's movement (Nicholson, 1994). This failure only strengthened the hands of movement's detractors. Marchand and Parpart (1995 : 8) rightly argued that while differences and multiple identities provide a welcome plurality and richness, in their extreme form they neither do assist to mount effective political action, nor do they assist in defending women's rights.

Globalisation and Women's Empowerment

The end of the Cold War, emergence of a global economy and rapid technological changes are all having unprecedented impact on various organs and sections of the community. The full and long-term impact of these changes is beyond comprehension at this stage. As a result of this changing environment, many critical national issues, such as population, financial markets, environment, technology transfer, human rights, that once would have been handled within national boundaries have been globalised (Sen, 1991), which, in many ways, are restricting the sovereign power of individual nation-states.

The structural adjustment policies, pursued by the multilateral agencies, with full endorsement of the G7 countries[21], have elements such as demand restraint, price decontrol, reform of trade regimes, financial sector reform, privatisation (Stewart, 1992). These impinge on the living conditions of all people, most adversely on low to middle-income people and in particular on women, as public investment in human resources and cuts in social expenditure take place (Elson, 1987). The rapid emergence of contract work, longer work shifts, dominance of part-time employment are few such examples. Sufferings endured by the Indonesian women and children, following their recent political and economic crises are an example. The women's movement cannot operate by ignoring this situation.

In a globalised economy, politically and economically weaker nations have little practical capacity to influence global policies, which have the potential to adversely impact on them. For example, the WTO provisions on subsidies, employment conditions, trade preferences etc. are bound to disproportionately impact on women, because of their relative inability to influence global policy outcomes. The widely reported news on the conduct of the Seattle WTO meeting, if it was true, supports this view.[22] Similarly, the proposed Multilateral Agreement on Investment (MAI) by the OECD, if ever adopted, will have profound impact, particularly on women.[23] These issues are serious concern for the future of the women's movement.

---

[21] USA, Canada, UK, France, Germany, Italy and Japan.

[22] A journalist (Madeleine Bunting) reported that during the Seattle meeting of the World Trade Organisation in November 1999 major multinationals paid enormous amounts for their ringside seats to enable them to manipulate its proceedings (The Canberra Times, 25 August 1999). While on its own this does not constitute an undue policy influence, when considered in a wider global political and economic context it creates concern as people with high spending power can invest in articulated policy development activities disproportionately, compared to those whose capacity to outlay is limited. During the GATT negotiations in the early 1990s it was found that on many instances the highly resourced delegations from the industrial countries outgunned and outmaneuvered delegations from individual developing countries on many complicated trade issues (Dasgupta, 1997)

[23] The draft MAI covers every kind of asset owned or controlled, directly or indirectly, by an investor and investors' rights. The Agreement, if ratified, will significantly reduce the capacity of the member countries to act independently

Even Germaine Greer, the doyen of the women's movement, acknowledged this in a recent radio interview.[24] She conceded that the women's movement has failed to achieve its original objectives and the influence of global economic structure (read capitalism) is responsible for this.

The increasing concentration of media ownership is a serious concern for the women's movement. Many women's issues often do not find sympathy with the oppressive governments or conservative social forces. In a competitive business environment, as commercial interests often take precedence over community obligations and interests, the anti-women forces may find it easier to control the public debate by putting commercial pressure to a limited number of media owners. There are signs that long-established quality media outlets are already tending to put commercial interest above community interests[25]. This is a critical issue globally, but more so in many developing countries, because when disadvantaged by oppressive government policies and poor governance practices voluntary agencies often find international public opinion and overseas sister agencies useful allies in support of their positions (Baden and Goetz, 1990).

The Need for a New Approach

It is clear that despite some successes, the women's movement is far from achieving many of its objectives, including equity and empowerment. In an uneven global political, economic and social environment there cannot be one strategy for all countries, as many

---

with regard to investment, particularly by foreign companies. All major industrialised countries are members of the OECD. Although the non-OECD countries will have nothing to do with the Agreement, it would be impossible for them not to succumb to the pressure to follow the OECD countries. Australia is the only IORC who is also a member of the OECD. Australia has decided not to ratify the Agreement in the present form.

24 In a pre-recorded interview with the *Australian Broadcasting Corporation* (Radio). The interview was aired at ABC's 2CN program (Canberra) between 4 p.m. and 6 p.m. on 21 April 2000.

25 A feature item on the newspaper industry broadcast on Channel Nine Television program on 1 November 1998 clearly indicated the possibility of such things happening.

aspects of the women's movement are complex and deep-rooted in their social structures.

Most IORARC countries have distinct ethnic, cultural and social entities. These differences demand that the focus and strategy of the movement need to be different, although the twin objectives of achieving equity and empowerment must remain the ultimate goal. A study in African women's issues is unequivocal that irrespective of their location, the women's movement have elements of context in common to form a standpoint fundamentally different from any that Western feminists construct (Steady, 1987).

Country and region specific focus does not necessarily imply the abandonment of the concept of international cooperation. On the contrary, it reinforces that all socio-economic movement must directly relate to the immediate needs of the society, if it were to achieve success. For example, there is no qualitative difference between industrial countries' concern of *cuts in social services* or *child minding centres* as opposed to developing countries' concerns of *high unemployment*' or *endemic poverty*, caused by the adoption of *structural adjustment policies*. The focus directly relates to the immediate needs of these respective societies. Movement's leadership is gradually grasping this distinction, as one activist writes, '*strategic motherhood*' is replacing the '*romantic sisterhood*' of the past.[26]

To achieve economic development, developing IORARC countries on the one hand have to comply with the economic policy setting demanded by investors, multilateral funding agencies, and economically and politically powerful countries. On the other hand, they need to address community concerns and issues, which often may conflict with economic policy settings.

Developing countries, therefore, must adopt innovative policy approaches to meet their own needs. Unfortunately, many developing country elite, in the past, has failed to do so. Often they have been overtly influenced by their educational upbringing in the West in recommending policy options on important issues. 'The tendency to essentialise and distort the lives of Third World women

---

[26] Agarwal, B. (1995), *From Mexico to Beijing*, *The Indian Express*, New Delhi., 6, October.

does not just occur in the writings of women in the North. It is also pronounced in some of the work of the Third World scholars trained in Northern institutions, particularly when writing for a Northern audience writes *Marchand and Parpart* (1995).

A globalised economy requires states and governments to follow internationally accepted *governance* principles, which focuses on creation of a strong *civil society*. This includes international covenants and instruments covering both economic and non-economic issues, and equality of sexes in all human endeavour and privileges conferred by the state (World Bank, 1994). Signatories to these instruments and covenants feel obliged to comply with them. Non-compliance does not necessarily bring any legal sanction, but the possibility of being identified as a non-conformer often leads to international embarrassment. The recent report by the UN Human Rights Commission on Australian Government's failure to override the controversial mandatory sentencing laws enacted by the Northern Territory and Western Australian Governments is an example.[27] Currently there are more than 170 major human, economic and cultural rights instruments, including individual and special groups' rights.[28] In practical policy terms they require governments to respond to the needs of citizens irrespective of their sexuality (Ray, 1998).

This new environment provides opportunity to women's movement to set their agenda within the boundaries set by governance and civil society issues, and various rights instruments. Within this frame, women's issues can be sensitised relatively easily in a non-threatening way, and in the process a coalition of

---

[27] The Federal Government has the Constitutional power to override all territorial laws. It can also override State laws if they conflict with Federal Government's external obligations. Constitutional experts acknowledge that the mandatory sentencing law violates human rights, and also in conflict with the racial discrimination law.

[28] 'Benchmark and Indicators for Economic and Social Rights in Development Assistance Programs,' an unpublished report by the Swinburne University of Technology and Deakin University (1996), Australia. The report was prepared for the Australian Agency for International Development.

men and women, urban and rural can be developed in support of their position (Das Gupta, 1991).

It is, however, worth noting that as former colonies most IORARC countries have had a long political and cultural encounter with the West and yet, many men have not forsaken hierarchical, authoritarian or patriarchal norms (Majumdar, 1997). In some instances this is created by a perception that the women's movement is detrimental to their self-interest, erodes their authority and power base. To overcome this situation, the movement needs to develop strategies to win their support or at least neutralise them from opposing the movement's objectives. One of the best ways to achieve this objective is to work through the existing political system and use the system to the movement's advantage.

Australian experience suggests that by increasing women representation in the Parliament through existing political structures, women could influence government policies better, and the movement's opponents find little scope to adversely influence the outcome. The leadership's strategy to achieve this goal was by raising funds and strategically directing them to get more women nominated by political parties in winnable parliamentary seats. With the group's support sixteen women (affiliated to the Australian Labour Party) were elected in the 1998 federal election, compared to only four in the previous election (Kirner, 1998).[29] It would, however, be wrong to attribute every win to the efforts of this group, but their role in getting women nominated in the winnable seats are beyond doubt.

A separate political set-up is unlikely to be a good strategy. An Indonesian study found that strong separate political set-up may at some point could be an obstacle to equality of sexes and real freedom (Douglas, 1980). Similarly, reservation of positions for women, either through appointment, nomination or election, has inherent weaknesses. It fails to encourage initiative, innovation, discourages competition. In extreme cases it promotes inefficiency, creates a feeling of dependency and creates animosity between

---

29 The group is known as EMILY (Early Money Is Like Yeast — it makes the dough rise).

those, who enter through the open and reservation systems respectively.

In certain circumstances, there certainly exists a case for reservation to attain short-term policy objectives, be it to minimise sexual imbalance or to provide better opportunities to disadvantaged groups. In such circumstances, there exist strong arguments for limiting its application for a specified period only. In India, a proposal exists before the Parliament to reserve 35 per cent of the seats for women. Some sections of the community are even suggesting that the policy should include a *caste* component as well. India's experience with the reservation policy to lift the economic and social conditions of socially disadvantaged group in the society has failed (which framers of the Constitution never contemplated to become a permanent feature), although it has now been pursued for more than 50 years (Ray, 1999 : 106-9).

South Africa's policy of reserved seats for women is enshrined in her constitution. Given the history of deprivation and disadvantages suffered by the community during the long apartheid struggle, the focus of the policy is understandable. However, if long-term difficulties are to be avoided this policy must be re-examined when the economic and political situation improves after certain period of time.

In this context the experience of the Women's Union in Vietnam is worth examining, although the country has a different political system from the IORARC countries. It has 11 million members and remains an arm of the Communist party where it plays an advocacy role for women's concerns, provides vehicles for promoting women friendly policies and monitors the outcome of policy interventions (Sobhan, 1992 : 57).

Conclusion

Women's empowerment is now widely recognised as a fundamental precondition for development. Whilst there are some general and universal policies needed to achieve the objective of improving the role and status of women, such as policies which aim at providing women with better access to education and health facilities, there are also specific lessons to be learnt from the experience of some developing countries. Indeed, policies aiming at women's empowerment must accommodate the historical and cultural needs of a country. For example, the success of the Bangladesh Grameen Bank in reducing the number of people (and particularly women) living in absolute poverty, and in lifting their dignity by empowering them to manage their own affairs within the Bank's operational principles offers lessons for the women's movement in some developing countries. Many social scientists, including economists, often make a mistake by considering the Bank's activities only in a financial context. From the women's perspective this is far from the reality. The Bank's philosophical base of genuinely working through the grass roots population, even though they may not be literate, extremely impoverished and marginalised in the society has provided women a feeling of ownership of the bank (Bornstein, 1996). It will be a mistake to follow the Bank's operational procedures blindly elsewhere. While the basic concept underpinning the Bank's activities may be replicated, the same degree of success, however, may not be achieved unless that feeling of ownership can be infused in the minds of the community to be served. The operational principles and procedures, therefore, must directly relate to the social and cultural nuances of the community to achieve the same degree of success.

The women's movement also needs to closely watch the functioning of bureaucracies. Experience suggests that the administrative structure and class character of the bureaucracies of many countries often is more a hindrance than a facilitator in introducing changes, as they feel threatened to lose their entrenched power base. Far from favouring the people they are required to serve, they often systematically implement laws in ways that strengthen their own position and that of the privileged in the society (Davidson, 1992).

This problem arises because most of the developing countries of the IORARC have not made any fundamental changes in their administrative structure following independence. Scholars such as Potter (1986) argue that many newly independent countries underestimated the strength of the bureaucracy they inherited, and failed to reform them in the post-independent period. This is clear from the Indian experience. The country has the unenviable record of completing more than 40 inquiries to reorganise its administrative structure, but the situation has not changed much since it obtained Independence in 1947, and one cannot claim that the women's situation has improved in any significant way in the post-independent India.[30] Besides Australia and Singapore, Malaysia and Tanzania have attempted to make fundamental changes in their administrative structure. Malaysia is considered to have some limited success, while Tanzania's efforts did not produce the expected result. There were a number of complex philosophical and economic reasons for the poor outcome of Tanzania's efforts.

The importance of public administration and good governance in achieving development objectives is increasingly recognised. In paying tribute to Arturo Israel, responsible for the World Bank's policy to consider non-financial issues in its funding considerations, the Institute of Administrative Sciences reiterated '... the presence of a strong environment of public administration and good governance' is essential to achieve development objectives (Pagaza, 2000). The women's movement should skilfully use this policy to its own advantage to achieve equity and empowerment objectives in the IORARC countries.

REFERENCES

Anand, A. (1992), Introduction in The Power to Change — women in the third world redefine their environment, Women's Feature Service, Zed Books, London, p. 3.

Attwood, H. (1996), 'PRA : What Is It and Why Should We Use It? And Illustrations of Poor People's Perceptions of Poverty and Well-Being as Disclosed through PRA Expenditures,' cited *in* UNDP (1997), p. 104.

Baden, S. and Goetz, A. M. (1997), Who Needs [Sex] When You Can Have Gender in Women, International Development, and Politics : The Bureaucratic Mire [Updated and expanded edition] (ed.) Staudt, K., Temple University Press, Philadelphia, p. 37-58.

30 For a detailed discussion of the Indian administrative reform issues see (Subramaniam 1992, Brown 1997, Marshall 1997 and Singh and Bhandarkar 1997).

Bhagwati, J. (1996), K.R. Narayan Oration, The Australian National University, Canberra, p. 9.

Bornstein, David (1996), The Price of a Dream, The University Press Ltd., Dhaka.

Brown, J. (1997), 'Gandhi and Nehru : Frustrated Visionaries?' *History Today*, Vol. 47, 90, September, History Today Ltd., London.

Buchori, B. and Bianpoen, C. (1996) Through Women's Eyes, IBRD, Washington, DC.

Chipp, S.A. and Green, J.J. (1980) Asian Women in Transition (eds.), The Pennsylvania University Press, University Parks and London, p. 1.

Chowdhry, G. (1995), Engineering Development? : Women in Development (WID), in International Development Regimes in Feminism/Postmodernism/ Development, (eds.), Marchand and Parpart. *Op. cit.*, pp. 26–40.

Dasgupta, B. (1997), On South Asian Trade : The Case for South Asia Free Trade Association in Dutta, D.K. Economic Liberalisation and Institutional Reforms in South Asia (ed.).

Das Gupta, S. (1991), Inputs in Development Planning : Decentralised Information System for Poverty Alleviation and Gender Equity in (eds.) Raj-Hashim, R. and Heyzer, N., Asia and Pacific Development Centre, Kuala Lumpu, p. 26.

Davidson, B. (1992), The Blackman's Burden, Random House, New York.

Douglas, S.A. (1980), Women in Indonesian Politics in Chipp and Green (eds.), *Op. cit.*, pp. 152-81.

Elson, D. (1987), The impact of structural adjustment on women : concepts and issues, The Institute for African Alternatives Conference, City University, London.

Emberson-Bain, A. (1994), De-Romancing the Stones : Gender, Environment and Mining in The Pacific in Sustainable Development or Malignant Growth? Perspectives of Pacific Island Women (ed.), Marama Publications, Suva, pp. 93–110.

Franklin, D. and Sweeney, J.L. (1988), Women and Corporate Power in Women, Power and Policy, (eds.), Boneparth, E. and Stoper, E. , Pergamon, New York.

Herz, B., Subbarao, K. Habib, M. *et. al.*, (1991), Letting Girls Learn : Promising Approaches in Primary and Secondary Education, World Bank discussion Paper No. 33, Washington.

The Institute for Development Studies (1996), 'The Power of Participation : PRA and Policy,' Policy Briefing Issue 7 (August), Sussex, cited in UNDP (1997), p. 104.

Jolly, M. and Macintyre, M. (1989), Family and Gender in The Pacific: Domestic Contradictions and the Colonial Impact (eds.), Cambridge University Press, Cambridge.

Kanter, R. (1977), Men and Women of the Corporation, Basic Books, New York.

Kirner, J. (1998), Co-convenor, Press Statement in Canberra, 1 November.

Koczberski, G. (1998), *Women in Development : a Critical Analysis*, The third World Quarterly, Vol. 19, No. 3. pp. 395 – 409.

Majumdar, D. (1991), *Poverty in Asia : An Overview in Gender, Economic Growth and Poverty*, in Raj-Hashim and Heyzer, *Op. cit.*, pp. 17-18.

Majumdar, V. (1997), A Few Hypothesis on Contexualising Women's Experience in Asia in Samaddar, *Op. cit.*

Marchand, M. and Parpart, J.L. (1995), *Feminism/Postmodernism/Development*, Routledge, London.

Marshall, P. (1997), The Making of the Hybrid Raj, 1700–1857, *History Today*, *Op. cit.*

Migdal, J.S. (1988), Strong Societies and Weak States : State Society Relations and State Capabilities in the Third World, Princeton University Press, Princeton, New Jersey.

Mitchell, S. (1995), Feminism, gender and development : What are Australia's policy options? in Gender and Development : The cutting edge, Australian Development Studies Network, Canberra, pp. 17-19.

Mohanty, C. (1991), Under Western Eyes : feminist scholarship and colonial discourses in Third World Women and the Politics of Feminism, (eds.), Mohanty, Russo and Torres, Indiana University Press, Bloomington, pp. 51–80.

Morna, C.L. (1992), The Power to Change : women in the third world redefine their environment., *Op. cit.* p. 39.

Moser, C.O.N. (1991), Gender Planning *in* the Third World : Meeting Practical and Strategic Needs in Gender and International Relations (eds.), Grant, R. and Newland, K., Open University Press, Buckingham, pp. 83-121.

Mukherjee, S. and I. (1995), The Constitution of India, World Press, Calcutta, pp. 91-99.

Narayan, Uma (1997), Dislocating Cultures : Identities, Traditions and Third World Feminism, Routeledge, New York, pp. 43–80.

Nicholson, L. (1994), Interpreting Gender in Signs 29/1, cited in Baden and Goetz, *Op. cit.*

Pagaza, I.P. (2000), International Review of Administrative Sciences, Vol. 6, No. 1, Sage Publications; Tribute to Arturo Israel (1940–2000).

Potter, D. (1986), India's Political Administration 1981-83, Clarendon Press, Oxford.

Ray, B. (1997), Indian Ocean Rim countries : Policy Challenges for Sustainable Development, Indian Ocean Centre, Curtin University of Technology, Perth, p. 1.

(1999), India — Sustainable Development and Good Governance Issues : A Case for Radical Reassessment, Atlantic Publishers and Distributors, New Delhi, pp. 48–81.

Ruthgeber, E.M. (1990), 'WID, WAD, GAD : Trends in Research and Practices, Journal of Development Areas, 24 July, Western Illinois University, pp. 492-502.

— (1995), Gender and Development in Action in (eds.) *Marchand and Parpart, Op. cit.*

Samaddar, R. (1997), Women in Asia : Work, Culture and Politics in South Asia and Central Asia (ed.), Vikash Publishing House, New Delhi.

Singh, P. and Bhandarkar, A. (1997), IAS Profile : Myths and Realities, Wiley Eastern, New Delhi.

Sen, G. (1991), Regional Overview in the Gender, Economic Growth in Poverty Situation at Macro Level in (eds.), Raj-Hashim and Heyzer, *Op. cit.*, p. 1.

Sivard, R. (1985), Women : A World Survey, World Priorities, Washington, DC., cited in World Resources 1994–95, The World Resource Institute (1994), OUP, New York, p. 46.

Sobhan, R. (1992), Planning and Public Action for Asian Women, The University Press, Dhaka.

Staudt, K. (1990), Gender Politics in Bureaucracy : Theoretical Issues in Comparative Perspectives in Women, International Development, and Politics : The Bureaucratic Mire (ed.), Temple University Press, Philadelphia. pp. 3–34.

Steady, F.C. (1987), African Feminism : A Worldwide Perspective in Women in Africa and the African Diaspora (eds.), Terborg-Penn, R., Harley, S. and Rushing, A., Howard University Press, Washington, DC.

Stewart, F. (1992), Can Adjustment Programs Incorporate the Interests of Women? in Women and Adjustment, (eds.), Afshar and Dennis.

Subramaniam, K.S. (1992), Political Violence, Social Movements and the State in India, Institute of Development Studies, University of Sussex, Brighton.

Tendler, Judith (1982), 'Turning Private Voluntary Organisations into Development Agencies : Questions for Evaluation, USAID discussion paper, Washington.

UN (1991), World's Women-1990, Trends and Statistics, New York, cited in World Resources 1994–95, World Resource Institute, New York, p. 45.

UNDP (1990, 1997, 1998 and 1999), *Human Development Reports*, OUP, New York.

Vohra, R. and Sen, A.K. (1986), *Status, Education and Problems of Indian Women,* Akshat Publications, New Delhi.

World Bank (1994), Development Practice, Governance, The World Bank's Experience, Washington, DC.

—(1995), World Tables, The Johns Hopkins University Press, Baltimore, p. 29.

— (1999), *World Development Report* 1998/99, Oxford University Press, New York.

APPENDIX

Table 1 : Showing Population Growth Trend in the IORARC Countries during 1980-1997.

Country	Development status	Population 1997 (millions)	Share of the World population	Share of the IORARC population	Popn. increase 1950-97 (Percentage)
Australia	Industrial	18.3	0.32	1.30	122.6
India	Developing	966.2	16.8	69.91	170.2
Sri Lanka	Developing	18.3	0.32	1.30	138.3
Indonesia	Developing	203.4	3.5	14.72	155.7
Malaysia	Developing	21.0	0.36	1.52	243.7
Singapore	Developing	3.4	0.06	0.25	233.3
Kenya	Developing	28.4	0.49	2.06	352.9
Madagascar	Least dev.	14.6	0.25	1.06	245.2
Mauritius	Developing	1.1	0.02	0.08	124.5
Mozambique	Least dev.	18.4	0.32	1.33	196.8
South Africa	Developing	38.8	0.67	2.81	183.6
Tanzania	Least dev.	31.4	0.55	2.27	297.9
Oman	Developing	2.3	0.04	0.17	461.9
Yemen	Least dev.	16.3	0.28	1.18	277.3
IORARC		1,381.9	24.1	-	-
World		5,743.7	-	-	128.3

Source : *Human Development Report* 1999, UNDP/World Resources, 1994-95, OUP, New York.

Table 2 : Showing Adult Literacy Rates in IORARC Countries in 1997

Country	1997 Adult literacy rate (Percentages)					
	Percentage of total population		Compared to industrial country popn. (Percentages)		Compared to world popn. (Percentages)	
	Female	Male	Female	Male	Female	Male
Australia	99.0	99.0	+0.4	+0.1	+27.9	+14.7
India	39.4	66.7	-59.2	-32.2	-31.7	-17.6
Sri Lanka	87.6	94.0	-11.0	-4.9	-16.5	+9.7
Indonesia	79.5	90.6	-19.1	-8.3	+8.4	+6.3
Malaysia	81.0	90.2	-17.6	-8.7	+9.9	+5.9
Singapore	87.0	95.9	-11.6	-3.0	+15.9	+11.6
Kenya	71.8	86.9	-26.8	-12.0	+0.7	+2.6
Madagascar	..	..	..	..	..	..
Mauritius	79.2	86.9	-19.4	-12.0	+8.1	+2.6
Moz'bique	25.0	56.7	-73.6	-42.2	-46.1	-27.6
S. Africa	83.2	84.7	-15.4	-14.2	+12.1	+0.4
Tanzania	62.0	81.7	-36.6	-17.2	-9.1	-2.6
Oman	55.0	76.9	-43.6	-22.0	-16.1	-7.4
Yemen	21.0	64.2	-77.6	-34.7	-50.1	-20.1
Ind. cou'ry	98.6	98.9	..	..	..	..
World	71.1	84.3	-27.5	-14.6	..	..

Source : *Human Development Report* 1999, UNDP, New York.

Table 3 : Showing GDP Growth and Women's Share of Earned Income in the IORARC Countries during 1980-1997

Country	GDP 1980 (Million)	GDP 1997 (Million)	Per-centage changes 1980-97	P/capita real GDP (PPP $) 1997	Female p/capita GDP as a % of male GDP (PPP $) 1997	Changes in p/capita GDP 1980-97 in 1987 US $
Australia	160,190	391,045	144	20,230	69.0	33.4
India	172,321	359,812	109	1,670	37.8	77.5
Sri Lanka	4,024	15,128	276	2,490	41.0	68.0
Indonesia	78,013	214,593	175	3,490	51.0	124.9
Malaysia	24,488	97,523	298	8,140	46.2	100.7
Singapore	11,718	96,319	722	28,460	50.0	157.1
Kenya	7,265	9,899	36	1,190	74.2	0.5
Madagascar	4,042	3,552	-12	930	61.9	-31.5
Mauritius	1,132	4,151	267	9,310	35.6	112.2
Moz'bique	2,028	1,944	-4	740	70.2	20.6
South Africa	78,744	129,094	64	7,380	45.4	-14.9
Tanzania	..	..	..	580	89.7	..
Oman	5,989	13,438	124	9,960	14.0	57.6*
Yemen	..	..	..	810	55.8	..
IORARC	549,873	1,336,498	143	..	..	..
Ind. C'tries	..	..	..	23,741	58.8	12.8
World	10,674,160	28,157,012	164	6,332	55.8	15.1

*Refers to 1980-1997.

Source : Columns 2-4 : *World Development Report* 1998/99, The World Bank, OUP, NY, PP. 212-13.

Columns 5-7 : *Human Development Report*, UNDP, OUP, NY, pp. 134-37; 151-54; 138-41.

Table 4 : Showing IORARC Countries' Rankings in Various Development Related Indexes in 1997

Country	Human poverty index (HPI)		HDI	GDI	GEM
	World ranking	% of popn. below income poverty line (1989-94)*	World ranking		
Australia	12	7.8 (1989-95)**	7	4	9
India	59	52.5	132	1112	95
Sri Lanka	33	4.0	90	76	80
Indonesia	46	14.5	105	88	71
Malaysia	18	5.6	56	52	52
Singapore	..	..	22	22	32
Kenya	49	50.2	136	113	..
Madagas'r	..	72.3	147	..	..
Mauritius	15	..	59	57	61
Moz'bique	79	..	169	138	59
S. Africa	31	23.7	101	84	18
Tanzania	54	16.4	156	126	..
Oman	39	..	89	85	..
Yemen	78	..	148	128	..
World av.	..	..	..	..	..

*Denotes $ 1 a day at 1985, PPP, $; **Denotes $ 14.40 a day at 1985, PPP $.

Source : *World Development Report* 1998/99, The World Bank, OUP, New York, pp. 212-13.

15 The Role of Education and Training in Asian Development : Problems and Prospects

Amir Mahmood

Introduction

There is an emerging consensus that human resource development is crucial in achieving a sustainable rate of economic growth.[1] Investment in human capital enhances the efficiency of productive factors and stimulates product and processes innovations (Becker, *et. al.* : 1990). Human resource development provides conditions that are conducive to achieve and enhance productivity and international competitiveness.

The purpose of this study is to assess the impact of human development strategies on economic development in some South-East Asian economies. Education and training are directly related to productivity growth and improvement in international competitiveness.

Educatior, Training and Inter-regional Growth Performance in Asia

The growth experience of the past few decades has established that the regions that have given priority to education and literacy have succeeded in achieving high rates of economic growth, international competitiveness, and better living standards. This explains why the East Asian economies, such as, the Republic of Korea, Taiwan, Singapore, Hong Kong, Indonesia, Malaysia, Thailand, and China, have outperformed other developing regions of the world, including South Asia. Table 1 reveals that although the

[1] Human resource development is a broad term, encompassing elements such as formal education, skills, knowledge, training, health and nutritional adequacy etc.

South and East Asian economies were almost at the same level of per capita income in the 1960s during the past three decades real GDP in East Asia grew at a faster rate than in South Asia.

Table 1 : Literacy, Education Spending and Growth

Indicators	1960			1993			Annual Rate of Change	
	South Asia	East Asia	E-S Gap	South Asia	East Asia	E-S Gap	South Asia	East Asia
GDP per capita (PPP $)	648	869	221	1370	11088	9718	2.3	8.0
Adult Literacy (%)	32	88	56	48	98	50	1.8.	0.5
Public Expenditure on Education (as % of GNP)	2.0	3.7	1.7	3.4	4.3	0.9	1.7	2.7
GNP per capita growth rate	1.4 (1965 -80)	1.5 (1965-80)	0.1	2.9 (1980 -93)	7.5 (1980-93)	4.6	-	-

Source : Haq, M. (1997), tables 1.2 -1.3 & author's calculations.

While the per capita income in the East Asian countries has grown at a rate of 7.5 per cent during the period 1980-93, the growth rate in South Asia was less than half that achieved by East Asia. Although public spending on education, as a proportion of GNP, has risen in both regions, the annual rate of increase of these spending in South Asia still lags behind the rate maintained by the East Asian economies. The adult literacy rate in South Asia in 1993 was almost half of the level achieved by the East Asian economies in the 1960s.

Although education is not the sole determinant of economic and social transformation, there is no doubt that higher literacy rates and appropriate education policies backed by public spending have played a major role in a rapid economic growth of East Asia. Figure 1 illustrates an interesting growth comparison between two countries (Pakistan and Thailand), representing the countries, that started off with almost similar level of per capita income but performed diversely due to, among other factors, their adherence to different approaches towards education.

Figure 1 : Comparative Growth Performance

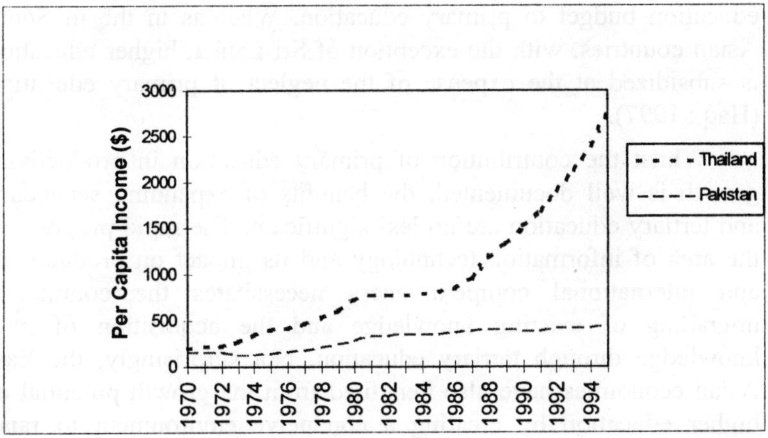

Source : World Bank (1997).

Given the significance of education and training and its positive spill-over effects, the conduct of public policy has an important bearing on exploiting the growth potential of education. In this respect, a vital tool to influence a country's level of human development is public-sector investment on education. Investment strategies that emphasize those areas of education that result in relatively higher social returns usually lead to efficient outcomes. By the same token an investment pattern that is skewed towards those sectors of education that are subject to a low social rate of return, lead to misallocation of resources and inefficiencies in the education system. This divergence between the social rates of return to investment in primary and tertiary sectors has important implications for resource allocation in the Asian economies. For instance, there is general agreement that countries with low levels of human resource development should emphasize the provision of primary education in their efforts to raise the rate of productivity growth. In this context relatively higher primary enrolment ratios of the East Asian economies (106 in 1980) point to a positive link between emphasis on primary education and their subsequent economic performance (UNESCO : 1997a). The Republic of Korea, Hong Kong, Thailand, and Malaysia allocate 70 per cent of their education budget to primary education. Whereas in the in South Asian countries, with the exception of Sri Lanka, higher education is subsidized at the expense of the neglect of primary education (Haq : 1997).

Whilst the contribution of primary education in productivity growth is well documented, the benefits of expanding secondary and tertiary education are no less significant. The rapid progress in the area of information technology and its impact on productivity and international competitiveness necessitates the continuous upgrading of existing knowledge and the acquisition of new knowledge through tertiary education. Not surprisingly, the East Asian economies have also benefited from the growth potential of higher education by creating a conducive environment to raise tertiary enrolment ratios (table 2).

Table 2 : Trends in Gross Tertiary Enrolment Ratios

Regions	Gross Tertiary Enrolment Ratio	
	1980	1995
South Asia	2.61	4.35
East Asia	10.16	23.6

Source : Author's computations based on UNESCO (1997a).

Table 2 provides a dismal record of South Asia in higher education. The South Asian tertiary enrolment ratio in 1995 was almost six times lower than the corresponding figure for East Asia. Further, unlike South Asia where tertiary education is heavily subsidized, the higher education in East Asia is largely self-financed. Like higher tertiary enrolment ratios, the number of scientists, engineers, and technicians, point to a country's commitment towards research and development and its capacity to adopt high-value added production processes. It is no coincidence, as table 3 indicates, that countries with higher per million personnel engaged in research and development, such as, the Republic of

Korea, Japan, and Singapore, have succeeded in acquiring and sustaining international competitiveness in high value-added industries.

Table 3 : Personnel Engaged in R & D in Selected Countries

Country	Scientists, and Engineers (per million)	Technicians (per million)
China (1995)	350	201
Republic of Korea (1994)	2636	317
Singapore (1995)	2728	353
India (1994)	149	108
Pakistan (1990)	54	76

Source : World Bank (1997)

Gender Issues in Education and Training

Gender equalities in education is an important pre-requisite for developing human capital. There is a general consensus that gender equalities in education and training result in higher female labor participation rates, greater output and higher productivity, a gradual drop in the fertility rate, an increase in income opportunities, and a drop in the proportion of people living in poverty. Whereas the East Asian countries have been successful in reducing the gender disparities in education, the poor performance in South Asian countries, as indicated by table 4, is a manifestation of its neglect of female education.

Table 4 : Women and Human Resource Development : Education Profile and Economic Activity

Indicator	South Asia	East Asia (Excl. China)	East-South Gap
Female Adult literacy (%) 1993	34	94	60
Female 1st, 2nd, and 3rd Level of Gross Enrolment Ratio (%) 1993	43	76	33
Female Mean Years of Schooling 1992	1.2	6.2	5
Female Economic Activity Rate	30	62	32

Source : Haq (1997).

There is no single dominating factor that could be held responsible for the extent of gender disparities in education that prevails in South Asia. In fact, there is a range of demand and supply side factors that obstruct gender equalities in education and have resulted in a low female adult literacy rate, a poor female gross enrolment ratio, and disappointing figures for mean years of schooling in South Asia (table 4). The female adult literacy rates achieved in East Asia are three times higher than the corresponding figures in South Asia. Similarly, the female gross enrolment ratio and mean years of schooling in East Asia have far exceeded the achievements of South Asia. The above record for female education has serious growth implications for a developing region such as South Asia, which accounts for 256 million of the world's 564 million illiterate women (UNESCO : 1997b). It is important to note that an important manifestation of East Asian emphasis on female education has been a relatively higher female economic activity rate.

As noted above, there exists a variety of demand as well as supply side factors that influence the pace of human resource development by impeding gender equalities in education. The demand side factors, including socio-economic and cultural aspects, play an important role in influencing the choices of parents and students. While political and institutional factors and issues relating to school influence the supply side of education services. A summary of such factors is presented in table 5.

Table 5 : Human Resource Development and the Factors Affecting Gender Equality in Education

Demand		Supply	
Socio-economic Factors	*Cultural Factors*	*Political and Institutional Factors*	*Factors Linked to the School*
• Poverty • Direct cost • Higher opportunity costs • Lower rates of return • Girls needed for household/agricultural tasks • Limited employment opportunities for graduates • Lower remuneration for women	• Parents' low level of education • Lower priority for girls' education • Girls education perceived as incompatible with traditional and/or religious beliefs • Early marriages and pregnancies • Skeptical attitudes towards the benefits and outcomes from educating girls	• Budget constraint • Structural adjustment programs • Inconsistent educational policies due to political instability • Poor quality of education programs • Ill-adaptation of education systems to local learning needs • Lack of clear strategy for women and girls' education • Limited employment prospects • Poor education policy formulation	• Limited school/classroom space • High school fees • Low proportion of female teacher • Untrained teacher/not sensitized to gender issues • School curricula in conflict with traditional culture • Orientation of girls/women to non scientific fields • School calendar incompatible with farming cycles

Source : Adapted from UNESCO (1997b).

In the context of female education, it is the interaction of the above forces that result in : limited access to schooling; low enrolment ratios; high school drop out rates; low female participation in scientific and technical fields; high proportion of illiterate women; scarce employment opportunities; reduced contribution to national economic and social development; limited bargaining power; and an absence from the political decision-making process (UNESCO : 1997b). It is, however, important to acknowledge that the relative intensity of the above outcomes will vary, as we have observed in table 4, from one region to another, depending on the relative strength of the forces that affect gender equalities in education. A validation of the above argument can be best seen by looking into the inter-country gender disparities in South Asia (see table 6).

Table 6 : Inter-Country Gender Disparities Profile : South Asia

Indicator	India	Pakistan	Bangladesh	Nepal	Sri Lanka	Bhutan	Maldives
Adult female literacy (as % of male)	40 (1970) 56 (1993)	35 (1970) 47 (1993)	35 (1970) 52 (1993)	12 (1970) 33 (1993)	80 (1970 92 (1993)	- - 47 (1993)	- - 99 (1993)
Female primary school enrolment (as % of male)	64 (1970) 81 (1993)	37 (1997) 61 (1993)	48 (1970) 82 (1993)	20 (1970) 6 (1993)	92 (1970) 99 (1993)	6 (1970) 71 (1993)	107 (1970) 100 (1993)
Female 1st, 2nd and 3rd level gross enrolment ratio (as % of male)	74 (1993)	49 (1993)	76 (1993)	61 (1993)	102 (1993)	- -	100 (1993)
Mean years of schooling (female as % of male)	32 (1970) 34 (1992)	25 (1970) 23 (1992)	29 (1970) 29 (1992)	33 (1970 31 (1992)	79 (1970) 79 (1992)	33 (1970) 33 (1992)	77 (1970) 76 (1992)
Economic activity rate (age 15+) (female as % of male)	43 (1970) 34 (1994)	11 (1970) 16 (1992)	6 (1970) 73 (1992)	52 (1970 48 (1992)	37 (1970 36 (1992)	52 (1970 47 (1992)	35 (1970) 30 (1992)

Source : Haq (1997).

Table 6 highlights that although the South Asian record of gender equalities in education is dismal, the performance of some of the countries in the region, such as Sri Lanka and Maldives, is commendable. In the context of South Asia, the indicators of gender equality in education in Sri Lanka are impressive. The same, however, cannot be claimed for some of the other South Asian economies, such as, Pakistan. While the overall situation of human resource development in Pakistan is disappointing, gender disparities in general and educational disparities in particular are appalling.

Within South Asia, Pakistan ranks lowest in most of the gender-related human development indicators. This result is disappointing given that Pakistan has enjoyed the highest rate of increase in real per capita income in South Asia during the past few decades.[2]

As noted above, there are various social, cultural, political, economic, and other supply side factors that determines the intro-regional gender disparities in education. The relative strength of these factors in obstructing gender equalities varies due to country-specific conditions. For instance, among other factors, the experience of Sri Lanka and Maldives reflects the commitment by their successive governments to pursue policies aimed at achieving gender equality in education. Other South Asian countries over the same period, however, failed to display similar results. Apart from a government failure, to realize the growth potential of female education in these economies, an interaction of various socio-economic, cultural, political, and economic factors have contributed to persistent gender gaps in education. Based on a gender profile of South Asian countries,[3] table 7 highlights the country-specific dominant factors that have been contributing to persistent gender disparities in education.

Whilst there are various country-specific conditions that hinder gender equality in education, there are also a set of generic factors that are common to the South Asian countries. For instance, the inside-outside dichotomy,[4] low government priority to female education, poverty, supply-side constraints, and urban bias in education planning have resulted in low educational attainment levels for South Asian women. The persistence of the above factors, in the presence of existing gender gaps in education, demand a

2 This implies significant foregone income gains for Pakistan due to investment on education over the past three decades (Nancy Birdsall, *et al.* : 1993).

3 See, World Bank (n.d.) for a detailed overview of gender profile of these countries.

4 This refers to situations where women are restricted to "inside" the home and are discouraged to work outside the home and face barriers in accessing education and other social services.

rethinking on the part of the South Asian countries towards the role of education in economic growth in general, and female education in particular.

Table 7 : Gender Disparities in Education and the Country Specific Factors : South Asia

Country –Specific Dominant Factors
Pakistan Fundamentalists' resistance to change traditional gender relations "Inside-outside" dichotomy Low government spending on education Shortage of girls' schools Shortage of female teachers Urban bias in access to education Girls needed for household/agricultural tasks
India "Inside-outside" dichotomy Urban bias in access to education Under-investment in girl education due to household/agriculture needs Poverty
Bangladesh "Inside-outside" dichotomy Poverty Household dependence on female child Labor Inadequate female teachers
Nepal Low spending on female education Ethnic beliefs and customs Poverty
Bhutan Ethnic beliefs and customs Poverty

Source : Author's adaptation of World Bank (n.d.).

Education and Training for Changing Comparative Advantage

With growing globalization of industries, technological advancement, discovery of new knowledge, and advancements in information technology, the productivity — enhancing human resource development strategies will likely to play a decisive role in efforts to acquire and/or enhance international competitiveness. In the presence of changing comparative advantage of industries, which put further pressure on enterprises to respond to sustain their competitiveness, the significance of skill acquisition and retraining becomes even more important. For instance, as China makes inroads into labor intensive manufacturing, enterprises in Indonesia and Thailand will come under increasing pressure to move into relatively more skill-intensive medium technology manufacturing. Such an industrial restructuring will require changes in skill and education requirements at the enterprise level (Tan : 1997).

Technological advancement and rapid globalization has also resulted in shorter product life, demanding workers to learn new skills quickly. Whereas the emergence of new knowledge has opened more business and employment opportunities, it also calls for flexible education and training systems to meet the changing industry needs (Silva : 1997). By the same token, failure to meet the above challenges by the Asian economies can lead to rising unemployment of unskilled workers and shortages of skilled workers.

As we have noted earlier, the growth experience of the past few decades validates claims that public investment in education and training bring high growth dividends. Alternatively, countries that have ignored the significance of education and training in the past are now finding it difficult to move towards the high value-added sectors. Apart from an emphasis on the provision of basic education, a rapid and sustainable economic growth for such economies would require a move towards tailoring of education and training programs to cater for high value-added and knowledge-based industries.

The above line of reasoning suggests that declining illiteracy ratios and high school enrolments is necessary but not a sufficient condition for achieving and sustaining international competitiveness. As highlighted by Low (1998), "human resource development has moved on from basic education and literacy to keeping up with structural and technological changes in the world economy" (p. 38). To meet the challenges of shifting comparative advantage, and to move from low-productivity production processes to high value-added production systems, rapid accumulation of skills, dissemination of new knowledge, and retraining is required. Among other factors, this transformation demands provision of education and training opportunities to generate skills and abilities that are compatible with changing industry requirements. Notwithstanding, the productivity potential of a skilled and trained labor force can only be achieved if their skills are indeed required by the industry and there exists a close coordination between educational/vocational institutions and employer groups and a well co-ordinated action on the part of government.

A failure to meet the challenges resulting from globalization can have serious labor market repercussions. There are, however, a few economies in East Asia that have been pursuing a coherent human resource development strategy to address labor market challenges. For instance, Singapore's Economic Development Board, and Economic Planning Board of South Korea have succeeded in executing forward-looking human resource development strategies to meet changing industry requirements and to move low skill, low value-added industries to skill-intensive, high value-added sectors (ILO : 1998).

Evidence to this effect, which contrasts the export orientation of South and East Asia, is given in table 8.

Table 8 : Export Roles in the Global Economy by Major Third World Regions

Regions	Primary Commodity Exports	Export-Processing Assembly	Component-Supply Subcontracting	Original Equipment Manufacturing	Original Brand Name Manufacturing
East Asia	X	X	X	X	X
South Asia	X	X			

Source : Adapted from, Gereffi : 1995.

It is evident that while the South Asian countries are still trapped in low to medium value-added manufacturing and primary commodity exports, some of the East Asian economies have successfully moved into sophisticated and high value-added production activities of Original Design Manufacturing (ODM) — a primary input in product innovation. Among other factors, the ability of the East Asian countries to meet changing industry needs through appropriate educational and training programs have enabled them to move into high value-added industries and enhance their competitiveness. An important aspect of the industrial transformation of East Asia has been their ability to convert the productivity gains into new investment and job opportunities.

Conclusions

This study highlights and assesses the impact of human resource development strategies on the development and competitiveness of South and East Asian economies with special focus on the role of education, training, skills, and gender disparities in education. It is argued that, among other factors, higher literacy rates; efficiency of allocation of resources among various education sub-sectors; acquisition and application of new knowledge; rapid accumulation of skills; skill-job requirement linkages; linkages between industry educational/vocational institutions; and efforts to reduce gender disparities in education, have played an important role in helping East Asian countries to create a conducive environment to achieve rapid economic growth. The study also examining the demand and supply side factors that obstructed the achievement of gender equality in education, and resulted in a low female adult literacy rate, a poor female gross enrolment ratio, low female economic activity rates, and disappointing figures for mean years of schooling in South Asia. With growing globalization, technological advancement, and the discovery of new knowledge, the productivity-driven human resource development strategies will play even a greater role in acquiring, sustaining, and enhancing competitiveness. A failure to meet these challenges may have serious employment and growth implications for the South and East Asian economies.

The study concludes that whilst investment in education and training is imperative to achieving sustainable productivity growth, the causation also runs backward where economic growth creates conditions for further human resource development that leads to an improvement in the skill and knowledge base of a work force. This circular relationship between economic growth and human capital thus provides a further impetus for a continuous upgrading of human capital through education and training.

REFERENCES

Barro, Robert J. (1991), "Economic Growth in a Cross-Section of Countries," *Quarterly Journal of Economics,* 106 : May, pp. 407-43.

Barro, Robert J, and J.W. Lee (1993), "International Comparisons of Education Attainment," *Journal of Monetary Economics*, Vol. 32, 363-94.

Becker, Gary S., Kevin M. Murphy and Robert Tamura (1990), "Human Capital, Fertility, and Economic Growth," *Journal of Political Economy*, 98 : S12-S37.

Birdsall, Nancy Ross, David, and Sabot, Richard (1993), "Underinvestment in Education : How Much Growth has Pakistan Foregone?" *The Pakistan Development Review*, 32 : 4 (winter 1993) pp. 453-99.

Denison, E.F. (1967), *Why Growth Rates Differ : Post-War Experience in Nine Western Countries,* Brookings Institution, Washington, DC.

Gapinski, James H. (1996), "The Economic Growth and its Components in African Nations," *Journal of Developing Areas*, 30, July, pp. 525-48.

Gereffi, Gary (1995), *Global Commodity Chains and Third World Development* quoted in Prokopenko, Joseph (1997), "Globalization, Alliances and Networking : A Strategy for Competitiveness and Productivity," *Enterprise and Management Development Working Paper*, Geneva : ILO.

Haq, M. (1997), *Human Development in South Asia 1997*, Karachi : Oxford University Press.

ILO (1998), *World Employment Report*, Geneva.

Levine, R., D. Renelt (1992), "A Sensitivity Analysis of Cross-Country Regressions," *American Economic Review*, Vol. 82, No. 4, September, 942-63.

Low, Linda. (1998), "Human Resource Development in the Asia-Pacific," *Asia-Pacific Economic Literature*, Vol. 12, No. 1, May.

Mankiew, N.G., D. Romer, and D. Weil (1992), "A Contribution to the Empiric of Economic Growth," *Quarterly Journal of Economics*, Vol. 107, No. 2, May, 407-37.

Oulton, Nicholas (1997), "Total Factor Productivity Growth and the Role of Externalities," *National Institute Economic Review*, Number 162, October, pp. 99-111.

Prokopenko, Joseph (1997), "Globalization, Alliances and Networking : A Strategy for Competitiveness and Productivity," *Enterprise and Management Development Working Paper*, Geneva : ILO.

Silva, de Sriyan (1997), "Human Resources Development for Competitiveness : A Priority for Employers", paper presented at the ILO Workshop on Employers Organizations in Asia-Pacific in the Twenty-First Century, Turin, Italy, May 5-13.

Tan, Boo Peng (1997), "Human Resource Development in Asia and the Pacific in the 21st century.

Century : Issues and Challenges for Employers and their Organisations, a paper presented at the ILO Workshop on Employer's Organisations in Asia-Pacific in the 21st Century, Turin, Italy, 5-13 May 1997.

UNESCO, (1997a), http://unescostat.unesco.org/indicator/indframe.htm.

UNESCO, (1997b), *Gender-Sensitive Education Statistics and Indicators : A Practical Guide,* Geneva.

UNDP, (1996), *Human Development Report*, New York : Oxford University Press.

World Bank (1980), *World Bank Report* 1980, New York : Oxford University Press.

World Bank (1997), *World Development Indicators (CD-ROM)*, Washington, D.C.

World Bank (n.d.), http//www.worldbank.org/html/prmgc/index.html.

16 The Application of Geographic Information Systems for Sustainable Catchment Management in India and Pakistan

S.R. Harrison
M.E. Qureshi
K.C. Roy

Introduction

Concern over Concern over degradation of natural resources including widespread clearing of native vegetation, soil erosion, soil salinity and waterlogging has been raised in both India and Pakistan. Government agencies and non-government organisations in both countries have acknowledged that sustainable use of natural resources is essential because the economies of both countries are natural resource based.

In addition to many other factors, effective, accessible and appropriate information systems are a key in for supporting sustainable management of natural resources. Geographical Information Systems (GIS) have been used effectively to support sustainable management of natural resources in various countries. GIS have been integrated with various other decision-support techniques, and applied to a wide variety of resource and environmental management problems. Developing countries face particular difficulties in adopting modern information technology, and this could be expected to be the case in India and Pakistan.

This paper provides an overview of nature and functions of environmental GIS as well as their integration with other models such as multicriteria analysis and the analytic hierarchy process. Applications in sustainable use of natural resources and in particular to catchment management are also discussed and an overview of natural resource degradation in India and Pakistan is presented. Finally, the potential application of GIS in catchment management in the context of Pakistan is examined.

Nature and Functions of GIS

Effective and accessible information systems are important to economic performance and strategic decision-making. From a geographical viewpoint, the trend towards advanced information systems has led to the design and use of GIS. There is no universal definition for computer systems manipulating geographic data and "geographic information systems" is a commonly accepted collective term (Bernhardsen, 1992). These systems are implemented with computer hardware and software functions, namely acquisition and verification, compilation, storage, updating, management and exchange, manipulation, retrieval and presentation, analysis and combination of geographic data (*Ibid*). The components of a GIS including computer hardware and software are discussed by Burrough and McDonnell (1998), who also provide a tool-based definition :

"GIS is a powerful set of tools for collecting, storing, retrieving at will, transforming and displaying spatial data from the real world for a particular set of purposes. The geographical (or spatial) data represent phenomena from the real world in terms of : (a) their position with respect to a known co-ordinate system, (b) their attributes that are unrelated to position (such as colour, cost, pH and incidence of disease) and (c) their spatial interrelations with each other which describe how they are linked together" (Burrough and McDonnell, 1998, pp. 11-12).

GIS have originated from two complementary sources. First, there is the field of graphic design systems (*e.g.*, Computer-Aided Design or CAD systems) which aim at visualising and graphically designing various objects in three-dimensional space. For planning purposes, such CAD systems have been helpful especially in the areas of infrastructure and land management. The second origin lies in spatial analytical systems development, which are used in spatial data analysis and planning. The latter development is more suitable for Decision-Support Systems (DSS) and image processing (Giaoutzi and Nijkamp, 1993).

A GIS contains spatially and thematically referenced data usually in a relational database, and interrogation and mapping facilities. It is a locationally defined, computerised database that answers queries of geographical or spatial nature (Lyons and Sharma, 1991) and is designed for ease of data entry and updating, and efficient storage with minimum data redundancy.

GIS are often regarded as a descriptive and systematic presentation of objects in geographic space; such objects may be multidimensional features which can be mapped *via* the georeferencing potential of GIS. In addition to description, GIS can play an important role in an explanatory stage of analysis and planning (Giaoutzi and Nijkamp, 1993).

Geographical data describe objects from the real world in terms of (a) their position with respect to a known co-ordinate system, (b) their attributes that are unrelated to position and (c) their spatial interrelations with each other (topological relations), which describe how they are linked together or how one can travel between them (Burrough, 1986). The coordinate system may be purely local, as in the case of a study of a limited area, or it may be that of a national grid or internationally accepted projection such as the Universal Transverse Mercator Coordinate System (UTM). All geographical data can be reduced to three basic topological concepts, namely the point, the line and the area (*Ibid*).

Giaoutzi and Nijkamp (1993) discussed four major functions of GIS, namely preparation, analysis, display, and management of geographic data. Preparation includes such functions as data collection, digitising point data, and editing. The purpose of the analysis function is to examine the data to create new data, with the aim of producing information. Display includes all operations which produce graphic output. These authors argued that from the viewpoint of model construction — and more generally of quantitative-empirical research methods — these GIS functions may supplement existing analysis techniques. However, they are by no means a replacement of such methods (*Ibid*).

GIS can process georeferenced data and provide answers to questions about the particulars of a given location, the distribution of selected phenomena, the changes that have occurred since a previous viewing, the impact of a specific event, or the relationships and systematic patterns of a region. GIS can perform spatial analysis of georeferenced[1] data to illuminate such specifics as the quickest "driving route" between two points, or the dependence of contested regional planning areas on the varying weightings of conflict parameters (Bernhardsen, 1992).

Many modern GIS can process data from various sources, including digital map data, digital images, video images, CAD data and various computer-based registers. Consequently, a GIS might be termed a "data mixing system" (*Ibid*). GIS offer a consistent representation of a set of geographical units or objects which — besides their location — can be characterised by one or more attributes (features or labels). Data in GIS can be represented by one of two data models : raster or vector. In a raster model data are represented as cell values in a grid. In a vector model, geographic data (object/features) are represented by points, lines and areas (or polygons). For analysing geographic information, there are various software packages available (such as ArcInfo and ArcView). These packages can utilise both raster[2] and vector data, and can convert among all these data types.

All such information systems may be highly important for planning the use of scarce resources, not only on a global scale but also on a local scale. Within this framework, spatial information systems are increasingly combined with pattern recognition, systems theory, topology, statistics and finite element analysis. GIS tools are currently modifying the perception of geography and planning (Giaoutzi and Nijkamp, 1993).

---

1 Georeferencing is usually expressed in terms of positions in Cartesian coordinates (such as Northing, Easting, Elevation) or in latitude and longitude. But other reference systems such as post codes and various area divisions used in map indexes and demographic studies are also employed.

2 An array of grid cells with each grid referenced by a row and column number representing the type or value of attribute being mapped.

In situations where complex environmental relationships exist, it has been found that data concerning different aspects of the physical environment can be used more effectively in combination than separately. One of the primary functions of a GIS is the combination and evaluation of disparate data layers for the purpose of providing "new information" (Evans and Myers, 1993). According to Burrough (1986), GIS should be thought of as being much more than means of coding, storing, and retrieving data about aspects of the earth's surface. In GIS, data can be accessed, transformed and manipulated interactively. GIS analyse and produce maps more rapidly, inexpensive and accurately than traditional non-automated methods. GIS can serve as test beds for studying environmental processes or for analysing the results of trends, or of anticipating the possible results of planning decisions (Burrough, 1986; Giaoutzi and Nijkamp, 1993).

While effective record keeping, analysis and management are important benefits of GIS in daily operations, the greatest benefits of GIS result from application to decision-making. GIS can quickly and accurately provide decision-makers with information in the most concise form : a picture. GIS produce maps and supporting tables of information that for centuries used to be difficult and time consuming to produce. GIS generate a multitude of relationships using information from varied sources and these are made immediately accessible to decision-makers, who can then spend their time considering strategic policy issues rather than extracting information (Giaoutzi and Nijkamp, 1993).

GIS provide a large range of analysis capabilities that will be able to operate on the topology or spatial aspects of the geographical data, and on the non-spatial attributes of these data. These analyses allow the user to work interactively to perform the analysis and synthesis required (Burrough, 1986). For example, in agricultural related decisions, GIS provide a powerful framework for assembling existing information about soil type, topography, agricultural enterprises and land degradation, as well as farmers' practices and attitudes to landcare. These data can be compiled for a target area, such as farm, stream catchment or local government area. In general, agricultural GIS typically have had only rudimentary economic analysis capabilities, while farming systems models have not handled spatial aspects well (Harrison and Sharma, 1996).

Development of GIS in Resource Management

Most aspects of land resource management require information on the current extent of features and the ways in which their distribution has changed over time. Such information can be collected by ground survey, aerial survey and satellite imagery. By capturing these spatial data on a computer-based GIS and overlaying various data sets, the land resource planner and manager have the capability to analyse changes in the distribution of features. This process plays an important role in assessing the impact of previous planning decisions and for carrying out inventories of existing procedures. By choosing appropriate modelling criteria, the possible future outcome of different planning decisions relating to resource use and conservation can be predicted using the analytical capabilities of the GIS (Deane, 1994).

The development of GIS for resource management can be seen in terms of three stages or levels, *viz.*, inventory, data integration and analysis and modelling (Harrison and Sharma, 1996). This conceptualisation reflects the view that to formulate policies for sustainable development there is need to understand the questions :

- What is the existing situation?
- What changes to the existing situation are taking place?
- What will the system be like in the future if the current management regime is continued?
- What will happen if alternative managements are imposed?

The simplest type of GIS is an inventory of resources and their characteristics. This base level operation provides a description of the present state of resources, and is a logical extension of current information recording systems. The system could include records of such variables as soils, crops, roads and climatic parameters.

The next level is the move away from isolated and stand-alone inventories to that of integrated databases. In such a system, data of various types and from various sources which form the basis of several databases are integrated into a single system. The requirements for such integration are well known : for textual and attribute data there is a need for some sort of common identifiers or keys; for graphic or map data a common co-ordinate reference system is required.

The highest level of GIS application is that of spatial analysis and modelling. This level includes possibilities ranging from relatively simple "what if" type calculations to more sophisticated process modelling.

As a tool, GIS are based on statistical-mathematical modelling, and in operation GIS are less suitable as a direct tool for explanatory or predictive modelling compared to conventional spatial modelling. However, some progress has been made, e.g. in the field of spatial location-allocation modelling, where traditional spatial interaction tools have been linked to a GIS representation of the resulting patterns and flows. Giaoutzi and Nijkamp (1993) argued that GIS are a more properly a tool for perception or visualisation methods for impact analysis rather than a direct impact tool (Giaoutzi and Nijkamp, 1993).

GIS Applications in Natural Resource Management

GIS have been applied in a number of areas of environmental and natural resource management, particularly in relation to forestry as a sustainable land use. For example, commercial forestry information systems were developed in the 1970s, to cover the whole gamut of operations including silviculture, inventories, plot management, harvest planning, replanting operations (Sharma *et. al.,* 1997). Other application areas in natural resource management include :

- catchment management (including riparian vegetation) (Le Maitre *et. al.*, 1993; Adinarayana *et. al.*, 1994; Bren, 1995; Lo, 1995; Petroeschevsky, 1997; Harrison *et. al.*, 1998; Shrestha *et. al.*, 1998);
- forestry on sloping lands (Zhai and Xian, 1994; Selman, 1992);

- monitoring land degradation and erosion risk (Garg and Harrison, 1992; Grunblatt *et. al.*, 1992; Mellerowica *et. al.*, 1994);
- landuse planning in degraded landscapes (Garg and Harrison, 1992; Fu and Gulinck, 1994);
- ecological restoration projects (Westman, 1991) and
- integrated models for policy applications (Schultink, 1992; Giaoutzi and Nijkamp, 1993).

In addition to the above studies relevant to natural resource management, Deane (1994) reviewed four case studies of GIS in the management of natural resources :

- Woodland resource mapping in Yemen, designed to produce a comprehensive database of the woodland resources of the whole country.
- Forest change monitoring in Tanzania study which examined in detail the changing patterns of forest cover to identify areas suitable for replanting with teak.
- Environmental sensitivity mapping which involved the examination of existing datasets covering the Black Sea in eastern Europe.
- Agricultural inventory involving use of remote sensing for monitoring crop areas and yields in a project in Europe.

Integration of GIS with Other Models for Decision Making Process

GIS have been applied in combination with other techniques in decision-support processes for natural resource management. A number of studies are summarised in table 1.

Table 1 : Integration of GIS with other Models for Natural Resource Management

Author and year	Type of supporting model	Policy applications area
Janssen and van Herwijnen (1989)	MCA and linear programming models	Optimal use of land in 118 regions
Grunblatt *et. al.* (1992)	Ecosystem model	Assessment of desertification and mapping
Le Maitre *et al.* (1993)	Integrated a GIS software on workstation and desktop computer database by using a standard relation database package	To associate spatial entities and to calculate spatial statistics
Littleboy *et al.* (1989)	Perfact soil loss model	Quantitative land suitability evaluation
McClean *et al.* (1995)	Decision support system to integrate economic, ecological and hydrological modelling capabilities	Land use related decisions
Negahban *et al.* (1994)	Decision support system with the integration of optimisation algorithms (linear programming)	Regional water quality planning
Fedra (1995)	Decision supports systems by integrating models, GIS and expert systems	Environmental impact assessment for water resource development projects and an air quality management system.
Mallawaarachchi *et al.* (1995)	Integrated GIS with mathematical programming	Assessment of land degradation costs in extensive areas
Elshorbagy *et al.* (1996)	Multicriterion evaluation model	Analysis of the irrigation water supply to a small sub-catchment
Villa *et al.* (1996)	Concordance method of MCA	Multi-objective evaluation of a park
Harrison *et al.* (1998)	Discounted cash flow analysis model	Estimated areas of riparian revegetation options
Shrestha *et al.* (1998)	Integrated remotely sensed data with socio-economic data	Sustainable watershed planning and management
Yeh and Li (1998)	Sustainable land development model (population growth model) using remote sensing and GIS	Impacts of agricultural land loss in a rapidly developing area

Janssen and van Herwijnen (1989) utilised GIS with the combination of multicriteria analysis MCA and linear programming to form a decision-support system. The system was made to rank 118 regions in Netherlands according to their suitability for combined land use and change in land use, to support decisions with a spatial dimension. Grunblatt *et. al.* (1992) applied a GIS in combination with simple ecosystem models to evaluate water and wind erosion, vegetation degradation and range utilisation, to assist in desertification assessment and mapping. Le Maitre *et. al.* (1993) developed a computer system by integrating GIS software on a workstation and a desktop computer database (PC system) using a standard relational database package. The GIS was used to generate the links that the PC system used to associate spatial entities such as land ownership boundaries, land management units and vegetation types. The system also calculated spatial statistics such as the area of a compartment or vegetation type or the length of a road or path.

Mellerowica *et. al.* (1995) combined the universal soil loss equation with a GIS in watershed planning. Littleboy (1996) integrated the Perfact model (developed to predict soil erosion in cropping areas in south-east Queensland) with a GIS for quantitative land suitability evaluation.

McClean *et. al.* (1995) developed a decision support system (DSS) which brought together large volumes of diverse, landuse-related data into a central database using GIS technology. They made available the data, as well as economic, ecological and hydrological modelling capabilities to the decision maker *via* a user-friendly interface designed for their project. Negahban *et. al.* (1994) developed a GIS-based decision support system which integrated a linear programming algorithms, to determine optimal management strategies for regional water quality planning in the Lake Okeechobee watershed in South Florida.

Fedra (1995) provided a useful discussion on GIS integration with other models in developing a decision support system for natural resource management. He described a number of examples from the work of the Advanced Computer Applications group at the International Institute for Applied Systems Analysis in Lexenburg,

Austria, including Environmental Impact Assessment (EIA) for water resource development projects and an air quality management system.

Mallawaarachchi *et. al.* (1996) integrated the spatial analytical capabilities of GIS with the constrained optimisation power of mathematical programming to facilitate the generation of composite data sets for extensive geographic regions. This was applied to assessment of land degradation costs in extensive areas of New South Wales, Australia.

Elshorbagy *et. al.* (1996) developed a multicriteria evaluation method as a decision aid for analysis of the irrigation water supply in a small sub-catchment in Thailand. They used GIS and simple formulae for the evaluation of performance of policy alternatives and coupled to a multi-objective decision support system shell using the DEFINITE software package.

Villa *et. al.* (1996) described a GIS-based method for evaluation of concordance between a set of mapped landscape attributes and a set of quantitatively expressed management priorities. They carried out a multi-objective evaluation of the park surrounding the Magnani-Rocca Foundation, a cultural institution located in Northern Italy.

Harrison *et. al.* (1998) used a GIS to estimate areas of riparian revegetation buffers in a small catchment in North Queensland and to produce maps. The discounted sum of estimated areas multiplied by the gross margin of sugarcane indicated the opportunity cost of each revegetation option.

Shrestha *et. al.* (1998) integrated remotely sensed data with socio-economic data, in a GIS for sustainable watershed planning and management in Nepal. Soil erosion status for particular areas of the watershed were generated by overlaying thematic map attributes, to identify areas of low, medium and high erosion. Similarly, Yeh and Li (1998) integrated remote sensing with GIS to evaluate the impact of unplanned urban growth, comparing actual development with optimal sustainable development. They identified landuse problems in both spatial and time dimensions and found that some land conversions are not at appropriate locations, and proposed land development which can meet the objective of sustainable development.

Environmental and Natural Resource Problems in India and Pakistan

The economies of India and Pakistan are mainly natural-resource based and their major sectors (agriculture, livestock, forestry, fishing and tourism) rely on these resources. A sustainable balance between present and future use of these resources is vital for the economies of both countries. They are faced by two mutually reinforcing problems : the seemingly persistent problem of poverty, and destruction of natural resources and environment. Like other developing countries, they are suffering a loss of biodiversity : animal and plant species known to have existed in the past have vanished, and many more are under threat of extinction. For example, in Pakistan expansion of human settlement and unlawful hunting practices have reduced the populations of animals such as the idex, snow leopard, wild ass, and houbara bustard to an endangered level, and a number of plant species are disappearing (Mumtaz and Mitha, 1996, p. 53).

Mumtaz and Mitha (1996, p. 53) observed how natural resources are being misused in Pakistan. According to their study : (a) only half of the urban excreta is disposed in sewers, (b) hazardous chemicals are disposed of in waterways, (c) motor vehicles emissions are excessive, (d) land is being lost to desertification, waterlogging and soil erosion, (e) destruction and degradation of forests is occurring, (f) wetlands are being drained and (g) the biological food-chain is being damaged. These authors identified key problems as :

- capture of Indus Basin runoff through development of large-scale irrigation schemes, reducing the scope for further increase in water supply;
- unlined canals which have proved to be extremely inefficient, losing large quantities of water in transmission;

- increasing contamination of groundwater and surface water from agricultural chemicals, and industrial and municipal wastes;
- threat to agricultural production due to land degradation. Only about 20 per cent (20 m ha) of the land area of Pakistan is classified as cultivable — equal to the area already under cultivation. Much of the land is of medium to poor quality, ravaged by water and wind erosion, waterlogging and loss of organic matter;
- untold long-term damage to the land and those who work on it due to widespread and unregulated use of pesticides;
- a rise in the watertable (to within 2 metres of the land surface) in Sind province, due to extensive use of irrigation, which has resulted into severe problems of waterlogging and salinity and
- 1.96 m ha of land in irrigated areas now covered by white salty crust and uncultivable.

Pakistan's estimated forest cover of 5.2 per cent is one of the lowest in the world. Forests have been used unsustainably and rapid reduction in forest cover has occurred over the last 30 to 40 years. The mangroves along the coast are under grave threat due to an increasing level of sewage and industrial pollution, increased salinity in the Indus delta, and through cutting for fodder and fuel (Mumtaz and Mitha, 1996).

Degradation of natural resources is occurring in all parts of Pakistan. In the hills, large areas have been denuded of their protective vegetation by people in search of fuel and timber and by animals in search of fodder. In the process, the natural habitat of plants and animals indigenous to Pakistan has been reduced markedly. Although the government has established seven national parks, 72 wildlife sanctuaries, and seven game reserves during the past 23 years, many of these areas are protected more in name than in reality (Reed, 1996, p. 233). Mumtaz and Mitha (1996) provided the following roots of these problems in Pakistan :

- economic and demographic pressures on a limited resource base;

- failure to manage natural resource sustainably;
- inadequate — or more often not strictly applied — regulatory measures and
- lack of co-ordination between the government departments and inability to deal with cross-sectoral issues.

Natural resource degradation is also critical in India. This was recognised in 1987 by the Government of India in its statistical abstract (Roy and Tisdell, 1992, Ch. 4). There was a decline in the total area of barren and uncultivated land, permanent pastures and grazing land, land under tree crops, groves and forests, from 80.5 m ha in 1968-69 to 71.5 m ha in 1984-85. Similarly, the total area of inaccessible state forests declined from 179,531 km^2 in 1951-52 to 160,421 km^2 in 1979-80. The most alarming decline was recorded in forest area owned by private individuals. Between 1951-52 and 1979-80, 45,100 km^2 of such forests disappeared (Government of India, 1987, reported in Roy and Tisdell, 1992, p. 76).

Exploitation of natural resources leading to environmental degradation is frequently a result of poverty. Poverty-led environmental degradation is responsible for much of the degradation of marginal lands, deforestation, overgrazing of fragile rangelands, cultivation of steep slopes and consequent soil erosion, flooding and loss of vegetative cover. Thus, while poverty accelerates environmental degradation, environmental degradation causes poverty. Such a self-perpetuating negative spiral is not an uncommon occurrence in developing countries.

GIS Use for the Management of Natural Resources in India and Pakistan

A search was carried out of the University of Queensland Library Database to locate references on use of GIS for management of natural resources in India and Pakistan. Database abstracts CAB, AGRICOLA AG&NR : STREAMLINE (Natural Resources) and ECONLIT were searched with the key words “GIS”, “natural”, “resources”, “India” and “Pakistan”, for the period 1991 to 1998 inclusive, on WinSPIRS software version 2.1. There were 10 references of GIS use relevant to natural resources for India. These are listed with author, year of publication, topic, methodology and findings in table 2.

Table 2 : GIS Use for Natural Resources Management in India

Author and Year	Topic	Methodology	Findings/achievements
Adinarayana *et. al.* (1994)	Mapping land use patterns in a river catchment using GIS	Used multi-temporal satellite imagery from different agricultural seasons to produce land-cover maps for the catchment, using knowledge-based re-classification. Digitised the drainage networks, elevation and other topographic and thematic data from maps. Used GIS to integrate these data sources and to provide tools for manipulation of the data.	Delineated spectrally inseparable classes and prepared maps. Developed various land use classes including wastelands to take appropriate preventive measures.
Murty and Venkatachalam (1992)	Delineation of erosion cells in a watershed using GIS	Spatial evaluation of erosions in a watershed using an erosion cell approach which uses the landform modifications caused by erosion process. GIS package (NRDMS-GIS) was used for the map analysis.	Delineated three components of the erosion cell, four basic maps, Landsat TM and field mapping. Different zones are described.
Menon and Bawa (1997)	Applications of a GIS, remote sensing and landscape ecology approach to biodiversity conservation in the Western Ghats	Used a landscape ecology and spatial analysis approach by integrating remote sensing and GIS. A correlation was estimated between deforestation and biodiversity.	Correlation was found between deforestation and biodiversity conservation in Western Ghats.

Author and Year	Topic	Methodology	Findings/achievements
Roy *et. al.* (1996)	Growing stock estimation of monoculture plantations using remote sensing techniques and a GIS — a case study in central Tarai Forest division, U.P.	Used inventory data, Landsat Thematic Mapper data and a geographical information for the area. Inventory data was collected at 85 sampling points selected by stratified random sampling technique. Growing stock estimation was also estimated at block and range level using the GIS.	Average volume/ha of the species was estimated and total growing stock in Central Tarai Forest Division was estimated, i.e. 1.26 m m^3.
Ravan and Roy (1997)	Satellite remote sensing for ecological analysis of forested landscape.	Satellite remote sensing data and a GIS were used. Landsat TM data were utilised to derive a community-level vegetation-type map and to measure species richness, biomass, physiography and patch characteristics such as size, shape, porosity and patch density. Analysed the impacts of disturbance on the landscape structure of three vegetation and management zones in the Madhav National Park, Madhya Pradesh, India.	Patch size and porosity are the most important parameters in discriminating differences in the ecological status of the 3 zones. Species diversity and biomass distribution significantly decreased as a result of increased human disturbance.

Author and Year	Topic	Methodology	Findings/achievements
Kushwaha *et. al.* (1996)	Interfacing remote sensing and GIS methods for sustainable rural development	A holistic approach was adopted considering the production and conservation functions of the ecosystem. Remotely sensed data were utilised to assess the natural resources of the area. A thorough analysis of climatic, socio-economic and natural resources was made.	A set of rules was formulated and the information integrated to prepare realistic action plans. These action plans have found wide acceptance due to their practicability and soundness.
Tiwari *et. al.* (1995	Remote sensing and GIS for management of Himalayan ecosystems	Remote sensing and GIS were used for the mapping of land use, forest, slope, soil, forest biomass and fuel wood/fodder availability of the Indian Himalayas.	Resource maps were prepared These maps can be used to generate additional information for management (such as calculation of soil loss)
Adinarayana and Krishna (1996)	Integration of multi-seasonal remotely-sensed images for improved landuse classification of a hilly watershed using geographical information systems	Multi-seasonal and multi-sensor remotely sensed data were used for mapping a land-use pattern of the watershed. The rasterised classified images and the relevant watershed resources were input and stored as separate layers in the GIS and then geometrically co-registered to a regular 30 m grid. Knowledge based rules were developed to manipulate the information database. Finally, the GIS improved and the land-use pattern map was classified.	Areal extent of final land-use map classes compared favourably with the natural conditions of the agro-climatic region of the watershed. The paper envisages future studies for watershed management policies.

Author and Year	Topic	Methodology	Findings/achievements
Ghosh *et. al.* (1993)	District level planning — a case study for the Panchmahals district using remote sensing and geographic information system techniques	Used the Composite Land Development Unit (CLDU) and the Service Centre Hierarchy (SCH) for natural and socio-economic resources, respectively. The CLDU map was derived from slope, soil, groundwater prospect and land-use information using GIS techniques.	Alternative land-use sites were recommended based upon the soil-slope conditions. Priority sub-watersheds in the district were identified for soil conservation measures.
Singh (1992)	Remote sensing and GIS as decision support systems in the Himalayas	Assessed the use of remote sensing and GIS in the monitoring of land use changes in both natural and anthropologically modified geosystems at regional and local levels by considering the following dimensions : (1) historical development of the geosystem, (2) current resource base, (3) feedback and side-effects of human activities, (4) socio-economic needs of the region and (5) forecasting of environmental transformation consequent upon development.	The results show changing forest distribution and a classification of land suitable for agriculture.

In all these studies, GIS has either been used separately or integrated with remote sensing to examine natural resources. These studies were carried out : to produce land cover maps for the catchment (Adinarayana *et. al.,* 1994); to evaluate erosion in a watershed (Murty and Venkatachalam, 1992); to examine the correlation between deforestation and biodiversity (Menon and Bawa, 1997); to estimate growing stock at block and range level of monoculture plantations; to derive a community-level vegetation map and analyse the impacts of disturbance on landscape structure, vegetation and management zones (Ravan and Roy, 1997); to assess the natural resources of the area by analysing climatic, socio-economic and natural resource data (Kushwaha *et. al.,* 1996); to produce maps of land use, forest, slope, forest biomass and fuel wood and fodder availability (Tiwari *et. al.,* 1995); to create maps and to classify landuse pattern of a watershed (Adinarayana and Krishna, 1996); to derive maps of slope, soil, groundwater prospect and landuse information (Ghosh, *et. al.,* 1993) and to monitor landuse changes in both natural and anthropologically modified geo-systems at regional and local levels (Singh, 1992). These studies indicate that there has only been limited application of GIS in the management of natural resources in India. Kumar (1994) identified and discussed four stages of GIS development in India, namely : (a) pioneer and research frontier phase; (b) formal development and government-funded research; (c) commercial phase and (d) routine phase. He argued that India is still at the second stage, and overall maximum use of GIS potential is yet to be explored and exploited.

In the case of Pakistan, not a single reference was located in the library search, suggesting that either there is little progress of GIS use in Pakistan or the applications are not reported in international literature. Personal communications indicate that some organisations in Pakistan — including the Soil Survey Department and World Wildlife Fund — are progressing towards compilation of digital data and GIS use (Ahmad, 1998). The World Wildlife Fund — Pakistan is one of the leading international organisations in the country but its GIS Lab has as yet only limited GIS datasets and is mainly making resource maps of specific project areas (Ashraf, 1998). Baseline data are being obtained from the Digital Chart of the World (DCW) at 1 : 1 million scale. For some projects, topographic sheets from the Soil Survey Department at 1 : 50,000 scale are being digitised. Recently, WWF-Pakistan has been involved in satellite image processing of SPOT XS data for the demarcation of Chilghoza Forest in the Suleiman Range area, close to Zhob in Baluchistan and at Daira Ismail Khan in the North-West Frontier Province (NWFP) (Ashraf, 1998). WWF also holds data for Wildlife Protected Areas of Pakistan, and the GIS Lab is digitising boundaries of these protected areas. The main theme of this exercise is to build protected areas of the Pakistan Information System where ground survey details will be linked with the spatial data of the protected areas, and ultimately made available on CD with multimedia (Ashraf, 1998).

Ashraf (1998) stated that "according to my knowledge, there are very few organisations using GIS in natural resource management … No national level GIS data are available." On the basis of this information, it would be difficult in the near future for the researchers to carry out projects relating to management of natural resources and the environment in Pakistan involving GIS data.

Inhibiting Factors of GIS Use in India and Pakistan

The above discussion reveals that progress on GIS in India and Pakistan has been limited. Sahay and Walsham (1996) reviewed literature on GIS implementation in developing countries and particularly in India. They identified so-called "inhibiting factors," as discussed below.

Data Scarcity

The first and most important impediment is lack of data. GIS need graphic and textual data in order to function. In developed countries much of the data needed for setting up GIS have been collected and are readily available, thus making GIS construction relatively easy, but data are less readily available in developing countries (Yeh, 1991). According to Sahay and Walsham (1996), data concerns are mostly technical in nature and relate to availability in appropriate scales and usability problems because of the over-dependence on remotely sensed data, quality problems due to maps being outdated, and non-standardised formats of data that are not supported by standard software. Collection of socio-economic data requires field surveys which are expensive and time consuming (Yeh, 1991).

Lack of Skilled Manpower

In India and Pakistan (as in many developing countries) there is acute shortage of people who are capable of understanding and using GIS, and also a general lack of awareness about GIS (Sahay and Walsham, 1996). The shortage of trained practitioners exacerbates the problem of providing GIS training.

Structural Concerns

These relate to decision-making styles and the forms of developing country organisations (Sahay and Walsham, 1996), including those in India and Pakistan. Decision-making is often confined to a central official who, despite inadequate knowledge about the technology, is responsible for taking critical decisions related to implementation. The sectoral form of organisation, coupled with an almost total absence of policies that enable coordination, often leads to duplication of efforts. Sahay and Walsham (1996) argued that in India, involvement of multiple actors, each with their own agendas and beliefs about GIS, makes the practice of GIS management an extremely complex task.

Financial Constraints

These are the key hurdle in implementation of GIS in India and Pakistan. Availability of data and trained manpower are directly related to availability of finance. Universities make slow progress in GIS development in India and Pakistan because of lack of funding. Whereas in developed countries, GIS progress is often led by teaching and research in the universities, this is not the case in developing countries (Yeh, 1991) including India and Pakistan. Finance constraints impede development and maintaining GIS systems, and also restrict the setting up and maintenance of training and research programs. Funding for a GIS project often comes as a part of an aid package that dries up long before the project is completed. The long lead time in implementing GIS also makes sustained funding difficult (Sahay and Walsham, 1996).

GIS-based Decision Support for Sustainable Use of Natural Resources in Pakistan

The concern over widespread degradation of natural resources has been acknowledged by Pakistani governments and non-government organisations. The Country's Sixth (1983-88), Seventh (1988-93) and Prospective Plans (1988-2003) reflect increasing evidence of recognizing the linkages among economic development, poverty alleviation, resource management and environmental protection (Reed, 1996, p. 234).

The national government has made a serious attempt to respond to the environmental crisis and to address future needs by commissioning and publishing the National Conservation Strategy (NCS). Developed through a consultative process involving policy makers, sectoral experts and non-government organisations, the NCS has identified priority actions for immediate attention : maintaining soils in crop lands; protecting watersheds, supporting forestry and plantations; restoring rangelands and improving livestock; conserving biodiversity; energy efficiency; and controlling pollution in streams (Mumtaz and Mitha, 1996, p. 58). The management of these issues at national levels demands their management at a local level.

To deal with these issues at a national level, many developed countries (such as Australia) adopt an approach which focuses on the sustainable use and management of resources at a catchment level, referred to as Integrated Catchment Management (ICM). ICM provides an opportunity for the owners and managers of land and water resources, in conjunction with the general community, to determine and mould future management. This approach is also relevant to developing countries including Pakistan, where implementation of ICM would ensure that decisions on land and water resource management are made on the best available information and take into account all relevant competing interests. One of the major elements of ICM is planting of trees and shrubs along streambanks and lakes which have degraded riparian zones. The effectiveness of riparian vegetation to protect land, water and natural habitat is well recognised (e.g. Raine and Gardiner, 1995).

Revegetation of degraded riparian zones removes land from agriculture, which implies opportunity costs of land as well as tree planting and maintenance costs. The wider the vegetation buffer the higher the costs and the greater the benefits, in terms of increased filtration of water runoff, streambank stability, reduced transport of nitrates and sediments and increased recreational values of streams due to improved quality of water.

Detailed surveys of an area will help to identify sites of soil erosion. On the basis of this information about soil erosion and riparian vegetation, the sites can be ranked and categorised in a catchment or region. The areas of highly categorised sites (prioritised on the basis of erosion and lack of riparian vegetation) can be estimated using GIS software ArcInfo and ArcView. The relevant information, such as property boundaries, parcel size and landowners (the Digital Cadastral Database or DCDB), land use pattern, and soil type and chemical properties) can be stored in a GIS database.

Estimation costs involved in growing trees and shrubs and the opportunity cost of riparian land requires particulars of the siting of riparian buffers and their size. GIS can also be used to examine where vegetation is most degraded, what locations are most vulnerable, how much crop land would be lost, and what is the current landuse pattern in the catchment. Multiplication of estimated areas (under any policy option) by gross margin of the particular crop provides estimates of the opportunity cost of land. The estimated costs can be used as an input to carry out a discounted cash flow analysis or a broad Cost-Benefit Analysis (CBA). Other benefits of riparian revegetation such as streambank stability, reduction in pollution (surface water quality) and reduction in soil erosion may be estimated either in dollar terms for CBA if possible, or else qualitatively for use in multicriteria analysis model, to compare policy options. GIS can be used with MCA and linear programming to develop a decision-support system. The GIS can also be used to create thematic maps of a particular catchment. Output can be integrated with MCA which recognizes the various criteria or objectives to be achieved and conflicting interests of stakeholder groups. An optimization technique can be used to determine preferred revegetation options.

The following are further applications where GIS could be used effectively.

1. Identifying areas where natural resources are degraded (such as deforestation, soil erosion, soil salinity and waterlogging).
2. Identifying areas where conservation practices are required.
3. Land use planning, including forest planning and management (especially on sloping lands).
4. Integrated catchment management (as discussed above), e.g. to examine the extent, distribution and boundary properties of land defined by buffer strips of different widths in a catchment as well as streambank erosion sites.
5. Facility siting such as power stations or tube-wells in a catchment.
6. Corridor analysis, e.g. roads in a catchment, electricity lines and adjacent land parcels.
7. Sites of disposal of wastes such as empty cans of pesticides and other chemicals.

There is great potential for GIS use in supporting resource use decisions in Pakistan similar to the studies discussed above, although data access will continue to be an impediment. The people in Pakistan have low incomes and it is difficult for them to develop GIS skills. Therefore, human development would be key in the development of GIS use in Pakistan.

Concluding Comments

Natural resources in India and Pakistan have not been used in a sustainable way. Sustainable use and management of these resources requires effective and accessible information systems. In many countries of the world (mainly developed countries), GIS have been used to assist in the sustainable management of natural resources. In India, there is evidence of GIS research, but there has been little integration with other models for effective management of natural resources. GIS have great potential for assisting in the management of natural resources in Pakistan; progress is being made in GIS development, but utilisation at a catchment level will take some time.

REFERENCES

Adinarayana, J. and Krishna, N.R. (1996), "Integration of Multi-Seasonal Remotely-Sensed Images for Improved Landuse Classification of a Hilly Watershed Using Geographical Information Systems," *International Journal of Remote Sensing*, 17(9) : 1679-1688.

Adinarayana, J., Flach, J.D. and Collins, W.G. (1994), "Mapping Land Use Patterns in a River Catchment Using Geographical Information Systems," *Journal of Environmental Management*, 42(1) : 55-61.

Ahmad, W. (1998), Personal Communication, Associate Professor, Department of Remote Sensing, Northern Territory University, Darwin.

Ashraf, S. (1998), Personal Communication, GIS Analyst, WWF-Pakistan, Lahore.

Bernhardsen, T. (1992), *Geographic Information Systems*, VIAK IT and Norwegian Mapping Authority, Chapter 1.

Bren, L.J. (1995), "Aspects of the Geometry of Riparian Buffer Strips and its Significance to Forestry Operations," *Forest Ecology and Management*, 75(1) : 1-10.

Burrough, P.A. (1986), *Principles of Geographical Information Systems for Land Resources Assessment*, Oxford Sciences Publications, Ch. 1, 2, 4, 5.

Burrough, P.A. and McDonnell, R.A. (1998), *Principles of Geographical Information Systems : Spatial Information Systems and Geostatistics*, Ch. 1, Oxford University Press, New York.

Cook, H.F. and Norman, C. (1996), "Targeting Agri-Environmental Policy : An Analysis relating to the Use of Geographical Information Systems," *Land Use Policy*, 13(3) : 217-228.

Deane, G.C. (1994), The Role of GIS in the Management of Natural Resources, *Aslib Proceedings*, 46(6) : 157-161.

Elshorbagy, A., Sharifi, A. and Perrier, A. (1996), Environment-Oriented Water Related Projects Appraisal, in *Transactions of the 16th International Congress on Irrigation and Drainage : Sustainability of Irrigated Agriculture — Irrigation Planning and Management : Measures in Harmony with the Environment,* Vol 1-C, Cairo, pp. 29-40.

Evans, B.M. and Myers, W.L. (1993), "A GIS Based Approach to Evaluating Regional Groundwater Pollution Potential with DRASTIC", *Journal of Soil and Water Conservation*, 45(2) : 242-245.

Fedra, K. (1995), *Decision Support for Natural Resources Management : Models, GIS and Expert Systems*, International Institute for Applied Systems Analysis, Laxenburg, http://www.iiasa.ac.at/ACA/papers/toronto.html.

Fu, B. and Gulnick, H. (1994), "Land Evaluation in an Area of Severe Erosion : the Loess Plateau of China," *Land Degradation and Rehabilitation*, 5(1) : 33-40.

Garg, P.K. and Harrison, A.R. (1992), "Land Degradation and Erosion Risk Analysis in SE Spain : A Geographic Information System Approach," *Catena*, 19(5) : 411-25.

Giaoutzi, M. and Nijkamp, P. (1993), Decision Support Models for Regional Sustainable Development : An Application of Geographic Information Systems and Evaluation Models to the Greek Sporades Island, Avebury, Sydney, Ch. 10.

Government of India (1987), *Statistical Abstract India*, New Delhi.

Ghosh, R., Goel, R.K., Lole, B.S., Singh, T.P., Sastry, K.L.N., Patel, J.G., Vanikar, Y.V., Thakker, P.S. and Navalgund, R.R. (1993), "District Level Planning : A Case Study for the Panchmahls District Using Remote Sensing and Deographic Information System Techniques," *International Journal of Remote Sensing*, 14(17) : 3163-3168.

Grunblatt, J., Ottichilo, W.K. and Sinage, R.K. (1992), "A GIS Approach to Desertification Assessment and Mapping," *Journal of Arid Environments*, 23(1) : 81-02.

Harrison, S.R. and Sharma, P.C. (1996), "GIS and Economic Models as Information Systems for Sustainable Development", in R.K. Sen and K.C. Roy, eds., *Sustainable Development and Environment : India and Other Low Income Economies*, Atlantic Publishers, New Delhi, Ch. 14.

Harrison, S.R. Qureshi, M.E. Sharma, P.C. and Tidey, M.E. (1998), Using GIS in Multicriteria Analysis of Riparian Revegetation Options, in *Proceedings of International Conference on Modelling Geographical and Environmental Systems with Geographical Information Systems* Vol. 1, Hong Kong Convention and Exhibition Centre, Hong Kong June 22-25.

Janssen, R. and van Herwijnen, M. (1989), Graphical Decision Support Applied to Decision Changing the Use of Agricultural Land, in Backman, M. and Krelle, W. eds., *Lecture Notes in Economics and Mathematical Systems*, Helsinki.

Kumar, N. (1994), "The Feasibility of GIS in the Indian Context," *Annals of the National Association of Geographers New Delhi*, 14(1) : 67-73.

Kushwaha, S.P.S., Subramanian, S.K., Chennaiah, G.C., Murthy, J.R. Rao, S.V.C.K, Perumal, A. and Behera, G. (1996), "Interfacing Remote Sensing and GIS Methods for Sustainable Rural Development," *International Journal of Remote Sensing*, 17(15) : 3055-69.

Le Maitre, D.C. van Wilgen, B.W. and Richardson, D.M. (1993), "A Computer System for Catchment Management : Background, Concepts and Development," *Journal of Environmental Management*, 39(2) : 121-42.

Littleboy, M., Silburn, D.M. Freebairn, D.M., Woodruff, D.R. and hammer, G.L. (1989), *Perfect : A Computer Simulation Model of Productivity Erosion Runoff Functions to Evaluate Conservation Techniques*, Queensland Department of Primary Industries, Brisbane.

Lo, K.F.A. (1995), "Erosion Assessment of Large Watersheds in Taiwan," *Journal of Soil and Water Conservation*, 50(2) : 180-83.

Lyons, K. and Sharma, P. (1991), *An Introduction to GIS For Land Management*, Australian Institute of Spatial Information Sciences and Technology, The University of Queensland, Brisbane.

Mallawaarachchi, T., Walker, P.A., Young, M.D., Smyth, R.E., Lynch, H.S. and Dudgeon, G. (1995), "GIS-Based Integrated Modelling Systems for Natural Resource Management," *Agricultural Systems*, 50(2) : 169-89.

McClean, C.J., Watson, P.M., Wadsworth, R.A., Blaiklock, J. and O'Callaghan, J.R. (1995), "Land Use Planning : A Decision Support System," *Journal of Environmental Management*, 38(1) : 77-92.

Menon, S. and Bawa, K.S. (1997), "Application of Geographic Information Systems, Remote-Sensing and Landscape Ecology Approach to Biodiversity Conservation in the Western Ghats," *Current Science*, 73(2) : 134-45.

Mumtaz, K. and Mitha, Y. (1996), *Pakistan Tradition and Change : An Oxfam Country Profile*, pp. 53-58, Oxfam, Oxford.

Murty, C.V.S.S.B.R. and Venkatachalam, P. (1992), "Delineation of Erosion Cells in a Watershed Using GIS," *Journal of Environmental Management*, 36(2) : 159-66.

Negahban, B., Moss, C.B., Jones, J.W., Zhang, J., Boggess, W.D. and Campbell, K.L. (1994), Optimal Field Management for Regional Water Quality Planning, Presented at the *1994 International Winter Meeting Sponsored by the American Society of Agricultural Engineers*, Atlanta Hilton and Towers, Atlanta, 13-16 December.

Petroeschevsky, A. (1997), Herbert River Catchment Co-ordinating Committee : Assessment and Mapping of Riparian Vegetation and Stream Bank Erosion on the Herbert Floodplain, Gatton College, The University of Queensland, p. 22.

Raine, A.W. and Gardiner, J.N. (1995), *RIVERCARE : Guidelines for Ecologically Sustainable Management of Rivers and Riparian Vegetation*, Occasional Paper No. 03/95, Land and Water Resources Research and Development Corporation, Canberra.

Ravan, S.A. and Roy, P.S. (1997), "Satellite Remote-Sensing for Ecological Analysis of Forested Landscape," *Plant Ecology*, 131(2) : 129-41.

Reed, D. (1996), "Case Study for Pakistan" in Reed, D. ed. *Structural Adjustment, the Environment, and Sustainable Development*, Earthscan, London, Ch. 10.

Roy, K.C. and Tisdell, C.A. (1992), "Technological Change, Environment and Sustainability of Rural Communities," in [Roy, K.C., Tisdell, C.A. and Sen, R.K. eds., *Economic Development and Environment : A Case Study of India*, Ch. 2, Oxford University Press, Delhi].

Sahay, S. and Walsham, G. (1996), "Implementation of GIS in India," *International Journal of Geographical Information Systems*, 10(4) : 385-404.

Schultink, G. (1992), "Integrated Remote Sensing, Spatial Information System, and Applied Models in Resource Assessment," Economic Development and Policy Analysis, *Photogrammetric Engineering and Remote Sensing*, 53 : 1229-37.

Selman, P. (1992), "An Investigation of the Potential for Landscape Ecology to act as a Basis for Rural Land Use Plans," *Journal of Environmental Management*, 35(4) : 281-99.

Sharma, P.C., Harrison, S.R. and Zhai, Y. (1997), "Development and Application of Forestry GIS Under Data Scarcity : A Case Study from the Three-Georges Area," PRC, in [Tisdell, C.A. and Chai, J.C.H. eds., *China's Economic Growth and Transition : Macroeconomic, Regional, Environmental and Other Dimensions*, Economics Conference Monograph No. 2, The University of Queensland, pp. 415-26].

Shrestha, S.S., Remigio, A.A., Murai, S. and Webber, K.E. (1998), "Watershed Management in Nepal Using Remote Sensing and GIS," in *Proceedings of International Conference on Modelling Geographical and Environmental Systems with Geographical Information Systems*, Hong Kong Convention and Exhibition Centre, Hong Kong, pp. 235-43, June 22-25.

Singh, R.B. (1992), "Remote Sensing and GIS as Decision Support Systems in the Himalayas," *Annals of the National Association of Geographers New Delhi*, 12 (1-2) : 103-13.

Tiwari, A.K. Kudrat, M. Manchanda, M.L. Singh, R.B. (1995), "Remote Sensing and GIS for Management of Himalayan Ecosystems," in Haigh, M.J. ed. *Proceedings of Third International Symposium on Headwater Control*, New Delhi, 6-8 October, pp. 329-38.

Villa, F., Ceroni, M. and Mazza, A. (1996), "A GIS-Based Method for Multi-Objective Evaluation of Park Vegetation," *Landscape and Urban Planning*, 35(4) : 203-12.

Westman, W.E. (1991), "Ecological Restoration Projects : Measuring their Performance," *Environmental Professional*, 13(3) : 207-15.

Yeh, A.G. (1991), "The Development and Applications of Geographic Information Systems for Urban and Regional Planning in the Developing Countries," *International Journal of Geographical Information Systems*, 5(1) : 5-27.

Yeh, A.G. and Li, X. (1998), "Sustainable Land Development Model for Rapid Growth Areas Using GIS," *International Journal of Geographical Information Science*, 12(2) : 169-89.

Zhai, Y. and Xian, M. (1994), "Suitability Analysis and Development of Lychee and Longon in the Three-gorge Area," *Resource and Environment in the Yangtze Valley*, 2(3) : 35-38.

17 Women's Empowerment, Sen's Entitlement Theory and Institutional Impediments in Rural India : the Case of Access to Education

K.C. Roy
C.A. Tisdell
A. Ghose

Introduction

Gender Empowerment has been recognised as a key to the improvement of the women in developing countries. One of the main means for gender empowerment is education to women so that they utilise their qualification to gain employment, which in turn will lead to economic independence. Increase of one's educational qualification leads to enlargement of the endowment factor, which is a part of Amartya Sen's work. However, Sen's theory of exchange entitlement does not fully take into the account the various social and institutional factors, which hamper exchange. In this paper we are more concerned with the issues of women's education and how the educational endowment of women provides exchange entitlement factors different from those of men due to social, cultural and institutional factors. An in-depth analysis is provided from field surveys and with theoretical aspects discussed on the basis of Sen's theory. The shortcomings of the theory have been noted and alternative solutions have been suggested for the extension of the theory and its application.

Sen's Exchange Entitlement, Endowment and Poverty Relationship : A Brief Review

The entitlement relation as proposed by Sen (1981) is one kind of ownership relation which could be obtained by the following four methods : Trade based entitlement, production based entitlement, own-labour entitlement and inheritance or transfer entitlement. One can exchange for other things what one owns. This exchange can take place either through trading, production or a combination of the two. *The set of all the alternative bundles of commodities that a person can acquire in exchange of what he or she owns may be called the 'exchange entitlement' of what he or she owns.*

The concept of entitlement is an advanced application of modern set theory with 'exchange entitlement mapping' as the relation which mathematically specifies the set of exchange for each ownership bundle. The Exchange Entitlement Mapping' or E-mapping, as set out by Sen originally (Sen, 1981), in short helps to identify whether a man or a woman will be exposed to starvation; in other words whether the exchange entitlement for his or her ownership could provide him or her with enough food. E-mapping specifies the exchange entitlement set of alternative commodity bundles for each endowment bundle.

The entitlement set of a person depends on two parameters, the endowment of a person (the ownership bundle) and the exchange entitlement. *The set of all such available commodity bundles in a given economic situation is the exchange entitlement of his endowment.*

Apart from the endowment or ownership factor, the key determinants of a person's welfare is his or her exchange entitlement. For example, labour is the natural endowment factor for most people, a part of the endowment set for them. However, the key factor for his/her welfare is whether he or she can find employment (this is whether he or she can exchange their endowment, or exchange entitlement), and if so, for how long and at what wage rate.

The exchange entitlement varies from person to person, based on his or her economic class structure as well as the modes of production of the particular economy. Even with similar endowment bundle, the exchange entitlement will vary depending on his or her economic prospects. For example, two people with same educational qualifications, in rural and urban areas will have different exchange entitlements. One of the main causes of rural urban migration is based on the entitlement exchange factor. One of the main factors in exchange entitlement differential is the gender factor. The gender factor, generically speaking, opens up a whole array of issues which have not been fully accounted for in Sen's theory of entitlement exchange.

With the gender issues now prevalent, and being one of the core issues of development, it is important that we combine the issue of development and the theory of entitlement. A host of issues come into play when we want to decide the factors of exchange entitlement of women. The issues are widely divergent, ranging from property rights to social customs, to gender empowerment measures for women's entitlement factors, to institutional and educational issues.

One of the main endowment factors in today's world is education, which is supposed to help one gain employment. The indicators for development as prescribed by World Bank and United Nations take into account the gross primary enrolment ratio for that purpose. However, education itself in the endowment set of a female doesn't necessarily improve her chances for exchange entitlement because of various social and institutional factors which are related to traditional and cultural ideology. The *ideology of seclusion* plays a pivotal role in significantly reducing gainful employment for educated women in rural sector of India.

Due to traditional custom of getting married in the right age, which is quite early, importance of getting a job takes a backseat. Primary surveys have been conducted in the rural hinterland of India to investigate whether increasing the endowment factor, by way of education to women, will lead to higher exchange entitlement. The surveys conclude that social custom, institutional impediments and ideology of seclusion are the main obstacles in the entitlement factor.

Some Comments

This endowment can lead to entitlements which when exchanged can lead to the removal of poverty and improvement in the socio-economic status of the individual on the assumption that there are no institutional deterrents to exchanging entitlements.

Since these deterrents exist, endowment does not automatically lead to this exchange of entitlement.

Women tend to suffer from these institutional impediments more than men do and among women, rural women suffer more than urban women do.[1] Sen was aware of gender differences. In later work (Anand and Sen, 1995), Sen has mathematically demonstrated that the exchange entitlement factor causes difference between male and female. However, he has not taken into account the institutional impediments, particularly the ideology of seclusion which is the key deterrent to the removal of poverty and empowerment of women in rural India.

Women's Access to Education, Employment and the Force of Institutional Impediments

Take the Case of Education

Education is an endowment which enables a women to use the skill and knowledge to obtain the entitlements. But due to gender discrimination embodying the 'ideology of seclusion' less attention is paid to and less emphasis is placed on the education of girls and females than on that of boys and males. As a result, females in villages and rural towns do not get the opportunity to acquire the same marketable skill and knowledge as the males. Even if they get the same endowment (education), it does not necessarily improve their entitlement exchange capacity due to institutional impediments although it helps reduce the population growth in the long run by making them aware of the beneficial effects of late marriage, use of contraceptives and of having fewer children. Hence, there is clear distinction between any education and appropriate marketable skills based education.

It is unfortunate that in the literature on women in development and on development studies in general (including Sen's study) such a distinction does not appear to have been made and the importance of skill based education in women's empowerment has not been

[1] (Agarwal 1989; Bhalla 1989; Chen 1989; Duvvury 1989; Jodha 1986; Roy and Tisdell 1993 a, b; Roy and Clark 1994; Roy, Tisdell and Sen 1992, 1995; Roy and Tisdell 1996.)

discussed. Thus the failure of girls and women in general and of rural girls and women in particular to acquire the appropriate education they choose, stems from the most powerful institutional deterrents called the ideology of seclusion which is the most powerful component of what we broadly term 'cultural impediments'. Furthermore, considerable emphasis has been placed in the literature on primary education being the key to the success of women's empowerment process. Therefore, primary school enrolment ratio has been used as a proxy to test the success of government's primary education programs. But in India, in rural areas, the actual enrolment ratio in primary schools generally is considerably below the ratio reported in the official statistics. This situation exists due to certain cultural impediments which include lack of work ethics, sense of responsibility and duty on the part of teachers which allow them to stay away from school during the school hours for carrying on their private business and on the part of government officials which allow them not to implement the rules and regulations properly and to penalise the teachers. Also even when the teachers are present, they may not be discharging their duties — although the students will pass their subjects. Even when the teachers impart adequate knowledge to their students, the education they obtain is mostly generalist and therefore does not help them in their empowerment process.

It should however, be noted that female teachers possess better work culture, greater sense of responsibility and are more motivated than male teachers.[2] However, in rural areas in India most primary schools are co-educational and are dominated by male teachers.

Parents also do not want to send their children to school due to these above noted factors as well as to the fact that the opportunity cost of sending children to school is loss of family income. These are all part of the same 'cultural impediment.' Hence, education does not always lead to the success of women's empowerment process in presence of the cultural impediments. Hence, Sen's theory and other studies on women in development do not seem to have recognised this fact.

---

2 Obtained through private conversation with students and parents during the field survey.

World Bank Study

A World Bank (1991) study found that the following factors impede women's progress towards achieving higher education :

1. Parental and societal attitudes towards the education of their daughters are important factors in the non-enrolment and higher drop-out rates of female children in families which have very limited income, assets and low rank in the caste and occupational hierarchies. Parents of these girls are illiterate or semi-illiterate agricultural labourers, small farmers and artisan families or are urban slum dwellers working in unorganised sector in low status jobs.
2. Since the level of family income is very low, the children of these families, specially girls, are required to work both within and outside the home. Banerjee's study (1989) found that between 1971 and 1981, there was a sharp increase in female child labour in rural areas. While the absolute number of boys in the rural labour force went down by 8 percent, the number of girls increased by 30 per cent.
3. The direct costs of education also deter families from sending their girls to school. Although there is no tuition fee for primary education in publicly funded schools, other expenses such as cost of books, other learning aids, uniforms and of transport can impose quite a heavy burden on poor families. Although some state-administered programmes offset some of the costs to scheduled castes and tribes, they do not cover all poor families.
4. Another important factor is the social perception about the return expected from girls' education. Since a girl once born will eventually get married, there is no long term return expected from investment in girls' education. Hence, for their future role as mother and unskilled workers, girls require little formal education.
5. Also the way the school system is run does not seem to provide an incentive to parents to send their children to school. Thus inconvenient location of schools, absence of

teachers, irregular functioning of schools, lack of basic minimum facilities such as blackboards, benches, table, chair etc., and single teacher school, exert a demoralising influence on parents' mind.

6. Also there is a particular scarcity of female teachers which affects girls' attendance at schools.

The Other Side of the Story

However, extensive fieldwork in rural hinterlands and in tribal belts in West Bengal, and private discussions and personal interviews with tribals reveals that there are other forces which work against women's empowerment, but which the World Bank failed to recognise.

Cost of and the Secondary Market for Education

The cost of education is high because there is gross inefficiency in the use of funds. A substantial part of the budgetary allocation to education is spent on wages and salaries of academic and non-academic staff in primary, secondary and tertiary institutions. A vast proportion of total income of educational institutions is derived from government grants which in 1985–86 accounted for 87.7 per cent of total funds available for expenditure by educational institutions (Government of India, 1995).

Primary and secondary education are the responsibility of state governments. The following table shows that the total state government expenditure on education which was only Rs. 68.8 billion in 1984 accounting for 22.7 per cent of total expenditure reached Rs. 205.3 billion in 1991 accounting for 23.2 per cent of total expenditure of states.

Table 1 : Expenditure on Education by State Governments

	1984	1985	1986	1987	1988	1989	1990	1991
1. Total expenditure of all State Governments (Rs. billion)	302.5	348.9	402.9	475.1	541.1	619.8	740.5	884.4
2. Total expenditure on education (Rs. billion)	68.8	82.2	91.7	107.0	126.8	157.0	183.4	205.3
3. 2 as % of 1	22.7	23.6	22.8	22.5	23.4	25.4	24.8	23.2

Source : IMF (1994) *Government Finance Statistics Year Book, 1994,* Washington D.C. : IMF

Hence, the higher cost of education cannot be due to low level of expenditure by government on education. This is due among other things to the fact that in India, although formal state schools, which absorb the overwhelming bulk of students, represent the primary education market, very little education is provided in these schools particularly in rural areas. Teachers in both rural and urban areas tend to provide the same education in the secondary education market through large scale private coaching. Thus while teachers earn comfortable salaries in primary market and even more than 100 per cent of their salaries in the *secondary* market, the parents are forced to bear the cost of enrolment in the formal market and the cost of teaching in the secondary market. Small farmers, tribals and scheduled caste families as well as low caste families doing odd jobs in informal sector in towns cannot afford such expenses. School and college teachers also belong to powerful unions and no government dares to flex muscles against these unions. Hence, degeneration of the educational system continues (revealed through private conversation with tribal elders during fieldwork).

Previous Field Study 1993

A 1993 field study by K.C. Roy (Roy and Tisdell, 1994) reveals that 93 per cent of all females interviewed agreed that lack of technical skill and knowledge limited their scope for employment of educated females. Also 79 per cent of them agreed that if guidance and opportunities were given to them, they would have completed technology-oriented degrees. Fifty-six per cent of the respondents agreed that male members in the family were given such guidance and help. Furthermore, more than 97 per cent of them agreed that information about the availability of technology, adequate facilities for training, credit to obtain and utilise technology would improve their access to technology which in turn would help them become economically independent.

Through private conversation, a number of respondents also revealed that even if girls and females in rural areas (villages and rural towns) receive education appropriate to their empowerment process they would be unable to utilise their education because the ideology of seclusion would prevent them from obtaining information about employment opportunities and from moving out of the confines of their surroundings in search of effective employment. In the same 1993 study more than 97 per cent of respondents agreed that equal opportunities with males is necessary for the employment of females. Thus, even if all the factors conducive to the progress of education and thereby to the empowerment process of rural women are present, derogatory customs embodying gender discrimination do prevent girls and females from achieving success in their empowerment efforts. They also mentioned that the type of education that girls and young females receive in villages and rural towns does not depend on what they consider appropriate to their empowerment process but on what is available within the proximity of their towns (even if that is inappropriate) and what family elders force them to take. Apart from the ideology of seclusion, poor economic status of rural families also prevent them from sending their female children to institutions located at distance places.

Field Study (1994–95)

One of the present authors (K.C. Roy) undertook a field study in a tribal area in rural West Bengal in recent past. It consisted of one survey of all girl students in class X (in exit year) in a secondary school. These students consisted of both tribal and non-tribal girls. The second survey interviewed all the female university graduates in that tribal region. This tribal region is in Midnapore district which is a part of Bengal, Orissa and Bihar tribal belt in India.

Field Survey 1 : Survey of All Students in the Top Class in A Girls' Secondary School in a Tribal Region in Midnapore District

The objective was to find out (i) the reasons for pursuing their current study; (ii) the influences of derogatory customs on the type and level of education they obtain; (iii) the effect of ideology of seclusion on the prospect of obtaining employment; (iv) the influence of customs on marriage and (v) the severity of the force of 'classic patriarchy.'

All students in grade X, which was the exit year for students for that school, were interviewed. After completing grade X, the students would have had to enrol in a higher secondary school or a college to compete grade XI and XII. These institutions are located at distant places. Some of the girls would have had to travel long distance every day or to stay at the school hostel. Such a move would have involved substantial expenditure on the part of the families and violated the rule of the ideology of seclusion. Total numbers of students interviewed was 90, of whom 31 were from tribal and scheduled caste families and 59 from upper caste families.

The results of the survey are presented in table 2.

The results of an earlier fieldwork summarised in previous paragraphs have already indicated that the type of education that women and girls were getting was not suitable for obtaining employment and therefore for the success of empowerment process. Now this fieldwork gives a better picture of the usefulness of education that girls in the rural hinterland are receiving.

Table 2 : Issues in Girls' Education and the Impact of Gender Discrimination

Items (1)	Girls of scheduled caste and tribal families				Girls of upper caste families				Grand total of all castes			
	Total respondent (2)	Yes response (3)	No response (4)	Yes/No as % of 2 (5)	Total respondent (6)	Yes response (7)	No response (8)	Yes/No as % of 6 (9)	Total respondent 2 + 6 (10)	Yes response 3 + 7 (11)	No 4 + 8 (12)	Yes/No as % of 10 (13)
1. Reasons for pursuing current study	31				59				90			
i) institutions close by home		30		96.8		53		89.8		83		92.2
ii very little expense for parents		28		90.3		53		89.8		81		90.0
iii) parents wanted it		24		77.4		35		59.3		59		65.6
iv) you wanted some kind of education		30		96.8		58		98.3		88		97.8
v) others – specify.		–		–		–						
2. Against the forces of social customs which enforce ideology of seclusion, would you pursue further studies at distant institution?			29	93.5		47		79.7			76	84.4
3. Would you pursue such further studies is such social customs do not exist?		30		96.8		59		100.0		89		98.9

	Girls of scheduled caste and tribal families		Girls of upper caste families		Grand total of all castes	
4. Derogatory social customs and traditions embodying gender discrimination greatly influence the type and level of education.	30	96.8	59	100.0	89	98.9
5. You prefer late marriage because you want to pursue further studies and acquire greater skills for obtaining employment.	25	80.6	55	93.2	80	88.9
6. Customary practice of marriage prevents you from realising your full potential.	30	96.8	59	100.0	89	98.9
7. Being female, it prevented you from taking job oriented education instead of generalist education	31	100.0	59	100.0	90	100.0
8. Discontinuing the traditional system of marriage without free choice is essential for the fuller development of women and society	30	96.8	59	100.0	89	98.9

	Girls of scheduled caste and tribal families				Girls of upper caste families				Grand total of all castes			
9. Who of the following enforces gender discrimination?												
i) village and family elders rather than youngers		30		96.8		45		76.3		75		83.3
ii) amongst elders females compared with males		30		96.8		49		83.0		79		87.8
iii) narrow minded younger females		9		29.0		22		37.3		31		34.4

Analysis of Survey 1 Results

For the question : reasons for pursuing current study, 96.8 per cent of girls from scheduled caste (S.C.) and Scheduled Tribes (S.T.) families and 89.8 per cent of upper caste (U.C.) families agreed that institutions close by home was one reason. The total affirmative response was 92.2 per cent.

To the second reason : very little expense for parents, 90.3 of S.C. and S.T. girls and 89.8 per cent of U.C. girls gave affirmative response. The total affirmative response was 90.20 per cent.

To the third reason : parents wanted it, 77.4 of S.C. and S.T. girls and 59.3 per cent of U.C. girls gave affirmative response, the total affirmative response was 65.6 per cent.

To the fourth reason : you wanted some kind of education, 96.8 per cent of S.C. and S.T. girls and 98.3 per cent of U.C. girls gave affirmative response. The total affirmative response was 97.8 per cent. There was no response to any other factors. Thus all the four factors played their part in leading the girls to take some formal education. No one mentioned that this education was appropriate and necessary for the success of their empowerment process. These girls also wanted some kind of education whatever the local institution can offer.

93.5 per cent of girls of S.C. and S.T. families and 79.7 per cent of girls of U.C. families reported that against the forces of social customs which confine them within the surroundings of their homes, they would not pursue further studies at a distant institution. This result is quite surprising because gender discrimination is generally more strictly imposed on girls in U.C. families than in S.C. and S.T. families. In answer to the question as to whether they would pursue such further studies if such social customs do not exist, 96.8 per cent of girls of S.C. and S.T. families and 100 per cent of girls of U.C. families reported they would. The total affirmative response was 98.9 per cent.

In response to the question as to whether derogatory social customs and traditions embodying gender discrimination greatly influence the type and level of education they receive, 96.8 per cent of girls of S.C. and S.T. families and 100 per cent of girls of U.C. families reported in the affirmative. The total affirmative response was 98.9 per cent.

When asked whether they would prefer late marriage because they would want to pursue further studies and acquire greater skills for obtaining employment, 80.6 per cent of S.C. and S.T. girls and 93.2 per cent of U.C. girls said 'yes'. The total affirmative response was 88.9 per cent.

When asked whether customary practice of marriage prevents a girl from realising her full potential, 96.8 per cent of S.C. and S.T. girls and 100 per cent of U.C. girls replied in the affirmative. The total affirmative response was 98.9 per cent.

To the question : being female, it prevented you from take job oriented education instead of generalist education, 100 per cent of S.C., S.T. as well as U.C. girls replied 'yes'. Naturally the total yes response was 100 per cent.

Also 96.8 per cent of S.C. and S.T. girls and 100 per cent of U.C. girls agreed that discontinuing the traditional system of marriage without free choice is essential for the fuller development of women and society. The total 'yes' response was 98.9 per cent.

When asked which of the three categories of people : (i) village and family elders, (ii) amongst elders, females rather than males and (iii) narrow minded younger females, enforces greater gender discrimination, the first category received 96.8 per cent affirmative response from S.C. and S.T. girls and 83 per cent affirmative response from U.C. girls. The total affirmative response for this category of people was 83.3 per cent. For the second category of persons, the affirmative response rate for S.C. and S.T. girls was 96.8 per cent and for U.C. girls was 76.3 per cent. The total affirmative response was 87.8 per cent.

For the last category of persons, the affirmative response rate was very low. Therefore, it would appear that while both village and family elders enforce gender restrictions on girls and women, female elders rather than male elders appear to be the principal actors in enforcing the ideology of seclusion on them.

Thus the results of the fieldwork support the argument that very little education is provided in educational institutions in rural areas, that the girls receive a particular education because the educational institutions are close by their homes, the expense is not high and parents want this education not because this education is helpful to them in their empowerment process.

Moreover, even if appropriate education is available at an institution located at a distant place, they cannot utilise that opportunity because of the enforcement on them of the ideology of seclusion.

Even if they receive such appropriate education they are unable to utilise this education to become economically independent because the social custom of parents arranging the marriage of their daughter as soon as they can and of daughters having no say in their own marriage.

Parents who fail to arrange successfully the marriage of their daughter tend to suffer from social humiliation.

The present system of formal education therefore has helped women and girls very little in their empowerment process. Appropriate education cannot be attained and empowerment process cannot be successful unless the quality of education is improved and derogatory social customs affecting women's empowerment are eliminated.

Field Survey 2 : Survey of All Female University Graduates (Tribals and Non-Tribals) in a Tribal Region in West Bengal

The female graduates interviewed were from upper castes, scheduled tribes and scheduled castes. All female graduates of that region were interviewed. The objective of this survey was to find out their perception of the influence of their education and of social customs on their empowerment process. Thus, the views of both current female students and of those who already completed their degrees are presented to get a clearer picture of the influence of education on the whole process of endowment, entitlement and empowerment of women in rural India. The results of this survey are presented in table 3.

Table 3 : Social and Cultural Impediments to Exchange Entitlement for Educated Rural Women

Items	Scheduled Caste			Scheduled Tribe			Upper Caste			Grand total of all castes		
	total	yes	%	Total	Yes	%	Total	yes	%	total	yes	%
1. Marriage age preference	9			13			15			37		
Late		7	(77)		9	(69)		12	(80)		28	(76)
Early		2	(22)		4	(31)		3	(20)		9	(24)
Reasons for late marriage												
1. Pursuit of higher studies		8	(88)		9	(69)		13	(86)		30	(81)
2. Economic independence		8	(88)		9	(69)		13	(86)		30	(81)
3. Children preference		8	(88)		9	(69)		13	(86)		30	(81)
4. Small family preference		8	(88)		9	(69)		13	(86)		30	(81)
2. Late marriage consequences												
1. Parents criticised		8	(88)		10	(77)		8	(53)		26	(70)
2. Ill treatment		8	(88)		10	(77)		9	(60)		27	(73)
3. Marriage a social responsibility		8	(88)		10	(77)		9	(60)		27	(73)
4. Full potential hampered		9	(100)		10	(77)		14	(93)		33	(89)

Items	Scheduled Caste			Scheduled Tribe			Upper Caste			Grand total of all castes		
	total	yes	%	Total	Yes	%	Total	yes	%	total	yes	%
5. Prefer freedom of choice		9	(100)		10	(77)		14	(93)		33	(89)
3. Employment												
1. Application of education		9	(100)		13	(100)		15	100		37	100
2. Obtaining employment by education		9	(100)		13	(100)		15	100		37	100
3. Ideology of seclusion an obstruction?		9	(100)		13	(100)		15	100		37	100
4. Social custom an obstacle?		9	(100)		13	(100)		15	100		37	100
5. Freedom of movement a problem?		9	(100)		13	(100)		15	100		37	100
6. Independent venture difficult due to ideology of seclusion?		9	(100)		13	(100)		15	100		37	100
4. Social Mobility												
1. Freedom of movement necessary?		2	(22)		13	(100)		15	100		30	(81)
2. Family allows it?		4	(44)		2	(15)		7	(46)		13	(35)
3. Taunting problem		8	88		6	(46)		5	(33)		19	(51)
4. Slander and gossip		8	(88)		8	(61)		6	(40)		22	(59)
5. Parent subjected to gossip		8	(88)		10	(77)		7	(46)		25	(67)
6. Parents criticised by grandparents		8	(88)		10	(77)		8	(53)		26	(70)
7. Becoming liability for family?		9	(100)		10	(77)		8	(53)		27	(73)
5. Gender discrimination												
1. Gender discrimination biggest hindrance		9	(100)		10	(77)		14	(93)		33	(89)
2. Neighbours and elders		9	(100)		6	(46)		6	(40)		21	(68)
3. Females vs males		9	(100)		9	(69)		14	(93)		32	(86)
4. Younger females		9	(100)		9	(69)		8	(53)		26	(70)

Regarding the issue of preferred marriage age, 77 per cent of the scheduled caste women and 69 per cent of the schedule tribe women said that they would prefer marrying at a late age, that is, after the age of 25. However, 86 per cent of the upper caste women prefer marrying late.

The various reasons for marrying late are as follows :

1. They want to pursue higher studies and acquire greater skills for obtaining employment.
2. They want to use their educational skills for economic independence.
3. Probability of having a larger number of children is higher with early marriage, which will leave them less time for work.

88 per cent of the scheduled caste women, 69 per cent of the scheduled tribe women and 88 per cent of the upper caste women agree to these points. In total 81 per cent of all the women surveyed agree to the following reasons.

However, they are very much aware of the late marriage consequences. One of the main problems is that their parent will be criticised. 88 per cent of the scheduled caste women, 77 per cent of the scheduled tribe women and 53 per cent of the upper caste women agree to that fact that their parents will have to face criticism. In total almost 81 per cent of the total women surveyed agree to this social problem.

Apart from parents being criticised, the women themselves are susceptible to ill treatment by their family members and neighbours. 88 per cent of the scheduled caste women, 77 per cent of the scheduled tribe women and 53 per cent of the upper caste women agree to this facet. In all 73 per cent of all the women are afraid of being treated badly.

To most women, and their parents, marriage becomes a social responsibility, rather than the welfare and happiness of the daughter. 88 per cent of the scheduled caste, 77 per cent of the scheduled tribe and 60 per cent of the upper caste women agree with this point of view. In total 73 per cent of the women surveyed agree to this.

However, 89 per cent of all the women surveyed agree to the fact that customary marriage prevents them from realising their full potential. 100 per cent of the scheduled caste, 77 per cent of the scheduled tribe and 93 per cent of the upper caste women support this view.

Therefore, the same 89 per cent of women also strongly support the fact that traditional practice of marriage should be discontinued, and freer choice are essential for the fuller development of women.

Employment

In regard to the questions relating to the issue of employment, 100 per cent of women from every caste agree to the statements as given below :

1. They would like to make their education useful in their single as well as their married life.
2. They consider obtaining employment to be the most important and effective way of making their education useful.
3. They agree to the fact being girls and women, elders will impose the 'ideology of seclusion' on them, as a result job prospects and vacancies do not easily reach them.
4. Social customs prevent them from journeying to distance places in search for employment.
5. Even if they manage to get a job, they might be forced to turn down the offer as their movements are mostly confined to the surrounding of their home.
6. Ideology of seclusion has kept their latent qualities relatively undeveloped and as a result they are unable to follow some independent profession or start some commercial venture.
7. Being female prevented them from taking some job-oriented education instead of generalist education.

It is important to note, that irrespective of high and low caste, all the women agree to the above mentioned points of view. Therefore, increasing their endowment set will not lead to entitlement exchange and removal of poverty until those social and institutional problems are removed.

Social Mobility

One of the first points in social mobility factor is how importantly it is viewed by the educated rural women. In other words is it necessary for them to have the freedom to move freely to meet and communicate with people to utilise opportunities for their development?

100 per cent of the scheduled tribe women and 100 per cent of the upper caste women say that it is necessary. Surprisingly only 22 per cent of the scheduled caste women think it is necessary. 44 per cent of the scheduled caste women 15 per cent of the scheduled tribe women and 46 per cent of the upper caste women said that their family allowed the necessary freedom of movement. In total only 35 per cent of the women said that their family allowed them the necessary freedom of movement. That is in the case of educated rural women in India, 65 per cent of the women are not allowed the necessary freedom of movement for their development.

However, there could be dire consequences if they are allowed to move freely. 88 per cent of the scheduled caste women, 46 per cent of the schedule tribe women and 33 per cent of the upper caste women agree that they would be subject to taunting by village and neighbourhood unemployed youths. In total 51 per cent of all the rural women surveyed agree that they would be subject to jeering if they were allowed to move freely.

Apart from being subjected to taunting by unemployed youth, they also would have to put up with slander and gossip by village and neighbourhood elders. 88 per cent of the scheduled caste women, 61 per cent of the upper caste women agree to this fact. In total 59 per cent of all the women agree that they would be confronted with slander and gossip problem.

The more painful fact for them is that their parents also would be subjected to neighbourhood gossip and criticism by elders. 88 per cent of the scheduled caste, 77 per cent of the scheduled tribe and 46 per cent of the upper caste women, in total 67 per cent of the women agree that this problem exists.

As a consequence, parents will be subjected to rebuke by grandparents and will be advised about the misbehaviour of the girl. 88 per cent of the scheduled caste, 77 per cent of the scheduled tribe and 53 per cent of the upper caste women, in total 73 per cent of all the women agree to this view.

Gender Discrimination

One of the main obstacles for women's development is gender discrimination. A number of social and religious customs are very powerful deterrents to women's empowerment. For example marriage without choice, dowry and other limitations on their freedom are the most important hindrance to social and economic progress in the country. 100 per cent of the schedule caste women, 77 per cent of the scheduled tribe women and 93 per cent of the upper caste women agree to this point of view. In total, 89 per cent of al the women surveyed agree to the problems relating to the gender discrimination.

Among those who practice gender discrimination :

- 100 per cent of the scheduled caste women, 46 per cent of the scheduled tribal women and 40 per cent of the upper caste women blame neighbours and elders, in total 68 per cent blame neighbours and elders.
- Within family 100 per cent of the scheduled caste, 69 per cent of the scheduled tribe and 93 per cent of the upper caste blames it on elders, specially on females compared to males. In total, 86 per cent blame it on elderly females.
- Generically 100 per cent of the scheduled caste, 69 per cent of the scheduled tribe and 53 per cent of the upper caste blame it on younger females. In total 70 per cent of them blame younger female for gender discrimination.

Non-Formal Education, Community Education and Derogatory Customs

The World Bank study (1991) admits that the 'enabling' quality of education, which allows women with primary and middle school education to enter secondary and tertiary occupations more easily than illiterate women, may be offset to some extent by the lesser 'need to work' among women in middle and high socio-economic groups as well as by traditional purdah-practices common among the middle class. Importantly a larger share of literate and educated women than illiterate ones enter into occupations outside the home, classified as 'non-household' occupations in the secondary sector. Even modest levels of education decrease rural women's participation in the primary sector. The study agrees that female education in India must be enhanced through both the formal school system and non-formal schemes. Adults and school drop-outs are critical target group in addition to younger school entrants. Also it further agrees that improving the quality of primary education would go a long way to increasing girls' participation. At the same time, non-formal education must be directed at girls whose need to work deprives them of the opportunity to attend formal school and provide them the equivalent of five years of schooling. These can encourage greater participation through the provision of incentives to girls. Furthermore, the provision of basic literacy and numeracy skills to adult women will enhance economic productivity and welfare. Production oriented skill training can also enhance women's earring capacity and open up new avenues of employment.

However, as our fieldwork has shown, gender discrimination is enforced not only on women and girls in U.C. families but also on women and girls in S.C. and S.T. families. Therefore, non-formal and formal education ought to be combined with community education of all village and family elders to convince them of the urgent need to discontinue the practice of 'ideology of seclusion'. World Bank's assessment of this problem of women's education in tribal India overlooks the urgent need for the removal of institutional impediments in the field of education of girls and females. Without this, no real progress can be made towards the empowerment of women.

Conclusion

Improvement of women's economic condition is considered to be one of the most important objectives in development issues. Both the World Bank and the United Nations have taken an active interest and participation in various projects trying to improve the economic situation of women. The effort of the United Nations have been reflected in first constructing the Gender Development Index (GDI) and then the Gender Empowerment Measure (GEM). Gender Development Index is an extension of Human Development Index which takes into account the gender issues into consideration. Both the GDI and HDI to a large extent is based on Sen's work on endowment and exchange entitlement, therefore they are limited to the same extent as his theory. For example, primary gross enrolment ratio, one of the measurements of women welfare is a part of GDI, which is based on the concept that education will lead to endowment and higher exchange entitlement.

However, social, cultural and institutional impediments which are very much country specific, have not been taken into account. For example the Panchayat Raj system in India has been lauded by World Bank as an extension of Gender Empowerment Measure. However, even the empowerment of women could be very much limited due to cultural impediments and ideology of seclusion.

Nevertheless, one thing that has been firmly established is that education is the most important prerequisite for uplifting of the status of women in general and of rural and poor women in particular. Education as prescribed by Sen's theory will certainly increase the endowment set of a women, however, the more important aspect of the theory lies in the exchange entitlement of that endowment. If there is no exchange entitlement for the endowment set of an individual, there will be no economic progress and the poor will remain poor.

From the two surveys conducted in a tribal area in West Bengal in India, it is evident, how strong the cultural impediments are. In spite of having a proper education, women fail to or even can't afford to get a job. Also as discussed earlier in the text, in South

Asian context enrolment ratio cannot be used as the most important indicator of progress of girls' and females' education, particularly in rural areas of India.

One of the biggest cultural impediments to improving women's status is the marriage factor. In both the surveys conducted, women prefer very strongly to have a late marriage. They wish to have a late marriage so they can further their career. The second survey pointed out very strongly that all of them want to get a proper job, however, being female they are automatically subjected to the ideology of seclusion and it is difficult for them to follow some independent profession or start some commercial venture. On these points the opinions are unanimous irrespective of caste and creed.

Another point which became obvious from the two surveys is that although most females prefer to have a late marriage, they are aware of the consequences of late marriage. Late marriage is looked down upon strongly in rural India. If the women are not married at early stage they will be subjected to various type of humiliation including taunting by youth, gossip by neighbours and criticism from elders.

Even the parents are not free from the social pressure which comes as the consequence of late marriage of their daughter. The pressure might become so high, that offspring seems to become more like a burden, to be rid of by a marriage. Under those circumstances marriage of the women becomes perhaps the most important thing in both the girl's and her parents' life.

Both the married and unmarried women are restricted from free movement in the rural hinterland. Even travelling too far to gain education is looked down upon. As a consequence, the prospect of getting a job becomes remote even with proper education. However, in most of the cases the education does not seem to be appropriate due to the same problem. For example when a technical qualification is perhaps essential to get a job, the education best suited to social and cultural norms are provided. This way even a graduate degree becomes somehow irrelevant for obtaining a job. In some cases, a women cannot even take up a job if it is offered to a far away place.

In view of these cultural impediments which include the social and traditional factors, education does not play a major role in the improvement of female economic condition. The Gender Empowerment Measure and the Gender Development Index loses much of its significance in the rural hinterland of India. The endowment factor definitely increases due to education, however, there is no exchange entitlement for such endowment factors. The measurement of women welfare by GDI and GEM, specially in the rural sector, at best can be termed as incomplete and insufficient. This paper concludes that there is a necessity for a social index, which will measure the various cultural impediments, with ideology of seclusion perhaps being of highest weight.

REFERENCES

Agarwal, B. (1989), "Rural women, Poverty and Natural Resources," *Economic and Political Weekly,* 24(43).

Anand, S. and Sen A. (1995), "Gender Inequality in Human Development : Theories and Measurement," *HDR Office Occasional Paper 19*, New York : UNDP.

Banerjee, N.K. (1989), "Trends in Women's Employment, 1971–81 : Some Macro Level Observations," *Economic and Political Weekly*, 16(25).

Bhalla, S. (1989), "Technological Change and Women Workers, Evidence from the Expansionary Phase in Haryana Agriculture," *Economic and Political Weekly,* 24(43).

Chambers, R. (1988), "Poverty in India : Concepts, Research and Reality," Discussion Paper 241, University of Sussex : Institute of Development Studies.

Chen, M.(1989), "Women's Work in Indian Agriculture by Agro-Ecological Zones : Meeting Needs of Landless and Landpoor Women," *Economic and Political Weekly*, 24(43).

Duvvury, N. (1989), "Women in Agriculture : A Review of the Indian Literature," *Economic and Political Weekly*, 24,(43)

Government of India (1995), *Economic Survey* 1994–95, New Delhi : Government of India.

IMF (1994), Government Finance Statistics Year Book — 1994, Washington D.C. : IMF.

Jodha, N.S. (1986), "Common Property Resources and the Rural Poor," *Economic and Political Weekly,* 21(27).

LTTP ://www.undp.org./gender/.

Rao, C.H.H. (1991), "Rural Society and Agricultural Development in Course of Industrialisation, Case of India," *Economic and Political Weekly,* 24(11, 12).

Roy, K.C. and Clark, C. (eds.) (1994), Technological Change and Rural Development in Poor Countries : Neglected Issues, New Delhi : Oxford University Press.

Roy, K.C. and Tisdell, C.A. (1993a), "Poverty Amongst Females in Rural India : Gender Based Deprivation and Technological Change," *Economic Studies,* 31(4).

Roy, K.C. and Tisdell, C.A. (1993b), "Technological Change, Environment and Poor Women — Specially Tribal Women in India," *Savings and Development,* 17(4).

Roy, K.C. Tisdell, C.A. and Sen, R.K. (eds.) (1992), *Economic Development and Environment : A Case Study of India,* Calcutta : Oxford University Press.

Roy, K.C., Tisdell, C.A. and Blomqvist, H.C. (eds.) (1996), *Economic Development and Women in the World Community*, C.T., London : Praeger.

Roy. K.C. and Tisdell, C.A. (1996), "Women in South Asia with Particular Reference to India," in Roy, K.C., Tisdell, C.A. and Blomqvist, H.C. (eds.) (1996), *Economic Development and Women in the World Community,* C.T., London : Praeger.

Sen, A.K. (1981), Poverty and Famines : *An Essay on Entitlement and Deprivation*, Oxford; Clarendon Press.

UNDP (1995), *Human Development Report*.

World Bank (1991), *Gender and Poverty in India,* Washington D.C. : World Bank.

World Bank (1996, 1995), *World Development Report,* New York : Oxford University Press.

Index

List of Contributors

DR. MEENA ACHARYA : Tanka Prasad Acharya Memorial Foundation, Institute for Integrated Development Studies, GA-1-286 Dillibazar, Kathmandu 1, Nepal
Tel : 977 1 472 405 Fax : 977 1 472 235

EMERITUS PROFESSOR D.J.J. BOTHA : Managing Editor, The South African Journal of Economics, Department of Economics, 4-44 EBW Building, University of Pretoria, 0002 Pretoria, South Africa
Tel : 27 12 420 3525 Fax : 27 12 362 5266

ASSOCIATE PROFESSOR RONY GABBAY : Senior Research Fellow, Department of Economics, The University of Western Australia, Nedlands WA 6907
Tel : 61 8 9830 2926 Fax : 61 8 9380 1016
Email : rgabbay@ecel.uwa.edu.au

ASSOCIATE PROFESSOR R.N. GHOSH : Senior Research Fellow, and Former Head, Department of Economics, The University of Western Australia, Nedlands WA 6907
Tel : 61 8 9830 1407 Fax : 61 8 9380 1016
Email : rghosh@ecel.uwa.edu.au

MR. ANANDA GHOSE : Department of Economics, The University of Queensland, Brisbane 4072
Tel : 61 7 3365 6429

ASSOCIATE PROFESSOR S.R. HARRISON : Department of Economics, The University of Queensland, Brisbane 4072
Tel : 61 7 3365 6577 Fax : 61 7 3365 7299

DR. SUNIL KUMAR : The University of the South Pacific, Fiji Centre, PO Box 1168, Suva, Fiji Islands
Tel : 679 382 049 Fax : 679 382 059

EMERITUS PROFESSOR PETER A. LONGTON : 64 Beatrice Road, Dalkeith WA 6009
Tel : 61 8 9386 4211

DR. AMIR MAHMOOD : Lecturer, Department of Economics, University of Newcastle, NSW 2308
Tel : 61 2 4921 5017 Fax : 61 2 4921 6919
Email : ecam@cc.newcastle.edu.au

MRS. ANITA MEDHEKAR-SMITH : Lecturer, Faculty of Business & Law, School of Management, Central Queensland University, Rockhampton QLD 4702
Tel : 61 7 4930 9220 Fax : 61 7 4930 9700
Email : a.medhekar@cqu.edu.au

DR. F.A. MOOG : Bureau of Animal Industries, The Philippines

ASSOCIATE PROFESSOR MALATI POCHUN : Department of Economics and Statistics, Faculty of Social Studies and Humanities, University of Mauritius, Reduit, Mauritius,
Email : Mpochun@dove.uom.ac.mu

DR. BIMAN C. PRASAD : Fiji Centre, The University of the South Pacific, PO Box 1168, Suva, Fiji Islands
Tel : 679 382 049 Fax : 679 382 059
Email : Chand.b@usp.ac.fi

MR. M.E. QURESHI : Research Officer, AHURI, Department : Geographical Sciences and Planning, The University of Queensland, Brisbane QLD 4072
Tel : 61 7 3365 6072 E-mail : e.qureshi@mailbox.uq.edu.a

MR. BINAYAK RAY : Visiting Fellow, Australian National University, Former Research Director, AusAID, Canberra, GPO Box 157, Canberra, ACT 2601
Tel : 61 2 6281 3362 (H)

MR. MAHENDRA REDDY : The University of the South Pacific, Fiji Centre, PO Box 1168, Suva, Fiji Islands
Tel : 679 382 049 Fax : 679-382 059

ASSOCIATE PROFESSOR K.C. ROY : Department of Economics, The University of Queensland, Brisbane QLD 4072
Tel : 61 7 3365 6577 Fax : 61 7 3365 7299
Email : roy@commerce.uq.edu.au

ASSOCIATE PROFESSOR LIAM RYAN : School of Management, Faculty of Business & Law, Central Queensland University, Rockhampton QLD 4702
Fax : 61 7 4930 9700, Email : l.ryan@cqu.edu.au

DR. M.A.B. SIDDIQUE : Director, Centre for Migration and Development Studies, Department of Economics, The University of Western Australia, Nedlands WA 6907
Tel : 61 8 9380 2964 Fax : 61 8 9380 1016
Email : asiddiqu@ecel.uwa.edu.au

DR. LAWSON SMITH : Lecturer, Faculty of Business & Law, Central Queensland University, Rockhampton QLD 4702
Tel : 61 7 4930 9220 Fax : 61 7 4930 9700

A/PROFESSOR SCHALK W. THERON : Department of Human Resources Management, Faculty of Economics and Management Sciences, University of Pretoria, South Africa

PROFESSOR C.A. TISDELL : Former Head, Department of Economics, The University of Queensland, Brisbane QLD 4072
Tel : 61 7 3365 6570 Fax : 61 7 3365 7299
Email : economic@commerce.uq.edu.au

BEGUM MEHERUNNESSA ZAMAN : D.Phil student, Geography Department, Waikato University, New Zealand
Email : bmz1@mailserv.waikato.ac.nz